ELLEN T. HARRIS

Handel
and the
Pastoral Tradition

London
OXFORD UNIVERSITY PRESS
New York   Toronto   Melbourne
1980

Oxford University Press, Walton Street, Oxford OX2 6DP

OXFORD   LONDON   GLASGOW   NEW YORK
TORONTO   MELBOURNE   WELLINGTON   CAPE TOWN
IBADAN   NAIROBI   DAR ES SALAAM   TOKYO
KUALA LUMPUR   SINGAPORE   JAKARTA   HONG KONG
DELHI   BOMBAY   CALCUTTA   MADRAS   KARACHI

© Ellen Harris 1980

First published 1980

ISBN 0 19 315236 3

British Library Cataloguing in Publication Data

Harris, Ellen T
    Handel and the pastoral tradition
    1. Handel, George Frideric. Operas
    2. Pastoral drama - Influence
    3. Music and literature
    I. Title
    782. 1′0924   ML410.H13   79-41703
    ISBN 0-19-315236-3

*Printed in Great Britain
by Ebenezer Baylis and Son, Limited
The Trinity Press, Worcester, and London*

Preface

The influence of pastoral drama on the birth of opera has long been accepted. The continuing role of the pastoral in determining musical styles throughout the baroque era, however, is less well known. In this book I will examine the relationship between pastoral drama and baroque opera.

Pastoral drama adhered to strict literary conventions. However, these changed, not only with time but also with nationality. In different countries and at different times within the baroque period, the conventions of pastoral drama led to distinctive musical styles and structures as attempts were made to reflect the text in a musical setting. By examining baroque opera from the point of view of the pastoral, many stylistic and structural elements can be explained which previously were confusing or perhaps misunderstood. Indeed, the present study has led to a completely new analysis of Purcell's *Dido and Aeneas* and a revaluation of its existing sources.

The ultimate goal of this study, however, is the music of George Frideric Handel. Not only was Handel a great composer of baroque operas, but he lived and worked in three countries. Thus it has been possible to study the national traits of the pastoral in the compositions of one man and also to judge his assimilation of these traits. Handel's traditional association with the pastoral was another reason for choosing his works as a focal point. But this turned out to be of less value than I had originally assumed, since the association has been based on Handel's use of pastoral interludes, such as his sicilianos, rather than on his settings of pastoral drama. Nevertheless, Handel did set many pastorals, some of which have not been recognized as belonging to that dramatic type, and studying them has led to a new interpretation of Handel's transition from Italian opera to English oratorio.

In 1733, with the production of *Deborah* and *Athalia*, Handel achieved his first major successes in the composition of English oratorio. In the same year his operatic enterprise lost the right to perform in its accustomed theatre. Yet Handel did not abandon Italian opera. Quite to the contrary, for six years he composed in no other form. Only then did he return, ultimately to the exclusion of opera, to the composition of English oratorio. A so-called 'difficult and obscure period', the years from 1733 to 1738 in Handel's life have previously been explained simply in terms of the composer's stubbornness and short-sightedness. An investigation of the dramatic pastoral, both literary and musical, clarifies Handel's composition during this period. The conventions of the German pastoral formed its basis.

Readers may wonder why there is no chapter on the pastoral in France. Although it can be argued that French traditions have always been somewhat idiosyncratic and nationalistic, and therefore atypical, their omission was based on the more practical ground that Handel never lived and worked in France. The French pastoral traditions have thus been treated only as an influence – see the chapters on Germany and England.

I hope that both literary and musical historians will find this book useful, if provocative. It is aimed, however, more toward the musicologist. I have felt free, indeed constrained, to quote liberally not only from the contemporary literary treatises and from pastorals themselves, but also from secondary literary sources. I have done this partly to support my arguments, and partly to give the musicologist a better feel for a body of literature with which he may be unfamiliar. This is particularly true in the first chapter where I attempt to define pastoral drama.

This book began its life as a dissertation at the University of Chicago (1976). Additional research and revision have followed, but its conclusions and arguments remain the same. I am extremely grateful to the Visiting Committee to the Department of Music, The University of Chicago, for a subvention which aided the book's publication. I am also grateful for the continuing support of the Music Faculty of the University of Chicago. In particular I wish to thank Robert Marshall, my dissertation adviser, for his careful and critical attention to the structure of this material, its balance, order, and stylistic presentation. Howard Brown, a reader of my dissertation as well, consented to read chapters of this book as they were produced and provided wise commentary, as did Suzanne Gossett, Pierluigi Petrobelli, Glending Olson, and Hester Lewellen.

To the friendship of Philip and Suzanne Gossett I owe continuous help and encouragement. Suzanne Gossett and Glending Olson helped to oversee my forays into the new and unfamiliar world of literary criticism; any errors which remain are due only to my own shortcomings. Pierluigi Petrobelli and Father John Fiore have helped me enormously in hammering out translations from the Italian. I wish also to thank my publisher, whose editing of the typescript improved the book in its final stages.

My researches began at the Music Library of the University of

Chicago and continued mainly in England. I would like to thank, for their enduring patience with my questions and requests, Hans Lenneberg, Music Librarian, and the staff of the Music Library of the University of Chicago; the staff of the British Library in all of its various divisions, but especially the Music Library which holds the vast majority of Handel's extant autograph manuscripts; Paul Woudhuysen, Keeper of Books and Manuscripts, Fitzwilliam Museum; Anthea Baird, Music Librarian, the University of London; Jane Harington, Music Librarian, Royal Academy of Music, London. I would also like to thank for help with enquiries and microfilm orders, the Württembergische Landesbibliothek, Stuttgart; the Gesellschaft der Musikfreunde, Vienna; and the Library of Congress, Washington, D.C. Specific scholarly debts I have tried to acknowledge in footnotes throughout the book.

Finally I have the honour of thanking my family, my husband John and our very special children Marian and Ann. During the writing and rewriting of this book they remained patient and tolerant; and gave me encouragement and love.

Ellen T. Harris
Columbia University

for my parents
Zelma and Roger Turner

Table of Contents

1*

Tables

Music Examples

Abbreviations used above:

BL   British Library
Eg   Egerton (Granville Collection)
RM   Royal Music Collection
DdT   Denkmäler deutscher Tonkunst
DTÖ   Denkmäler der Tonkunst in Österreich
PAPTM   Publikation älterer praktischer und theoretischer Musikwerke
RAM   Royal Academy of Music

CHAPTER I

An Introduction to the Pastoral

The best introduction to this study would be a simple and clear definition of pastoral drama. Unfortunately this is not possible. The most obvious definition – shepherds and shepherdesses engaged in amorous pursuits against an idyllic pastoral backdrop – immediately calls to mind any number of exceptions and qualifications. For example, these shepherds are generally aristocratic and not realistic. Often, they represent contemporary figures from politics or religion. Sometimes the characters reflect events in the author's life. At other times they may allegorically represent states of mind. And so one would continue.

It is difficult to find adequate definitions of any large genre which develops over many years and differs in national characteristics. Aristotle's definition of tragedy provides one example which has existed for centuries as a model for other attempts. Unfortunately Aristotle himself could not try his hand at a definition of pastoral drama, for even though pastoral poetry can be traced back to the classics – the *Idylls* of Theocritus and the *Eclogues* of Virgil – pastoral *drama* is a modern form developed during the waning years of the Renaissance in response to changing dramatic tastes. At this time Aristotle's writings were particularly influential, but whereas he could treat tragedy and comedy as the two opposing kinds of drama, the baroque era rarely saw either of these types in its pure form. Instead it witnessed their combination in the new form of tragicomedy, of which the pastoral was one example.

When Guarini wrote *Il pastor fido* (1685), perhaps the most famous of the early pastoral dramas, he faced many critical objections. These, and Guarini's own defence, were mainly concerned with the validity of the larger genre of tragicomedy – suspect specifically because it was not sanctioned by Aristotle.[1] Guarini argues that classical tragedy is no longer pleasing to his age and describes modern comedy as totally debased. He ends his justification of tragicomedy with a definition which exactly parallels the form of Aristotle's definition of tragedy. The pastoral in its turn is justified as a type of tragicomedy.

---

[1] See Nicholas Perella, *The Critical Fortune of Battista Guarini's 'Il Pastor Fido'* (Florence: Leo S. Olschki, 1973) for a thorough study of the continuing controversy surrounding *Il pastor fido*. Allan H. Gilbert (ed.), *Literary Criticism: Plato to Dryden* (New York: American Book Co., 1940) contains a good translation of much of Guarini's *Compendium of Tragicomic Poetry* (1599), as well as excerpts from Aristotle's *Poetics* containing the definition of tragedy.

The major dramatic genre of the baroque era, and especially of opera, being tragicomedy, the student of baroque operatic traditions must remember that the Aristotelian polarity of tragedy and comedy no longer obtains. Instead the contrast is between various kinds of tragicomedy – the most important being pastoral and heroic drama – which include both serious and comic elements. Often, however, heroic drama is wrongly equated with tragedy and contrasted with comedy, leaving the pastoral as an incidental dramatic type.[2] Such alignments distort the picture of baroque opera and drama in which the pastoral played a major role. Although pastoral drama is a type of tragicomedy, Guarini's definition of this genre will not suffice for the pastoral. Thus the problem of a definition for the pastoral remains.

As with other dramatic types, the pastoral was not a static form. It changed greatly during the seventeenth century and differed according to national characteristics. Indeed, precisely because of this mutability, no writer on the pastoral has attempted a comprehensive definition of the genre. Beginning, however, with the superficial and inadequate description given at the outset of this chapter – shepherds and shepherdesses engaged in amorous pursuits against an idyllic pastoral backdrop – it is possible to study those aspects of action, of plot, of characterization, and of setting which alter this basic conception and enlarge it. These elements can be studied here without the strict regard to chronology and nationality which will be necessary in the following chapters, and their analysis will hopefully lead to a basic understanding of the pastoral in all its various guises. Such an understanding is essential to any study of baroque operatic traditions.

One of the most important elements in a definition of the pastoral is that its action represents a wooing or courtship, the lover's seeking, and winning or losing, of his beloved. Thus stories involving marital bliss or conjugal discord are of extreme rarity.

In the pastoral married love and wedded bliss are almost contradictions in terms. No pastoral poet, at least when keeping his inspiration within the bound of the genre, has felt any inclination to raise his humble eclogue to the level of a solemn epithalamium, or to drown the quiet music of his idyll under the

---

[2] Today's more common division of opera into 'serious' and 'comic' types was a development principally of the eighteenth century and closely connected with the burgeoning classicism in music and literature. Handel, like his contemporary Bach, was more tied to the older seventeenth-century baroque traditions than to the modern rococo style. One example of this is Handel's dependence on older seventeenth-century librettos. Winton Dean in *Handel and the Opera Seria* (Berkeley: University of California Press, 1969), p. 38, has shown the pitfalls in interpreting Handel's librettos by means of the later eighteenth-century comic-serious polarity. In this book and the earlier *Handel's Dramatic Oratorios and Masques* (London: Oxford University Press, 1959), Winton Dean has single-handedly brought Handel scholarship into the twentieth century. His careful research, close attention to manuscript sources, and obvious delight in the music itself stand as a model to all those who would follow in his path.

noise of wedding bells. This in spite of the fact that so many pastorals end with a marriage which in the course of the story was more hoped for than expected; and which is postponed as late as possible . . . in order to permit all possible digressions and divigations about subtler or more attractive forms of love.[3]

Because pastoral plots almost always revolve around a complicated love intrigue, the following description of one late Renaissance pastoral 'is remarkable . . . only for being so unremarkable an example of Renaissance Italian pastoral drama'.[4]

Caught in a maze of emotion complicated by a transvestite joke, [the characters] hold forth in various metres, singly, in duets, trios, and a final octet, on love, nature, illusion, love of nature, the nature of love, the illusion of love, the nature of illusion, and so forth.[5]

Mythological and magical elements always play an important role in these plots, and from the very beginning the amorous pastoral contained scenes of religious ceremony and sacrificial rites. The intrinsic nature of these ceremonial elements probably led to the earliest of the pastoral adaptations, or 'pastoralizations' of material not obviously pastoral. Indeed, the poets adapted some non-pastoral material merely because it contained mythical and magical scenes. They were drawn especially to Ovidian love stories involving transformations, for example, 'Acis and Galatea', 'Apollo and Daphne', and 'Orpheus and Eurydice'.[6] This type of pastoral adaptation was to become particularly prevalent in operatic librettos. Simon Towneley Worsthorne has described the typical librettos of the Venetian public opera houses in the middle of the seventeenth century:

Although the more popular plots were woven around historical or purely imaginary melodramatic stories, the old type of *favola pastorale*, deriving from the classical eclogue through the academies of the renaissance still had some following; but the final result in a libretto is a bastard child. Tasso's *Aminta*, for example, is far removed from such librettos as Persiani's *Le Nozze di Teti e di Peleo*, in which the pastoral landscape is filled out with figures from classical mythology.[7]

---

[3] Renato Poggioli, *The Oaten Flute: Essays on Pastoral Poetry and the Pastoral Ideal* (Cambridge, Massachusetts: Harvard University Press, 1975), p. 55.

[4] Louise George Clubb, 'The Making of the Pastoral Play: Italian Experience between 1573 and 1590' in *Petrarch to Pirandello: Studies in Italian Literature in honour of Beatrice Corrigan*, ed. by Julius A. Molinaro (Toronto: University of Toronto Press, 1973), p. 47.

[5] Ibid., p. 46. The play described is Luigi Pasqualigo's *Gl'Intricati: pastorale* (Venice, 1581).

[6] In *Pastoral Poetry and Pastoral Drama* (London: A. H. Bullen, 1906), p. 36, Walter Wilson Greg writes that 'Another of the outlying realms of the pastoral is the mythological tale, more or less directly imitated from Ovid.' Clubb, 'The Making of the Pastoral Play,' p. 67, gives both 'real magic and Ovidian metamorphosis' as 'stock elements of the genre'.

[7] Simon Towneley Worsthorne, *Venetian Opera in the Seventeenth Century* (Oxford: Clarendon Press, 1954), p. 128. This opera by Cavalli, with a libretto by Persiani, was performed in 1639.

The principal characters in a pastoral were normally non-specific and nondescript. The elevated historical and mythological figures of heroic or epic modes were avoided. At the same time, however, the characters were not base or rude, as in the contemporary comedy or farce, but were bestowed with a grace and elegance fit for the highest court. Still, they were elegant nobodies. One can imagine even now the sixteenth-century Italian heroes such as Orlando or Rinaldo, or the important comic figures of Pantalone and Zanni, but who were Dorinda, Amarilli, or Silvia? Each was only one of an apparently unlimited supply of lovelorn nymphs. This characteristic is succinctly illustrated in a modern criticism of Goethe's *Faust* where Helen of Troy is made queen of Arcadia: 'But to live within Arcadia Helen was not needed; any Phyllis would have served'.[8]

The nymphs and shepherds of Arcadia may have been nonentities in themselves, but they walked with the gods. And the shepherds' natural relations with the gods lent authority to the pastoralizations of Ovidian stories of transformation. At the same time, however, the inclusion of these stories within the pastoral corpus served to change somewhat the nature of the pastoral character. One recognizes Eurydice, Daphne, and Galatea as identifiable characters with individual histories. Moreover, their success in Arcadia led to still other kinds of pastoralizations and the inclusion of characters from a 'rank fit for epic and tragedy',[9] often associated with the use of 'magic from the *romanzo* tradition'.[10]

Just as the pastoralists used the stories and characters of Ovidian mythology, they also borrowed from the Italian epic poetry, especially that of the sixteenth century. The pastoral episodes of these, for example the story of Erminia among the shepherds in Tasso's *Gerusalemme liberata*, and the story of Angelica and Medoro in Ariosto's *Orlando furioso*, became a storehouse for pastoral conceits.

The dark wood confirmed by Dante as landscape for human error had also for the late Cinquecento poet the specific aspect of labyrinth of love, reminiscent of Horace and Petrarch but primarily identified with *Orlando Furioso*, in which [the dark wood represents] fictional 'fact', principle of plotting, and, continually, simile. . . . The [pastoral] playwright's recognition of Ariosto's importance to the genre is expressed in their including him in prefatory genealogies and in their plundering of *Orlando Furioso*. . . .[11]

Furthermore, it seems clear that there was a particularly close relationship between the magical elements borrowed from Ariosto and the

[8] George Santayana, *Three Philosophical Poets: Lucretius, Dante, and Goethe* (Cambridge, Massachusetts: Harvard University Press, 1910; reprint ed., New York: Doubleday, Anchor Books, 1953), as quoted by Poggioli, *The Oaten Flute*, p. 52.
[9] Clubb, 'The Making of the Pastoral Play', p. 54.
[10] Ibid., p. 53.
[11] Ibid., p. 64.

metamorphoses borrowed from Ovid. 'Even when not directly quoted, *Orlando Furioso* is often evoked by the presence of didactic sorcerers resembling Atlante or Melissa, and by pastoral transformation, especially those of the loquacious arboreal variety, in which Ariosto's particular blend of the amorous cause from Ovid and Petrarch with the monitory effect from Virgil is dominant.'[12]

Such pastoral episodes within the epic or other non-pastoral work have been termed 'pastoral oases' by Renato Poggioli. 'Such "oases" appear in the *Aeneid*, the *Commedia*, the *Furioso*, the *Lusiados*, *Don Quixote*, and *As You Like It*. One of the most beautiful, and the most typical of them, is in Tasso's *Gerusalemme liberata* (vii).'[13] In operatic librettos, however, these episodes lose their status as oases and stand by themselves as pastorals. This point is crucial for the definition of an operatic pastoral, or, for that matter, of contemporary pastoral drama. Just as the pastoral oases do not make the Italian epics any less heroic, so a pastoral episode does not alter the otherwise heroic structure of a play or an opera. In fact, when such an oasis does appear in a play, this means that the play itself cannot be a pastoral. In a pastoral the Arcadian landscape must envelop the entire world. Thus it is a peculiar feature of the pastoral theme that its inclusion in a non-pastoral composition does not disturb that work's mode, yet an interruption of the pastoral world, by making that world an oasis, does destroy the pastoral mode. Only excised from their original context, do these oases become fully fledged pastorals.[14] Thus as early as 1619 Marco da Gagliano set to music a libretto entitled *Il Medoro* by A. Salvadori, based on the Medoro-Angelica episode in *Orlando*. In 1633 M. A. Rossi set Rospigliosi's *Erminia sul giordano*, adapted from the pastoral "oasis" in *Gerusalemme*. Throughout the baroque era such pastoral librettos continued to be popular.

Another type of pastoralization, less well documented but often implicit in the use of scenes from epic poetry, involves the use of stories and characters from the tradition of medieval romance. Between this literary form and the pastoral there exist many points of contact. For example, the importance and quality of the process of wooing cannot be overemphasized in a discussion of either tradition. In both it serves to delimit the realm of the genre. In fact, its lack has been used to

---

[12] Ibid.

[13] Poggioli, *The Oaten Flute*, pp. 9–10. In *Gerusalemme liberata* Poggioli refers to the story of Erminia among the shepherds.

[14] It will be seen that Handel was very careful to observe the distinction between 'oases' and pastorals in his compositions. Pastoral scenes were treated differently than pastoral operas, the former depending quite heavily on the use of the siciliano, whereas this style was rare or totally absent in true pastorals. See the discussions below on *Il pastor fido*, *Amadigi*, and *Ariodante*.

explain why certain works cannot belong to the tradition of courtly love:

In *Erec* . . . the later rules of love and courtesy are outraged at every turn. It is indeed a love story; but it is a story of married love. . . . This, in itself, is an irregularity; but the method of wooing is worse. *Erec* sees *Enide* in her father's house, and falls in love with her. There are no passages of love between them: no humility on his part, no cruelty on hers. Indeed it is not clear that they converse at all. . . . Later, when they are seated, the father and the guest talk of her in her presence as if she were a child or an animal. *Erec* asks her in marriage, and the father consents.[15]

The crux of the difference between this story and one belonging to the sphere of medieval romance or pastoral lies in the concept of duty. Love, at least 'true love', cannot be dependent on duty; it must be won, not commanded. In addition, it must be secretive and jealously guarded from the needs and desires of society. Thus, in *Il pastor fido* Amarilli is constrained to marry Silvio by her duty to her father, who has arranged her betrothal to spare the Arcadian society continued human sacrifice. It is crucial for the sake of the pastoral that this duty be denied, which it is, and for the circumstances to allow 'true love' to triumph, which they do.[16] It is just this concept of duty which bars marital love from the stories of courtly love.

Conjugal affection cannot be 'love' because there is in it an element of duty or necessity: a wife, in loving her husband, is not exercising her free choice in the reward of merit. . . . Conjugal love is not furtive, and jealousy, which is of the essence of true love, is merely a pest in marriage. . . . The love which is to be the source of all that is beautiful in life and manners must be the reward freely given by the lady, and only our superiors can reward. But a wife is not a superior. . . . As your own wife, for whom you have bargained with her father, she sinks at once from lady into mere woman. How can a woman, whose duty is to obey you, be the *midons* whose grace is the goal of all striving and whose displeasure is the restraining influence upon all uncourtly vices?[17]

---

[15] C. S. Lewis, *The Allegory of Love: A Study in Medieval Tradition* (New York: Oxford University Press, Galaxy Book, 1958), p. 25. *Erec* is by Chrétien de Troyes who lived in the second half of the twelfth century.

[16] The separation of the goals of society from those of the pastoral has also been cited by Richard Cody, *The Landscape of the Mind: Pastoralism and Platonic Theory in Tasso's 'Aminta' and Shakespeare's Early Comedies* (Oxford: Clarendon Press, 1969), p. 46: 'The *Aminta* thus differs markedly from a non-pastoral, such as the *Mandragola*. For all its concern with the courtship of lovers, one of whom is feverish and the other coldly chaste, Machiavelli's is a play about society, not passion – the politics of sex. . . .'
The lack of marital subjects and the concept of duty in pastoral plots may explain why the apparently similar stories of Orpheus and Eurydice and Admetus and Alcestis have traditionally been treated so differently; Orpheus has become in some ways the patron saint of the pastoral whereas Admetus and Alcestis remain outside the genre. Aside from the fact that Orpheus is a shepherd and Admetus a king (in the Golden Age shepherds were kings), the story of Orpheus is about a couple in love, a sudden loss, a bereavement, and a decision to regain the initial idyllic state against all odds. It is a selfish decision. The story of Alcestis is about a married couple, illness, the needs of society, and a sacrifice.

[17] Lewis, *The Allegory of Love*, pp. 36–7.

In many of their aspects the literary traditions of the medieval romance and the pastoral seem to suggest a parent-child relationship. The pastoral appears to have borrowed from the earlier mode not only the concept of wooing, but also the general anonymity of the characters reflected in the stereotyped situations wherein the actors can retain no identity other than 'Mistress' or 'Lover' rather than 'nymph' or 'swain'. 'Nymph and shepherdess are not personalities but images of woman. In this they conform to that transparency by means of which pastoral could so readily become opera. As one listens to the arias of Silvia or Dafne it is clear that Tasso writes not a comedy of manners, but a *Romance of the Rose* adapted to the stage. Like shepherd and satyr, these are figures in a play of shadows and represent a lover's inner life collectively.'[18]

The settings of these stories also seem to have affected the renaissance descriptions of the Arcadian pastoral landscape, itself borrowed from the classical eclogues and bucolics of Theocritus and Virgil. The following description of the traditional hedged garden is strikingly similar to the most common representations of the Arcadian Golden Age. 'Turning his back on the nominal subject of his poet, he [Claudian] carries us away to a mountain in Cyrus which the frosts never whiten and the winds never beat. On the mountain head is a meadow guarded by a *hedge of gold* [added emphasis], and all within it blooms unsown. . . . Only the sweetest song-birds live in its copses. . . . *Juventas* also is there and he has shut *Senium* out from the garden.'[19] One can also see a parallel between the allegorical representation of the court as an enclosed garden and Tasso's use of the pastoral to represent actual figures at the Ferrarese court.[20] The differences lie in the change from a walled garden as a limited oasis to the pastoral landscape as an entire world.

The mood of courtly love permeated the pastoral and left an important mark which sometimes blurs the borders of the later tradition. Surely this relationship added authority to the courtliness of otherwise natural

---

[18] Cody, *The Landscape of the Mind*, pp. 54–5.

[19] Lewis, *The Allegory of Love*, pp. 74–5. Claudian came to Italy in A.D. 395. He wrote the work described here, an Epithalamium on Honorius' marriage, in 398. It is just possible that the poetry of courtly love retained some of the important traditions of the classical pastoral poetry until the rebirth of the pastoral in dramatic form during the Renaissance. Greg (*Pastoral*, p. 6) writes, 'Having inspired Ovid and Vergil, and been recognised by Lucretius, it [the concept of a Golden Age] passed as a literary legacy to Boethius, Dante, and Jean de Meuny [the second author of the *Roman*]. . . .' See also Paul Piehler, *The Visionary Landscape* (London: Edward Arnold, 1971), Chapter 5: 'The Landscapes of Vision,' pp. 70–83, for an interesting discussion of the pastoral landscapes in medieval romance literature.

[20] See Eugenio Donadoni, *A History of Italian Literature* (New York: New York University Press, 1969), Vol. I, p. 255: 'The sincerity of the poetry [in *Aminta*] also is due to the fact that the poet, behind the transparent curtains of pastoral poetry, sketches the milieu of the court of Ferrara with himself as the spurned lover in the character of Aminta . . .'

shepherds, and pastoralizations of stories from the tradition of the medieval romance exist in something of a never-never land between the two traditions. Spenser's *Faerie Queene*, for example, is considered by C. S. Lewis the last English exponent of the tradition of courtly love and by W. W. Greg as one of the first examples of pastoral.[21] Some baroque operas, similarly, are distinctly treated as pastorals, though their plots are infused with courtly love and their characters are without the normal pastoral disguises.[22] This treatment may be explained by the basic duality of the baroque operatic tradition (courtly love is not heroic) as well as by the close similarities of the two literary genres.

As in the medieval love stories, the use of allegory is persistent in the pastoral. 'One could say, at least in a certain sense, that almost all pastoral poetry is allegorical because it deals only rarely with shepherds in the literal sense of the term: in the main it uses the shepherd's disguise to give an idealized representation of the withdrawn artist, or the retired poet, of the solitary lover, or, more generally, of the man for whom private life is the highest value on earth.'[23] This intrinsic use of allegory seems to push both genres toward the conscious representation of religious subjects. In the poetry of courtly love this direction is suggested by the similarity of the religious hierarchy to that of love's divinities. In the pastoral, religious, mystical, and sacrificial elements had played a large role from the beginning, but it was the pastoral images in Christian symbolism that were strong enough to make such a transformation of the pagan world into the Christian not only possible, but at least as plausible as that which changed Daphne into a tree.

Pastoral traits can be found not only in the legend of the Nativity but also in the story of Christ's mission and teachings, as related by the Gospels: think of Jesus entering Jerusalem riding a donkey, or choosing his apostles among the humblest of the humble, the fishermen, of whom he makes his angler of souls; think especially of the parable of the herdsman who abandons a flock of ninety-nine sheep to find again the hundredth one, which is missing and must be lost in the wilderness. It is from this parable, so meaningful and suggestive, that Christianity later derived the most poetic of all its allegories, representing both Christ and the new faith under the figure of the good shepherd, carrying back on his shoulders the little sheep once lost. Christian symbolism seems

---

[21] *The Faerie Queene* is obviously indebted to the Italian epic as a primary source. Yet the relationship between the epic and the pastoral has also been shown to be important. The general interdependence of these many literary genres, fascinating as it may be, must here be passed over with only a mention and left in the more capable hands of literary historians. The reader is referred to the works listed in the Bibliography by Clubb, Cullen, Fleming, Greg, Lewis, and Praz.

[22] Handel's *Ariodante* (1735) is one such example where a specific attempt is made to connect the story with the pastoral tradition. See below, Chapter VI, 'Handel's Stylistic Maturity.'

[23] Poggioli, *The Oaten Flute*, pp. 121–2.

able to translate into idyllic imagery even the highest moment in sacred history, the Passion of Christ and the Redemption of Man, the martyrdom and immolation of the Son of God. That moment, which transcends the most heroic and tragic visions ever shaped by the human mind, still allows itself to be represented under the pastoral emblem of *agnus dei*, the sacrificial lamb washing away all the sins of the world with its blood.[24]

The equation of the Golden Age with the Garden of Eden, or as something attainable in the hereafter, also pertains, as do the many pastoral images within the psalms, the most familiar being 'The Lord is my Shepherd'. The religious pastoral, however, did not generally serve as a song of praise, but as a didactic or corrective tool.

It is obviously by something more than a mere coincidence that the Catholic priest or the Protestant minister came to be called a *pastor*: the origins of this name go back as far as the evangelical parable of the lost sheep, or at least as the early Christian symbol of the good shepherd. The negative aspect of such an analogy was bound to tempt all the critics of the worldly and temporal aims of the religious and ecclesiastical polity: all those who blamed the Church for harbouring too many bad shepherds among the tenders of its flocks, and even of raising to its highest seat a wolf in sheep's clothing. In brief, the allegorical pastoral turns the praise of pastoral life into an indictment of the bad shepherds of the Church; and if it evokes an ideal of bucolic purity and idyllic innocence, it is only to make more severe its condemnation of the pastors who betray it.[25]

These pastorals were often set not as dramas but as poetical treatises, and it can hardly be a surprise that such allegorical and didactic treatises do not find their way into the corpus of operatic librettos. Their undramatic means and their ultra-corrective aims are hardly suitable for such a purpose. Yet their lesser relation, the pastoral morality, played, in constrast, a large role indeed.

The very first Roman opera, *Rappresentazioni di anima e di corpo* (1600) by Emilio de'Cavalieri, was of such a type. Thus also was *Eumelio: Dramma pastorale* (Rome, 1606) by Agostino Agazzari and *La Catena d'Adone: Favola boschereccia* (Rome, 1626) by Domenico Mazzocchi. In the early years of operatic production, the pastoral morality formed the most important sub-category to the more lascivious, mythological pastoral performed at Florence. Its influence was far-reaching; even the first extant German opera, *Seelewig* by Sigmund Staden, is subtitled *geistliche Waldgedicht*.[26]

The morality is easily adapted to the pastoral vein. As in the pastoral, the setting of a morality is usually in some way secluded or cut off from daily life. Often it is completely outdoors, a landscape, forest, or garden. After all, Jesus was tempted in a wilderness, Adam and Eve in a garden.

[24] Ibid., p. 121.
[25] Ibid., p. 94.
[26] This work is discussed in detail in Chapter III, 'The Pastoral in Germany.'

The subject of a morality, like a pastoral, is of a wooing or courtship, and the characters are easily equated with those of the pastoral. Equally anonymous, or here, perhaps, universal, the soul is represented in most cases by the young nymph. Temptation and Good Conscience are her two suitors, represented by the omnipresent Arcadian satyr and the lovelorn, but faithful shepherd. It is clear that pastorals could easily be turned into moralities. When Guarini was criticized for the explicit immorality of *Il pastor fido* he simply devised an allegorical programme which explained how the actions of his characters represented the triumph of innocence over licentiousness.[27]

The allegorical and specifically religious use of the pastoral has always had critics. 'The preposterous mixture of pagan and Christian motives . . . was indeed one of the most persistent as it was one of the least admirable characteristics of pastoral composition.'[28] The realistic pastoral developed in reaction to this type. Such a realistic portrait of the shepherdly life, however, found no place in an operatic genre, where unreality was such a virtue. It destroyed the sense of a world set apart; it invariably played havoc with the proper essence of wooing, and it gave a distinct and generally comic identity to the characters. Those writers connected with baroque opera always argued forcefully against its intrusion. Giambattista Doni specifically warned against the use in librettos of the 'sordid and vulgar shepherds who today may be found guarding the sheep'.[29] Metastasio wrote that 'between the language of real and theatrical shepherds there should be the same proportion of difference as the best writers usually observe between real and theatrical princes';[30] and Hunold prescribed that 'the shaving room for the rams, cheese from sheep's and goat's milk, and other stinking material must be omitted'.[31] The use of rustic pastoral types in opera was, therefore, restricted to the comic interlude in a more serious story, and such operatic characters did not derive from the pastoral tradition at all, but from the rustic stereotypes found in the Commedia dell'Arte.[32] These characters never seem to appear as protagonists.

All of the various types of pastoral detailed above were developed by the end of the sixteenth century, and almost all found an immediate

[27] See Perella, *Critical Fortune*, p. 27: Mirtillo = perfect man, Amarilli = true happiness and honest love, Dorinda = natural love, Corisca = bestial love, etc.

[28] Greg, *Pastoral*, p. 41.

[29] Giambattista Doni, 'Trattato della Musica Scenica,' *Lyra Barberina*, ed. by A. M. Bandini (Florence: Ex Typis Caesareis, 1763), ii, p. 16.

[30] Quoted and translated in Dorothy Irene West, *Italian opera in England (1660–1740), and Some of its Relationships to English Literature*, An Abstract of a Thesis (Urbana: University of Illinois, 1938), p. 7.

[31] Hunold, Christian Friedrich [Menantes], *Die allerneueste Art, zur reinen und galanten Poesie zu gelangen* (Hamburg: G. Liebernickel, 1707), p. 348.

[32] See, for example, Helmuth Christian Wolff, *Die Barock Oper in Hamburg: 1678–1738* (Wolfenbüttel: Möseler Verlag, 1957), i, p. 183.

place in the early operatic librettos. Moreover, as the pastoral drama and its operatic counterpart spread out of Italy into other European countries, both began to take on specific, national attributes as well. Many of these pastoral types, the versions and the national variants, could be distinguished by their different settings. Although the landscape of the pastoral seems at first to be its most universal trait, it takes on many different guises which are both meaningful and important. The amorous pastoral could be set in mythological Arcadia, or in Sicily, or on Mt. Parnassus. In the English versions these settings were generally transformed into forests such as those of Arden or Sherwood. The morality could use the image of a Garden of Eden, which like Arcadia is lost forever, or point to a new Arcadia in Paradise or the Elysian Fields. A courtly pastoral might not even have an outdoor setting as long as the terrain was in some sense isolated or mysterious. Islands abound. In pastorals taken from the epic romances the location is often completely magical and imaginary. The only requirement seems to have been that for the duration of the pastoral the setting represents a world of its own outside the realm of the real or typical world.

As a single genre, then, the pastoral exists in many diverse guises. Its main attributes, existing throughout all of the many variations, only seem to be: the use of a setting complete in itself and divorced from the real world in time and place; a plot that involves a wooing, courtship, or quest which, except in the morality, is divorced from duty and society and may be won or lost; and a set of generalized characters that remain undelineated except when a non-pastoral has been used as a source. The plurality of the versions of the pastoral has caused a great deal of confusion, and many attempts have been made to define the genre by its variety. In fact, modern theorists of the pastoral have often resorted to the use of antithesis in attempting to clarify the genre's manifold elements. Unfortunately, each seems to have chosen a different set of elements to contrast, and this has only created more confusion of its own. The theories about the English pastoral form a good example.

W. W. Greg distinguishes 'pastoral orthodoxy' (as exemplified by the works of Guarini and Tasso) from 'a more spontaneous' (or realistic) style. 'Thus it is possible to trace two distinct though mutually reacting tendencies far down the stream of English literature, and to this double origin must be referred many of the peculiar phenomena of English pastoral work. There was furthermore a constant struggle for supremacy between the two traditions, in which now one now the other appeared likely to go under.'[33] J. E. Congleton's definitive *Theories of Pastoral Poetry in England* contrasts the 'neo-classic' (mythological) with the

[33] Greg, *Pastoral*, p. 68.

'rational' (naturalistic) pastoral – the latter developing into the 'romantic' (idealistic or utopian) pastoral.[34] Furthermore, in discussing the English origin of the pastoral, Congleton opposes the use of allegory with the 'imitation of rural life'.

Because allegory remained an important element of English pastoralism, many modern writers base their antitheses on the different ways in which it was used, rather than on whether it was used or not. Homer Smith distinguishes an allegory that signifies abstract qualities from one that represents real characters or events in disguise.[35] Patrick Cullen contrasts the 'Arcadian' pastoral which 'takes as its pastoral ideal the *pastor felix* and the soft life of otium'[36] and the 'Mantuanesque' pastoral which 'takes as its ideal the Judeo-Christian *pastor bonus* . . . largely opposed to the shepherd of worldly felicity'[37] – the former satirizing the artifices of courtly life, the latter aiming at revealing religious corruption.

The plurality of the antithetical theories is confusing, and this even when dealing only with the English adaptation of the pastoral. None of the categories are irrelevant or non-existent, but one searches in vain for a common thread that would yield the 'Universal Antithesis'. One obvious and simple alternative, a list of all the traits of the pastoral, only some of which can be covered in the above theories, has now been attempted by Poggioli.

Like the theorists preceding him, however, Poggioli begins with a dichotomy, in this case the pastoral of happiness and the pastoral of innocence. Unlike his predecessors, he then describes the important categories which developed out of these basic concepts: the Christian pastoral, the funeral elegy, the pastoral of self, and the pastoral of solitude. In addition Poggioli goes on to describe almost thirty less important variants: the pastoral of animal life, Biblical pastoral, pastoral of childhood, courtly pastoral, erotic pastoral, pastoral of friendship, political pastoral, urban pastoral, and so on. Poggioli's theories are comprehensive and his analyses acute. Any serious student of the pastoral must henceforth be greatly indebted to him. Yet his theories are too complex, the types described too numerous, to lead towards a basic understanding of the genre. Furthermore, neither the antithetical theories nor a comprehensive list can illustrate the mixture of features in any one work.

[34] James E. Congleton, *Theories of Pastoral Poetry in England: 1684–1798* (Gainsville, Florida: University of Florida Press, 1952).
[35] Homer Smith, 'Pastoral Influence in the English Drama,' *PMLA*, xii (1897), pp. 355–460.
[36] Patrick Cullen, *Spenser, Marvell, and Renaissance* (Cambridge, Massachusetts: Harvard University Press, 1970), p. 2.
[37] Ibid., p. 3.

One answer lies in the use of a simple matrix which illustrates the basic form any work might take without detailing every stylistic deviation an author might use within that form.

TABLE 1
Literary Pastoral Forms

Shepherd Type	Literary Style	
	Allegoric	Lyric
Idealistic	1	3
Realistic	2	4

Thus there are four main types.

1. Idealized or 'Golden Age' shepherds presented in an allegorical framework;
2. Realistic or rustic shepherds presented in an allegorical framework;
3. Idealized or 'Golden Age' shepherds presented in a mode of pure lyric beauty; and
4. Realistic or rustic shepherds presented in a romantic appreciation of the 'natural life' or for comic effect.

This schema recognizes the two criteria by which the pastoral must be described: the goal of the author, and the literary method used to achieve that goal. Part of the reason why the antitheses of the various literary critics cannot be reconciled with one another is that they mix elements from both sets of criteria. Pastoral operas as well as pastoral dramas may be found in all four categories.

Handel's operatic pastorals fall into the third category, which includes original pastoral dramas (*Il pastor fido*, 1712, 1733, 1734), Ovidian transformation stories (*Acis and Galatea*, 1708, 1720, 1732, etc.), and the adaptations of epic poetry (*Amadigi*, 1715). This category encompasses, in fact, most pastoral literature and is the characteristic Italian form. The pastoral moralities fall clearly into the first category, as do the generally non-musical Christian pastorals. Both the literary form of the realistic pastoral and the burlesque, rustic scenes of the operatic mode belong in the fourth. There is some overlap between the first and the third, as in the case of Tasso's *Aminta*, which is in the main an example of the lyrical mode but is in part autobiographical and therefore allegorical. This type of allegory, having no didactic intent, however, can for purposes of definition be generally disregarded. For example, the importance of the allegory in Spenser's *Shepherds Calendar*, discussed below, does not reside in its autobiographical aspects, but in those dialogues which deal with ecclesiastical or court affairs. Thus 'allegory', whether or not it refers to real personages, is here taken to

have a corrective or moralistic aim. Except for a few works of Theocritus, the second category, also allegorical, is peculiarly English.

It may strike the reader that so complicated a subject as the literary
pastoral should find no place in a discussion of baroque opera. However,
one can only begin to understand and explain the stylistic differences
between the heroic and pastoral modes which occur in the baroque
operatic scores when one can identify the various types of pastorals
which occur in the librettos. To attribute differences of scale, for example, to purely superficial reasons, such as financial difficulties or
festive, royal occasions, is to beg the issue entirely. Rather, one should
ask, given certain external circumstances, what type of libretto would be
most suitable. For example, it is much more informative to learn that
composers wrote pastorals when they were required to write a festive
choral opera than to say they wrote choruses in their pastorals because
they were performed on festive occasions. Pastorals were used for other
than royal and festive performances, and their characteristics remained
the same. In each country, however, the literary traditions created a
different set of characteristics.

It should not be surprising that Italy, Germany, and England, having
developed by the end of the seventeenth century widely divergent types
of literary pastorals, produced different types of operatic pastorals as
well, each distinctly reflecting the national literary conventions. The
character of these scores falls generally into two categories: one dependent on the text, one not. The first represents those things presented
in the libretto which affect the entire make-up of an opera before any
music is written. The use or lack of choruses, the use of the *da capo*
convention and 'exit aria', the strict alternation of aria and recitative,
and the use or lack of comic characters are all examples. Within these
limitations, however, a composer may interpose a stylistic identity of
his own, and this represents the second category. He can, for example,
determine the vocal ranges and vary the instrumental accompaniments.
He controls the harmonic plan and the metrical variety. He may, of
course, slavishly follow the poetic foot and rhyme scheme of his libretto,
as does Staden in *Seelewig*, but he may also, like Kusser in *Erindo*,
faced with multiple verse forms for arias, come up with unchanging
bipartite solutions. The composer may raise recitative into song and
change song into recitative as Lawes does to Milton's *Comus*; or he
may add and delete choruses, as Purcell does in *Dido and Aeneas*.[38]

Handel, too, made all these kinds of adjustments. Faced with innu-
merable *da capo* aria texts, he found seemingly endless ways to set them.

[38] All these operas are discussed below; those by Staden and Kusser in Chapter III, 'The
Pastoral in Germany,' and those by Lawes and Purcell in Chapter IV, 'The Pastoral in
England.'

He freely altered arioso, arietta, recitativo accompagnato and secco, and aria sections without strictly adhering to his libretto. On occasion he added instrumental symphonies, ballets, and choruses.[39] The way in which a composer reacts to any specific text reveals a great deal about his conception of that dramatic form, and composers did not typically set pastoral and heroic texts in the same way. That is, the stylistic differences to be found between these kinds of operas are not only those dependent on the text.

The analysis of musical and literary pastorals in Italy, Germany, and England in the seventeenth century reveals for each country a national literary pastoral tradition and a distinct musical reaction to that tradition. When Handel lived and worked in each of these countries he adjusted his pastoral style to the prevailing pastoral traditions. In the competitive atmosphere of the 1730s when the fortunes of the heroic *opera seria* were failing and contemporary events called for musical celebration, Handel's familiarity with three national pastoral types was an important factor in his survival. The pastoral also formed the bridge for his 'conversion' from the *opera seria* of the 1720s to the oratorios of the 1740s.

The dramatic pastoral had been the most important element leading to the birth of opera. In addition, throughout most of the seventeenth century it provided the only alternative to heroic *opera seria*. Finally the synthesis of its national varieties led to some of the most important operatic developments of the eighteenth century. In this last, Handel led the way.

---

[39] For the best general discussion of Handel's reactions to his librettos see Dean, *Opera*, 'The Libretto,' pp. 36–53, and 'Aria and Recitative,' pp. 152–84.

CHAPTER II

The Pastoral in Italy

THE BIRTH OF THE DRAMATIC PASTORAL

The dramatic pastoral was born in Ferrara, 1554, in the form of a play entitled *Il sacrifizio* by Agostino de'Beccari. So says Giambattista Guarini, author of the most renowned of all pastoral dramas, *Il pastor fido*.

It must always be understood that though, in respect to the persons introduced, pastoral poetry recognizes its origin in the eclogue and the satyr drama of the ancients, yet as to form and method it can be called something modern, since we have from antiquity no example of such a drama in Greek or Latin. The first of the moderns who had the courage to do it and succeeded was Agostin de'Beccari, a respected citizen of Ferrara, to whom alone the world should assign the happy invention of such a poem.[1]

One hundred years later, in one of the most thorough baroque histories of Italian literature, Giovanni Maria Crescimbeni concurs completely, and indeed cites Guarini. 'There is no doubt whatsoever that the origins of this dramatic type are to be recognized in [classical] comedy for the form and in the eclogue for the content.'[2] And after describing the subjects of these eclogues which lead up to the pastoral drama, he writes:

All these things were elements of good pastoral poetry represented scenically, which dramatic type was finally to be born about 1555 [in *Il sacrifizio* by Beccari] . . .; and if this play does not have all the most refined features of a most perfect comedy, it has enough to bestow upon the author the boast of invention, as he himself does in the prologue of that work, and as Guarini and others after him agree.[3]

As Crescimbeni was one of the founding fathers and first president of the Roman Arcadian Academy which championed the failing fortunes of the pastoral drama in word and deed, his writings on the pastoral also have special claims to attention.

---

[1] *Compendio della poesia tragicomica* (1599), translated in Gilbert (ed.), *Literary Criticism*, p. 531.

[2] Giovanni Maria Crescimbeni, *Commentarii intorno all' Istoria della Poesia Italiana* (London: Presso T. Becket, 1803), ii, p. 212. Crescimbeni's principal critical works are *Dell'Istoria della Volgar Poesia* (Rome, 1698), the *Commentarii* (Rome, 1702–11), both of which were republished together in Rome, 1714, and *La Bellezza della Volgar Poesia* (Rome, 1700). All these works were republished together in Venice, 1730–1.

[3] Crescimbeni, *Commentarii*, ii, pp. 218–19. Crescimbeni deals thoroughly with all other claims of precedence and explains their lack of priority.

In this century W. W. Greg's encyclopedic *Pastoral Poetry and Pastoral Drama* remains the best modern history of the dramatic pastoral. He, too, notes the modernity of the form and cites Guarini. 'We shall find that the pastoral drama comes into being, not through the infusion of the Arcadian ideal into pre-existing dramatic forms, but through the actual evolution of a new dramatic form from the pre-existing non-dramatic pastoral.'[4] He describes the drama's evolution 'from its germ in the non-dramatic eclogue',[5] and its birth in the work of Beccari where 'the author boldly announces the novelty of his work', and he explains that 'Guarini bore out Beccari's claim'.[6]

Guarini, Crescimbeni, and Greg are thus in total agreement about the birth of the dramatic pastoral, and in the three centuries separating their works they are the major historians of the genre. Because the way in which the dramatic pastoral was born affected its subsequent history and, as will be seen, its relationship with music, such concurrence is important. It is not unanimous. In fact, Crescimbeni and Greg must both deal with conflicting theories.

Some consider either Poliziano's *Favola d'Orfeo* or Niccolò da Correggio's *Cefalo* (1487) the first pastoral drama. For example, Richard Cody, writes, 'It is in the *Orfeo* (*c.* 1480) that Platonic theory and Orphic mythology first coincide in a pastoralism that anticipates Tasso's. Guarini, an Aristotelian in criticism, omits all mention of this from the *Compendium*, preferring to acknowledge Beccari's *Sacrifizio*(1554) as the prototype. But Poliziano's little play remains the classic instance in this mode of the nexus of doctrine and poetry.'[7] Although it is certainly true that during the heyday of pastoralism and pastoralizations the stories of Orpheus and Cephalus were widely used, neither played a fundamental role in the development of pastoral drama.[8]

. . . Critics who would see in them the origin of the later pastoral drama have to explain the strange phenomenon of the species lying dormant for nearly three-quarters of a century, and then suddenly developing into an equally individualized but very dissimilar form. It should, moreover, be borne in mind that contemporary critics never regarded the Arcadian pastoral as in any way

---

[4] Greg, *Pastoral*, p. 155.
[5] Ibid., p. 156.
[6] Ibid., pp. 174–5.
[7] Cody, *Landscape*, p. 30.
[8] Of Orpheus little need be said. The story of Cephalus also made frequent operatic appearances, for example, *Il Rapimento di Cefalo* (Florence, 1600), *Il Ratto di Cefalo* (Ferrara, 1650) and *L'Aurora in Atene* (Venice, 1678). See below, p. 26.

In this and later discussions dealing with seventeenth-century operatic literature, I am deeply indebted to Thomas Walker who generously made available to me his unpublished catalogue of seventeenth-century Italian operatic librettos indexed by title and supplemented with a catalogue of the characters as they appear in the lists.

connected with the mythological drama, and that writers of the pastoral themselves claimed no kinship with Poliziano or Correggio, but always ranked
themselves as the followers of Beccari alone in the line of dramatic development.[9]

Nevertheless, lack of poetic quality in *Il sacrifizio*, noted by Crescimbeni, has led some critics to seek another source for the dramatic
pastoral. By using this criterion, however, the important distinction
between pastoral poetry and drama is overlooked. Greg's words
'dramatic development', give the best clue for resolving the problem
of the pastoral's origin. When critics show a line of development
from Poliziano to Tasso's *Aminta*, they refer not to a dramatic form
but only to a specific aura or atmosphere. Indeed, the content of
the dramatic pastoral can be traced to the eclogue, as Guarini and
Crescimbeni agree. Tasso's play itself was often called an eclogue, and
divorced from the main line of dramatic pastoral poetry it can still be
discussed that way. The proposed developmental line from Poliziano
and Sannazaro to Tasso, then, leads inevitably to a discussion of
pastoral poetry, of idylls and oases. The line from Beccari to Guarini
leads to the dramatic pastoral and to opera.

It is difficult to define the characteristics of even the first dramatic
pastorals.[10] Of our three principal authorities Crescimbeni's comments
are by far the most revealing and indicate the close relationship between
pastoral drama and opera. In discussing the developments prior to the
invention of the dramatic pastoral he explains that the nascent forms
took on many titles ('favola', 'commedia', 'commedie rusticali',
'egloghe', and so on). After 1554 'favola' became the most prevalent.[11]
It is also the commonest subtitle for early opera up to 1750.

Crescimbeni writes that the form and metre of the poetry varied
considerably and was often mixed within one work, but that the most
typical were *versi sdrucciolti sciolti*, or unrhymed twelve-syllable lines
with an accent on the antepenultimate syllable (often mixed with
shorter lines). The older eclogues (such as Poliziano's *Orfeo*) had used
terza rima, the mythological plays (such as Correggio's *Cefalo*) *ottava
rima*.[12] The move away from regular rhyme and verse length proved

[9] Greg, *Pastoral*, pp. 168–9.
[10] Greg writes (ibid., p. 2), 'little would be gained by attempting to give any strict
account of what is meant by "pastoral" in literature. Any definition sufficiently elastic to
include the protean forms assumed by what we call the "pastoral ideal" could hardly have
sufficient intension to be of any real value.'
[11] Crescimbeni, *Commentarii*, pp. 212–14.
[12] Ibid., pp. 214–15. Greg, *Pastoral*, p. 170, writes, 'so too in the matter of metrical form,
the strict *terza rima* of the earlier examples came to be diversified with *rime sdrucciole*, and by
being intermingled with verses with internal rime [sic], with *ottava rima*, *settenari* couplets,
and lyrical measures.'

critical to musical settings. The metrical form of the early pastorals may be found in almost all early operas.[13]

As the eclogues grew in length it first became necessary to divide them into three or four acts and then into five acts with additional divisions into scenes.[14] The characters in these dramas grew from 'every sort of rustic people' to include sylvan deities, satyrs, spirits, centaurs, demi-gods, infernal deities, and even 'such men as by chance pass from the city to dwell in the wood.'[15]

Thus in *L'Egle* (Ferrara, 1545) by Giambattista Giraldi Cintio, the most important play in the development of pastoral drama immediately prior to Beccari's, one already finds *sciolti versi*, five acts divided into scenes, and the introduction 'of many satyrs, and other woodland deities laying snares for the nymphs.'[16] It is not entitled 'favola' but 'satira' and represents a 'solitary attempt to revive the "satyric" drama of the Greeks'.[17] This, however, is not primarily why it is disallowed the title of the first pastoral drama. The difference appears to lie not in the drama itself but specifically in its use of music.

Crescimbeni explains the importance to the developing pastoral of prologues in verse and of epilogues after the end of the drama 'in the form of singing choruses'.[18] He also emphasizes the importance of dance and what might be called choral ballets.

And finally, [the proto-pastoral dramas] have no other display and ornament except for some ballets and singing choruses such as one finds in the above-mentioned *Cefalo*, in which there is a chorus of nymphs which sings a *barzel-letta*, and a ballet of satyrs, and another chorus of nymphs that, singing, lead another dance; and in *Tirsi* by Castiglione and by Gonzaga, in which there is a *moresca* and a chorus of shepherds; and in *Maggio* by Mescolino, where there are several choruses of shepherds and nymphs; and in that by Casio da Narni,

[13] Gary Tomlinson ('Ottavio Rinuccini and the *Favola Affettuosa*,' *Comitatus*, vi (1975), p. 6) attributes the metrical qualities of Rinuccini's operatic *favole* to Sperone Speroni's tragedy *Canace* (1541), rather than to pastoral precedents, because 'Rinuccini shows a similar mixture [to Speroni] of seven- and eleven-syllable verse in the bodies of his *favole* . . .' However, Tomlinson has not considered the exceptional nature of *Canace*, which has often been noted in discussions of the pastoral and opera. 'Reasons are not lacking to explain the facility with which music so quickly took possession of the dramatic pastoral and especially its metrical form: even if the use of *endecasillabi* alternated with *settenari* and some kinds of these last had been continued from earlier examples, and even if it [this metrical form] has been criticized in *Canace*, where it mostly developed, because it was contrary to the decorum of tragedy, such metres still properly belong to the pastoral, helping to give suaveness and agility, and are especially well-suited to the sighs and songs of the shepherds and nymphs.' (Àngelo Solerti, *Gli Albori del Melodramma* (Milan, 1904/5; reprinted ed., Hildesheim: G. Olms, 1969), i, p. 13.)

[14] Crescimbeni, *Commentarii*, p. 216.

[15] Ibid., p. 217. Tomlinson, 'Ottavio Rinuccini,' pp. 2–3, finds no pastoral precedent for Rinuccini's use of characters from a divine realm.

[16] Crescimbeni, *Commentarii*, p. 218.

[17] Greg, *Pastoral*, p. 439.

[18] Crescimbeni ,*Commentarii*, p. 215.

which finishes with a *moresca*; and in many others that would be excessive to cite.[19]

In conclusion, Crescimbeni lists three qualities which uniquely define the pastoral. First is their metric structure which emphasizes *versi sciolti, mescolati d'ettasillabi*, and second 'that they admit a prologue, and choruses, both speaking and singing, and a *Commus* or *Epicarmus* epilogue, which is a chorus appearing after the end of the last act'.[20] 'Third, they were the first dramas that were completely ornamented with music, and as we said above they were represented on the stage by singers and not by actors; and they earned both the greatest applause and following.'[21]

The qualities given by Crescimbeni thus show this new genre as uniquely dependent on song and dance. It is neither a surprise nor a coincidence, then, that in his discussion of 'Musical Dramas: Their Origin and Present State'[22] he again singles out Beccari's *Sacrifizio*, here as the first drama to include whole scenes meant to be set to music,[23] and goes on to say that by the end of the century pastorals were set to music from beginning to end.[24]

What slowly becomes clear is that this new drama was 'opera', if only in an incipient form. Some of the music from the production of Beccari's work has survived. Written by Alfonso della Viola it is not essentially different from that sponsored by the Camerata half a century later, although in these early examples it lacks sophistication.[25] But even Peri's *Euridice* was likened to 'the chanting of a passion',[26] an analogy particularly apt for della Viola's music.

---

[19] Ibid., p. 217.
[20] Ibid., p. 223.
[21] Ibid., p. 224.
[22] Ibid., Chapter XI, pp. 236–44.
[23] Ibid., p. 238.
[24] Ibid., p. 239.
[25] Excerpts from this scene have been printed in Donald J. Grout, *A Short History of Opera* (New York: Columbia University Press, 1947), p. 32. See Henry W. Kaufman, 'Music for a *Favola Pastorale* (1554)', in *A Musical Offering: Essays in Honor of Martin Bernstein*, ed. by Edward H. Clinkscale and Claire Brook (New York: Pendragon Press, 1977), pp. 163–82, for an edition of all extant music and further bibliography. See also Jessie Ann Owens, 'Music in the Early Ferrarese Pastoral: A Study of Beccari's *Il sacrifizio*', to be published in the *Proceedings* of the International Congress on Renaissance Theatre in Northern Italy: The Court and the City (1400–1600) at Barnard College and Harvard University (13–17 November 1978).
[26] Claude V. Palisca, 'Musical Asides in the Correspondence of Emilio De' Cavalieri', *MQ*, xlix (1963), 351.

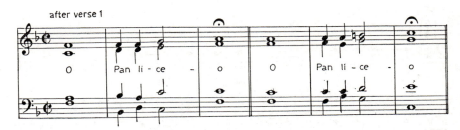

One can recognize here, in incipient form, the fluidity of metre associated with the solo recitative style, alternating between groups of two, three, and four syllables. There is a strong sense of tonal centre: cadences to the 'tonic' (F) are relieved by a few inner cadences to the 'dominant' (C).

The choral responses, in contrast to the solo monody, can be strictly measured in common time. They illustrate the type of choral setting favoured by the Camerata in which no musical obstruction interfered with the understanding of the text. The three responses are varied – the second being the most elaborate. The first two close with half cadences on the dominant (certainly the tenor would sing B natural in the penultimate measure of the second response). Only at the last response is there a full (plagal) cadence.

Ferrara saw the production of at least three other dramas with music by della Viola: Giraldi Cintio's *Orbecche* (1541), a 'pre-pastoral'. and two important pastoral dramas, Alberto Lollio's *Aretusa* (1563) and Agostino Argenti's *Lo fortunato* (1567). It also saw the production of the two most famous examples of the pastoral genre: Tasso's *Aminta* (1573) and Guarini's *Il pastor fido* (1581–90). These two works were responsible for making the pastoral both widely popular and widely imitated. In the next century this popularity and imitation were the causes of the pastoral's demise, but for the moment it was the glory of Italy.

Both *Aminta* and *Il pastor fido*, like their predecessors, were intimately connected with music. Guarini himself described the original setting to music of the 'blind-man's bluff' scene by Luzzasco Luzzaschi; the music was written first. [27] And even before its first performance or production, short lyrical excerpts became favourite texts for madrigal composers. [28]

In his *Dialoghi* Tasso himself advocated the union of music and poetry. [29] Working toward the achievement of this union he became a close friend of Gesualdo and 'frequenter of Gesualdo's academy'. [30] Later he developed friendships with Laura Giudiccioni and Emilio de' Cavalieri who collaborated with him in a production of *Aminta* with Cavalieri's music in Florence, 1590. [31] Finally, Ottavio Rinuccini, the man most often associated with the 'birth of opera', was a disciple of Tasso's and as 'the first opera librettist, merely continued in the tradition of the Tasso pastoral.' [32]

The idea that Rinuccini's part in the development of opera was not revolutionary, or even planned, is not without its opponents. Most recently, Barbara Hanning has tried to show through a detailed study of Rinuccini's prologues, and especially that of *Euridice*, that 'Rinuccini, the principal poet among the theorists and composers of humanist persuasion, who, in the spirit of experimentation and reform, formulated the new genre of opera, did indeed have a program – one which was deeply influenced by the Greek, and especially Aristotelian, concept of

[27] Giambattista Guarini, *Il pastor fido* (Venice: Gio. Battista Ciotti, 1602), pp. 149–50. See Iain Fenlon, 'Music and Spectacle at the Gonzaga Court, *c.* 1580–1600', *PRMA*, ciii (1976–7), pp. 90–105.

[28] A. Hartmann, Jr., 'Battista Guarini and *Il Pastor Fido*', *MQ*, xxix (1953), p. 424.

[29] Torquato Tasso, *Dialoghi*, ed. by Ezio Raimondi, 3 vols (Florence: G. C. Sansoni, 1958). See especially 'La cavalletta overo de la poesia toscana', II, 2, pp. 611–68. For a modern discussion see Romain Rolland, *Some Musicians of Former Days*, translated by Mary Blaiklock (New York: Henry Holt and Co., 1915), p. 64.

[30] Gustav Reese, *Music in the Renaissance* (1st ed., rev.; New York: W. W. Norton and Co., 1959), p. 569, see also p. 430.

[31] Ibid., p. 569; Grout, *Opera*, p. 36; Rolland, *Some Musicians*, pp. 65–6.

[32] Reese, *Renaissance*, p. 569; see also Grout, *Opera*, p. 36 and Rolland, *Some Musicians* p. 67.

the powers and function of music.'[33] This programme purportedly aimed at resuscitating the *style* rather than the form or content of classical tragedy. That is, the practice of having a drama performed completely in song was meant to reflect the character of ancient drama.[34] Hanning admits, however, 'that both of Rinuccini's early libretti, *Dafne* and *Euridice*, belong [in form and content] entirely to the realm of the pastoral clearly defined by Guarini',[35] and further that Rinuccini's opera texts owed their 'allegiance to the new genre of tragicomedy, the aim of which, as had been argued by Guarini, was precisely to purge melancholy'.[36]

All writers of these 'new forms' in the late Renaissance strove to validate their work by finding for them a classical basis. Thus, the classical derivation sought by the Camerata for the new operatic genre only embodies the general temper of the time which insisted on such justifications,[37] and says nothing about the modern development of a literary genre which was specially related to music. In fact, the Camerata's invocation of classical precedents is strikingly similar to that of Guarini in his *Compendium*.[38]

With knowledge of Aristotle equal to that of his opponents, he [Guarini] sets out to show that what he has done is countenanced by the very letter of the *Poetics,* or at least that his methods follow directly in the course of development from hints in the exposition of the Greek philosopher. Latin comedy, too, offers him justification. His process reminds one of the use of the Bible by sectaries. . . . They show how everything in their doctrine is supported by Sacred Scripture, and there is no reason to doubt their sincerity; yet one can hardly suppose that in forming their opinions they really started out from a Scriptural basis. They followed their own reason or their own liking, and they sought for justification of what was already accomplished and seemed good to them.[39]

Without knowing what lay ahead, the first writer of the dramatic pastoral actually gave birth to the dramatic operatic form, which in time would outgrow its origin in the pastoral and outlive it.

[33] Barbara Hanning, 'Apologia pro Ottavio Rinuccini,' *JAMS*, xxvi (1973), p. 261.
[34] Ibid., p. 252.
[35] Ibid., p. 241. It might be questioned just how clearly Guarini actually defined the genre of the pastoral as opposed to tragicomedy in general.
[36] Ibid., p. 246.
[37] See also Claude V. Palisca, 'The Alterati of Florence, Pioneers in the Theory of Dramatic Music' in *New Looks at Italian Opera: Essays in Honor of Donald J. Grout,* ed. by William W. Austin (Ithaca: Cornell University Press, 1968), pp. 35–6.
[38] *Il pastor fido* was written between 1581 and 1590. Mei's letters were written between 1572 and 1581. Galilei's *Dialogo* was published in 1581, the *Compendium* in 1599, the 'Dedication' to the libretto of Rinuccini's *Dafne*, the 'first opera', in 1600.
[39] Gilbert, *Literary Criticism*, pp. 504–5. Crescimbeni also uses this method in a justification of his pastoral play, *Elvio,* in the fifth dialogue of the *Bellezza.* Here one would be led to believe that in writing on tragic poetry Aristotle really had pastorals in mind.

The pastoral was thus not simply a subcategory of opera; the pastoral *was* opera. Not until the advent of public opera, and especially the opening of the Venetian theatres, did pastoral opera become a 'type', and then it rather quickly lost favour. In general, after this time, the operas which were the most successful were of an entirely different cast.

OPERATIC CHANGE AND CONTINUITY

Although various travelling companies presented opera as a public spectacle some years before the opening of the Venetian opera houses,[40] the decade of the 1630s was a period of striking developments in operatic traditions.[41] Up until that time the pastoral had remained dominant. Opera had been a formal, courtly entertainment. It was sophisticated, often allegorical, and basically lyrical, rather than dramatic. It was almost always written for an 'occasion'.

In time the fashion of having dramas completely set to music outlived its origin in the pastoral drama. The association of music and drama had been natural to the pastoral and had afforded a certain realism to this use of music. It was understood that Orpheus should sing, and the same ability in his companions was accepted by analogy. This is not to say that the dramatic pastoral was realistic. On the contrary, it was regularly criticized for lack of realism.[42] Contemporary shepherds certainly did not behave in this way. Before one could justify the continuous singing, therefore, it was necessary to accept Guarini's description of classical shepherds living in mythological times. Toward the middle of the seventeenth century Doni clearly indicates this need. 'About the pastoral . . . I would say that since this type [of play] is usually more poetic and abstract than are comedies and the [spiritual] representations, and is usually composed on amorous subjects and in a florid and polished style (as may be seen in *Aminta* and *Il pastor fido*) it is thus possible to allow it to have musical settings of all its parts, especially since gods, nymphs and shepherds of that oldest age in which

---

[40] See Lorenzo Bianconi and Thomas Walker, 'Dalla *Finta Pazza* alla *Veremonda*: Storie di Febiarmonici,' *Rivista Italiana di Musicologia*, x (1975), pp. 379–454, for a discussion of the activities of these academies. Bianconi and Walker use the terminology of Giovan Domenico Ottonelli in explaining the stylistic changes occurring in operas of the 1640s, which generally may be seen to be moving away from the courtly (le principeche) and academic (le accademiche) types to the commercial (le mercenarie). To a great extent this parallels the change from pastoral and mythological subjects to heroic and historic ones.

[41] See Grout, *Opera*, p. 84.

[42] See Nino Pirrotta, 'Early Opera and Aria' in *New Looks at Italian Opera*, pp. 80–1, where he writes of Peri's and Rinuccini's concern 'to provide a justification for their departure from reality.' Dismissing the classical justification as 'fashionable, but too simple and also . . . difficult to maintain,' Pirrotta states, 'More effective in the long run was the built-in defense which gave "recitar cantando" a motivation by endowing the protagonists of opera with the most exceptional gifts for music and by placing them in the very special climate of the pastorale.'

music was natural and speech almost poetic are introduced.'[43] And a little later he states it directly. 'Nor will anyone deny that to introduce shepherds so lovely, as if they were brought up in court and regularly trained in dance and gymnastics, is against verisimilitude . . . we ought not to imagine that the shepherds which are introduced [into these plays] are the sordid and vulgar kind that today look after animals.'[44] That is to say, the use of singing was only realistic when the shepherds were not.

The pastoral subject, then, and not its so-called classical origin, gave a justification for musical settings which in time became unnecessary. In fact, these settings which had formed an important part in the birth of the dramatic pastoral took on a life of their own. The dramatic pastoral, born of Beccari and della Viola, was fully realized in the works of Tasso and Guarini, and continued with the collaboration of Peri and Rinuccini. Opera was born in the 1630s of the pastoral.

The birth of music drama as an independent form, signalled by the change from pastoral to tragic, epic, or simply human plots, was neither easy nor casual. As early as 1600 Cavalieri refers to the story of Caccini's *Il rapimento di Cefalo* (9 October 1600) as tragic and thus an objectionable subject for an operatic libretto.[45] It is interesting that Cavalieri should make so narrow a distinction and it indicates once again that mythological dramas were not considered at that time to be linked with the pastoral. It would be fifty years before such stories were regularly pastoralized. Indeed, the story of Cephalus itself is identified as a pastoral in two later adaptations: *Il ratto di Cefalo* (Ferrara, 1650) and *L'Aurora in Atene* (Venice, 1678).

In *Arianna* (1608), another mythological tale, Rinuccini and Monteverdi made the next attempt at setting a tragedy to music. 'The experiment, however, more daring than we realize, caused no little concern at the Mantuan court, where the plot was felt to be too dry — too human, that is; for it is a fact that, while the fishermen of Naxos, replacing the shepherds and nymphs of Arcadia in the plot of *Arianna,* can still praise the primeval simplicity of their life, the pastoral aura and the blessed innocence of the Golden Age have completely abandoned Theseus, Arianna, and their retainers.'[46] Still, the mythological atmosphere was retained, as were the lyrical Arcadian-like choruses. In fact, mythological operas differed very little from the strict pastoral in musical form.

[43] Doni, 'Trattato,' p. 15.
[44] Ibid., p. 16.
[45] As translated in Palisca, 'Musical Asides,' pp. 351–2. See also Pirrotta, 'Early Opera,' p. 50. Pirrotta dates Cavalieri's letter 24 November 1600.
[46] Pirrotta, *Early Opera*, p. 91.

Like the contemporary pastorals, *Arianna* is built of recitative soliloquies and connecting, lyrical choral movements. There is no rapid dialogue, and only the first scene, sung by Venus and Amor, is without chorus. The *Coro di Soldati* are Teseo's comrades, just as the shepherds are Orfeo's. Indeed the soldiers are given no opportunity to be martial in their one scene, the embarkation of Teseo and Arianna on Naxos (an island, of course), but rather sing such lines as, 'Be your sweet dreams happy and content; and may you awake in the fair dawn of the morning more tranquil still.'[47] No doubt somewhat uncomfortable at using soldiers for such a purpose, Rinuccini replaces them after this scene with the inhabitants of the island, the *Cori di Pescatori*, who can sing pastoral conceits without blushing.

Using the opening of the Venetian opera houses as a convenient dividing point, then, one may say that before 1637 the mythological and pastoral stories were treated alike musically. After 1637 they were considered to belong to the same literary type as well. Both operatic types contributed to the formation of the Venetian, or post-1637, pastoral, a form descended from the sixteenth-century model, but already different from it. Side by side with heroic or historical (although far from historically accurate in most cases) operas, such as Monteverdi's *L' incoronazione di Poppea* (Venice, 1643), from which all pastoral elements are excluded, the Venetian pastoral existed from the opening of the public opera houses until about 1650, after which it slowly died out.

As operatic taste shifted from the pastoral to the heroic, from formal tableaux to dramatic intensity, during the years from 1637 to 1650, the chorus became the first casualty. The choruses in the pastorals had usually functioned as a purely lyrical element, often contributing to the formal structure of large scenes but not often to the drama. As such they had no place in the new music drama. However, the crowds themselves remained and played an important role in the action.

It was easier for the [producer] to create a magnificent crowd-effect without the bother of a chorus master, and more profitable for the [composer] to compose for solo voices, contenting the chorus with short exclamations, 'alla caccia', 'all'armi', 'viva', 'vittoria', and so on, which could be sung by almost any member of the crowd. Therefore, although the size of what is termed the chorus in the lists of the casts increases in the later operas, it is in fact only the crowd or *comparse* which grows, as a liking for battle or other grand scenes requiring a lavish stage-effect necessary to the historical plots becomes necessary.[48]

[47] *Arianna*, in Solerti, ed., *Gli Albori*, ii, p. 155, ll. 195–8.
[48] Towneley Worsthorne, *Venetian Opera*, p. 54.

This may be seen by comparing the librettos for Monteverdi's *Orfeo* and *Poppea*. In the former, the libretto lists three choruses: the nymphs and shepherds, the infernal spirits, and the shepherds who dance the *moresca* at the end of the opera.[49] In *Poppea* six groups are listed: the students of Seneca, the consuls, tribunes, lectors, and choruses made up of the fairy-like creatures associated with Virtue and Love who sing the Prologue. Except for a chorus of Seneca's students (II, iii), built around the repeated and effective phrase, 'Don't die, Seneca, oh no,' and a general rejoicing at the accession of Poppea in the last scene, the choruses function as stage properties. Their contribution to the drama is no longer musical, lyrical, or formal, but dramatic, visual, and, usually, silent.

To illustrate the distinction with examples closer together in time, one may compare *Poppea* with a pastoral libretto by the same librettist, Giovanni Francesco Busenello. *Gli Amori d'Apollo e di Dafne* (1640) calls only for a chorus of nymphs and another of muses. Both appear in large, choral, lyrical scenes which could rightly be termed choral ballets. In the last of these the nymphs spell out Dafne's name in flowers. As in the earlier pastorals, the choral repetitions often determine the formal structure of those scenes in which the chorus appears.

It should be noted that the word 'coro' in the libretto's list of characters did not imply a 'chorus' in modern English terminology but merely a group of people. This fact is made particularly clear in Orazio Persiani's *Le Nozze di Teti e di Peleo* (1639), another Venetian pastoral. Persiani calls for thirteen choruses but indicates that four of them 'dance' ('Coro . . . che ballano') and that one does combat ('Coro di Tritoni Combattenti'). This last group does no singing at all and neither do three of the four 'dancing choruses'. And four of the remaining eight choruses which do sing make additional silent appearances. Act I uses the 'choruses' most: of the eleven scenes, seven call for a 'chorus' on stage. In scene i the *Coro di Dei* sings. The *Coro di Cacciatori* sings in I, ii, while the *Coro di Cavalieri* simply appear. In I, iii, the *Coro di Cavalieri* and the *Coro di Ninfe* sing while the *Coro di Cacciatori* remain silently on stage. The *Cavalieri* and the *Ninfe* remain on stage for scene iv, and the former combat the *Coro di Tritoni*. In I, v, the *Coro di Demoni* appear and sing; in I, viii, the *Driadi*, *Oreadi*, *Nereidi*, and *Aure* each sing separately and then together. Finally in I, xi, the *Coro di Ninfe* sings once more.

In the Venetian pastoral the choruses played an important musical and formal role even if they were also used silently for crowd scenes. But

---

[49] The original libretto by Striggio did not end happily, but with the traditional tragic finale of the myth. Of course, the adoption of the happy ending, and especially the use of a 'choral epilogue' followed by a danced *moresca*, definitely attach the final version to the conventions of the sixteenth-century literary pastoral.

the Venetian heroic opera typically used the chorus only in the latter function. To pick a famous example, Cicognini's *Giasone* (1649), set by Cavalli, calls for six choruses. The first appearance of any of these is in the last scene of the first act (I, xv) where the *Coro di Spiriti* sings six lines in the 'stanza degli Incanti de Medea', as it is called in the libretto. In fact, this scene turns out to be the only one in the entire opera which calls for a singing chorus, and in it the chorus contributes nothing to the musical form. The other five choruses perform only as extras.

As already explained, the 'early pastoral' and the 'Venetian pastoral' opera are different in a number of ways. The first was an independent musical drama, the latter a kind of opera performed in Venice which included pastoralizations as well as pastorals. In many ways the pastoral operas of Venice were more like the heroic operas than the early pastorals. The Venetian opera (a catch-all term, for these traits appear equally in other Italian cities) was divided into three acts, not five. Unlike the early pastoral, the operas from the second third of the century did not normally close with a choral epilogue whether or not they used the chorus in other scenes. For example, there is no chorus in the final scene of *Gli Amori d'Apollo e di Dafne*, of Persiani's *Le Nozze di Teti e di Peleo*, or Cicognini's *Giasone*; nor was Busenello's *Poppea* set with a choral finale. The pastoral and heroic operas of Venice shared equally in the developing contrast of recitative and aria, the replacement of recitative soliloquies with rapidly-paced dialogue, and the inner expansion of each act.[50] Their difference lay in the lyrical and often patently undramatic nature of the pastoral. This showed in the greater proportion of solo lyrical passages to recitative and almost invariable use of the singing chorus, which in the heroic drama was all but eliminated.

Many still believe that the use, or non-use, of a chorus depended only on the availability of funds. 'The choruses will not always play so important a role. Is that to say, as Kretzschmar has held, that they are about to disappear? Not at all. If they are employed less it is for reasons of economy, not of principles.'[51] This statement neglects the importance of the literary influences on opera. Moreover, it is apparent from the librettos that large crowds continued to be used for stage effects even when they were not asked to sing. 'Unlike the size of the orchestra,

[50] Two of the best discussions of Italian operatic developments remain unpublished: about Venice, Thomas Walker, 'Francesco Cavalli and the Beginnings of Opera in Venice: Notes and Observations' (unpublished typescript); and for Rome, Margaret Murata, 'Operas for the Papal Court with Texts by Giulio Rospigliosi,' unpublished Ph.D. dissertation (University of Chicago, 1975).

[51] Henri Prunières, *Cavalli et l'Opéra Venetian au XVIIe Siecle* (Paris: Les Editions Rieder, 1931), p. 52.

2*

which can be explained as dependent largely upon finance, the size of the chorus is governed, if ultimately by finance, more immediately by *taste*.'[52]

The pastoral does not seem to have been popular with public operatic audiences. It was performed on the Venetian public stage for less than fifteen years. After 1650 it becomes exceedingly rare. When in the last decade of the seventeenth century a number of literary men including Crescimbeni founded the Arcadian Academy of Rome and established a programme to revitalize and reform Italian literature, the heroic operas of the mid-century were particularly damned. Originally composed of those men of letters who had surrounded Queen Christina of Sweden, the Arcadian Academy quickly mushroomed to include at least 114 'colonies' outside of Rome, and even outside of Italy, and boasted after twenty-two years 'mille e trecento' members.[53] Queen Christina, a convert to Roman Catholicism, had fled to Rome after abdicating her throne. Her apparently scandalous and none-too-private life caused the Pope to back away from his initial joyous reception of her, but Christina has commended herself to posterity by remaining, through all of her Roman residence, a staunch supporter of the arts.[54] From 1680 to 1684, for example, Alessandro Scarlatti served as her *maestro di cappella*, and many of his first operas were written in fulfilling the responsibilities of this position. The Arcadian Academy was founded in Christina's honour one year after her death in 1689 by members of her former artistic circle.

The stated purpose of the Academy was to defend Italian poetry against contemporary criticism and to restore it to its former glories by opposing the mannered artificiality of the seventeenth century with simplicity and naturalness.[55] The Arcadian name, chosen after a chance comment at one of the early meetings, reflected this aim. The academy's members would themselves become simple shepherds and restore Italy to the Golden Age of Arcadia.

No one was admitted into this Academy without first taking on a pastoral name. At meetings the members assumed pastoral manners and participated in literary games wherein the poets competed with one another at extemporizing pastoral verse in the manner of shepherds

[52] Towneley Worsthorne, *Venetian Opera*, p. 83.

[53] Giovanni Maria Crescimbeni, *Storia dell'Accademia degli Arcadi* (London: T. Beckett, 1803), p. 6. This work was originally published in Rome, 1712. For more information on the Academy, see the references to Baretti, Crescimbeni, Donadoni, Fehr, Gravina, Muratori, Paget, Portal, and Robertson in the Bibliography.

[54] For more information on Queen Christina see Gaetano Compagnino, Guido Nicastro, and Giuseppe Savoca, eds., 'Cristina di Svezia e il suo circolo' in *Il Settecento: L'Arcadia e l'eta della riforme*, Vol. VI, p. 1, of *La Letteratura Italiana: Storia e Testi*, ed. by Carlo Muscetta (Laterza: Bari, 1973), pp. 37–9, and the bibliography for that section, p. 66.

[55] See John George Robertson, *Studies in the Genesis of Romantic Theory in the Eighteenth Century* (Cambridge: Cambridge University Press, 1923), pp. 4–5.

from Theocritus's *Idylls*. The reed pipes of the god Pan served as a symbol for the 'shepherds' of this Academy, the late Queen Christina was their 'basilissa', or empress, and the Baby Jesus was chosen as their protector, for simple shepherds of Bethlehem had been the first to be told of the saviour's birth.[56]

The adoption of pastoral mannerisms might suggest that these literati championed the cause of pastoral literature. However, they condemned the literature of the seventeenth century, and especially operatic librettos, both heroic and pastoral. Thus the Arcadians' views on the pastoral in drama has had many interpretations. Although even a cursory glance at the Arcadian's output would be enough to belie such an opinion, some modern scholars go so far as to say the pastoral was banned. 'One should not be misled by the stage effects of the Arcadian Academy, the name itself, and the pastoral pseudonyms of its members. This was a fashionable frivolity, and seems to have originated more or less playfully. Actually, the programme of the Academy was, or at least developed into, something that might be called rather "anti-pastoral".'[57]

In the same article, Nathaniel Burt refers to the sixth dialogue from Crescimbeni's *Bellezza*. He writes,

The Sixth Dialogue . . . closes with a discussion of 'comedy' according to classic and Aristotelian definitions, and as exemplified by the Roman and Renaissance comic playwrights. . . . The dialogue concludes with a short history of the pastoral, and of what we should call 'opera', treated, of course, as a purely literary, never as a musical, form. Here both the pastoral and the *dramma per musica*, which is considered a direct product of the pastoral, come in for severe castigation, indicating what were some, at least, of the Arcadians' special objections.[58]

By failing to place it within the context of Crescimbeni's oeuvre, however, Burt has misinterpreted this short passage; he therefore mistakes precisely what it was to which the Arcadians objected. Burt states that the pastoral is condemned, but this is surely not so. In the previous dialogue, Crescimbeni takes his own pastoral play, *Elvio*, as the perfect example of a modern application of Aristotle's rules on tragic poetry. A closer examination of the sixth dialogue shows that Crescimbeni is not condemning the pastoral or opera per se, but the extravagances of the seventeenth-century style which were particularly blatant in those genres. He especially condemns Giacinto Andrea Cicognini as the dramatist most responsible for the development of

[56] Campagnino, Nicastro, and Savoca, eds., 'L'Accademia d'Arcadia' in *La Letteratura Italiana*, Vol. VI, 1, p. 40. Note the connections made at the outset by the Arcadians between contemporary life, classical mythology, and Christianity. Christina, Pan, and Jesus make a strange 'amour a trois', but each represents a particular aspect of the pastoral genre.
[57] Nathaniel Burt, 'Opera in Arcadia,' *MQ*, xli (1955), p. 151.
[58] Ibid., p. 155.

this style, and he singles out Cicognini's *Giasone* (1649) as particularly bad.

Crescimbeni and his Arcadian followers objected to the lack of choruses in these heroic dramas, to a form where as many as fifteen or twenty scenes were crowded into a single act, to the association of kings and heroes with buffoons and servants, to the destruction of the rules of poetry, and to the lack of regard for elocution and rhetoric in a genre which elevated music over words.[59] With the formation of the Academy in 1690 an official attempt was made to turn contemporary literature toward naturalness and simplicity. To Crescimbeni this meant that the pastoral of the sixteenth century became an ideal form.

None of the librettos known to have been written by Cicognini are pastoral, and Crescimbeni only connects them with that genre by virtue of their being set entirely to music. Crescimbeni does not condemn early pastorals nor opera in general. He praises works which show a return of good taste, singling out those of the Venetian librettists Domenico David and Apostolo Zeno.

During his lifetime Zeno wrote thirty-five librettos by himself and fifteen more with his collaborator, P. Pariati, whom he took on as an assistant in 1705. His first three operas were pastoral: *Gl' inganni felici* (1695; Pollaroli), *Tirsi* (1696; Ariosti, Lotti, Caldara), and *Narciso* (1697; Pistocchi).[60] Their appearance can definitely be related to the Arcadian movement's wish to restore Italian drama's international reputation by returning to Italy's most renowned 'modern' dramatic form, the pastoral. In fact, in *Narciso* Zeno quotes directly from his renaissance sources and returns to the old five-act structure.[61] Act II, iii, of *Narciso* copies Act IV, vii, of Guarini's *Il pastor fido*; and Act III, viii, of the same opera copies the second eclogue of Sannazaro's *Arcadia* (1489–1504),[62] the first attempt to revive classical pastoral poetry in the vernacular.[63]

---

[59] Giovanni Maria Crescimbeni, *La Bellezza della volgar poesia* (Rome: G. F. Buagni, 1700), p. 129. See also Burt, 'Arcadia,' pp. 155–6. That Cicognini served as a scapegoat seems clear enough. William C. Holmes, 'Giacinto Andrea Cicognini's and Antonio Cesti's *Orontea*' in *New Looks at Italian Opera*, p. 117, writes, 'Great as Cicognini's reputation was to his contemporaries, he soon became an object of derision to later writers, anxious to reform what they considered to be the barbarous state of the Italian stage.'

[60] The opera *Dafne* (1696) only mentioned and attributed to Zeno in the *MGG* article on Ariosti by Werner Bollert, is no doubt identical to that entitled *Tirsi* (1696).

[61] A few of the pastorals written during the Arcadian revival try to revive the form as well as the spirit of the early pastoral. These, therefore, often include the lyrical and formal choruses omitted from the more modern Italian pastoral and can usually be traced by their use of five, rather than three acts. One such example is Frigimelica-Roberti's *Il Pastore d'Anfriso* (Venice, 1695), set by Pollaroli, which includes thirteen characters and eight different choruses in its five acts. See Chapt. III, p. 73.

[62] Max Fehr, *Apostolo Zeno und die Reform des Operntextes* (Inaugural Dissertation, University of Zurich; Zurich: A. Tschopp, 1912), p. 68.

[63] See Grout, *Opera*, p. 31. 'The pastoral poem was firmly established by Sannazaro's *Arcadia* (1504). . . .'

The quotation of earlier works, at least in pastorals, was considered a sign of erudition and was further an attempt to equate one's work with its important predecessors. Jacopo Sannazaro's *Arcadia* already illustrates this by its extensive borrowings from the classics.[64] In borrowing from contemporary works there was the added motive of competition. Guarini, for example, borrows many elements from Tasso's *Aminta*, thus heightening the two Ferrarese poets' rivalry. The quotations used by Zeno, therefore, are not a sign of lack of interest on his part, nor an indication that 'Zeno is . . . here as unoriginal as possible.'[65] They are simply a part of the pastoral style, and one that is often encountered in operatic librettos where it has the added motive of positively identifying a work as pastoral. Although Zeno rarely returned to the pastoral after these first plays, he recognized the importance of the genre. He writes in his biography of Guarini that *Il pastor fido* is 'no less an unique ornament of its country than of Italian poetry'.[66]

Eumene, Zeno's fourth libretto, was the first to present 'a great historical personality of note',[67] and it was to plots involving such characters that Zeno thereafter remained attracted. In these as in the pastorals he displayed his learning – citing in his *Argomenti* more than eighty classical and modern historical sources.[68] These historical works also aimed at the revitalization of Italian drama, but the emphasis was dramatic rather than lyric.

As Robert Freeman says, Zeno was not a leader of the movement to reform the libretto.[69] Freeman here refers to Zeno's heroic dramas, but he might equally have included the pastorals. Freeman shows that Crescimbeni in *La Bellezza* (1700) was the first to praise Zeno's work, but even higher praise is reserved for a pastoral written by Cardinal Pietro Ottoboni, *Amore eroico tra i pastori*.[70] During the early years of Zeno's career, moreover, his librettos were generally pastoral and it is only to these that Crescimbeni referred. By 1702, when Crescimbeni started publishing his *Commentarii*, he no longer mentions Zeno, 'but stresses the dramatic merits to be found in what he calls the "favola pastorale", particularly in Cardinal Pietro Ottoboni's *Adonia*. . . .'[71] By then, Zeno had turned from pastoral composition. In Crescimbeni's

---

[64] See Anthony Thorlby, ed., *The Penguin Companion to European Literature* (New York: McGraw-Hill Book Company, 1969), p. 694.
[65] Fehr, *Zeno*, p. 68.
[66] Apostolo Zeno, 'Vita di Gio: Battista Guarini,' *La Galleria di Minerva, overo Notizie Universali*, i (1696), 78–9.
[67] Fehr, *Zeno*, p. 55.
[68] Ibid., p. 56.
[69] 'Apostolo Zeno's Reform of the Libretto,' *JAMS*, xii (1968), pp. 321–41.
[70] Crescimbeni, *Bellezza*, p. 141. See also the *Commentarii*, p. 224.
[71] Freeman, 'Zeno', p. 328. See Crescimbeni, *Commentarii*, pp. 243–4.

earlier work, *L'Istorii* (1698), the one libretto praised by name is also a 'dramma pastorale', *L'Endimione* by Abate Alessandro Guidi.

Crescimbeni's emphasis on the pastoral is hardly accidental. His remarks on Zeno's works, then, do not constitute an important critical commentary, as Freeman seems to believe. Rather they simply emphasize Crescimbeni's own crusade to restore the dramatic pastoral to its original character. He rejects neither the pastoral nor music drama; what he decries is the deterioration of literary quality found in some examples of these genres during the seventeenth century, and he understandably credits the Academy and its members with the proper revival of good taste.

But as much success as the pastorals had from their birth until well into the seventeenth century, their reputation then began to decline, . . . because the quantity produced, almost without number, had sated Italy (especially because many of those written were tasteless and clumsy, and almost all of them on the same subject as *Aminta* and *Il pastor fido*, changed and elaborated in various ways). . . . But returning to that which one hopes for in pastorals, even if the defective qualities of modern drama remain, we may cite some prudent authors who, as much as the corruption of the modern theatre allows, have tried to restore in their pastorals some of the rules which had made them highly esteemed during the seventeenth century. It so happens that among them one ought to give first place to the most illustrious Shepherd of Arcadia, Crateo Ercinio [Cardinal Pietro Ottoboni]. . . .[72]

The pastoral was condemned not so much in itself but as a catalyst. All literary critics seemed to agree that the recognition of pastoral drama as a legitimate form somehow led directly to the most degenerate period of Italian literature, which was represented most clearly by the 'drammi' of Cicognini. Some, like Crescimbeni, laid the blame on the new-fangled idea of having plays sung, so that writers and composers began to strive toward the unusual rather than dramatic substance.[73] Others laid the blame on the dramatization and expansion of the original literary pastoral without Aristotle's authority. They argued that the pastoral was synonymous with lyricism and as such intended to be short. The pastoral subject was seen to be incompatible with drama; its transformation into that form had caused drama's decline. Giasone De Nores, Guarini's first critic, whom he answered with his *Compendium* (1599), attacked the pastoral drama in part for this reason.[74]

The criticism of pastoral drama for passing the bounds set by Aristotle and those demanded by verisimilitude, along with the

---

[72] Crescimbeni, *Commentarii*, pp. 226–7.
[73] Ibid., and *Bellezza*, p. 129.
[74] See the discussion of Guarini's early critics in Perella, *Critical Fortune*, pp. 18–19.

'improper' elevation of rhetoric, remained strong throughout the seventeenth century. It is striking, therefore, that as a general rule the Arcadian Academy, though composed of declared literary reformers, supported Guarini and the pastoral.

The very striking feature of the Arcadian reaction for us is the unusual place Guarini has in it. For what we see is that it is rather on Marino and the Marinists that the axe of disapproval falls and that Guarini is most often rescued from the general critical carnage. Not always, to be sure; there are those who see him closely linked to Marino and single him out as one of the very first to lead Italian poetry astray. But most often, Guarini is kept just on this side of the line which divides the history of modern Italian poetry into the classic greats and the apostate corrupters.[75]

Of the detractors, Gianvincenzo Gravina (1664–1718) was one of the best known. With Crescimbeni, he was one of the original fourteen Arcadians; and because of his prominence as a legal authority it fell to him to compose the rules of the Academy which, of course, included all the pastoral regulations. It cannot be assumed, therefore, that Gravina was totally anti-pastoral. Like the earlier seventeenth-century critics, he was opposed to the expansion of the pastoral genre and felt that the eclogue was its true form. His argument, not inherently Aristotelian, rests on the lack of verisimilitude in the expanded pastoral form. Pastoral literature, says Gravina, should consist of 'nothing other than a simple discourse among shepherds, and competitions among them in versifying – considering that among uncultured and uneducated persons, subjects suitable for a long treatise, or those of great intricacy, will not, in all likelihood, arise. . . .'[76] With this point of view Gravina is able to applaud enthusiastically the pastoral drama *Tancia* (Siena, 1612) by Michelangelo Buonarroti (the younger), which is placed in the sub-category of 'egloghe rusticali' by Crescimbeni.[77] And he grudgingly accepts Tasso's *Aminta* and the adaptation of that drama by Antonio Ongaro (scene by scene) into a piscatory drama, *Alceo*, 'a story of the coast which nevertheless preserves a large amount of the proper simplicity.'[78] Gravina uses Guarini's *Il pastor fido* to illustrate the worst offences of the genre.

[Guarini] even transposed [the life of] the courts into the shepherds' huts by transferring the emotions and customs of the antechamber and the trickiest

---

[75] Ibid., p. 85.
[76] *Prose di Gianvincenzo Gravina*, ed. by Paolo Emiliani Giudice (Florence: Barbèra, Bianchi e Co., 1857), p. 137.
[77] *Gravina*, p. 138. See also Crescimbeni, *Commentarii*, p. 225; and Greg, *Pastoral*, p. 434. Not surprisingly, *Tancia* reappears as an opera in Florence, 1638, perhaps adapted by Buonarroti himself, for he signs the dedication.
[78] *Gravina*, p. 138.

dealings of the back-rooms to the characters of his *Pastor fido*; he placed precepts on the regulation of the political world into the mouths of shepherds, and thoughts so considered [into the mouths] of the amorous nymphs that they seem to have graduated from the schools of today's speechmakers and epigrammists. Nothing then is left of the pastoral to these shepherds and nymphs except their rustic dress and the darts [of love]; and on the other hand, the sentiments and expressions so noble in themselves lose their worth from the illogicality of their location, like a cypress painted in the middle of the sea.[79]

Gravina did not object to the pastoral, not even to the pastoral drama, but only to the elaborate and lengthy pastoral drama illustrated by Guarini's *Pastor fido*.[80] As a result of the efforts of the Arcadian Academy, and specifically of men like Crescimbeni, the pastoral dramas reappeared in force at the end of the seventeenth century. As a result of the continued literary criticisms, however, they reappeared not in their sixteenth-century form, but in a new guise. At the same time, the dramatic pastoral returned to the operatic stage after an absence of almost a quarter of a century.

The periods in the seventeenth century during which the pastoral found favour on the operatic stage can be illustrated most easily by noting the appearances of important pastoral texts throughout that time. For example, the story of Orpheus and Eurydice occurs frequently in the earliest operatic productions:

> Florence, 1600; *Euridice*; Rinuccini-Peri
> Florence, 1600; *Euridice*; Rinuccini-Caccini
> Mantua, 1608; *Orfeo*; Striggio-Monteverdi
> Florence, 1616; *Il Pianto d'Orfeo*; Chiabrera-Belli
> [sung as an intermezzo between the acts of Tasso's *Aminta*]
> Rome, 1619; *La Morte d'Orfeo*; Landi-Landi

In the middle of the century the theme recurs only once:

> Rome, 1647; *L'Orfeo*; Buti-Rossi

A libretto by Aurelio Aureli in 1673, however, saw numerous productions:

---

[79] Ibid. In criticizing the use Caccini made of ornamentation the 'Peri faction' had used this same analogy of the cypress tree one hundred years earlier. See Pirrotta, 'Early Opera,' p. 64, n. 62. It is probable that neither Gravina nor the Peri faction intended the Biblical reference (*New English Bible*, Luke 17: 6): 'If you had faith no bigger even than a mustard-seed, you could say to this sycamore-tree, "Be rooted up and replanted in the sea"; and it would at once obey you.' The quotation does underscore, however, that both Peri and Gravina lacked sufficient faith in Guarini's Golden Age shepherds to believe that such rhetoric and musical ornaments could have been natural.

[80] Gravina is also known to have praised the contemporary pastoral *Endimione* by Alessandro Guidi. See Eugenio Donadoni, *A History of Italian Literature* (New York: New York University Press, 1969), I, p. 299.

Venice, 1673; *L'Orfeo*; Aureli–Sartorio
Palermo, 1676; *L'Orfeo*; Aureli–Sartorio
Naples, 1682; *L'Orfeo*; Aureli–Sartorio
Piacenza, 1689; *L'Orfeo*; Aureli–Sabatini
Rome, 1694; *L'Orfeo*; Aureli–Sabatini
Bologna, 1695; *L'Orfeo, o sia Amore spesso inganna*;
    Aureli–?
Savona, 1697; *Orfeo a torto geloso*; Aureli–?

And there was one other late production as well:

Vienna, 1683; *La Lira d'Orfeo*; ?–Draghi

Similarly, the mythological story of Narcissus and Echo was first 'pastoralized' during the early years of Venetian operatic theatres.

Venice, 1642; *Narciso et Ecco immortalati*; Persiani–
    [Cavalli?]

It reappears with a vengeance in the last two decades of the century, often specifically labelled 'favola boschereccia':

Naples, 1682; *Il Narciso*; Lemene–Borzio?
Cremona, 1683; *Il Narciso*; Lemene–?
Mantua, 1689; *Il Narciso*; Lemene–?
Milan, Parma; Vienna, 1699; *Il Narciso*; Lemene–?
Ansbach, 1697; *Il Narciso*; Zeno–Pistocchi

The list could be extended. Operas referring to shepherds or shepherdesses in their titles, for example, appear in 1640 and 1641, and in 1693 and 1695. The story of Apollo and Daphne is present in 1597 and 1608, again in 1640, 1647, and 1656 (all by Busenello and Cavalli), in 1660, and then finally in 1679, 1690, 1695, and 1699. The examples from 1660 and 1679 are exceptional: in fact, very few pastorals appeared from 1650 to 1680. On the other hand, there were concentrations of such stories in operas produced in 1600–20, 1637–50, and 1680–1700. The pastoral revival at the end of the century may conveniently be said to begin with the first known opera of Alessandro Scarlatti, *Gli equivoci nel Sembiante* (Rome, 1679). Like many of his first operas *Gli equivoci* is a pastoral and associated with Queen Christina and her coterie in Rome.

THE NEW OPERATIC PASTORAL IN ITALY

In their private, courtly function, Scarlatti's pastorals recall those of the beginning of the century. However, their style and form conform to contemporary musical criteria; they utilize the modern musical vocabularies, and, like the heroic opera, generally avoid the use of chorus. The continuing criticisms of the elaborate dramatic pastoral had led to an avoidance of complexity, spectacle, and unnatural length in the texts. Composers mirrored this conception in their settings. The revitalized operatic pastoral was rarely conceived in its renaissance form but was a diminutive version of the heroic and mythological operas performed concurrently in the public operatic houses. The number of scenes in these pastorals was reduced, often to half that in an heroic opera. There were usually no more than four or five characters – two couples and a confidant. The musical style was simplified and concise. A strict avoidance of contrast of any type became the stylistic ideal.

Scarlatti's first opera is one of the earliest examples of this new type.[81]

'Gli Equivoci nel Sembiante' is on quite a small scale, as was suitable to a private performance. It is a very innocent little drama, containing four characters only. *Clori* is in love with *Eurilla* and *Eurilla* with *Clori*; but the unexpected arrival of *Armindo*, *Eurilla*'s exact double, produces confusion, further complicated by the jealousy of *Lisetta*, and it is only after three acts of sighs and recriminations that matters are cleared up. There is not much scope for variety . . .; but Scarlatti at least provided a good many pretty little airs. . . . The airs are never very remarkable, though always pleasant.[82]

Even though it was not so intended, Dent's description of *Gli equivoci nel Sembiante* gives a good general picture of the new Italian operatic pastoral. It is as easily applied to any of Scarlatti's later pastorals as to this, his first, and is typical of all pastoral operas after the middle of the seventeenth century.

Another of Scarlatti's early pastorals, *La Rosaura*, or *Gli equivoci in amore*, may serve as an example. Written in 1690 for private festivities celebrating two marriages in the Ottoboni family,[83] the first two of its three acts have appeared in a modern edition.[84]

The story of *Rosaura* revolves around two pairs of lovers who, quite typically, must live through many reversals and much heartache before the proper pairs can be united. Elmiro arrives in Cyprus (islands being second only to Arcadia as pastoral locations) to marry Climene. He

[81] *Chi la fa se l'aspetta* (Bologna, 1667 and Rome, 1672) may actually be the first. The librettist and composer are both unknown, as is any occasion for which the opera might have been written. Entitled 'favola pastorale per musica,' it already illustrates the reduction of scenes from about twenty to ten an act, and the use of only four or five characters – two couples and either a comic servant or elderly adviser. The vast majority of these operas, however, date from the decade of the 1690s. Scarlatti's pastorals in this vein remain some of the very first.

[82] Edward J. Dent, *Alessandro Scarlatti: His Life and Works* (London: Edward Arnold, 1960), pp. 25 and 34.

[83] Dent, *Scarlatti*, p. 63. The double wedding was of Princess Tarquinia Colonna with Prince Marco Ottoboni, Duke of Fiano, and of Princess Cornelia Ottoboni with Prince Urbano Barberini (Alfred Lorenz, *Alessandro Scarlatti's Jugendoper: ein Beitrag zur Geschichte der italienischer Opera* (Augsburg: Dr. Benno Filser Verlag G. M. B. H., 1927), p. 130).

[84] Edited by Robert Eitner in *Gesellschaft für Musikforschung: Publikation Aelterer Praktischer und Theoretischer Musikwerke* (*PAPTN*), xiv (Facsimile ed., New York: Broude Bros., 1966).

falls immediately in love with Rosaura without knowing her name. His friend Celindo, unaware that Elmiro's new desire is his own Rosaura, is persuaded in friendship's name to pretend to woo Climene in order to free Elmiro from his promise to wed her. Rosaura overhears this pretended wooing, from which point the incriminations and accusations take flight. Elmiro tries to win Rosaura, while Celindo continues to feign love to Climene, who only rebuffs him to pine for her lost Elmiro. At the end, rather unconvincingly, the correct unions occur. Throughout this story a fifth character, Lesbo, a servant to Celindo, adds to the complexity and delivers comic commentary.

As in *Gli equivoci nel Sembiante*, there is little in *Rosaura* to distinguish it from contemporary opera other than its dimensions. There is no chorus, and there is not even any ensemble writing in the three so-called duets. In two of these the participants are each given one long uninterrupted solo; in the third the style consists of 'a simple aria divided between two voices'.[85] There are no ballets nor any descriptive symphonies. Many (approximately half) of the arias have simple *basso continuo* accompaniment. The instrumental accompaniments and ritornellos are typically written for three strings with continuo. There is only one aria with solo obbligato in these first two acts: Rosaura's 'Non dar più pene', Act II, iii ('Con un solo Violino e Violoncello senza Cembalo').[86] The score appears to make no use of any winds, although these may have been present in some instances to double the strings.

Of *Rosaura's* thirty-six published arias, twenty-five are designated *da capo*. Three more are written out in ternary form (ABA). The distinction here, however, is more apparent than real. In the primary manuscript source for the modern edition there are no *da capos* indicated by that sign.[87] The reason for writing out all of the arias seems to be the regular omission of the ritornello from the *da capo*. In 'Tu vai cercando' (I, vi), where the ritornello is only two measures long, for example, it is still omitted. And even when there is a motto opening followed by an instrumental interlude, as in 'Un cor da voi ferito' (I, v), this too is omitted in the repetition. Only seven arias are binary without any repetitions; one is strophic.[88]

---

[85] Dent, *Scarlatti*, p. 55.

[86] Quoted from one of the manuscript sources preserved in the British Library (Add. 31513).

[87] The most complete source, and presumably the earliest, is British Library Add. 31513. In this there are no signed *da capos*. Another very complete score, but lacking the prologue, symphony, and final scene, is British Library Add. 14167, in which the repeated sections of the *da capos* are signed. British Library Add. 31488 contains only Act iii, vii, the 'death' scene of Rosaura, transposed down an octave for tenor voice. There is only continuo accompaniment.

[88] Even the form of these strophes is ABA, however, and in British Library Add. 31513 the second strophe is missing.

The arias are mainly in common time (twenty-five), with nine in
3/8 and two in 3/4.[89] They conform to a regular length; the voice
parts of the A (that is, repeated) section of the *da capo* are close to ten
measures in every case. The B sections tend to be the same length or a
little longer.[90] The rhythmic nature of these pieces achieves regularity
in most cases; the melodies are generally conjunct or triadically based
in the harmony. There is a good deal of phrase repetition and little or
no pause in the musical flow.

The contrast between the A and B sections of the *da capos* is not
great; often the B section derives from a motive in A or begins with the
same head motive before developing different material.

Ex. 2

[89] It should be noted that none of these arias are in the 'pastoral' metre of 12/8, another
indication that this style was generally reserved for pastoral episodes in non-pastorals.
[90] The pieces in 3/8 are generally double or more this length. However, they are regularly
barred in 6/8 in the modern edition, and, indeed, the feeling is **of 'di due battute.'**

poi mi to - glies - ti e poi mi to - glies - ti e mi più non

è nò nò nò nò, e_____ mi più non è.

All of these stylistic traits point to a musical adaptation of the simplicity inherent in the late seventeenth-century literary pastoral. The regularity of length, form, and metre in the arias in general and the relationships of theme and size between the two sections of the *da capo* arias all point to a pastoral consistency translated into music. Even the regular omission of the opening ritornellos points to a conscious diminution.

In only one scene does Scarlatti move away from this musical simplicity, consistency, and regularity. Act III, ii, contains the confrontation of one betrothed couple. Rosaura, lamenting Celindo's apparent love for Climene, sings 'Rendete, rendete al mio core.' The A section, in E minor, 'Largo ed affettuoso', is in common time; the B section, in 12/8, 'Andante', cadences on B minor. The return to A is written out and interrupted four measures before the end by Celindo's entrance.[91] In their duet which follows, 'Cruda – Infido', there is also a complete change of metre and style between sections.

Particularly interesting throughout the opera is Scarlatti's use of lengthy musical repetition to create large formal sections. In Act II, vii,[92] Climene soliloquizes on her situation in the aria, 'Non farmi più languir', a full *da capo*. In the next scene, Lesbo, Celindo's servant, enters to deliver to Climene a letter meant for Rosaura, which the latter has rejected and ordered brought to her supposed rival. Climene also rejects it angrily, and ignoring Lesbo returns her thoughts to Elmiro. The musical setting of these new words is a repetition of her former aria, with only minor changes in the B sections.[93]

[91] See pp. 170–2 of the printed edition. In the manuscript BL Add. 31513 the aria is not as effectively broken off. The *da capo* is shorter and ends after the first statement of the text (after five measures) with a double bar. In Add. 14167, and in the edition, the *da capo* is extended for three more measures into the middle of the text's second statement and is broken off abruptly.

[92] In the modern edition Act II has two scenes designated 'iv' and the rest follow in sequence. Thus from scene v on, the numbers used here are one ordinal higher. Moreover, the first scene iv is lacking in Add. 31513; a solo scene for Lesbo appears instead. The second scene iv in the modern edition corresponds to scene v of Add. 31513.

[93] Eitner writes in the introduction to this edition that the two middle sections are different (p. 106). This is hardly the case. In fact, the continuo lines are identical, and the vocal lines are only slightly differentiated.

Ex. 3

1. Non far mi più lan   —   guir,   Non far mi

2. Con-so-la i miei de   —   sir,   Con-so-la i

più lan — guir   ca-ro, ca-ro,   ca-ro, deh vie-ni, deh   vie-ni a me,

miei de — sir   ca — ro, ca — ro,   deh per pie-tà,__ deh   per pie-tà,

ca — ro, ca — ro,   ca — ro, deh vie-ni, deh   vie ni a   me.

ca — ro, ca — ro,   deh per pie — tà,__ deh   per pie tà.

1. Bel - tà · for-se più va - ga il cor___ t'im - pia -

2. Mos-tra-ti, mos - tra - ti chi ___ 't'a - do - ra, poi di ___ ch'io mo -

-ga ò pur, ò___ pur t'ar-res - ta, ò pur t'ar-res-ta il

-ra e gran fa - vor sa - rà,___ e gran fa-vor sa -

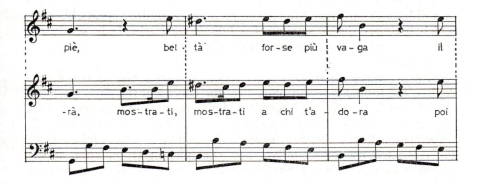

piè, bel - tà · for - se più va - ga il

-rà, mos - tra - ti, mos-tra-ti a chi t'a - do - ra poi

[da capo]

A similar situation occurs for Elmiro in scene ix. Here Elmiro sings twenty-one measures followed by Celindo singing seventeen measures of a different character. After some recitative, Elmiro repeats his part, which becomes the A section of a full *da capo* aria. It is surely not accidental that the first measure of the continuo part in both 'B sections' is identical.[94]

In many ways these large-scale repetitions over one or two scenes replace the formal function played by the chorus in the early pastoral. The change is in order with the altered dimensions of the genre, and the repetitions help to maintain the lyrical quality of the pastoral formerly associated with the choral refrains. This quality is also heightened by the restricted use of recitative. For example, in II, x, after an abnormally long section of recitative for this opera (fifty-three measures), Elmira sings an aria, followed without pause by Climene singing an aria, and then, still without pause, Rosaura sings an aria. After six additional measures of recitative, Climene sings another aria.[95]

These lyrical qualities and the opera's other stylistic features reflect

[94] See pp. 204–7 of the printed edition.
[95] British Library Add. 14167 includes yet another aria for Elmiro, 'Ah, crudel.'

the continuing criticisms of the early pastoral drama's elaborate nature. The opera is short. There are few attempts at variety. Musical form, metre, and motive are kept as consistent as possible. Even the orchestral accompaniments are held apparently to the minimum of three string parts and continuo. The stylistic trait which would become the most important feature of the revitalized operatic pastoral, however, was the use of a strong melodic relationship between the two sections of the *da capo*.

Almost none of these traits appear in Scarlatti's heroic operas. For example, where *Rosaura* (1690) has in its three acts seven, ten, and eight scenes, respectively, *Eraclea* (1700) has eighteen, eighteen, and sixteen, and *Marco Attilio Regolo* (1719) has sixteen, eighteen, and fourteen.[96] Compared with *Rosaura*'s five characters, *Eraclea* has nine and *Marco Attilio Regolo* eight. Both heroic operas include more ensembles and descriptive symphonies than the pastoral. *Marco Attilio Regolo* has choruses and ballets. The instrumentation of *Marco Attilio Regolo* is especially rich, calling for oboes, cornetti, trumpets, and horns in addition to the strings and continuo. In the dance of the young Carthaginians (I, i), the stage directions refer to bagpipes, castanets, and jingles. In the *sinfonia* (I, v), horns are called for on the stage. Even *Eraclea*, however, calls for obbligato flutes and trumpets.

The arias of both *Marco Attilio Regolo* and *Eraclea* seem to be quite evenly distributed between the use of duple and triple metre, common time (C) and 3/8 prevailing by far. As in the pastoral, the *da capo* form predominates, but the *da capo* is generally signed and the ritornello repeated. The A sections (again counting 3/8 in double bars) are not of regular length, but often fall between twenty and thirty measures. The B sections are about half that length and thematically differentiated from the repeated section. The only case in either opera of an identical motive beginning both sections is in a mock-pastoral duet from *Eraclea*, 'Son lupo d'amore', sung by the opera's comic couple.[97] It is predictably set in 12/8 metre, the pastorale metre for non-pastorals. Totally absent in *Rosaura*, it makes relatively frequent appearances in both *Eraclea* and *Marco Attilio Regolo*.

---

[96] Modern editions of both *Eraclea* (ed. by Donald J. Grout, 1974) and *Marco Attilio Regolo* (ed. by Joscelyn Godwin, 1975) have appeared in the Harvard Publications in Music, *The Operas of Alessandro Scarlatti*, Donald J. Grout, general editor.

[97] The use of mock-pastoral scenes is discussed more fully in the commentary about Keiser's *L'inganno fedele* in Chapter III. The text of 'Son lupo d'amore' is translated in the modern edition:

'Alfeo: I am a lovewolf, my beautiful Lilluccia.
Livio: If you want a lamb, my beloved, I am here.
Alfeo: My heart is already pounding with avid desires.
Livio: Eh, eat if you're hungry; don't stand still like that.
　　　I am a lovewolf, etc.'

Ex. 4

The arias in *Marco Attilio Regolo* are always separated by recitative.[98] In the first act the range varies from four measures to eighty-four; most frequently the length of these recitatives is between forty and sixty measures. The use, however limited, of choruses, symphonies, ensembles, and ballets seems to make unnecessary the use of large-scale repetitions, such as appear in *Rosaura*. When the chorus was first omitted from Venetian opera, it was maintained in the pastorals. After a thirty-year absence from the stage, however, the operatic pastoral was re-established in a new form without chorus. The appearance of large concerted pieces in heroic opera completed the circle. As the operatic pastoral shrank, the heroic opera grew.

Rosaura was written ten years before *Eraclea* and almost thirty before *Marco Attilio Regolo*, and the differences between it and the later operas are partly due to operatic developments during that time. A pastoral opera written by Scarlatti in 1710, however, shows that to a large extent the form of the pastoral was stable during this period and different in conception from heroic opera.

La fede riconosciuta has three pairs of lovers who go through the usual tribulations caused by disguises, misunderstandings, and jealousies before uniting properly at the end. Dent remarks with some surprise on the simplicity of the musical score, saying that if one did not know otherwise, *La fede riconosciuta* could have been written for a private amateur performance.[99] The reason for this, of course, is the opera's

---

[98] The recitatives from *Eraclea* do not survive, but the libretto indicates that in it, too, the concerted numbers did not come consecutively with no break.

[99] Edward J. Dent, 'A Pastoral Opera by Alessandro Scarlatti,' *The Music Review*, xii (1951), p. 11. The occasion calling for this opera is described in the libretto: 'Dramma

simplicity of style. As Dent describes it, *La fede riconosciuta* is a perfect example of the musical pastoral form.

The scene is laid in Arcadia, and the characters are all nymphs and shepherds. . . . The literary style follows the 'Arcadian' convention of the period, and so does the behaviour of the characters, but we must accept it for what it is, and within its convention—we must remember that it is specifically called a *divertimento* [in the dedication] – its affectations have a certain 'Dresden china' charm and grace, together with an agreeably humorous atmosphere. . . . Each act [there are three] has about a dozen arias (including ariosi and duets) practically all of which are in *da capo* form. . . . All the *arias* are simple in style and there is not much in the way of elaborate coloratura. The compass, for all the voices, is restricted.[100]

The orchestra consists for the most part of strings in various combinations from unison violins with continuo to the full quartet. The flute appears but once as an obbligato instrument; the oboe appears once as an obbligato, and in the closing ensemble it doubles the violins. There is no chorus, nor are there any descriptive symphonies.

Scarlatti again uses large-scale repetition. In II, v, Elpina sings 'Mi stai nel core come un bambino', a full *da capo*. Following some recitative with Falcone, the scene ends with the A section of the aria set as a duet for both characters. In the last scene of Act II,[101] snippets from the B section of Elpina's aria appear in her opening recitative. Moreover, the opening duet of III, v, derives from the closing duet of Act II.

All of these scenes involve Elpina and Falcone, the two comic characters who lend respite to the self-made tribulations of the two young pairs of lovers. In *Rosaura*, the comic character Lesbo was often involved in the scenes with large-scale repetition. Perhaps at this time the comic characters replaced the lyrical and formal aspects of the early operatic chorus. Shortly they would be relegated to the ends of acts only, and then to intermezzos.[102]

Pastorale per musica da rappresentarsi nel Teatro di S. Bartolomeo nell' Autunno del 1710 per l'ingresso felice dell'Ill. e Ecc. Sig. Co. Carlo Barromeo consigliero di Stato . . .' (Ibid., p. 7.)
[100] Ibid., pp. 8 and 10–11.
[101] This final scene is numbered xiii in the manuscript preserved at the Fitzwilliam Museum, Cambridge, but is actually xii because scene vii, containing the part of a shepherd (Aminta) later omitted, has been excised. Similarly in Act I, scene v has been excised, leaving ten scenes rather than the eleven numbered in the autograph.
[102] The surviving sources for *Eraclea* may represent just such a progression in the use of comic scenes. See Grout, 'Introduction,' *Eraclea*, p. 5. The manuscript of *Marco Attilio Regolo* (British Library Add. 14171) may also illustrate such a progression. In this source the various comic scenes have been grouped together at the ends of acts. The numbering of the scenes, however, follows the original order, in Act I, for example, skipping from scene vi to ix. As these changes occur where one number has been interpolated into the score in a strikingly different and formalistic hand, and they do not correspond to any surviving libretto, it seems likely that Scarlatti may have altered his original score for a performance which never occurred. See Godwin, 'Introduction,' *Marco Attilio Regolo*, pp. 7–8, where he discusses the possibility of a London performance.

Carlo Francesco Pollaroli's setting of *La fede riconosciuta* is presumably later than Scarlatti's because the character of Elpina is dropped, and Falcone, who becomes Lupino, is mostly devoid of his comic characteristics; he serves simply as elder confidant to the 'faithful' shepherdess, Dorinda.[103] This diminishes the size of the opera still further. The three acts of Scarlatti's version had ten, twelve, and eight scenes; Pollaroli's have nine, ten, and seven.

As in the earlier pastorals, Pollaroli's instrumentation is quite limited. The strings and continuo constitute almost the entire orchestral timbre. Oboes are called for in the overture and in one aria: 'Si crudel barbara sorte', at the end of Act II; they probably are used for doubling elsewhere. Of the twenty-eight arias, nine are accompanied by continuo alone. In five more the violins play 'unisono'. The opera has no choruses, symphonies, or ballets.

Ex.5
A Section

B Section

<hr />

[103] This manuscript is preserved at the Library of the Royal Academy of Music, London. It is not the same as Pollaroli's *L'Innocenza riconosciuta* (Venice, 1717) listed in *MGG* under 'Pollarolo' (Vol. 10, col. 1422).

The most interesting aspect of this opera is Pollaroli's use of a melodic relationship between the two sections of the *da capo*. He never uses a motivic or head-motive relationship as does Scarlatti. Instead, he sets up two themes in his A section and quotes the second at the opening of the B section. Often the theme is quoted at pitch. Pollaroli uses this stylistic mannerism whenever he is faced with a text describing nature or utilizing images of nature, such as 'Di gigli e di rose amore', 'Ditemi dolci aurette', 'Se al monte mi segui amor', and 'Ai fiori del prato', and in a few other instances as well, especially when there are word resemblances between the texts of the two sections. An example of such a relation may be seen in 'Ai fiori del prato' (Ex. 5).

During his long career, Pollaroli wrote numerous pastorals. One of his first was a setting of Zeno's libretto *Gl'inganni felici* (1695), his only setting of a Zeno pastoral. After producing three pastoral librettos, however, all highly praised by Crescimbeni,[104] Zeno returned to the pastoral world only when he had what might be termed a specific commission. On the completion of one of these pastorals (*Imeneo*, 1727), Zeno wrote to a friend, 'I have finished a pastoral as well as I am able considering my weariness and my age. Even for poets, old age has little grace in matters of love.'[105]

Zeno's *Aminta*, 'Dramma regio-pastorale', was performed in Florence in the autumn of 1703. The composer is unknown, and it is Zeno's only work to have its first (and only?) performance in that city. It is not unlikely that *Aminta* was commissioned for a private performance. Zeno's other pastorals were written at Vienna for the birthday (28 August) celebrations for the Empress Elizabeth Christina. *Semiramide* (18 August 1725) and *Imeneo* (30 August 1727) were both performed outside in the garden of the country palace, La Favorita, built by Leopold II. *Enone* (28 August 1734) may also have been presented outdoors as it was certainly privately performed at the Favorita.[106] The music for all three was composed by Antonio Caldara.

Caldara (1670–1737) was an Italian composer of wide repute. His formal positions included that of Maestro di cappella at the Mantuan court (1700–7) and for Prince Ruspoli in Rome (1709–16), and Vice-Kapellmeister (under Johann Joseph Fux) for Emperor Charles VI (formerly King Charles III of Spain) in Vienna (1716–36).[107] At

---

[104] See above, pp. 33–4.
[105] Letter 716, written to the Venetian poet, Luisa Bergalli, quoted by Fehr, *Zeno*, p. 67.
[106] Ibid., p. 138.
[107] See Ursula Kirkendale, *Antonio Caldara: Sein Leben und seine venezianisch-romischen Oratorien* (Graz: Hermann Bohlaus Nachf., 1966), pp. 21–102.

different times in one year, 1708, he composed for Cardinal Ottoboni in Rome, for King Charles III of Spain in Barcelona, and for the opera in Venice. Caldara's vocal compositions include operas, oratorios, cantatas, serenatas, canons, and masses, few of which are available in modern editions. While in Vienna he was regularly required to compose vocal works for festive occasions. 'From the year of his appointment, he composed a large festival opera every year for the name-day of the Emperor (4 November), and in addition about every other year, and from 1732 on every year, an opera or serenata for the birthday of the Empress (28 August), and in some years . . . he supplied a serenata or *festa teatrale* for the birthday of the Emperor (1 October) or the name-day of the Empress (19 November) . . .'[108] It was for these occasions, especially the Empress's birthday (at which time the performances could be outdoors), that the pastoral was needed.[109] These works were not massive *opere serie* but closer to *feste teatrali* or *serenate*.

While in Vienna Caldara managed in addition to his duties as Kapellmeister to work for the Archbishop of Salzburg, Franz Anton Graf von Harrach.[110] From 1716 to 1727 Caldara wrote at least twelve operas for Salzburg all dedicated to the Archbishop.[111] The fourth of these was *Dafne: dramma pastorale per musica*, written by the Munich court poet Abate Biani and performed in July of 1719, probably for the opening of the garden theatre now known as the *Heckentheatre* in Mirabell Park.[112] As it is available in a modern edition it may serve as an example of the early eighteenth-century pastoral *feste teatrali* which were often performed outdoors.

As in other pastorals, there are few characters. The main soloists are Dafne, soprano; Febo (Apollo), alto (surely sung by a castrato);[113] Aminta, a shepherd in love with Dafne, tenor; and Peneo, a water-god, Dafne's father, bass. In the prologue, before the entrances of the other characters, Apollo is joined by three planets: Giove, Venere, and Mercurio, who, not coincidentally, are bass, soprano, and tenor – these roles were almost certainly sung by the same people playing Peneo, Dafne, and Aminta. The planets do not return until the epilogue, by which time Aminta has been turned into a plant; Dafne, into a laurel tree; and Peneo, into a river. There is no chorus, although in the third act there are stage directions calling for a group of hunters with Peneo

---

[108] Ibid., pp. 84–5.
[109] Fehr, *Zeno*, p. 67.
[110] Kirkendale, *Caldara*, p. 89.
[111] Constantin Schneider, ed., *Dafne* by Antonio Caldara, *DTÖ*, xci (Vienna: Österreich Bundesverlag, 1955), p. xiv.
[112] Ibid., p. xv.
[113] Ibid.

and Dafne, and later, shepherds with Aminta. As there are directions for a ballet to close the first two acts (with no indication of either topic or music), one can perhaps assume the dancers were used in Act III as the 'crowd'. The dances themselves have no obvious connection with the opera, its composer or librettist. Like the intermezzi attached to this opera, both of which survive without music, they surely served as divertissements.

The plot generally follows the well-known myth with a few original alterations and adaptations, some of which were to enable the soloists to play dual roles. The imaginative libretto brings a good deal of life to both Apollo and Dafne. The set changes are extraordinarily simple and well suited to an outdoor performance. Act I takes place in a flowering wood; Act II, by a river with many trees on its banks; Act III, in a park with a mountain in the background.

The accompaniments are also simple. In general, Caldara uses only strings, sometimes singling out the violin as solo obbligato. The most striking instance of the latter occurs at the end of Act I where the aria takes on the character of a concerto grosso. Other tone colours are sparingly used. Both the opening trio (prologue) and the final 'chorus' (epilogue) employ additional instruments; in the body of the opera there are only three instances, each for a heightened nature scene. In Act II, i, Apollo hears a nightingale singing and addresses his own song to the bird. This 'nightingale song' is accompanied by pizzicato strings and oboe obbligato, the cembalo remaining silent. In Act II, v, Peneo sings an apostrophe to fishing, and is accompanied by two oboes, bassoons, and basso continuo. Finally Dafne opens Act III with a hunting song which along with strings and cembalo uses two hunting horns.

Of the twenty-nine vocal pieces, twenty-seven are in *da capo* form, Of these, twenty-one are in major keys, sixteen of which modulate to related minor keys in the middle section. There are slight differences in the use of the ritornellos which tend to reflect the scope and weight of each aria. The most striking musical feature throughout the opera, however, is the consistent use of material from the A section in the B section, which increases the opera's simple lyric and non-dramatic impact. In some of these arias an accompanimental figure is borrowed for the B section which may have been of only minor importance in the A section. Like Scarlatti, but unlike Pollaroli, Caldara almost always identifies the resemblance by using the same head motive to begin both sections. Indeed he takes this technique to extremes, often repeating material so integral to the A section that the B section becomes little more than a variation.

The ritornello of 'O cara dolce' (Act I, i) begins in the violins with an eight-bar phrase (Example 6a). When the voice enters it is given an extended version of the antecedent four bars after which the strings pick up the consequent phrase. This latter phrase is never put into the voice. In the B section, the voice is given a new antecedent phrase, but the consequent phrase, still in the strings, remains the same (Example 6b). This exact phrase in the strings is then repeated concurrently with the voice; and finally three measures before the *da capo*, the strings bring back the head motive of the antecedent phrase of the A section ritornello (Example 6c).

Ex.6
(a) Ritornello (violins)

(b) beginning of B Section (voice and violins)

Tu   so - la. d'og - ni   stel - la   sor - mon - ti   la   bel -

- tà

(c) ending of B Section (voice and violins)

do - lor di   mor   te, ——————— do - lor,   do - lor di   mor - te

In 'Dite bene' (Act I, iv) the continuo part of the two sections varies melodically only in degree. It is, of course, in a different key.

Ex.7

In some cases such as in 'Tanti raggi' (Act II, ii) the B section actually begins with a repetition of the A ritornello in the tonic key, only modulating at the entrance of the voice. That is, the parallelism between the two sections is emphasized by moving the double bar from after the repetition of the opening ritornello to before, creating varied strophes with identical instrumental introductions.

Ex.8

In 'La bella rosa' the vocal part of the B section is simply a transposition of the A section's primary theme with an elongated cadence. This cadenza, with its cadential formulae, begins at the point in the A section where the theme begins its melodic development coupled with textual repetition.

Ex.9

Such relationships are not incidental to Caldara's style. They occur in fully two-thirds of the arias of this opera. Moreover, one may associate this particular style in Caldara's works, at least tentatively, with the pastoral.[114] In an earlier pastoral opera, for example, *Selvaggio eroe* (1707), the relationship occurs in about half the arias.[115] In Caldara's heroic opera *Andromaca* (1724), however, it appears less than once in each act.[116] Finally, the highest percentage of arias which show this type of relationship occurs in Caldara's cantatas, each of which is a miniature pastoral.[117]

[114] Kirkendale, *Caldara*, pp. 171–5, does not include this trait as a mannerism of the oratorios. The religious vocal music of Caldara in print reveals little dependence on the *da capo* form at all.

[115] Twenty-five arias from *Selvaggio eroe* have been preserved at the British Library (RM 23.f.5).

[116] This opera is preserved in autograph as well as in a good eighteenth-century copy (which I was able to study on microfilm) at the Gesellschaft der Musikfreunde, Vienna.

[117] The following cantatas, published in *DTÖ*, lxxv (Vienna: Universal-Edition A.G., 1932), ed. by Eusebius Mandyczewski, are datable to before 1716.

1712 (no. 6)	'D'improvviso' for alto
October 1715 (no. 7)	'Soffri mio caro Alcino' for alto
December 1715 (no. 3)	'Che prodigio' for soprano
January 1716 (no. 1)	'È qual cosa' for soprano
April 1716 (no. 5)	'Astri' for alto
August 1716 (no. 4)	''Io crudele' for soprano

In these cantatas there are fourteen arias. Thirteen are designated *da capo*; the fourteenth is ABA. All but one of the *da capo* arias show distinct thematic relationships between the A and B sections. Robert Freeman, 'Opera without Drama' (Unpublished doctoral dissertation, Princeton University, 1967), p. 222, argues nevertheless that one must reject the idea that, 'in the corpus of Caldara's arias, specific kinds of texts imply specific varieties of musical setting.'

THE INVOLVEMENT OF THE CANTATA WITH THE PASTORAL

Whereas the pastoral mode in opera remained relatively rare, perhaps because its smaller size was inconsistent with the genre, it reigned supreme in the cantata. By the middle of the seventeenth century, when pastoral operas were on the wane, Marc' Antonio Cesti could set a text ridiculing the use of familiar pastoral conceits.

> But soft; listen! Let's let the amorous songs go by the board; everyone is sick of listening to these things; there is nothing to listen to but
>> 'Little eyes to die, heart, to die.'
> And dealing with such rubbish: 'Phyllis', 'Lilla', 'fair orbs', 'eyes I would call you, but you are stars'; stuff so irritating the world is thoroughly fed up with it by now. . . .[118]

Despite this, however, the amorous pastoral theme never lost its popularity. What Gloria Rose has written of Giacomo Carissimi (1605–74) holds equally well for Caldara, A. Scarlatti, and even George Frideric Handel: 'Regardless of author, the texts of the cantatas deal almost exclusively with one subject – love; more specifically, with the lament of a lover, dying of unrequited passion.'[119]

Like Caldara, Alessandro Scarlatti excelled in the field of opera and in the cantata. His librettists were often men who formed and ran the Roman academy and with whom Handel assuredly associated: among them Ottoboni, Zappi, and Panfili.[120] Scarlatti's style in these works is similar to that in his pastoral operas. The cantatas were everyday occurrences; they were concerts, not dramatic performances, and they drew on a continuous development of almost one hundred years. Nevertheless, their styles and subjects and those of pastoral opera were similar – lyric refinement and homogeneity being primary goals. The musical difference between these forms lies only in the reduced need of the cantata composer to underscore continually the pastoral nature of his text. That is, as the cantata generally contained two or three arias and rarely grew beyond five, the arias themselves did not need to be as constrained. As overdramatization was unlikely without the use of action, scenery, or props, the composers had a freer hand with both harmony and form. Compared with *La Rosaura*, the melodic writing in Scarlatti's pastoral cantatas is less repetitive. There is also a greater variety of metres, fewer designated *da capos*, and more distant harmonic modulations.[121]

---

[118] Translated by David Burrows in *Antonio Cesti*, The Wellesley Edition Cantata Index Series, i (Wellesley, Mass.: Wellesley College, 1964), p. xv.
[119] Gloria Rose, 'The Cantatas of Giacomo Carissimi', *MQ*, xlviii (1962), p. 206.
[120] See Hans Engel, 'Kantate', *MGG* vii, col. 559.

It is important to remember, however, that these differences are often only a matter of degree. The strong literary criticisms of the dramatic pastoral had created many constraints on its use. These could be relaxed somewhat in the composition of the smaller cantata; but even though freed from an exact consistency, the cantata style was essentially the same as that in the larger forms. However, the literati did encourage the use of pastoral themes in the cantata, since it was considered more appropriate there.

It should come as no surprise, then, that neither of the two operas composed by Handel during his brief Italian residence was a pastoral. Handel moved in the company of many of the greatest Arcadians whose musical and literary tastes would have been known to him. His music from this period shows that he was increasingly sensitive to these tastes. During the years in which Handel apparently wrote most of his one hundred Italian cantatas, he was employed by the Marquis Ruspoli and intimately connected with the Arcadian Academy. These cantatas are almost exclusively pastoral.

With the aid of the Ruspoli documents about a third of these are datable, providing a strong foundation for the stylistic dating of the entire set. The chronology shows that Handel arrived in Italy with a well-developed dramatic sense and departed having mastered the lyrical Italian pastoral style as well. In order to examine the effect of the Italian pastoral on his musical style, these cantatas will be studied in a later chapter. It is necessary first to understand how the pastoral had developed in Germany and how Handel understood this genre before he arrived on Italian soil.

---

[121] See the following cantatas, all available in modern editions: 'Quando amor vuol ferirmi', 'Lascia, deh lascia', 'Solitudine amene', 'Su le sponde del Tebro', and 'Arianna' (probably composed about 1707). These cantatas contain a total of fifteen arias.

CHAPTER III

The Pastoral in Germany

THE ORIGIN AND CONTINUED POPULARITY OF THE PASTORAL
IN GERMANY

At the beginning of the seventeenth century, German culture fell under the spell of two particularly strong influences. The first was an infatuation with anything foreign;[1] the second, in seeming contrast, was a strong sense of nationalism. Paradoxically, however, this nationalism was itself the result of foreign influence, for German societies devoted particularly to purging the vernacular of foreign elements, and encouraging the use of German in all forms of literature, developed in imitation of the late sixteenth-century Italian societies, and especially the 'Accademia della Crusca' (founded 1582) of Florence. In simultaneous satisfaction of the two trends, Germany in the early seventeenth century was flooded with translations. Among these the late renaissance pastorals of Italy stand out in number and importance,[2] especially as they to a great extent determined the character of German literature for the next century and a half. The most popular of these and the one with the most influence on the future of German literature and music drama was Guarini's *Il pastor fido*.[3]

It was first translated into German by Eilgerus Männlich in Mülhausen in 1619.[4] Later translators included Statius Ackermann (Schleusingen, 1636), Georg Philipp Harsdörffer (Nuremberg, 1644), Hofmann von Hofmannswaldau (1652–9, published in Breslau, 1678), and Hans von Abschatz (1668). Although more translations were to follow in both the seventeenth and eighteenth centuries, von Hofmannswaldau's and von Abschatz's became the most popular.

Of the only two musical settings of *Il pastor fido* known to have been written in Germany in the seventeenth and eighteenth centuries, the

---

[1] See especially Lawrence Marsden Price, 'English > German Literary Influences: Bibliography and Survey,' *Modern Philology*, ix (1919–20).

[2] For more information on the importance of the pastoral in Germany, see Gustav Andreen, *Studies in the Idyl in German Literature* (Rock Island, Illinois: Lutheran Augustana Book Concern, Printers, 1902), p. 20.

[3] *Il pastor fido* seems to have been translated during the baroque era more into German than any other language.

[4] Leonardo Olschki, *Guarini's 'Pastor Fido' in Deutschland: Ein Beitrag zur Literaturgeschichte des 17. und 18. Jahrhunderts* (Leipzig: H. Haessel Verlag, 1908). See especially Chapter II: 'Die deutschen Übersetzungen des Pastor Fido,' pp. 27–76.

first, by Heinrich Schütz (Dresden, 1653), was set to a German libretto by Ernst Geller ('Der getreue Schäfer; oder Der getreue Hirte' with a ballet, 'Arkadischer Hirtenaufzug'). The second, by Nikolaus Adam Strungk (Brunswick, 1678), was a setting of the Hofmannswaldau translation.[5] However, though few operas were based on Guarini's drama, it could still be hailed at the beginning of the eighteenth century as an important, if not the most important, source of the operatic pastoral.

Afterwards, however, upon the nuptials of Duke Carl Emanuel of Savoy, the incomparable Guarini offered *Il Pastor Fido*, which Hoffmannswaldau and Abschatz have translated into German. Capellmeister Cesti, if my memory serves me right about the name, set the aphorisms and morals as arias. Then all musicians and poets thought further about this until they came up with a suitable recitative, and in its place, where an aphorism ought to be, devised an aria. Thus is *Il pastor Fido* a source of all opera.[6]

Although the knowledge of history displayed here is weak, since Charles Emmanuel I (1562–1630), to whom Guarini dedicated *Il pastor fido* on the occasion of the Duke's marriage to Catherine of Austria (in 1585),[7] died when Cesti was but ten years old, it is interesting to note the belief that opera grew out of a desire to set to music the entirety of *Il pastor fido*, not just the 'pretty madrigals'.[8] No such suggestion ever appears in Italy.

Although *Il pastor fido* itself never became particularly popular as a German operatic libretto, it nevertheless inspired an indigenous German pastoral literature which often borrows from it by paraphrase or quotation. And so closely was the German pastoral associated with music that the title 'Pastoral' began to imply music.[9]

Using only the *Handbuch zur Geschichte der Barockoper*, it is possible to derive a fair idea of the number of operatic pastorals written in

---

[5] Renate Brockpähler, *Handbuch zur Geschichte der Barockoper in Deutschland* (Emsdetten/Westfalen; Lechte, 1964), pp. 89 and 134. Olschki states that *Il pastor fido* was never set to music in Germany (*Guarini's 'Il Pastor Fido'*, p. 123), and Gustav Friedrich Schmidt (*Die frühdeutsche Oper und die musikdramatische Kunst Georg Caspar Schürmann's* (Regensburg-Gustav Bosse Verlag, 1933), p. 57) notes only the Strungk-Hofmannswaldau collaboration.

[6] Hunold, *Die Allerneueste Art*, p. 395, paragraphs ccliv and cclv.

[7] The one musician known to have been working for Charles Emmanuel I at the time of his wedding is Alfonso Ferrabosco (the elder). No music survives of a setting for *Il pastor fido*. For the gala performance in Florence, 1589, the musical sections were composed by Luzzasco Luzzachi. See above, Chapter II, p. 23

[8] When Johann Mattheson writes more than thirty years later, 'If one of us were to write that Cesti, even though he lived so recently, was the founder of opera, wouldn't that same writer show his ignorance of music history?' (*Der vollkommene Kapellmeister* (Hamburg: C. Herold, 1739; facsimile reprint, ed. by Margarete Reimann, Kassel: Barenreiter Verlag, 1954), p. 24, paragraph xxxiii), he clearly is referring to Menantes's error. The mistaken attribution to Cesti, however, lasted almost a century, ending up finally in the *Historisch-biographisches Lexicon der Tonkunstler* (Leipzig: Breitkopf, 1790–2) by Ernst Ludwig Gerber.

[9] See especially Olschki, *Guarini's 'Il Pastor Fido'*, p. 122, and Andreen, *Idyl*, p. 21, n. 3.

Germany between 1627 and 1745. Counting those operas subtitled 'Pastorale', 'Schäferspiele', etc., and adding those with 'Schäfer' or 'Arcadia' in their titles and works whose titles indicate a known pastoral story, such as 'Orpheus' or 'Acis and Galatea', yields 114 operatic pastorals. This simple accounting omits those works where pastoralism is only implied, such as in 'La fede ninfa', in addition both to the many foreign pastoral operas performed in Germany during those years and to the large body of repeated or revised productions. It therefore underestimates the total number of compositions. Nevertheless, it helps illustrate the geographical centres for the production of operatic pastorals, shifting from Dresden to Brunswick to Hamburg, and finally dying out at Gotha. It also shows that although the most active period for the production of pastoral opera occurs in the last decade of the seventeenth century, pastoral operas continued to be produced regularly throughout the Baroque era. This was not the situation in Italy. Andreen says that in Germany 'the flood of pastoral literature . . . came in two large waves: the former, the smaller wave, reaching its highest point about the middle of the seventeenth century. After a subsidence this was followed by a larger wave, reaching *its* highest point about the middle of the eighteenth century.'[10] But he rarely treats operatic librettos, and when he does, he does not always identify them as such. By plotting the life cycle of the musical pastoral alongside that of the pastoral drama, however, one sees that there was a consistent production of dramatic pastorals in Germany, an 'operatic wave' coming between the two 'literary waves'. Reprinted below is the 'Drama' section of a table given in Andreen's study with the operatic figures added.[11]

These figures suggest that pastoral opera and pastoral drama begin simultaneously, indicating their common inspiration, but do not develop simultaneously. Rather, there is a single continuous development, with the literary 'waves' appearing from 1640 to 1680 and from 1730 to 1780, and the operatic pastoral in the interim, from 1680 to 1730. Evidently when opera was at its strongest in Germany it attracted most literary creative ability. At least this appears true for the pastoral. Certainly there was a close connection between pastoral literature and pastoral opera. Rather than a deterioration, one might say that for fifty years the operatic pastoral was a *substitute* for pastoral drama.

---

[10] Andreen, Idyl, p. 24.
[11] Table 2 is taken from Andreen, *Idyl*, p. 72. It is an abbreviation of the whole; here only two categories are reproduced in addition to the 'totals'. This is why the 'total' rarely equals the real total of the two rows above.

TABLE 2

The Growth Patterns of the Literary and Operatic Pastorals in Germany (1620–1800)

	1620–1629	1630–1639	1640–1649	1650–1659	1660–1669	1670–1679	1680–1689	1690–1699	1700–1709	1710–1719	1720–1729	1730–1739	1740–1749	1750–1759	1760–1769	1770–1779	1780–1789	1790–1799
Literary (Andreen):																		
drama	2	4	4	2	4	3	1	1	1		3	28	8	4	5	1		
pastorals	1	9	16	16	9	4	4	1	1	5	4	10	15	14	11	4		2
Total	*3*	*23*	*23*	*21*	*14*	*8*	*6*	*2*	*6*	*12*	*52*	*41*	*44*	*44*	*16*	*9*		
Operatic (Harris):																		
miscellaneous			1	3	4	4	8	14	16	11	11			4				
Dresden								1	1	1								
Brunswick								10	2	2								
Hamburg								5	3	1								
Gotha	1						1	1		3	2	1						
Total	*1*	*1*		*4*	*6*	*6*	*10*	*30*	*18*	*17*	*16*	*12*	*5*	*2*				

THE BEGINNINGS OF OPERA IN GERMANY

Heinrich Schütz's *Daphne* (1627) is commonly considered the 'first German opera'. The score is no longer extant; the libretto was translated and adapted from Rinuccini's Italian pastoral (*Dafne*, 1597) by Martin Opitz.[12] Opitz stands at the forefront of the seventeenth-century German literary movement. His work typifies the two dominant literary trends in Germany in the early seventeenth century and their resolution. He sounded the call to a return to the vernacular in his *Aristarchus, sive de contemptu linguae Teutonicae* (1619) and later in his *Buch von der deutschen Poeterei* (1626). He was a member of the first German literary society, 'Die fruchtbringende Gesellschaft' or 'Palmenorden', founded in 1617. And he devoted much of his life to 'translations, or paraphrases, of foreign works, whose importance consists in the fact that they created the literary diction of Germany, and became the standard for succeeding writers.'[13] Not surprisingly many of these translations were of pastorals, *Daphne* being the first. Opitz also wrote an original pastoral play, *Hercynie* (1628).

Because Schütz's setting has not survived, it is impossible to study the collaboration of two masters in their respective fields. In fact, it seems that all of Schütz's dramatic music is lost. Four operatic works apparently followed *Daphne*, all produced in Dresden and, like *Daphne*, occasional compositions. All would seem from their titles to be pastoral-mythological, and all four are entitled 'Ballett' or 'Singend Ballett'.

> 1638 *Orpheus und Euridice, Sing-ballett* (Five Acts)
> librettist: August Buchner, based on Alessandro Striggio's 'Orfeo' (Mantua, 1607)
> occasion: the wedding of the Saxon Electoral Prince Johann Georg II and the Brandenburg Princess Magdalene Sibylle (14 November).

> 1650 *Singend Ballett von dem König Paris und der Helena*
> librettist: David Schirmer
> occasion: the double wedding of the sons of the elector, Duke Moritz and Duke Christian to the sisters Hedwig and Christiane of Schleswig-Holstein.

> 1653 *Der getreue Schafer* (Der getreue Hirte) with a ballet: 'Arkadischer Hirtenaugzug'
> librettist: Ernst Geller, based on Guarini's *Il pastor fido.*
> occasion: the name-days of
> Hr. Joh. Georg of Sachsen Rührfurst

----

[12] *Daphne* was written to celebrate the marriage of Princess Luise of Saxony and Landgraf Georg von Hessen-Darmstadt at Torgau (Grout, *Opera*, p. 37).
[13] Andreen, Idyl, p. 21.

Hr. Joh. Georg of Sachsen Ruhrprinz
Hr. Joh. Georg of Sachsen (24 June).

1655 *Ballett der Glückseligkeit*
librettist: David Schirmer
occasion: the birthday of Johann Georg I (5 March).[14]

What little can be said about these dramatic productions and about *Daphne* in particular has to be based on the surviving librettos. In his thorough study of Schütz's life and works, Moser has compared Rinuccini's text and Opitz's paraphrase. He finds that 'while [Opitz] has in part transcribed literally, he has frequently, on the other hand, eliminated the dramatic and merely retained the lyrical elements, or has even enlarged on their idyllic nucleus.'[15] Of one specific section of the libretto, he suggests that 'it is likely . . . that Schütz did not set this in the actual *parlando* recitative style but as a solo concert.' Moser concludes that 'the concept "opera" seems to be applicable only with some reservation in the case of Schütz's "Dafne"', 'since choruses and solo concerts seem to have far outweighed the real *stile rappresentativo*. Therefore one should almost speak rather of a concert and madrigal presentation than of an actual *dramma per musica*'.[16]

Moser has based his judgement on early Florentine practice, perhaps because this libretto was indeed used in 1598. But the first attempts at opera did not in fact indicate its future development. The lyric element soon became more and more important – first in the chorus and dance, and then in the aria. In a later Italian setting of Rinuccini's original libretto this direction is already apparent. 'Early seventeenth-century composers of opera whose training and technique allied their styles to those of the previous polyphonic era and whose tastes were not ultra-modern welcomed the opportunity to write multi-part choruses. *Dafne*, an opera performed in Mantua in 1608, shows its composer, Marco da Gagliano more at ease in the choral than monodic sections.'[17]

Apart from the fact that it would already have been out of date to

---

[14] See Brockpähler, *Handbuch*, p. 134, for a general listing. About 'Orpheus' see Hans Joachim Moser, *Heinrich Schütz: His Life and Work*, translated by Carl F. Pfatteicher (Saint Louis: Concordia Publishing House, 1959), pp. 166ff., and Moritz Fürstenau, *Zur Geschichte der Musik und des Theaters am Hofe zu Dresden* (Dresden: Rudolf Kuntze, 1861–2; facsimile edition, Leipzig: Edition Peters, 1971), pp. 102ff. About 'Paris' see Moser, *Schütz*, pp. 188ff., and Fürstenau, *Dresden*, pp. 117f. About 'Schafer' see ibid., p. 130. About 'Glückseligkeit' see ibid., pp. 131f. Brockpähler attributes all four to Schütz. Moser allows the first two; and Fürstenau accepts only the first. In every case, those not assigned to Schütz are considered anonymous.

[15] Moser, *Schütz*, p. 393.

[16] Ibid., pp. 394 and 396.

[17] Michael F. Robinson, *Opera Before Mozart* (London: Hutchinson University Library, 1966), p. 57.

write in the style of Peri and Caccini in 1627, Schütz and Opitz were probably keeping in mind the tastes of the Elector. As Robinson writes, 'the changes seem designed'.[18] In any event, the traits noted in the libretto and presumed in the music are just those that form the basis of the continuing pastoral style in Germany. This style can be equated neither with the earliest operatic monodies nor with the heroic 'aria-opera' of Venice. Rather it belongs to that short period in between, to the Venetian pastoral, when opera first achieved a certain balance among its various elements: monody, aria, recitative, chorus, and ballet. This remained the format for operatic pastorals in Germany even after the general style and subject matter of operas in both Italy and Germany moved in other directions.

The earliest extant German opera, *Seelewig*, 'a spiritual pastoral', was composed by Sigmund Theophil Staden to a text by Philipp Harsdörffer. It was published at Nuremberg in 1644. The opera is allegorical and aims at being didactic as well as entertaining. Its librettist, Harsdörffer, is, like Opitz, an important figure in the history of German baroque literature.

As with Opitz, Harsdörffer's output illustrates clearly the literary trends of the seventeenth century. For example, Harsdörffer founded his own *Sprachgesellschaft* at Nuremberg in 1644. 'Der Pegnitz Schafer' imitated the earlier 'Fruchtbringende Gesellschaft' to which Opitz had belonged.[19] Harsdörffer's own academy was aimed at the production of large quantities of German poetry. In this endeavour, Harsdörffer was exemplary.

He is credited with no less than forty-seven volumes of poetry and prose, and with his famous *Poetischer Trichter die Teutsche Dicht- und Reimkunst, ohne Behuf der lateinischen Sprache, in sechs Stunden einzugiessen*, or more shortly, *Der Nürnberger Trichter* (1647–53), he gave the German Baroque poets a hand-book which was more to their taste than the simple instructions of the *Buch von der deutschen Poeterey* [by Opitz, mentioned above]: and indeed, it carried in all seriousness the Opitzian doctrines to a point of absurdity. Another work by Harsdörffer, *Frauenzimmer Gesprech-Spiele* (1641–49), a compilation of informatory dialogues from French, Italian and Spanish sources in eight parts, was also widely read in its day.[20]

---

[18] Ibid., p. 82.

[19] Hans Engel states ('Pastorale' in *MGG*, x, col. 939) that this society was the model for the Roman 'Accademia Arcadia'. This seems unlikely. Between Italy and Germany in the seventeenth century the direction of influence flowed predominantly or exclusively northward. There is no reason to suspect that the group of men who formed Queen Christina's coterie would have had to look so far for a model. Many Italian societies devoted to nationalistic causes had preceded it - such as the Accademia della Crusca (1582). The choice of the pastoral scheme was motivated by the sought-after new simplicity in literature and was, of course, affected by the Arcadians' attitude toward pastoral literature.

[20] J. G. Robertson, *A History of German Literature*, 6th edition, ed. by Dorothy Reich (London: William Blackwood, 1970), p. 185.

Frauenzimmer Gesprech-Spiele (Gesprächspiele) contains both *Seelewig* and a short treatise on the literary pastoral.

Like Crescimbeni, Harsdörffer views the pastoral as a mixed form. He declares a preference, however, for the versified pastoral[21] and says that political allegory plays a large role. Political topics are well suited to the occasional and courtly use of the pastoral, which can be tailored to announce, criticize, or congratulate.

Although Harsdörffer's own pastoral appears not to have served an occasional or courtly function, it is allegorical. Just as the political pastorals are not what they seem, neither is the moralistic *Seelewig*. Its characters do not represent actual men but men's passions. That is, *Seelewig* is an attempt to present morally instructive information within the entertaining trappings of the contemporary pastoral. Harsdörffer explains this aim in the *Gesprächspiele*.

The use of enjoyable plays is a fine and wholly fruitful experience for the young. . . . There are now . . . three kinds of dramatic art: treating of either tragedy, comedy, or the middle type of Pastorals. . . . Of both the first we can read many in our language; of the last, however, there are still few to be found. . . . I think that in the pastorals translated from the Italian, the graciousness is wholly lost – as when delicate plants are transplanted into a hard soil and not correctly affixed, such as in the German translations of *Aminta, Il Pastor Fido* and others (these examples are well known).[22] Not only have the poetical stories of these been transmitted in unmetrical speech but also there is a great difference between this one and that in artistic decoration and handling. . . . I will myself venture to prove that pastorals are not impossible in our tongue.[23]

In the course of Harsdörffer's pastoral a young nymph Seelewig (soul) is enticed by the talk of another nymph Sinnigunda (sensuousness) and the flirtations of three shepherds, Kunsteling (artifice), Reichmut (wealth), and Ehrelob (power), to enter into the dominion of the satyr Trügewalt (deception). She is saved, however, by the steadfastness of her matronly adviser Gwissulda (conscience) and the friendship of the nymph Herzigilda (wisdom). There are choruses of nymphs, shepherds, and angels.

Some commentators have dismissed both the plot and the music of this 'first' German opera as puerile. Moser calls it 'a clumsily cadencing, stickily moving affair full of much unintended comedy'.[24] Grout says

---

[21] *Frauenzimmer Gesprächspiele* (Nuremberg: Wolfgang Endtern, 1643–57), v, 316.

[22] It is worth remembering that Harsdörffer himself was the third person to translate *Il pastor fido* into German. It appeared the same year as this volume of the *Gesprächspiele*, 1644.

[23] Harsdörffer, *Gesprächspiele*, iv, 30–2. This section is reprinted in Robert Eitner, '*Seelewig*, das älteste bekannte deutsche Singspeil von Harsdörffer und S. G. Staden, 1644: Neudruck,' *Monatschefte für Musik-Geschichte*, xiii (1881), p. 61. In the original this section is part of a conversation.

[24] Moser, *Schütz*, p. 396.

simply, 'there is evidence of some effort to write in the recitative style, but Staden has not acquired the knack; consequently, most of the songs are short melodies, and nearly all are in strophic form.'[25] Both writers feel that Staden falls short in a supposed attempt to write in the Italian monodic style. Here again, however, the Florentine criterion has biased their critical judgement. Only a few writers have recognized the innovative aspects of Staden's score. 'The composition shows us that the Nurembergers could be musically original and did not have to depend on the Italian style. Thus, they had nothing to do with recitative; all narratives and speeches are set in a measured and melodic song-style, similar to the way in which the Florentines composed the small prologues to their operas.'[26] *Seelewig* is presented in the *Frauenzimmer Gesprächspiele* in a manner typical of that work, with many interruptions for didactic discussions of the material.[27] Using these comments as a guide, one can investigate the presumed intentions of the author and composer.

The sections which he values most highly are those in which the musical setting serves to emphasize the rhyme scheme of the poem. Although not differentiated in the commentary, two musical techniques are used. The more common reflects the rhyme scheme in parallel repetitions of the melody and bass line. For example, in 'Künsteling, ich muss dir klagen' (Trügewald: I, ii), the rhyme scheme is *ababcc*; Staden sets this so that the melody and bass line follow the same pattern.

Ex.1

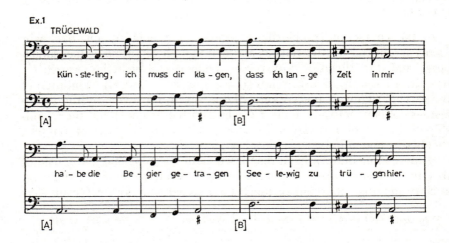

[25] Grout, *Opera*, p. 115.

[26] Hermann Kretzschmar, *Geschichte der Oper* (Leipzig: Breitkopf & Härtel, 1919), p. 155.

[27] The *Gesprächspiele* itself is in dialogue form. The character who guides the musical commentary is named Cassandra.

The second technique for emphasizing the rhyme scheme utilizes metre and rhythm. There is a simple example in Act III, ii, 'Schnelleilende Wellen' (Seelewig), where the rhyme scheme *abab* calls forth the metrical pattern 6/4–C–6/4–C. In another example, 'Zerfliessender Spiegel' (Künsteling: I, i), the form of the sonnet, here *abba abba ccd eed*, is illustrated:

metre: C 3 C   3
rhyme scheme: a bb a ccdeed

The rhyme scheme of the poetic quatrains is further emphasized musically by the distinct rhythmic structure of the 'a' and 'b' lines which, although differentiated from each other, never contradict the underlying dactylic poetic foot.

Only after the rhyme scheme and the poetic foot of the poem are reflected securely in the metre and rhythm does Staden take the liberty of setting up the voice and melodic bass lines so that they gently oppose this poetic structure.

rhyme scheme: a b b a ccd eed
melody and bass: a b a b   c   c

Thus the poetic *octave* (the two quatrains) of this sonnet shows the following musical-poetic relationships – both complementary and contradictory.

rhyme scheme: a b b a
(musical) metre: a b b a
rhythmic patterns: a b b a
melody: a b a b
bass: a b a b
poetic foot ⎱
musical rhythm ⎰ dactylic throughout

Ex.2

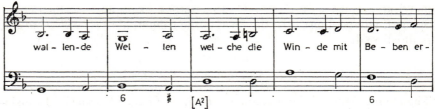

In addition to concerning himself with questions of scansion and structure, Staden also attempts to characterize the persons in the opera and their feelings. Sometimes this is accomplished by means of a song's rhythm and tempo. One such example occurs in Act II, i, where Sinnigunda's part is in $\frac{3}{2}$, presumably in a quick tempo, and uses syncopation within the measure: Seelewig's part, however, is in $\frac{4}{4}$, in a slower tempo and, rhythmically straightforward. Harsdörffer specifically mentions the aptness of the musical characterization in this scene.[28]

In other scenes which include long dialogues, Staden connects a specific four-measure melody and bass pattern with each character.

[28] Harsdörffer, *Gesprächspiele*, iv, p. 86.

Thus in Act I, v, for example, where Herzigild (H), Gwissulda (G), Sinnigunda (S), and Seelewig (W) are conversing, the following pattern evolves:

rhyme scheme: a a b b c c d d e e f f[29]
bass and melody: A B A C A C D C B B C A
character: H G H S H S W S G G S H

creating a musical rondo-like scheme despite the poem's rhyming couplets.

For some of the characters this kind of motivic identification seems to be extended throughout the opera. The most convincing example occurs at Trügewald's infrequent appearances, where the motive is emphasized by the use of a "grosses Horn".

Ex.3

I,vi ; III,i   I,ii

In fact, Staden uses this kind of instrumental characterization through-out the opera. Harsdörffer comments: 'One should observe about the music that for each act one hears a prelude or instrumental symphony, and just as the nymphs incline to strings, lutes, and flutes, and the shepherds to shawms, transverse flutes, and flageolets, so the large horn is appropriate to Trügewald.'[30]

Staden's plan for the overall structure of the opera makes use not only of an instrumental prelude to each act – each characterizing a different set of people – but also of important choral movements at the close of the last two acts. The first act, which lacks the choral finale, is the only act to include an internal sinfonia. In this way Staden apparently tried to balance the first act musically with the two which included texts for chorus.

Quite apart from the accident of being Germany's first extant opera, and apart from the fame of its author, Harsdörffer, *Seelewig* is interest-ing because of Staden's musical setting. The preceding analysis should have demonstrated, among other things, that to compare *Seelewig* with the operas of Peri and Caccini is completely invalid. The 'stile rappre-sentativo' of these Florentine works is isolated in time and place, and

---

[29] Each couplet has an internal rhyme, thus: a a = x a x a, b b = y b y b, etc.
[30] Harsdörffer, *Gesprächspiele*, iv, p. 162. The lack of instrumental or motivic characteriza-tion for the title role may well be attributable to the fluctuations of spirit inherent in it.

even within the corpus of the composers using it.[31] The defects of this style were soon recognized – among them 'the lack of clear, consistent musical organization'.[32] If *Seelewig* must be compared with an early Italian opera, it should be Cavalieri's *Rappresentazione di anima e di corpo* (1600), with its 'moralizing purpose and allegorical figures'. The *Rappresentazione* also uses the chorus 'more extensively than . . . the earliest operas, and several of the solo songs are not in monodic recitative but are distinctly tuneful and popular in character.'[33]

The title page of *Seelewig* includes the words 'Gesanweis auf italiänische Art gesetzet'. What this refers to is the art of the 'seconda prattica', the supremacy of words over music, the importance of declamation, and composition in two real parts, *basso continuo* and solo voice. Staden's use of evenly barred measures, strong rhythms, strophic song forms, and general musical organization do not contradict those stylistic features. They make them more lyrical. Presumably Schütz's opera, *Daphne*, was also more lyrical than its Italian original. Lyricism, an early feature of German opera, and the regular use of chorus and dance, remained conspicuous features of the German pastoral.

THE LATER SEVENTEENTH-CENTURY REPERTOIRE

After the first group of pastorals at the Dresden court (1627–53) and the single example at Nuremberg (1644), the centre for German pastoral opera passed to Brunswick–Wolfenbüttel (1660–1710). As in Dresden, Brunswick's opera was courtly (a public theatre was opened only in 1690). The works initially presented there seem to be similar to those by Schütz, and his presence probably explains the geographical shift. Schütz served as Kappellmeister at the Brunswick court in 1638 and 1639; from the year 1655 he had the (honorary?) title of *Obercapellmeister von Haus aus*.[34]

The first pastoral known to have been performed in Brunswick is a ballet: *Ballet der Natur, oder Fürstliche Frühlingslust im Wechsel von Balletten und Singspiel-Szenen* (1660). The text of this 'singend-Ballett' was by the Duke Anton Ulrich, the music by the Duchess Sophie Elisabeth. It is quite likely that both contributors were influenced directly by the earlier Dresden examples.[35] Although the operatic

---

[31] Grout, *Opera*, p. 38.

[32] Ibid., p. 49.

[33] Ibid., p. 38. A more specific comparison to Agazzari's *Eumelio*, 'dramma pastorale' (1606), will be made by the author in a forthcoming article.

[34] Brockpähler, *Handbuch*, p. 86. For references about Schütz in Brunswick-Wolfenbüttel, see Moser, *Schütz*, pp. 165, 176, and especially 204.

[35] The duchess was a student of Schütz, and works of hers have been mistaken for his. Moser allows that Schütz might have 'polished' them.

pastoral soon took on a more dramatic form than is apparent in such singend-Balletten, their festive atmosphere was never completely lost.

After Strungk's musical setting of Hofmannswaldau's translation of *Il pastor fido* (1678), an *Orpheus* (1684), and an Italian pastoral (1691), there appear on the Brunswick stage works by its most important librettist, Friedrich Christian Bressand. From 1690 to 1699, during which time he was court poet, Bressand is credited with writing twenty-four operas, at least eight of which (1693–9) are clearly pastoral. The others are mostly mythological, such as *Ariadne* and *Jason* (both 1692) and *Hercules* and *Plejades* (both 1693), though a few, e.g. *Cleopatra* (1691) and *Porus* (1693), are more historical. Eight of Bressand's librettos were set by Keiser, seven by Kusser, and two by Krieger.[36] Five other composers are known to have set at least one.

From 1693 to 1702, Bressand's librettos also appear with regularity at Hamburg. Although he did not hold any position there, Bressand must sometimes – perhaps often – have been present. Clearly he was highly esteemed. In fact, there seems to have been a very strong professional relationship between the opera houses of Brunswick and Hamburg. Johann Theile, Hamburg's first Kapellmeister (1678–9), worked in Brunswick as Kapellmeister from 1685 to 1689. Both Kusser and Keiser went immediately from their directorial posts in Brunswick to similar positions in Hamburg. And Gottlieb Fiedler, the poet who on Bressand's death in 1699 replaced him as court poet, later became a familiar librettist at Hamburg as well.

Two of Bressand's operas appeared in Hamburg in 1693, five in 1694. At least five of these seven had appeared the previous year in Brunswick.[37] The first was a pastoral. In fact, it is the first pastoral that can be so identified to play at Hamburg. The list of contemporary pastorals performed in Hamburg suggests that they derived almost entirely from Brunswick influence and especially from Bressand.[38] Those performed before Handel's *Florindo* and *Daphne* are:

---

[36] According to Brockpähler, *Handbuch*. The statistics gathered from Käte Lorenzen, 'Bressand,' in *MGG*, ii, cols. 302–3, would be slightly different; that is, two librettos with settings by Kusser and one with a setting by Keiser are not included in this list of Bressand's work. In addition, one libretto with a setting generally attributed to Keiser is here attributed to Georg Bronner: *Procris und Cephalus* (1694).

[37] From 1695 to 1698 no opera written by Bressand was played at Hamburg. Posthumously, from 1699 to 1702, there were ten, seven of which had appeared first elsewhere.

[38] Pastoralism was not unknown in Hamburg in the earlier seventeenth century. Johann Rist (1607–67), pastor and founder of the 'Elbschwan Orden' (1660), a Hamburg academy of poets, is known to have written two, both with incidental music: *Des edlen Daphnis aus Cimbrien Galathée* (Hamburg, 1642), music by Rist and H. Pape; *Des edlen Daphnis aus Cimbrien besungene Florabella* (Hamburg, 1651), music by Peter Meier. Nevertheless, the frequent appearance of the pastoral at the Hamburg opera seems to have been dependent especially on Bressand's influence and the Brunswick tradition.

1693	Erindo (Bressand–Kusser)
1694	Echo und Narcissus (Bressand–Bronner)
1694	Königliche Schäfer (Bressand–Keiser)
1694	Wettstreit der Treue (Bressand–Krieger)
1697	Der geliebte Adonis (Postel–Kusser)
1698	Atalanta (Mauro–Steffani)
1699	Ismene (Bressand–Keiser)
1702	Euridice and Orpheus (2 operas: Bressand–Keiser)
1708	Florindo and Daphne (2 operas: Hinsch–Handel)

Bressand's *Echo, Wettstreit,* and *Euridice* had been performed earlier in Brunswick, *Ismene* in Salzthal. *Atalanta,* an Italian work, was brought to Hamburg by Kusser and translated by Gottlieb Fiedler.[39] *Florindo* and *Daphne,* therefore, are the first pastoral operas in Hamburg not to be associated in some way with Brunswick, but even they are influenced by the traditions apparent in Bressand's œuvre. Bressand's librettos, in fact, preserve a very interesting picture of the 'common practice period' of German baroque operas. They illustrate the clear textual differences between the German operatic pastoral during the decade of its greatest popularity and the German heroic-mythological opera.[40]

Bressand's pastoral dramas are exclusively in three acts. Except for his first libretto (*Cleopatra,* 1691) all his heroic operas are in five acts. This reverses the contemporary situation in Italy, for midway through the century the Italians had given up the five-act structure in their operas, returning to it only in a few late seventeenth-century examples, and these rare cases, illustrating an attempt to recapture the spirit of late renaissance Italian drama, occur in pastoral rather than heroic opera.

The reason so many German historical and mythological operas of this period should be in five acts is somewhat difficult to assess. However, the influence of French classical tragedy on German drama of the time was certainly great. Bressand was particularly attracted to it. Like his predecessors, he was an active translator, and many of his translations are of classical French drama, including Corneille's *Rodogune* in 1691, La Calprenède's *Hermenegildus* in 1692, and Racine's *Athalia* in 1694. While Bressand's heroic operas retain a French dramatic tradition in their act structure, however, the general alternation of

---

[39] Kusser was influential in bringing many foreign operas to Hamburg. There were six by Steffani, one by Pallavicino, and *Acis et Galathée* by Lully. See Wolff, 'Johann Sigismund Kusser und sein Einfluss in Hamburg,' in *Barockoper,* i, pp. 233–40.

[40] This discussion of Bressand's librettos is based on those copies which are preserved in Wolfenbüttel. See *Libretti. Kataloge der Herzog August Bibliothek Wolfenbüttel,* xiv (Frankfurt am Main: Vittorio Klostermann, 1970). In general the attributions in this catalogue agree with those in Brockpähler, *Handbuch* and not Lorenzen, *Bressand.*

recitative and aria certainly owes its origin to contemporary Italian musical practices. In contrast, Bressand's pastoral operas do not reflect the contemporary musical style of the Italian pastoral. Although generally in three acts, the diminutive Italian pastoral lacked the large choral and ballet scenes so integral to the German traditions. An interesting situation ensued, therefore, when Apostolo Zeno wrote a pastoral, *Narciso* (1697), to be produced at Ansbach. His previous two operas (1694 and 1695) had also been pastoral and had adhered to the brief three-act Italian style. In attempting to follow the German traditions, Zeno correctly enlarged his underlying structure. He not only included important choral scenes, however, but also expanded the libretto to five acts. Apparently Zeno equated the German conventions with the contemporary but rare Italian pastoral which imitated renaissance models and had five acts.[41] Zeno's confusions and intentions seem clear enough from a comparative study of the Italian and German pastoral styles; they are verified in later Italian versions of the libretto where, although the five-act structure remains, the text is always cut 'to follow the [Italian] custom of brevity'.[42]

Bressand actually uses choral movements in both heroic and pastoral operas, but he treats them differently. In the pastorals, the chorus plays an integral and natural role in the development of the story. In the heroic opera it is extraneous and only serves for spectacle. Bressand's *Porus* (1693) for example, which tells of the conflict between Porus and Alexander the Great, opens with a short 'viva' chorus in honour of Alexander, an acclamation of six lines. The fourth act ends with a chorus of Indians which includes a ballet. In the middle of the last act there is a battle chorus ('all'armi'). Both this and the Indian chorus are similarly constructed and typical of Bressand's heroic choral style. The chorus opens the scene with a text of four or five lines, the first one or two repeated at the end. This (not necessarily the rhyme scheme) may be represented: a(b) cde a(b). The scene then unfolds soloistically with recitative and aria, closing with the repeated line(s) of the chorus. In *Porus* the entire opera closes with a single line for chorus, a textual repetition of the reconciliation of the two heroes: 'It is the most beautiful victory which conquers with generosity.'

Bressand's other heroic operas are similar. They often open with a short chorus but usually close with a perfunctory choral line or two.

---

[41] Zeno's use of five acts for *Narciso* is his first use of such a structure, and it is the only five-act libretto among his first nine operas. From 1704 to 1718 Zeno used a five-act structure in three out of eighteen librettos, all heroic, and from 1719 to 1726 seven out of thirteen librettos are in five acts. Thus two decades after the period under discussion Zeno seriously experimented with five-act librettos, but after the single example of *Narciso* (1696), none were pastoral.

[42] From the libretto preserved at Wolfenbüttel (1124).

Where there are choruses within the body of the opera, the same structure is used: a short choral opening with a choral line at the end. Elaborate choral finales are very rare. Indeed, this appears to be an important
distinction between the use of chorus in the German heroic opera and
the pastoral. In the former the choruses are apt to be short and at the
beginnings of operas, acts, or scenes. In the latter the choruses are
longer, more elaborate, and more frequent, and they usually serve as
finales. Only two of Bressand's heroic operas contain choruses of this
pastoral type. The first, *Cleopatra* (1691), is Bressand's first libretto
and contains other unique differences from the rest of his œuvre.[43] The
second, *Ariadne* (1692), is also an early work, but more important,
perhaps, is the ambivalence with which this particular story had been
held ever since the Rinuccini–Monteverdi production of 1608. The
mixed pastoral-heroic nature of its plot continued to place this operatic
subject in a special category of its own.[44]

Except for *Ismene* (1695), the elaborate choral scene plays a large
role in all Bressand's pastorals. For example, in *Echo und Narcissus*
(1693) one of the choral scenes (I, xiii) serves to introduce the river
gods, among whom is Cephisus, the father of Narcissus.[45] First the
chorus sings two strophes, each a set of two interlocking rhymed couplets (abab cdcd). Then it dances, probably to an instrumental repetition
of the choral movement. A single river god (male) and naiad (female)
follow with a duet of three lines (aab) which is repeated. They then
dance. Finally the opening two-strophe chorus is repeated, creating a
huge choral *da capo* over an entire scene.

In another scene of *Echo und Narcissus* (III, xi) the shepherds,
hunters, and nymphs try to distract Narcissus from the fatal fountain.
They sing four lines. Afterwards the stage directions read: 'Here some
of the people begin to dance in order to distract Narcissus.' Then two
nymphs sing an eight-line text, after which they dance as well. Confusion
interrupts when Narcissus tries to get away, and there is a substantial
amount of dialogue. The chorus begins to dance once again. 'Finally
Narcissus tears himself free and returns again to the fountain.' The
shepherds drain the fountain. At the end of the scene the opening chorus
is repeated, and 'everyone dances together'.

[43] It is Bressand's only libretto to contain a mythological prologue and the only heroic
opera in 3 acts.

[44] An *Ariadne* by J. G. Conradi (Hamburg, 1691) also shows an important use of solo-
choral-ballet scenes rare in the heroic opera. See George J. Buelow, '*Die schöne und getreue
Ariadne* (Hamburg, 1691): A lost opera by J. G. Conradi rediscovered,' *Acta Musicologica*,
xliv (1972), pp. 108–21.

[45] This paternity becomes somewhat of a pastoral tradition. The fathers of both Daphne
and Galatea are also water-gods. See the discussion below on the libretto for Handel's
Florindo and *Daphne*.

Erindo (1693), Bressand's first pastoral, was set by Johann Sigismund Kusser. Many of the arias, duets, and simple choruses were published in 1694, and lacking the original manuscripts, a modern edition has been based on this material.[46] Even though preserving only a part of Kusser's setting, the score provides important insights into the musical settings of Bressand's pastorals.

Whereas Bressand's model for his pastoral librettos seems to have been the earlier Venetian-style pastoral, Kusser's compositional style is not similarly anachronistic. Like *Daphne* and *Seelewig*, *Erindo* consists of a libretto based on the structure of older Italian forms set in a modern musical style. Contemporary Italian musical practice in the pastoral, however, had been simplified to match the brevity of the text. Only in France had the musical style appropriate to the older literary pastoral form been both cultivated and expanded.[47] As a result, whereas the German heroic opera drew on French literary traditions and a contemporary Italian musical style, the German pastoral appears in *Erindo* to acknowledge an older Italian literary tradition while drawing on French opera for musical inspiration.

As in many other countries, the impetus for opera in France had derived from the pastoral. During the first half of the seventeenth century the pastoral poetry of Ronsard inspired musical settings. Then, shortly after mid-century, the leap was made to opera. In 1655 de Beys and La Guerre collaborated on *Le Triomph de l'Amour sur des Bergers et Bergères*, subtitled a 'pastorale . . . mise en musique'. The two collaborations of Perrin and Cambert, *Pastorale* (1659) and *Pomone* (1671), were also pastoral. Cambert's final effort before Lully achieved his operatic monopoly was pastoral as well: *Les Peines et les Plaisirs de l'Amour* (1672). The subtitle of this work, 'pastorale héroique', distinguishes it from comic pastorals, such as *Pomone*, which had a more rustic than mythological atmosphere. Indeed, the mythological characters of the 'pastorale héroique', which became the more important of the two types, conferred an almost noble bearing on the shepherds and shepherdesses. Lully continued in this vein with another pastoral in mythological guise, *Les Festes de l'Amour et de Bacchus* (1672).

Lully's operas were not, of course, all pastorals. But the form and style of the tragédie lyrique had been set by the musical idiom of the

---

[46] Edited by Helmuth Osthoff in *Das Erbe deutsche Musik: Landschaftsdenkmale, Schleswig-Holstein*, iii (Brunswick: Henry Litolff's Verlag, 1938). After the first performance of *Erindo*, nine of the arias received new texts. In this edition the libretto contains the old words, while the text underlay includes the new.

[47] See Joseph Kerman, *Opera as Drama* (New York: Vintage Books, 1952), p. 53.

pastoral and never lost that flavour.[48] The subjects of late seventeenth-century French opera, when not pastoral (such as Lully's *Acis et Galatée* of 1686 and Destouches's *Issé* of 1697), were neither historical nor heroic but either mythological or legendary.[49] Many, such as *Amadis* (1684), contain extended pastoral scenes, and these are usually connected with spectacle and the ballet. In Rameau's first pastoral ballet, *Les Fêtes d'Hébé* (1739), where the three art forms of poetry, music, and dance are personified, the traditional relationship between pastoral and dance is illustrated clearly. Whereas Poetry is played by Sappho, and Music by Tyrtaeus, Dance is represented neither by a famous dancer nor by Terpsichore, the muse of dance, but by a *pupil* of Terpsichore, the shepherdess Eglé.

When French elements were brought into the more heroic and historical atmosphere of Italian and German opera, this was usually to mark specially pastoral or lyrical moments. Chorus and dance were little used in late seventeenth-century Italian opera, whether heroic or pastoral. In Germany, however, they generally remained features of the pastoral.[50] This is especially true of Kusser's *Erindo*. After studying what remains of the score it comes as no surprise that Kusser is thought to have studied with Lully during the eight years he lived in Paris.[51]

The primary difficulty in studying *Erindo* today is the fragmentary nature of the material. Many choral scenes especially are no longer extant. For example, the entire fourth scene of Act I, a dialogue between Erindo and the shepherds' chorus, is completely lacking. In Act I, scene v, the second chorus only is missing. This single omission, however, illustrates the kinds of important musical questions left unanswered. First, was this chorus a 'second verse' of the previous one within this same scene? Such a musical repetition would have unified the scene, and there are strong implications for such a musical solution: the poetic metre and rhyme scheme of the two sections of texts match, and there is a similarity in the words.[52] Second, does Erindo's aria follow immediately after this second chorus, or is there an instrumental interlude? Although there is no direction in the printed source, the

---

[48] Cuthbert Girdlestone (in *Jean-Philippe Rameau: His Life and Work,* 2nd edition (New York: Dover Publications, Inc., 1969), p. 109) writes, 'French opera had therefore a heavy pastoral heredity. Italian [opera], too, was well laden with it. . . . The new genre [tragédie lyrique] could not help being "pastoralized" from one source or the other.'

[49] The relationship of such stories to the pastoral world is discussed in Chapter I.

[50] For more information on French opera and its use of the pastoral see in the Bibliography Demuth and Girdlestone, and the relevant sections of Grout, Robinson, and Kerman.

[51] Grout, *Opera,* p. 121.

[52] These reasons are in addition, of course, to the second chorus's musical omission from the printed source, which in itself could imply a repetition of the first setting.

second chorus could easily have ended with some sort of instrumental postlude or 'ballo'. Erindo's aria, itself, however, would bring the scene to a close in the same key as that of the opening chorus.

In Act II, viii, a choral response-extension of the servant's drunken song is lacking (which may or may not have been a musical extension), as is the 'Entrée der Schäffer' which closes the act and may or may not have been related musically to vocal music heard previously within the scene. The last scene of the third and last act is similarly defective; missing are the opening chorus, the final ensemble of the two sets of lovers (a quartet?), and any mention of the repetition noted in the libretto of the last chorus after the duet for two shepherds.[53] In these choral scenes, therefore, there is little opportunity to analyse closely Kusser's dramatic talent.

In studying Kusser's melodic style, the modern student is on firmer ground. Forty-four numbers are printed in the published selection. Nineteen are *da capo*, nineteen are in binary dance forms, and six are through-composed. It is in the dances that Kusser seems to lean most heavily on Lully.[54] Those named in the score include the gavotte, the minuet, the branle, the bourrée, the galliarde, and the passepied. They all follow the formal pattern $a: \|: b$, where b is at least twice as long as a. As they never include any return to a material, these dance pieces contrast with the *da capo* forms. As the texts of these dances have greatly varied rhyme schemes, one may conclude that the musical forms were not suggested by the poetry but imposed upon it. That is, the prevalence of dance forms cannot be attributed to Bressand's libretto, which itself does not derive from a French source, and the poetic patterns Kusser adapts to the binary form are extreme in their differences.

---

[53] In the modern edition of this work, Osthoff has compiled a list of those lyrical numbers omitted, but unfortunately it appears to be neither complete in itself, nor accurate. In all, Osthoff omits listing the extensions of two solo pieces which are printed (i, iii: no. 8; and ii, viii: no. 36), two important choral repetitions (ii, vi; and iii, vii), one Entrée (ii, viii), and one aria (iii, ii), while including one aria (ii, vi: no. 28) which is simply one of the nine arias which are given with the alternate text in the score. The other text substitutions occur in nos. 1, 3, 5, 25, 34, 35, and 42.

[54] When Kusser 'borrows' from Lully, he uses the French forms, not the style *per se*. That is, Lully 'vocalized' the binary dance form in France; Kusser popularized it in Germany. Yet in Kusser's operas these dances are placed in an Italian milieu of aria and recitative; they substitute for the *da capo* or another aria form. The melodic line of these pieces is more Italianate than French. Throughout the history of German baroque opera, the French influence was of this type; it resided in the use of certain forms and formats.

a	b
a	a
aa	abbcc
abab	cc
aa	bb
abab	ccdd
ab	ab
ababcdcd	eeff
abab	cdcd
aa	a

This method contrasts with Staden's, who allowed his composition to play a subordinate role to the poetry. Thus one may properly ask whether the musical function of these dances is formal, dramatic, or decorative.

The dances are used in three distinct situations: for the ensembles of shepherds and shepherdesses, for the concluding or exit number of a scene (somewhat in the manner of a Shakespearean couplet),[55] and for the especially 'pastoral' numbers – the nature scenes.[56] The first use is natural: all eight of the shepherds' choruses are dances, and it is appropriate that the choral numbers, themselves a pastoral element, should be set in the form most closely connected by Kusser with the pastoral style, as will be seen below.

The second use of the dance normally comes after an important scene and just prior to the exit of one or more of the principal characters. For example, after the first scene (in which the young nymph Eurilla learns of her father's intention to return to Arcadia from Laconia, and during which there are three *da capo* arias using much baroque artifice, including ritornellos, motto openings, musical word paintings and long *passagi*) Eurilla sings an exit aria – the first dance piece – which is completely syllabic and straightforward with no instrumental introduction. Like the Shakespearean couplet, this dance breaks the dramatic (musical) flow; it is a period. Similar examples occur in numbers 10, 27, 29, and 40.

In their third use the dances underline a particularly pastoral moment, usually an emotional outpouring directed toward some inanimate natural element. 'Ihr, o Baume', No. 8, and 'Schöne Wiesen, edle Felder', No. 12, are both in 3/2, both in major with predominantly whole and half-note motion. Both have simple continuo accompaniment. 'Ihr, o silberreine Wellen', No. 31, is in common time, in the minor mode, and has a constantly recurring rhythmic pattern in the voice, ♪♫ ,

[55] Grout uses the same analogy in discussing the strong metrical closures in the *Euridice* operas by Peri and Caccini (*Opera*, p. 45).
[56] Pollaroli similarly singles out his nature scenes in *La fede riconosciuta* by the use of the monothematic *da capo*, as Caldara does by the use of instrumental obbligatos in *Dafne*. See above, Chapter II.

which is surely meant to convey the sound of the flowing water. In each case the dance form is used with a rhythmically repetitious melodic line to depict an exquisite nature scene; and curiously, each is marked 'con affetto', the only times such a designation appears in the opera.

The choral movements, binary dance forms, and the essential and integrated use of the larger ensemble, including chorus and ballet, illustrate Kusser's conception of the pastoral in music. In *Erindo* he strengthens the German operatic pastoral tradition which maintained an out-dated Italian literary model by infusing it with contemporary French musical forms. Even in Kusser's hands, however, the German operatic pastoral was not without the common Italian operatic forms and techniques. Indeed, by his distribution of various national styles, Kusser was able to characterize musically the major personality traits of his main soloists.

The story of *Erindo* is typical of all apolitical, romantic pastoral texts – two pairs of lovers suffer through misplacements of affection; but with the help of parents, friends, and advisors the original couples are reunited at the end. Erindo, an older shepherd, is serious, fatherly, and living on his happy memories. Eurilla, his daughter, is the faithful but naïve shepherdess. Daliso, her suitor, is strong, determined, and looking to the future. Cloris, the 'other shepherdess', is emotional and impulsive. Tisbo, Erindo's servant, plays the part of the buffoon, mocking, both sober and inebriated, the lovers' various pangs. The musical settings of their arias are accurate depictions of these characters' basic personalities, as well as of the texts.

Three-quarters of Erindo's arias are *da capos*. Like his thoughts, they return to previously-heard material. Eurilla is characterized by having more dances than anyone else. Moreover, most of her arias include obbligato instruments.[57] She is the true shepherdess. Daliso is the only soloist to have through-composed arias; he is characterized as not looking back. Of Cloris's four *da capo* arias, three have important metre changes in the *B* sections reflecting her constantly fluctuating moods. Interestingly, one of Daliso's arias also has a metre change, and this occurs while he is temporarily under Cloris's spell. Daliso's two dance pieces occur while he is thinking of the absent Eurilla.

Of the two arias printed for Tisbo, one is perfectly square and straightforward, with relentless quarter-note motion and a voice part that doubles the continuo line in unison. The second illustrates a drunken Tisbo with a hesitant and broken vocal line over a rolling bass ostinato

---

[57] Kusser's use of the instrumental obbligato to heighten nature scenes within a pastoral opera antedates Caldara's by thirty years.

with a perpetual ♩ ♫♩ rhythm. The use of chromaticism adds to the depiction. These styles used for Tisbo set him off immediately as the comic servant. On the one hand he is amused to watch his master and others above him struggle in the throes of love; on the other, his drunkenness generates a little intrigue of its own.

Kusser, like many German composers of the Baroque era, succeeds in blending many national styles. From the contemporary Venetian opera, he adopts the *da capo*, the rich use of obbligato instruments, and long-spun triadic melodies; from French and especially Lullian opera, the chorus, ensemble numbers, and dance forms.[58] He overlays these foreign characteristics with traits usually identified as German – rhythmic freedom and syncopation, melodic basses, and well-planned modulations. Kusser can be given credit for formulating an international operatic style unique to Hamburg. 'He imported a kind of singing unknown up to that time, and took great pains to improve everything in the performance of music, and to adjust it to the genuine Italian taste; for this reason and because he also showed a leaning toward the French style, he has won great praise.'[59]

The pastoral was the perfect vehicle for this synthesis. Although it could be said that the pastoral in Germany did not develop – many of its characteristics were old-fashioned or out-moded compared with modern Italian opera, the French music drama represented a contemporary form where some of these same characteristics had been cultivated. Moreover, Kusser seems to have identified the French influence particularly with the pastoral. Perhaps it is significant that the first foreign opera to play in Hamburg was Lully's *Acis et Galatée*. The performance was arranged by Kusser.[60] It was especially in the pastoral that opera in Germany found a balance of its own. By 1707, the now traditional German pastoral style was given the official sanction of a definition in the treatise of a leading contemporary librettist.

Christian Friedrich Hunold, who wrote under the pseudonym of 'Menantes', came to Hamburg at the age of nineteen in 1700. He was quickly caught up into the city's operatic life.[61] In 1707 he published his encyclopedic treatise, *Die allerneueste Art, zur reinen und galanten Poesie*

---

[58] For listings of these and other foreign traits in Kusser's opera, see Wolff, *Barockoper*, pp. 235–9, and Osthoff, in Kusser, *Erindo*, p. vi.

[59] Mattheson, *Ehrenpforte*, p. 189, translated in Beekman C. Cannon, *Johann Mattheson, Spectator in Music* (New Haven: Yale University Press, 1947), pp. 23–4.

[60] See Brockpähler, *Handbuch*, p. 201, and Wolff, *Barockoper*, p. 234.

[61] For information on the life of Hunold, see Friedrich Wilhelm Wodtke, 'Hunold', *MGG*, vi, cols. 960–3.

zu gelangen.[62] In the first part of this treatise Hunold discusses the various literary genres which are set to music (Chapter 8: 'Von generibus Carminum'). Hunold orders his categories by overall size in groups of ascending order; he ends with the following four species: cantata, serenata, pastoral, and opera. Although he thus considers the pastoral an independent genre, Hunold immediately associates it with opera. 'A *pastourelle* or a *pastoral* is also analogous to an *opera*.'[63] This statement perhaps is meant to show where the break occurs in his ordering, to separate the cantata and serenata from the larger categories. As he says, 'it differs, however, from both *opera seria* and a *serenata* in that it is smaller than the former and bigger than the latter.'[64]

Hunold mainly describes the pastoral of the lyrical, unrealistic type. 'The characters will be especially shepherds and shepherdesses. Still one occasionally sees hunters, gardeners and gods, etc., with the single condition that a shepherd must be the protagonist.[65] . . . The dramas are mainly of the type of Latin and Greek *Pastorelle*, which one called *Eclogas* and *Bucolica* in school, of which Theocritus and Virgil are the consummate masters.[66]

Like Doni a half a century before, Hunold bans the occupations of real shepherds. 'The shearing room for the rams, cheese from sheep's and goat's milk and other stinking material must be omitted; instead, everything should be modestly and charmingly presented.[67] Unlike Harsdörffer, Hunold only mentions the allegorical pastoral in passing, but his recognition of the importance of spectacle throughout a pastoral opera is significant. 'It is indeed accepted and makes the work more pleasing when one adds to it certain *Entréen*. In the course of the plot, however, during any one scene, these can be called Ballet or Masquerade.'[68] Not only is the French terminology significant, but it should be remembered that Hunold describes *Il pastor fido* as the 'source of all opera'.[69] In this treatise, therefore, both the literary model and the modern musical inspiration for the German pastoral tradition are implied; they form the basis for the explicit definition.

There can be little doubt that Hunold was describing contemporary German practice. At any rate, it is no surprise that the treatise by

---

[62] The treatise is known to have been based on lectures given by Erdmann Neumeister to whom the work is sometimes attributed.

[63] Hunold, *Die allerneueste Art*, p. 347.

[64] Ibid. This distinction may be true of the text *per se*, but with the extended musical settings, the pastoral became larger than either of the other types.

[65] Ibid.

[66] Ibid., p. 348.

[67] Ibid.

[68] Ibid., p. 347.

[69] Ibid., p. 395.

Barthold Feind, *Gedanken von der Opera* (1708), tends to corroborate Hunold's definition. Like Hunold, Feind was a librettist. From 1705 to 1715 he collaborated on twelve operas, eight composed by Keiser. Feind's short treatise is not encyclopedic; as its title indicates, it is simply a collection of thoughts. In fact, along with a treatise on poetry, the *Gedanken* is actually a foreword to a collection of Feind's librettos and poems.[70] One can discern nevertheless that Feind, like his colleagues, thought of the pastoral as an independent genre. Indeed, it seems as if Feind thought that, as a genre, the pastoral was too plentiful. 'In pastorals, shepherd-poems, eclogues or shepherd-plays, one mainly treats the love intrigues as first described by Theocritus, Virgil, Horace, etc. There are enough examples.[71] When Feind mentions the general importance of chorus and dance in opera, he lists the various opportunities for their use. Most are stock situations in the contemporary pastoral. 'When many people can be found on the stage at one time, one must seize the opportunity for choruses and *Entrées*, especially when there is news of victories, peace, sacrificial offerings, battles, witchcraft, funerals, feasts, etc.[72] Not surprisingly these situations are very similar to those mentioned by Harsdörffer when he is discussing the pastoral.[73]

It is clear that by the beginning of the eighteenth century, both musicians and writers in Germany considered the pastoral to be an independent and important genre with characteristics of its own. This German pastoral form, with a large and elaborate structure and integral use of chorus and ballet, remained important throughout the history of German baroque opera. After the first decade of the eighteenth century, however, it was not unchallenged. Contemporary Italian forms and styles which made such inroads into other kinds of opera began to affect the German pastoral as well, notably in the works of Reinhard Keiser.

Of Reinhard Keiser's many operas, only a small handful appear in modern editions.[74] One, *L'Inganno fedele* from 1714, is subtitled an

---

[70] The full title reads: *Deutsche Gedichte besthehend in musicalischen Schau-Spielen, Lob-Gluckwünschungs-verliebten und moralischen Gedichten, ernst- und schertzhafften Sinn- und Grabschriften, Satyren, Cantaten und allerhand Gattungen sammt einer Vorrede von dem Temperament und Gemühts-Beschaffenheit eines Poeten und Gedanken von der Opera.*

[71] Feind, *Gedanken*, pp. 101–2.

[72] Ibid., p. 102–3.

[73] See the discussion of Harsdörffer above.

[74] And these are widely scattered:

Croesus (1710), ed. by Max Schneider in *Denkmäler deutscher Tonkunst, Folge* 1. *Neuauflage.* Bd. 37–8 (Wiesbaden: Breitkopf & Härtel, 1958).

L'Inganno fedele (1714), 'Erlesene Sätze,' ed. by Max Schneider in ibid.

'heroic pastoral'. Unfortunately the full score of this opera is lost, but, like Kusser's *Erindo*, selected pieces were published at the time and have been preserved.[75] *L'Inganno fedele* is apparently Keiser's last pastoral.[76] The style follows that of the Italian *opera seria* as do Keiser's larger, 'grand' operas, but it is simplified and the dimensions are miniaturized. That is, *L'Inganno fedele* is in the Italian pastoral form.

Of the twenty-three pieces included in the printed selection, twenty are in *da capo* form. In these there are no startling rhythmic, metric, or harmonic effects. For example, ten modulate to the dominant, five to the relative minor, and one to the relative major. No aria includes a metric change, and all are similar in style. Six numbers are in common time; the rest are in simple triple or compound: $3/4$ (2), $3/8$ (3), $6/8$ (7), $6/4$ (1), $12/8$ (4). All of the pieces in $12/8$ are siciliano-andante types; their special Italian derivation is emphasized by three of the four having Italian texts.[77] The only other Italian text occurs during the 'performance' of an 'Italian cantata' at the beginning of the third act.

The twenty-three pieces of *L'Inganno* illustrate the most important facet of the Italian, and Keiser's, pastoral idiom – an exaggerated simplicity, consistency, and diminution of the Italian *opera seria* style. None of the stylistic features in *L'Inganno* are inherently pastoral, but a statistical comparison of three of Keiser's operas, *L'Inganno*, *Croesus* (1710), and *Octavia* (1705) illustrates how the pastoral effect derives from a difference in their use.

Jodelet (1726), ed. by T. Zelle *Publikationen älterer . . . Musikwissenschaft*, Bd. 18 (Leipzig: Breitkopf & Härtel, 1892).

Octavia (1705), ed. by F. Chrysander in *Händelgesellschaft Handel's Werken*, Supplemente 6 (Leipzig: Stich und Druck der Gesellschaft, 1902).

Tomyris (1717), ed. by Klaus Zelm in *Die Oper*, (Munich: G. Henle Verlag, 1975).

[75] The selection was arranged by Cyrill von Wich, the English Resident in Hamburg to whom Johann Mattheson served for many years as secretary. The full title reads, 'Erlesene Sätze aus der Opera *L'Inganno fedele* bestehend in Sing-Sachen für verschiedene Stimmen mit und ohne Instrumente nebst einer Italiänisher Cantata mit dem Accompagnement der Flute traveriere.' See Keiser, 'Erlesene Sätze aus *L'Inganno fedele*,' edited by Max Schneider in *Denkmäler deutscher Tonkunst*, xxxviii (Leipzig: Breitkopf & Härtel, 1912).

[76] The pastoral was the first opera to be performed at Hamburg after the plague. On this account it included a prologue and epilogue giving thanks to Apollo and the muses. See ibid., p. viii.

[77] Keiser's opera is one of the rare cases of a pastoral opera utilizing the metre of $12/8$ in a number of pieces. It may be that in Germany the use of the Italian pastoral style needed the underscoring of sicilianos set to Italian texts. It should also be noted that although, like Scarlatti, Keiser here emphasizes the use of one metrical type, he chooses triple rather than duple. Handel would do the same in *Acis and Galatea* (1718).

TABLE 3

Reinhard Keiser: The Pastoral and the Opera Seria

	L'Inganno (1714)	Croesus (1710)	Octavia (1705)
Solo pieces	23	47	49
da capo	20	11	26
	(*c.* 90%)	(*c.* 25%)	(*c.* 50%)
duple metre (2/4, C, ₵)	6	21	13
	(*c.* 25%)	(*c.* 50%)	(*c.* 25%)
triple metre (3/4, 3/8)	5	13	12
	(*c.* 25%)	(*c.* 25%)	(*c.* 25%)
compound metre (6/8, 9/8, 12/8, 6/4)	12	13	24
	(*c.* 50%)	(*c.* 25%)	(*c.* 50%)

L'Inganno has only about half as many solo pieces (three are known to be missing from this printed selection), and they all have nearly the same form. Unlike the pastoral, *Croesus* and *Octavia* contain a striking diversity of method—arias interrupted by recitative, recitative flowing in and out of highly charged arioso sections, and forms which lead one to expectations that are dashed in new beginnings. *L'Inganno* lacks these dramatic situations and even shows a high proportion of thematic relationships between the A and B sections of the *da capos*. The frequency of these relationships is not so great as was seen in the pastoral operas of Pollaroli and Caldara, but they occur notably more often than in *Croesus* and *Octavia*.[78] Keiser's less frequent use of this important feature of the Italian pastoral style derives from the freedom with which he, being in Hamburg, is able to treat the Italian *opera seria* conventions: since his non-pastoral operas include more diversity than their Italian counterparts, less simplicity, regularity, and diminution are necessary in *L'Inganno* to make the pastoral effect. However, three particular examples of the monothematic *da capo* stand out.[79]

'In 'Se vivo' the rhythmic pattern of the continuo is identical throughout the A and B sections. The melodic lines of both the bass and the vocal part of the B section are clearly derived from the A section as well.

[78] In all of *Croesus*, there appear only three *da capo* arias with related sections: 'Alle Freude leicht verstellt,' 'Mir gefällt in seinem Munde,' and 'Elmir! Elmir! wo bleibest du?' None of the relationships, however, are as strong as those in *L'Inganno*.

[79] Other good examples may be found in 'Per compiacerti,' 'Locken die auch,' and 'Ich weis es wohl!'

Ex. 4

In 'Sterb ich in so schönen Armen' the B section begins as a simple variation of the A section.

Ex. 5

With 'Ihr holden Wangen' the B section is basically nothing more than the A section transposed. The entire aria may be analysed as: a_1 ‖: a_2 :‖ A ‖ a_2' a_1' *da capo*. There is no ritornello, and the instrumental interlude (capital A) is based on identical thematic material.

Ex.6

As Keiser's dependence on the monothematic *da capo* aria lessened, he increased his use of the *Entréen* typical of the German pastoral traditions and evident from the synopsis of Johann König's libretto given in the modern edition.[80] During the first act, two of the characters come in from a hunt accompanied by many other hunters and attendants. After the main action the act ends with a 'Tantz von Jägern und Hirtenknaben, welche durch einen Bären verjagt werden, der Tantz beschliesset' (Dance of the hunters and shepherds, which ends on account of a bear being chased out) – clearly a pantomime-ballet. Similarly, the second act ends with a dance portraying a procession of 'threshers, harvesters, priests, nymphs and children', on their way to worship the goddess Hertha. Finally at the end of the opera there is a general merry-making. Compared to *Erindo*, these ensemble scenes appear less integrated into the main story. They are not as extraneous, however, as the ballets found in *Croesus* which have literally nothing to do with the protagonists of the story, and were omitted, probably on account of the cost, without apparent detriment to the opera's second run in 1730.[81]

The importance of dances and processions in the Hamburg pastoral can be partly explained by their use in the earliest German operas, which were pastoral in nature and closely allied with ballet. This tradition is also the result of adopting an out-dated Italian style. Its maintenance in Germany is due both to the simultaneous development of pastoral and heroic opera and to the lack of a strong reformatory literary movement as in Italy. The later Germanic pastorals continue this tradition of ensemble and dance, and one may even find it in operas like *L'Inganno* which are otherwise stylistically derived from the Italian musical pastoral.

One important feature of pastoral music of Germany, both in complete operas and pastoral interludes, is the use of old or folk instruments. *Croesus* offers an example of this in a pastoral interlude which opens the second act. In an introductory bipartite F major ritornello in 6/8 an obbligato 'zuffalo' is added to the strings. The 'zuffalo' is a folk instrument similar to a flute and associated with shepherds.[82] Extended pedals, first on the tonic and then on the dominant, add to this rustic effect by creating a drone bass like a bagpipe. The compound metre as well is associated traditionally with folk melodies.

The first vocal line in this scene derives from the ritornello. Only the instrumentation changes, adding two oboes and two bassoons and

[80] Schneider in Keiser, *L'Inganno*, pp. viii–xi.
[81] Ibid., p. vii.
[82] Sibyl Marcuse, *Musical Instruments: A Comprehensive Dictionary* (Garden City, New York: Doubleday & Co., Inc., 1964), p. 601.

omitting the zuffalo. The key, metre, and use of a drone bass continue. The vocalists are at first two shepherds (man and woman), who are joined in the repetition by (their?) four children. The stage directions indicate that they should accompany themselves on 'schalmeien' (shawms) and 'sackpfeifen' (bagpipes).

The characteristics displayed in this scene are just those that with continued use became indelibly associated with pastoral interludes – compound metre, simple harmonies, major tonalities, pedal points or drones, and classical wind instruments or old and folk instruments.[83] They were used less frequently in pastoral opera – which, of course, hardly needed a pastoral interlude. But *Erindo*, for example, makes use of this style to augment the pastoral feeling. In *L'Inganno* these kinds of interludes are parodied.[84]

The comic element in *L'Inganno* is centred on two older servant-like characters: Grulla, an old widow of a fisherman and foster-mother (nurse) of one of the leading men; and Elpin, a herdsman of cows and goats (specifically *not* a shepherd). Grulla is generally ineffective in all of her wheelings and dealings. When she attempts to drive off some dancing gypsies, for example, they quickly return and finish their dance. She steals one of Elpin's animals in order that she may demand a kiss before returning it, but Elpin deliberately misunderstands and thrashes her instead. And finally after Elpin grudgingly pledges her his love, he dutifully returns to serenade her; but Grulla is asleep, and she continues to sleep soundly throughout the whole scene.

Elpin's serenade is in 6/8, A major, and includes moderately long tonic and dominant pedals. Elpin has brought along a shepherd to accompany him; his friend's instrument is the cowhorn. When Grulla cannot be awakened, the two celebrate their relief, dancing and playing on their cowhorn and bagpipe. The listener laughs not only at Grulla and Elpin, but at the obvious parody of the stereotyped pastoral interludes included in *opera seria*.

To the extent that Kusser's pastoral style was French, Keiser's is Italian. And just as Kusser incorporated French forms into the pastoral idiom of Germany, so Keiser introduced the Italian pastoral style. Keiser's first opera, the pastoral *Adonis*, shows the early influence of Kusser, Keiser's teacher and predecessor, and of the French operatic forms in general.[85] The overture is written in the Lullian style. There

---

[83] In Italy this style had been stereotyped further, using 12/8 metre and the *da capo* form.

[84] *L'Inganno* does, however, contain three serious siciliano-type arias; 'Per compiacerti,' 'Se vivo' (see Example 4, above), and 'T'amero se m'ami.' Scarlatti's *Eraclea* also contains a parody of the siciliano style. See above, pp. 45-6.

[85] Hugo Leichtentritt, *Reinhard Keiser in seinen Opern* (Berlin: Tessarotypie-Actien-Gesellschaft, 1901), pp. 12–17.

are choral conclusions and additions to the arias similar to those seen in Kusser's *Erindo*. There also appear songs in bipartite form – a:‖:b, and others named after dances, such as the Courante, Sarabande, Minuet, Bourrée, and Gigue. The finale is a small Lullian 'chaconne-rondeau' set for chorus with the middle section taken by two sopranos. It parallels the form of *Erindo*'s final movement. Very shortly, however, Keiser turned from this style to the Italian model. *Ismene* (c. 1697) is already very similar to *L'Inganno*. The characters are all individual shepherdesses and shepherds: this is Bressand's only pastoral not to include any choruses.[86] Unfortunately the score is lost, for this opera is singled out by Johann Mattheson as the perfect example of the pastoral form.

Mattheson was surely Handel's closest friend in the operatic circles of Hamburg;[87] he composed operas, held the position of cembalist, and sang leading roles as well, including those in Handel's *Almira* (1705) and *Nero* (1705). Moreover, he was esteemed as a man of letters and published prolifically throughout his lifetime. His collected writings on music 'form an encyclopedic exposition of musical life, art, and thought in Germany of the eighteenth century'.[88] The culmination of his musical theories came with the publication in 1739 of *Der vollkommene Kapellmeister*.[89]

Like Hunold, Mattheson treats the pastoral as a separate and independent genre. In Chapter XIII of the second part of his treatise, 'Von der wirklichen Verfertigung einer Melodie, oder die einstimmigen Gesänge samt dern Umstände und Eigenschafften' (On the correct composition of a melody, or the song for solo voice, including its connotations and characteristics), Mattheson describes vocal and instrumental genres according to their melodic style, ranking them by size and complexity. He includes the same four categories as Hunold and places them in the same order but with additions: cantata, duet, trio, chorus, serenata, ballet, pastoral, and opera. As with Hunold, the placement of the pastoral genre within this ordering indicates Mattheson's conception of the form.

---

[86] Leichtentritt (*Keiser*, pp. 17–18) writes that the opera contained a ballet at the end of each act and included twelve additional pantomime-ballets. These are not marked in the libretto preserved at Wolfenbüttel. Were they included it would only heighten the relationship to *L'Inganno*.

[87] Many documents attest to this fact, including an extant letter from Handel to Mattheson during the latter's trip to Amsterdam (1704), the many references to this friendship in Mattheson's later works, and their continued correspondence after Handel's departure from Germany. See Otto Erich Deutsch, *Handel: A Documentary Biography* (London: Adam and Charles Black, 1955), pp. 10–13, 86–9 and 393–4; and Erich H. Müller von Asow, *The Letters and Writings of George Frideric Handel* (London: Cassell and Company, 1935).

[88] Cannon, *Mattheson*, p. 83.

[89] Ibid., p. 200.

To Mattheson the pastoral was neither as episodic as the ballet nor as dramatic as the opera, yet contained elements of both forms.[90] That is, although based on a consistent plot, the pastoral still depended for its dramatic effect on just that type of spectacle, dance, and chorus found in the ballet. Mattheson, however, criticizes those who believe that the more complex vocal species, which include the pastoral, are different in their physical arrangement rather than in their melodic composition. Here Mattheson seems to be attacking the more traditional German pastoral in favour of the Italian style. He writes that since pastoral texts are based on 'an innocent, modest love' and 'an unadorned, innate and pleasant naïveté', then

he who will accordingly set a pastoral to music that will gain applause, must make an effort to create melodies which express innocence and naïveté. He must feel as amorous, or even more, as if he acted the role of the protagonist in the pastoral. . . .

The heroic pastoral, which introduces kings and princes disguised in costume, as well as gods and machinery, certainly requires a raised style to which belongs elocution and formality. However, the previously mentioned main distinction [melodic composition] must stand out above all else. And when a prince appears as a shepherd he must also sing like a shepherd.[91]

As is evident from works such as Keiser's *L'Inganno*, however, the Italian pastoral style was not adopted in Germany without concessions to the traditional German format. Although Mattheson clearly favours the 'pure' Italian form, he implies the true situation by placing his pastoral definition between the *singend-Ballett* and opera rather than before both of them; and he grudgingly admits, after insisting that the pastoral should not be characterized by its 'physical arrangement' nor by its 'cheerfulness and exultation, nor by sumptuous parades', that 'indeed, the shepherd has his entertainment as well as other people; which one finds, however, to be simpler, more childish, and suitable to the land-lover. So the pastoral often has parades and games; but these are not necessary, only pleasing.'[92] Mattheson's strong preference for the Italian pastoral style reflects a general shift in taste in Germany. Yet Mattheson does not accept readily the changes that were made in the Italian tradition when it was adopted, nor the fact that the older German style was never totally abandoned. After

---

[90] The 'ballet' described here was a vocal genre: *singend-Ballett*. It depended more on spectacle than substance and was constructed on loosely connected episodes rather than a plot. Its musical components generally consisted of an alternation of pantomimed dance and narrative choruses. There could be solo roles and solo singing.

[91] Mattheson, *Kapellmeister*, pp. 218–19.

[92] Ibid., p. 219.

all, Mattheson's example of a perfect pastoral is not contemporary with his treatise, but an opera composed more than forty years before.

Unlike both Harsdörffer and Hunold, Mattheson never mentions the allegorical pastoral. He identifies two types of pastoral stories dependent on the type of character involved. The terms, 'heroic' and 'comic', by which Mattheson describes these two types are rarely found in contemporary librettos and scores, and actually seem to be translations of the late seventeenth-century French descriptive terminology. Gustav Schmidt could find only two German instances of their use: Fux's *Componimento, pastorale eroica : La decima fatica d'Ercole* (1710) and Keiser's *L'inganno fedele, oder der getreue Betrag : heroisches Schaferspiel* (1714).[93] Nevertheless, Mattheson's terms are descriptively accurate. Most German pastorals fall into the heroic category, including as they do Roman or Greek gods and persons of noble heritage in a rustic setting. Handel's two pastorals, *Florindo* and *Daphne* (1708), are also of this type. Of the fewer pastorals in the comic vein, Schmidt gives Neumeister's *Daphne* as an example,[94] and Keiser's *L'inganno*, although called 'heroic', has definite comic-rustic characteristics.

The German pastoral opera, then, regardless of the influences acting upon it, had more dances and was more choral and more lyrical (less dramatic) than other operatic types. It never became so visual as did the French opera, nor so soloistic as the Italian. It preserved a middle road between much exaggerated and one-sided experimentation, and was perhaps a real possibility only in a country peripheral to more innovative operatic production. It is probably no coincidence, therefore, that the first 'reform operas' of Christoph Willibald Gluck, the mid-century German-born synthesizer of operatic trends, were pastoral. The character of Gluck's genius is never attributed, even in part, to the operatic influences of his homeland; yet the traditions of the German pastoral, which synthesized Italian and French characteristics, probably in fact played no small part.[95]

The beginning of opera in Germany was represented by the musical pastoral, and the form never lost favour. It did not suffer literary constraints. In fact, from 1680 to 1730, the popularity of the operatic pastoral form greatly impeded the production of any purely literary

---

[93] Schmidt, *Frühdeutsche Oper*, p. 59.
[94] Ibid., p. 55; see also on that page, n. 72.
[95] Note, for example, the striking similarities between the opening scene of Telemann's *Damon* (Leipzig, 1719, and Hamburg, 1721) and Gluck's *Orfeo ed Euridice* (Vienna, 1762 (and Paris, 1774)). Both operas are readily available in the collected works of their respective composers.

German pastoral drama. The German pastoral borrowed from the French and from the Italian, but it never gave up its own original underlying dramatic structure, which in other countries was not maintained. The German pastoral was a unique genre.

4*

CHAPTER IV

The Pastoral in England

INTRODUCTION

Unlike Italy, Germany, and other countries on the European continent, England never developed a strong musical-pastoral tradition. For many reasons this is surprising. Italian pastoral drama was imported at the end of the sixteenth century; and the number of Italian editions, English translations, and English adaptations in the seventeenth century attests to its continued popularity. Moreover, at the time of the Italian pastoral's first appearance, the availability and vitality of English artistic talent, both literary and musical, was greater than at any previous time in English cultural history.

In the field of secular vocal music one can point to the oustanding groups of lutenist song-writers as well as to the English madrigalists. Instrumental music was also particularly strong, represented in music for various consorts and for the virginal. To measure the relative strength of Elizabethan and Jacobean drama one need only mention Shakespeare and Jonson. Indeed the combination of these elements, song, music, and drama, already existed in the court masque which parallels such precursors of opera as the Italian *intermedio* and the German *singend-Ballett*. Why then in this extremely fertile soil did opera not develop as on the continent? The answer lies in England's reaction to pastoral drama.

At the end of the sixteenth century in England, neither musician nor dramatist was looking for new directions, as in Germany, or for novelty, as in Italy. English pride had reached a peak; political and religious security had been achieved. The prevalent styles in music and literature were strong, independent, and nationalistic. In such an environment foreign forms such as opera and pastoral drama were accepted only on England's own terms; and these were not conducive to their development either separately or together.

ORIGINS OF THE ENGLISH LITERARY PASTORAL

The first major literary work in England to make use of the pastoral motif is Edmund Spenser's *Shepherds Calendar* (1579). Not a drama, but a symmetrically ordered series of eclogues, or pastoral dialogues, it derives its title from the artificial arrangement of the poetic sections according to the months of the year. Spenser's poetry, however, reveals two of the most important characteristics of what would become the continuing literary, and especially dramatic, pastoral tradition in England and may represent the source of the specifically English pastoral conventions.

The first important trait is the use of allegory. Spenser's aim was to write of serious matters while apparently describing the pastoral life. Although some of the allegory is, as in Tasso's *Aminta*, autobiographical, its main use is to present political and religious criticisms in only slightly veiled form.

The second important trait of *Shepherds Calendar* is Spenser's portrayal of his shepherds. He substitutes traditional English names for those of the refined shepherds of Arcadia; the names such as 'Hobbinol', 'Colin Clout', 'Diggon', and 'Cuddie' reflect the atmosphere of the work. Moreover, Spenser aims not at an elevated literary style but uses a dialect in a 'rough, accentual meter'.[1] This dialect is not based on any historically known accent but is derived by Spenser from an antiquated literary prose style. Thus even in picturing rustic shepherds, Spenser does not turn to a realistic portrayal, partly on account of the moralistic intent of the poem; the rustic shepherds serve Spenser's allegory but do not exist in themselves.

Of the rustic and allegorical tendencies in English pastoral writings, the allegorical element was the first to be emphasized.[2] The only two treatises written before the turn of the sixteenth century which include sections on the pastoral reflect this early emphasis. The first, written by William Webbe in 1586, describes the methods and aims of the ancient pastoral, but could just as easily refer to the *Shepherds Calendar* published only seven years before.

Although the matter they [Theocritus and Virgil] take in hand seemeth commonlie in appearaunce rude and homely, as the usuall talke of simple clownes, yet doo they indeed utter in the same much pleasaunt and profitable delight. For under these personnes, as it were in a cloake of simplicitie, they would eyther sette foorth the prayses of theyr freendes, without the note of flattery, or enueigh grieuously against abuses, without any token of bytterness.[3]

---

[1] Greg, *Pastoral*, pp. 93–5.
[2] This emphasis is reflected in the preface to *Shepherds Calendar*, which is perhaps by Edward Kirke, a friend of Spenser's (Greg, *Pastoral*, p. 83). See also Congleton, *Theories*, p. 41.
[3] William Webbe, *A Discourse of English Poetrie* (1586), in *Elizabethan Critical Essays*, ed. by G. Gregory Smith (London: Oxford University Press, 1904), i, p. 262.

Three years later, George Puttenham acknowledges that many feel
pastoral poetry to be the earliest form of literature because 'the shepherd's life was the first example of honest fellowship'.[4] He himself
considers this unlikely, however, due to the pastoral's typically
allegorical content.

> But for all this, I do deny that the *Eglogue* should be the first and most ancient
> forme of artificiall Poesie, being persuaded that the Poet devised the *Eglogue*
> long after the other *drammatick* poems, not of purpose to counterfait or
> represent the rusticall manner of loves and communication, but under the vaile
> of homely persons and in rude speeches to insinuate and glaunce at greater
> matters, and such as perchance had not bene safe to have bene disclosed in any
> other sort. . . . These Eglogues came after to contain and informe morall
> discipline, for the amendment of mass behaviour . . .[5]

These theorists, and the *Shepherds Calendar* itself, show the early
English pastoral as infused with allegory with a moral or corrective aim.
Spenser's use of rustic images would in time play an equally large role
in determining the character of the English pastoral. His rustic English
names are borrowed directly in George Peele's *Arraignment of Paris*
('A Pastorall presented before the Queenes Majestie, by the Children of
her Chappell' in 1581), 'Hobbinol', 'Diggon', and 'Colin', replacing
the Italian 'Tirsis' and 'Aminta'. Sir Philip Sidney, author of the pastoral
romance *Arcadia* (*c.* 1580), might be dismayed by Spenser's use of dialect: 'The *Sheapherds Kalendar* hath much Poetrie in Eclogues: indeede
worthy the reading, if I be not deceived. That same framing of his stile
to an old rustick language I dare not alowe, sith neither *Theocritus* in
Greeke, *Virgill* in Latine, nor *Sanazar* in Italian did affect it.'[6] But he
too used 'burlesque characters of the rustic tradition' to balance his
more courtly shepherds.[7] And as much as forty years later Ben Jonson
followed this tradition by using names from popular English romance,
'Aeglamour', 'Lionel', 'Clarion', 'Mellifleur', 'Amie', and 'Alken'.

The use of rusticism in English pastorals served to increase its comic
possibilities. Sometimes this humorous element softened the allegorical
intent, creating a work more comic than sharp. In time this satirical
quality replaced the allegory so prevalent in the early pastorals. Spenser's work, however, remained the basic model for English pastorals in
all the years to come. Simultaneously with its appearance, England was
also introduced to the Italian pastoral ideal, which proved not as
popular.

[4] George Puttenham, *The Arte of English Poesie* (1589) in *Essays*, ii, p. 39.
[5] Ibid., p. 40.
[6] Sir Philip Sidney, *An Apologie for Poetry* (*c.* 1583, printed 1595) in *Essays*, i, p. 196.
[7] Greg, *Pastoral*, p. 150.

THE ITALIAN INFLUENCE

The first English translation of Tasso's *Aminta*, made by Abraham Fraunce (*c.* 1558–*c.* 1633), appeared in 1591 in 'The Countesse of Pembrokes Ivychurch'. With it was published the first Italian edition in England of *Il pastor fido* – the first Italian edition of *Aminta* had appeared a decade before.

Il pastor fido was first translated by an anonymous hand in 1602. In 1630 Jonathan Sidnam made a new translation, but this was never published. *Aminta* reappeared in 1638 in a translation probably by Henry Reynolds.[8] The most influential pastoral translation of the seventeenth century appeared in 1647 – Richard Fanshawe's *Il pastor fido*. Re-issued in 1648, it saw two further editions between 1660 and 1700 and was reprinted in 1736. In 1676 it was adapted to the stage by Elkanah Settle: this version was reprinted in 1677, 1689, and 1694. During these years two more translations of *Aminta* had also appeared by John Dancer (1660) and John Oldmixon (1698).

The number of translations of these two works alone attests to the popularity of the Italian pastoral drama among the English reading public. As early as 1606 Ben Jonson wrote in *Volpone* about Guarini:

> All our English writers,
> I mean such as are happy in the Italian,
> Will deign to steal out of this author, mainly:
> Almost as much as from Montagnie:
> He has so modern and facile a vein,
> Fitting the time, and catching the court-ear![9]

Other pastoral dramas were also available in multiple or single translations,[10] and copies were available in French 'for such as happened to be more familiar with that language.'[11]

As popular as these plays were and continued to be, they exerted no lasting influence on English pastoral drama. If anything the influence went in the opposite direction. The main traits of English pastoral drama had already been established by Spenser, and Guarini was regularly criticized for his lack of 'decorum' in making shepherds speak in

[8] See ibid., p. 238.
[9] *Volpone*, III, ii.
[10] See Greg, *Pastoral*, pp. 235–51; Jeanette Marks, *English Pastoral Drama from the Restoration to the Publication of the 'Lyrical Ballads': 1660–1798* (London: Methuen and Co., 1908), pp. 153–6 and 172–6; and Mary A. Scott, 'Elizabethen Translations from the Italian', *PMLA*, xi (1896), pp. 377–484.
[11] Greg, *Pastoral*, p. 238, n. 1; see also C. P. Brand, *Torquato Tasso: A Study of the Poet and his Contribution to English Literature* (Cambridge: Cambridge University Press, 1965), pp. 280–1.

the manner of the court.[12] Jonson, for example, says that 'Guarini in his *Pastor Fido* kept not decorum in making shepherds speak as well as himself could.'[13] Similar criticisms were made by Dryden, Edward Phillips, and Addison, among others.[14]

Some translators of these Italian masterpieces tried, therefore, to anglicize the plays on which they were working. In this Abraham Fraunce is conspicuous. 'Tasso never brings the lovers face to face, but Fraunce concludes his version with some rustic lovemaking . . ., and he introduces the vocabulary of the English shepherd: "Hoblobs", "curld-pate boy", "oaks, briars and hawthornes", "sheephookes", "waggs", "hugs", "thimbles", and "Redbreasts". The result is a lively but crude pastoral . . .'[15] The Italian shepherd, idealized and courtly, was never fully accepted in England.

PRE-COMMONWEALTH PASTORAL DRAMA

Samuel Daniel (*c.* 1563–1619) is correctly regarded as the first English playwright to have succumbed to the influence of the Italian pastoral.[16] Indeed, Daniel's sonnet which prefaces the first English translation of *Il pastor fido* seems to indicate that he had been in Italy and had there met Guarini.[17] Daniel's *Queen's Arcadia* (1605) and *Hymen's Triumph* (1614) include direct parodies of scenes by Guarini as well as by Tasso. Such imitations had always played a role in the Italian pastoral style. Nevertheless, analysts of the English pastoral have in general been critical of direct parody and have overlooked that what is most Italianate in Daniel's pastoral dramas is the use of quotation, not the subject matter itself.[18] That is, Daniel interweaves obvious Italian borrowings into a plot dependent on large quantities of English satire.

---

[12] It is interesting to note that in response to similar criticisms of Guarini's pastoral, Italy maintained the pastoral's lyrical nature while adjusting its size and form. England, on the other hand, in general rejected the artificial lyricism entirely.

[13] From *Ben Jonson's Conversations with William Drummond of Hawthornden* (1619), ed. by G. B. Harrison (London: John Lane, The Bodley Head Ltd., 1923), p. 5. On p. 3 Jonson condemns Sidney for the same fault.

[14] Perella, *Critical Fortune*, pp. 111–16.

[15] Brand, *Tasso*, p. 279.

[16] See Ashley H. Thorndike, 'The Pastoral Element in the English Drama Before 1605,' *MLN*, 4 (1899), col. 229; Greg, *Pastoral*, p. 251; John Leon Lievsay, 'Italian *Favole Boscaresce* and Jacobean Stage Pastoralism' in *Essays on Shakespeare and Elizabethan Drama*, ed. by Richard Hosley (Columbia, Miss.: University of Missouri Press, 1962), p. 320; and Perella, *Critical Fortune*, pp. 66–7.

[17] See Perella, *Critical Fortune*, p. 65.

[18] For a more complete discussion of borrowing as a characteristic of the Italian pastoral style, see above, Chapter II, pp. 32–3.

In *Queen's Arcadia* a group of modern townspeople attempt to disrupt the idyllic Arcadian atmosphere. Although one can trace such characters to the coarse Corisca in *Il pastor fido*, Daniel has multiplied and manipulated them in his own way. He uses a 'subtle wench' who attempts to lead the nymphs astray while ostensibly showing them the latest fashions; a courtier type who entices the nymphs with his 'urbane manners'; and a series of quack professionals including a doctor, lawyer, and evangelist. One can easily imagine the humour with which these characters would have been played. Of course, by the end of the play, all are successfully banished. Daniel's attempt to graft English pastoral realism onto the classical Italian model, then, occurs mainly through his use of comic satire to criticize or deride contemporary evils. This combination, moreover, seems to have been relatively successful. It was not imitated, however. When afterwards the balance swung toward the Italian element, failure was certain.[19]

Although John Fletcher's *The Faithful Shepherdess* does include some English pastoral elements, its main thrust in characterization and plot is Italian. When first produced (*c.* 1608) it immediately failed. In 1610, when it was first published, four of England's leading writers prefaced the play with poems denouncing the stupidity of popular judgement. Fletcher himself added a petulant defence of his 'innocent shepherds', deriding the taste for realism.

It is a pastorall tragic-comedy, which the people seeing when it was plaid, having ever a singular guift in defining, concluded to be a play of country-hired Shepheards, in grey cloakes, with curtaild dogs in strings, sometimes laughing together, and sometimes killing one another; and misling whitsun ales, creame, wasel, and morris-dances, began to be angry.[20]

But no such defence could turn the tide.

Contemporary public taste ultimately answered the question: 'Should authors of pastorals be guided by the great ancient critics and pastoral poets, or should they follow the natural enlightenment of reason and keep their eyes on English landscapes and English shepherds?'[21] The use of comic satire, of 'native characters and comic rusticity' became for the English pastoral its most distinctive trait.[22] Coupled with this was a

---

[19] See Greg, *Pastoral*, p. 264, about the uncertain date of the first production.

[20] Fletcher, 'To the Reader' in *The Faithful Shepherdess* in *The Works of Francis Beaumont and John Fletcher*, ed. by Arnold Glover and A. R. Waller (Cambridge: Cambridge University Press, 1906), ii, p. 522.

[21] Congleton, *Theory*, p. 75.

[22] R. Warwick Bond, 'Note on the Italian Influence in Lyly's Plays' in *The Complete Works of John Lyly* (Oxford: Clarendon Press, 1902; facsimile edition, Oxford: Clarendon Press, 1967), ii, p. 474.

more prevalent use of a forest atmosphere instead of the pasture, and a substitution of the English hierarchy of witches, goblins, and fairies for the Italian mythological apparatus. This direction was evident in drama even before the introduction of the dramatic English pastoral. In John Lyly's mythological plays, *Gallathea* (1584) and *Love's Metamorphosis* (1588–9), which are generally considered the forerunners of a more strict pastoral drama, 'the usual allusions to sheep and goats are almost entirely suppressed, Lyly substituting forestry, with which he was more familiar'.[23] Even in Fletcher's *Faithful Shepherdess* 'the English folk-lore witches, fairies and goblins are mixed with Greek nymphs and shepherds'.[24]

By the time of Ben Jonson's *Sad Shepherd* (pub. 1640), the last major pastoral before the Commonwealth, the genre was totally anglicized. The characteristics of the English pastoral drama are well-exemplified in Jonson's work in which the pastoral form was combined with the fable of Robin Hood and his merry men, and the forest atmosphere with realistic English swains substituted for the Golden Age shepherds of Arcadia. Moreover, the changes of scene and character led to a greater use of humour, burlesque, and satire. What did this mean for the development of a musical-poetical pastoral tradition?

In Italy the pastoral developed out of a trend toward pure lyricism. The Golden Age of shepherds became idealized as a time of pleasurable and idyllic perfection. The poets were not aiming at a useful, moral, didactic, or even a forceful product, but at one that was beautiful. One will recall that Guarini's *Pastor fido* was criticized as being only a string of madrigals, and not dramatic.[25]

The English pastoral tradition, on the other hand, as initiated in *Shepherds Calendar*, was never particularly oriented toward a musical setting. The dialect, rough verse, and moralistic overtones ruled against it. For example both the lyrical sections and the dialogues of Spenser's *Shepherds Calendar* were patently unsuitable as song texts.

> Ye Gods of love, that pitie lovers payne,
> (If any gods the paine of lovers pitie)
> Looke from above, where you in joyes remaine,
> And bowe your eares unto my dolefull dittie:
> And, Pan, thou shepheards God that once didst love,
> Pitie the paines that thou thy selfe didst prove.

[23] Ibid., p. 484.
[24] Smith, 'Pastoral Influence,' p. 410.
[25] See Robinson, *Opera Before Mozart*, pp. 47–8, for a good discussion of the musical qualities inherent in the Italian pastoral drama.

Thou barrein ground, whome winters wrath hath wasted,
Art made a myrrhour to behold my plight:
Whilome thy fresh spring flowrd, and after hasted
Thy summer prowde, with Daffadillies dight;
And now is come thy wynters stormy state,
They mantle mard, wherein thou maskedst late.[26]

Hobbinol: Diggon Davie! I bidde her god day;
  Or Diggon her is, or I missaye.

Diggon: Her was her, while it was daye-light;
  But now her is a most wretched wight:
  For day, that was, is wightly past,
  And now at earst the dirke night doth hast.

Hobbinol: Diggon, arede who has thee so dight?
  Never I wist thee in so poore a plight.
  Where is the fayre flocke thou was wont to leade?
  Or bene they chaffred, or at mischiefe dead?[27]

Rustic realism created a strong impediment to musical settings of English pastoral literature. It was lack of realism inherent in the Golden Age of Arcadia which rendered continual singing possible in the Italian pastoral and encouraged the growth of opera. Whereas an Italian theorist like Gravina could rail against the elevated language coming out of the mouth of a simple nymph, the practising authors and musicians of this style, from Guarini to Metastasio, defended that practice and kept it in use. In Italy and Germany, Doni and Hunold specifically warn against the use of realistic and crude scenes. In both of these countries musical pastorals flourished. Because of the naturalization and nationalization of the pastoral in England, the proper poetic medium for musical settings was rarely, if ever, achieved. In fact the difference between the English and Italian types of pastorals was already so pronounced by the end of the sixteenth century that Shakespeare in *As You Like It* (1599) was able to burlesque both traditions. All strata of shepherds are included – the ideal, the courtly, and the rustic; and all of them are presented in exaggeration.

Phebe and Silvius are the idealized, Golden-Age shepherd couple. They are cardboard characters playing out the roles of unrequited lover and cold beloved and serve as Arcadian objects to which the main characters are able to respond. The style of their utterances can be shown from one of Silvius' outcries in II, 4.

---

[26] Edmund Spenser, 'January Eclogue', *Shepherd's Calendar*, ed. by C. H. Herford (London: Macmillan and Co., Ltd., 1932), p. 15.
[27] Ibid., 'September Eclogue,' p. 64.

> O, thou didst then never love so heartily;
> If thou rememb'rest not the slightest folly
> That ever love did make thee run into,
> Thou has not loved.
> Or if thou hast not sat as I do now,
> Wearying thy hearer in thy mistress' praise,
> Thou hast not loved.
> Or if thou hast not broke from company
> Abruptly, as my passion now makes me,
> Thou hast not loved. O Phebe, Phebe, Phebe!

In response to this speech which he has overheard, Touchstone, the Clown, reminisces on his own more rustic follies in love. The contrast in style and content is overwhelming.

> I remember, when I was in love I broke my sword upon
> a stone and bid him take that for coming a-night to
> Jane Smile; and I remember the kissing of her batler,
> and the cow's dugs that her pretty chopped hands had
> milked; and I remember the wooing of a peascod
> instead of her, from whom I took two cods, and giving
> her them again, said with weeping tears, 'Wear these
> for my sake.' We that are true lovers run into strange
> capers; but as all is mortal in nature, so is all nature in
> love mortal in folly.

Two of the lords in attendance upon the banished duke also play upon both sides of the pastoral coin in responding to their new rustic life (II, 5):

> *Amiens:* Who doth ambition shun
> And loves to live i' th' sun,
> Seeking the food he eats,
> And pleased with what he gets,
> Come hither, come hither, come hither.
> Here shall he see no enemy
> But winter and rough weather.

> *Jaques:* If it do come to pass
> That any man turn ass,
> Leaving his wealth and ease
> A stubborn will to please,
> Ducdame, ducdame, ducdame!
> Here shall he see gross fools as he,
> An if he will come to me.

The courtly lovers who become involved in traditional pastoral pursuits seek refuge in the forest of Arden, which has the dual atmosphere of Sherwood Forest and Arcadia. Orlando leaves his poetic love letters on trees – a common pastoral device in Italy and already used in England by John Lyly in *Love's Metamorphosis* (c. 1580). And Rosalind tests Orlando's love while she is disguised as a man. These familiar 'pastoralisms' are cheerfully derided throughout by Touchstone; and even though the lovers are happily united at the end – could one doubt it? – the trials and tribulations which they have overcome are belittled by the rapid attainment of the same end by their siblings (V, 2).

> There was never anything so sudden but the fight of two rams and Caesar's thrasonical brag of 'I came, saw, and overcame'; for your brother and my sister no sooner met but they looked; no sooner looked but they loved; no sooner loved but they sighed; no sooner sighed but they asked one another the reason; no sooner knew the reason but they sought the remedy: and in these degrees have they made a pair of stairs to marriage, which they will climb incontinent, or else be incontinent before marriage: they are in the very wrath of love, and they will together: clubs cannot part them.

Shakespeare's comedy had no rivals in its day, but a century later pastoral satire was revived by the group of writers with which Handel particularly associated himself. Pastoral burlesques were an out-growth of the humour inherent in all English pastoral drama and developed simultaneously with serious English pastorals. In countries where the classical pastoral was predominant, humour, satire, and burlesque were never an intrinsic part of the style.

The closest foreign approach to this comic-burlesque style was in Germany, where Mattheson divided the pastoral genre into two forms: the rustic-comic and the heroic. Only one play, however, could be identified with the comic type, the divisions therefore seeming more theoretical than practical. But *L'inganno fedele* did contain comic scenes in which the literary pastoral conventions were burlesqued by König, and where Keiser, recognizing the intent, burlesqued the musical pastoral conventions as well. These cases, however, appear as adjuncts to a basically Italianate tradition. Furthermore, the latter example underscores Germany's marriage of the musical and literary pastoral which never occurred in England. Although it is true that many of the English pastoral plays included incidental music, this was part of a general theatrical tradition not uniquely connected with the pastoral.

THE ROLE OF MUSIC IN PRE-COMMONWEALTH DRAMA

The dramatic use of stage music became an important part of Elizabethan and Jacobean theatre. The impetus for the insertion of music came not, however, from the lyrical pastoral elevated into song, but rather from imitation of the court masque, discussed below, and the ready availability of musicians of professional calibre.[28] As a result, perhaps, of its non-pastoral origin, music in English plays represented a dramatic device, not simply a lyrical interlude. It was never raised to a position where, as in opera, it sustained or carried the drama. Music never was used except where it was natural and realistic.[29]

In plays of the period, persons on stage react to music being played on or off the stage. This device helped to define character or to change, end, or divert the action. The characters who sang were musicians, people of the lower classes, or 'unnatural' persons. 'Characters of exalted stations seldom sang.'[30] 'Shakespeare inherited the tradition of songs by the clown, the vice, or the devil. It was expected that madmen would sing on the stage . . . , all to the infinite delight of the groundlings; [and] that fairies and witches would converse in a peculiar strain, half-incantations, half-song.'[31]

This 'realistic' use of music for 'unrealistic' characters had in other countries made the pastoral the perfect musical vehicle for operatic development. Golden Age shepherds are meant to sing and dance and play their pipes. The Orpheus legend is based on the power of song. Thus it took but a small leap to intensify in pastorals all speech into song, and then to move away from pastorals into the intensified emotions of more heroic people. At least, it appears to have happened that way in Italy and Germany. In England one only sees a glimmer of this possibility.

In what is perhaps the earliest English attempt at pastoral-mythological drama, the *Arraignment of Paris* (1581) by George Peele, there is a very prolific use of music, both choral and solo. In this adaptation of the familiar story of the golden apple, the goddesses could be expected to sing, as could Paris, the shepherd. The pastoral element is further enlarged by giving Paris a pastoral sweetheart, Oenone, and by adding other pastoral characters: Colin, 'th'enamoured shepherd', and Thestylis, 'a fair lass'.

In the first act alone, there is an echo song for two choirs (a very standard musical-literary device), a solo for Pan ('the god of shepherds')

[28] See R. W. Ingram, 'Operatic Tendencies in Stuart Drama,' *MQ*, xliv (1958), p. 490; see also John H. Long, *Shakespeare's Use of Music: A Study of the Music and its Performance in the Original Productions of Seven Comedies* (Gainesville, Florida: University of Florida Press, 1955), p. 4.

[29] Some definitions are needed in the use of this terminology. As it will be seen below, it is not necessarily (or normally) the 'natural' or 'realistic' *characters* who sing, but those for whom *singing* would be 'natural' or 'realistic'. Therefore, many supernatural and unnatural characters, quite naturally, sing rather than speak.

[30] Long, *Shakespeare's Use of Music*, p. 3.

[31] John Robert Moore, 'The Function of the Songs in Shakespeare's Plays' in *Shakespeare Studies* (Madison: University of Wisconsin Press, 1916), p. 81.

and a love-duet for Paris and Oenone.[32] In the third act Colin sings of his cruel lover, Oenone sings of her false lover, and Thestylis sings a simple folk tune. In addition, a chorus of priests sings a choral dirge – again, not an unrealistic musical function. One can accept quite naturally the use of music in any religious ceremony which might be incorporated into a play.

There are two exceptions to a strict adherence to 'realistic' singing in *Arraignment of Paris*. In Act II Helen of Troy is given a solo although she clearly does not fall into an English category of a singing character. Interestingly, however, her song is in Italian and Italianate in style. Perhaps Peele and his anonymous musical collaborator(s) felt this device gave them the liberty to break the rule of musical naturalness.[33] Finally there is a large and integrated musical finale which includes an instrumental consort, a choir, and three soloists.

This scene, however, is an epilogue sung to the glory of the Queen of England, to whom, in recognition of her surpassing beauty and chastity, the goddesses forfeit their claims to the golden apple. Although it does provide a pleasant and definitive finale, this scene does not form a part of the dramatic action. One might better say that it functions as a short masque attached to a public stage production, a technique which was to become very popular later. The 'Masque of Hymen' which concludes *As You Like It* is one example.

Peele's play had in it all the necessary elements for the birth of an English pastoral opera. That Peele himself saw the pastoral form as uniquely musical is evidenced by the fact that his 'only tragedy, like the tragedies of his contemporaries, is entirely bare of songs'.[34] On the other hand, *Arraignment* contributed to the impossibility of an English opera by fixing the barriers between those who could sing and those who could not.

Partly on account of this English philosophy of the place of music in drama – 'English poets could never accept the idea of a normal man expressing himself in song'[35] – and partly on account of the English literary development of the pastoral style away from these idealized Golden-Age shepherds for whom singing was natural and necessary,

[32] For a more complete description of this score see Long, *Shakespeare's Use of Music*, pp. 5–7; and Greg, *Pastoral*, pp. 216–24.

[33] Of two possible explanations, one is that a song in Italian was considered a performance within a performance. Thus presented, an Italian song becomes wholly natural. The second, more fascinating, explanation is that the use of Italian actually excused the requirement for realism.

[34] Moore, 'The Function of the Songs in Shakespeare's Plays,' p. 79.

[35] Edward J. Dent, *Foundations of English Opera* (Cambridge: Cambridge University Press, 1929), p. 8.

the germ of an English pastoral opera, inherent in Peele's work, was never developed.[36] And it is possible that without a pastoral foundation, in which intensified song appears naturally, that the leap to 'less natural' opera is impossible.

One might expect the situation to be different in the English court masques. After all, here the mythological-pastoral element remained stronger than on the public stage, and the apparent union of the various arts would seem to be an important step toward opera. 'The connexion of the pastoral with the masque began very early,' Greg writes, 'and may well have been more constant than we should be tempted to suppose from the isolated examples that remain. The union was a natural one, for the pastoral whether in its Arcadian or chivalric guise, was well suited to supply the framework for graceful poetry and elaborate dances alike, while the rustic and burlesque elements were equally capable of furnishing matter for the anti-masque, when the form had reached that stage of structural elaboration.'[37] That is, the masque in its various elements could have been perfectly directed toward the development of the operatic style. In Italy, the courtly inter-medio had played such a role, as did the *ballet de Cour* in France. Mythological pastoralism prevailed in both. In England this never happened.

After stating that the pastoral was apparently the perfect subject matter for the masque, Greg is unable to find any strict masques which make use of it. 'Although the mythological element is everywhere prominent, the pastoral is comparatively of rare occurrence in the regular masque literature of the seventeenth century. This, considering the adaptability and natural suitability of the form, is rather surprising. Probably the masque as it evolved itself at the court of James I needed a subject possessing a traditional story, or at least fixed and known conditions of a kind which the pastoral was unable to supply.'[38] He discusses briefly a group of early pastoral pageants or entertainments which are distinctly not masques, and more often mentioned for their influence, not on the masque, but on the development of English pastoral drama.[39] 'The first strict masque of a pastoral character that we meet with is that of Juno and Iris, with the dance of nymphs and the

---

[36] D. M. Walmsley ('The Influence of Foreign Opera on English Operative Plays of the Restoration Period', *Anglia*, lii, [1928]) sees *Psyche* (1773) by Thomas Shadwell and Matthew Locke as influenced by *Arraignment* (1581). This seems highly unlikely in view of the texts, scores, and separation in time. It is not even particularly likely that Shadwell and Locke even knew of the *Arraignment*. The more common and plausible thesis of French influence through Molière, Quinault, and Lully is presented by Dent, *Foundations*, pp. 4 and 105ff.

[37] Greg, *Pastoral*, p. 370.

[38] Ibid., p. 378. Quite possibly the mythological element inhibited the use of the pastoral since its Anglicized form rejected this framework.

[39] See especially, Thorndike, 'Pastoral Elements,' cols. 235–7.

"sun-burnt sicklemen of August weary", introduced by Shakespeare into the *Tempest.*'[40]

Masques introduced into stage plays of the Jacobean and Caroline eras fall into a special category, but none can be called a 'strict masque'. The form was specific, elaborate, and independent, not a part of something else or a simple dramatic device to be inserted here and there for entertainment value. The vast popularity of the masque caused elements of the form to be borrowed in public stage plays, but the most central feature, the 'raison d'être', of the genre, the 'taking out' or the social dancing of the masquers with the members of the court, was always missing in these adaptations.

The form of the masque was relatively fixed. First was a Prologue, spoken or sung, which gave some excuse for the impending entrance of the formal dancers, or masquers. This section was the only one in which the dramatist could fully exercise his art; it was here that the plot, or full-fledged drama, could be developed. After the introduction of the dance, the writer's function was wholly subsidiary to the choreographer's. 'When it has led up to the masquers' the dramatic element of the masque has 'served its purpose'.[41]

After the Prologue came the Entry of the masquers and their first dance. The Main Dance followed after a brief interlude, either spoken or sung, during which the dancers could rest. Then followed the Revels or the 'taking out', which was, for much of the audience, the highpoint of the evening. The masque closed with a final dance of the masquers leading to their exit.

Thus the masque form was always dependent first on the dance. 'The masque . . . was not what most literary historians make it appear. By virtue of its origin the masque was, in the first place, dance, and naturally, dance music – and by virtue of its history, in the second place spectacular entertainment. Only in the third place was the masque literature, whereby the song-text, with its music, easily maintained a certain degree of preponderance over monologue or dialogue'.[42] There was constant opposition to the extension of the literary aspects of the masque – from the impatient dancers, the audience eager to arrive at the moment of their participation, and by those responsible for the scenic devices. In the first decade of the seventeenth century, the spectacular and episodic nature of the English masque was enlarged by the addition of subsidiary dance sections, a device borrowed from the

[40] Greg, *Pastoral*, p. 378.
[41] Herbert Arthur Evans, ed., *English Masques* (London: Glasgow, Blackie and Son, 1897), p. li.
[42] Otto Gombosi, 'Some Musical Aspects of the English Court Masque,' *JAMS*, i (1948), p. 3.

French *ballet-masquerade*.[43] Called 'antemasques' by some because of their position before the Entry dance, 'anticmasques' by others because of their comic nature, these additions were called 'antimasques' by Ben Jonson whose concept of the masque as a literary form led him to treat these episodes as important sub-plots.[44] 'It seems to me extremely likely that he deliberately invented the term antimasque and used it instead of the form anticmasque in the hope that he would be able to emphasise the fact that the antimasque was meant as a foil, and not as a mere entertainment.'[45]

The direction taken by Jonson was not particularly favoured, especially after the accession in 1625 of Charles I and His French Queen Henrietta Maria. After six years of their reign Jonson was replaced – 'he was never again asked to prepare a great Court masque'.[46] From the dramatic potential exhibited in Jonson's masques, the form slipped into a succession of unrelated, but spectacular episodes.

It is hardly necessary to emphasize that without a drama there could be no opera. Furthermore, the vocal element, even in Jonson's masques, was strictly regulated. In fact, as in the stage drama, the main characters did none of the singing or dancing,[47] and the dancers neither spoke nor sang.[48] The 'strict masque' was never an integrated art form which an English pastoral-operatic style might emerge, even if more masques had been written on pastoral subjects.

Thus in neither of the two main types of English dramatic production in the first half of the seventeenth century, the public theatre and the court masque, did there develop any viable musical-pastoral tradition. The developments which led to a unique English pastoral drama did not generally produce a text suitable for musical setting. The contemporary musical philosophy discouraged the use of music in stage presentations except in specific instances and for special effects. And finally, the English masque never made much use of pastoral elements, and in itself was not an integrated artistic event.

---

[43] Enid Welsford, *The Court Masque: A Study in the Relationship Between Poetry and the Revels* (New York: Russell and Russell, Inc., 1962), p. 185.

[44] See Dolora Cunningham, 'The Jonsonian Masque as a Literary Form' in *Ben Jonson: A Collection of Critical Essays*, ed. by Jonas A. Barish (Englewood Cliffs, N.J.: Prentice-Hall, Inc., 1963), pp. 160–74.

[45] Ibid., p. 186.

[46] Ibid., p. 220.

[47] Dent, *Foundations*, p. 23.

[48] Evans, *English Masques*, p. xxxiv.

OPERATIC DEVELOPMENTS OF THE COMMONWEALTH AND
RESTORATION

Although no operatic type was developed, imitated, or borrowed
during the Jacobean and Caroline eras, music had become an important
part of theatrical performances. With Ben Jonson the masque had taken
on more literary pretensions, and this development had created more
opportunity for dramatic or operatic musical settings. For these 'literary
masques' Nicolas Lanier had instigated the use of the declamatory ayre
and *stilo recitativo* based on the Italian practice.[49] However, the subsequent history of the masque prevented the immediate development
of an English operatic genre. In fact, with the institution of the Commonwealth in 1642 the court masque reached its end. Furthermore, the
Puritans banned all theatrical performances. Thus one might expect
that there continued no possibility for the birth of an English operatic
genre. But, as it happened, it was the Interregnum which saw the
beginnings of English opera, and, most likely, even caused it.

Music was treated by the Puritans as an issue separate from theatre.
Theatre was banned. And although ecclesiastical music was also banned,
secular music was not. 'In fact, statistics show that throughout the
period of Puritan supremacy music was performed as regularly as ever
before. In an anonymous *Short Treatise Against Stage-Plays* (1625) we
find the statement that "music is a cheerful recreation to the mind that
hath been blunted with serious meditations".'[50] Since musical performances were allowed, it was only necessary for someone to realize
that by setting a drama to music it could be performed.

Sir William Davenant took that step in May of 1656 producing *The
First Day's Entertainment at Rutland House, by Declamations and Music:
After the Manner of the Ancients*.[51] The music is lost. The structure of
the composition followed exactly the implications of the title.

Prologue:	1. Music
	2. Prologue
Act I:	3. Musical interlude
	4. A declamation against public enter-tainment by Diogenes

[49] For a complete discussion of Lanier's contributions to English dramatic music, see
McDonald Emslie, 'Nicolas Lanier's Innovations in English Song,' *ML*, xli (1969),
pp. 13–27.
[50] Sigmund Gottfried Spaeth, *Milton's Knowledge of Music* (Weimar: R. Wagner Sonn,
1913), p. 9.
[51] William Davenant was born in 1606 and considered by some to have been an illegitimate
son of Shakespeare. He replaced Ben Jonson in 1637 as Poet Laureate under Charles I, for
whom he produced many masques. Davenant was a staunch royalist and commuted for a time
between Queen and King in Paris and London. He was twice imprisoned for his views; and
once freed from the Tower of London on a plea from John Milton. He was respected by
his peers.

5. Musical interlude
6. A declamation for public etertainment by Aristophanes
7. Music: song and chorus

Act II:
8. 'A Consort of Instrumental Music after the French Composition'
9. A declamation on the pre-eminence of Paris by a Parisian
10. Music 'imitating the *Waites* of London'
11. A declamation on the pre-eminence of London by a Londoner
12. Music: final song

Epilogue:
13. Epilogue
14. Musical conclusion

Whatever the impact of these politically charged speeches,[52] one will hardly concede that this is an opera. As Dent writes, 'the entertainment, it will be seen, was really little more than what nowadays would be called a "lecture-recital in costume".'[53]

Evidently it was meant to be a precursor of things to come.

> Think this your passage, and the narrow way
> To our Elisian field, the Opera.[54]

In September 1656 Davenant produced *The Siege of Rhodes*, considered by most commentators to be England's first opera.

There is little doubt that *The Siege* was sung throughout, but again, the music is lost. Also, it was, unlike the *First Day's Entertainment*, a dramatic production – a play set to music. Perhaps it was too daring an undertaking, for Davenant's later two efforts signal a retreat. *The Cruelty of the Spaniards in Peru* (1658) consists of six *Entries*. Each presents a flat scenic display, a spoken commentary by the Priest of the Sun on that display, a 'commenting' chorus ('after the manner of the ancients') and a ballet (except in the first Entry, where acrobatics are substituted). In *The History of Sir Francis Drake* (1659) a minimal plot structure creeps back in. Six episodes from Drake's life are presented as *tableaux*, again called Entries. For each there is a painted flat, a musical introduction, a dance, and a chorus. There are a few songs. The Priest of the Sun in *Peru* is replaced by real dialogue which (it remains

---

[52] Dent wryly notes (*Foundations*, p. 53), 'The speeches are lengthy and tedious, but were perhaps appreciated by an audience accustomed to Puritan sermons.' For a sensitive analysis of the drama in Davenant's *Entertainment*, see Eugene Haun, *But Hark! More Harmony: The Libretti of Restoration Opera in English* (Ypsilanti, Michigan: Eastern Michigan University Press, 1971), pp. 52–62.
[53] Dent, *Foundations*, p. 54.
[54] Davenant, 'Prologue to *The First Days Entertainment* (1656)' quoted in Haun, *Libretti*, p. 58.

unclear), was either spoken or set in *stilo recitativo*. Neither of the last two presentations of Davenant attained the dramatic integrity of *The Siege of Rhodes*. But all three are 'dramatic' and musical. Together they comprise Davenant's total contribution during the entire Commonwealth period to stage drama. The question always asked is: What were Davenant's intentions? In the main, the answer given is that Davenant 'was not really attempting to start English opera as a primary object of his efforts. His first desire was to get the theatres re-opened and plays (naturally, his own) performed'.[55] Recently, this point of view has come into question. 'Davenant had sufficient initiative and influence to enable him to mount the first production of such a work [opera] in England. Also, he was the first to call them by the name which was then acquiring currency in Italy and France'.[56] Nevertheless, when *The Siege of Rhodes* was revived in the Restoration, it was acted as a play, not sung.[57] Furthermore, when Davenant placed excerpted versions of *The Cruelty of the Spaniards in Peru* and *The History of Sir Francis Drake* in his *The Playhouse to be Let* (1663), where various troupes audition to use the theatre, the first is called 'historical dancing', and second, a 'Heroique story in *Stilo Recitativo*'. Moreover, it is difficult to overlook the testimony of John Dryden, an admirer of Davenant although a far superior poet, and a collaborator with him in the 1670 adaptation of *The Tempest* by Shakespeare.

For heroic plays . . . the first eight we had of them on the English theatre was from the late Sir William Davenant. It being forbidden him in the rebellious times to act tragedies and comedies, because they contained some matter of scandal to those good people who could more easily dispossess their lawful sovereign than endure a wanton jest, he was forced to turn his thoughts another way, and to introduce the examples of moral virtue writ in verse, and performed in recitative music. The original of this music, and of the scenes which adorned his work, he had from the Italian operas; but he heightened his characters (as I may probably imagine) from the example of Corneille and some French poets. In this condition did this part of poetry remain at his Majesty's return, when, growing bolder, as being now owned by a public authority, he reviewed his *Siege of Rhodes*, and caused it to be acted as a just drama.[58]

[55] Dent, *Foundations*, p. 65.
[56] Haun, *Libretti*, p. 51.
[57] In accordance with his personal theory, Dent assumes *The Siege* 'was originally written not as an opera but as a play' (*Foundations*, p. 65). When Davenant 'found it impossible to produce it as a play, . . . he decided to turn it into an opera by cutting it down . . . (Ibid., p. 66). Haun writes, 'On the contrary, it seems more reasonable to suppose that the drama as first written was intended for music and later altered into a play' (*Libretti*, p. 70). This point of controversy begs the issue. Regardless of Davenant's first intention, the experiment was not repeated. Davenant's brand of opera did not survive the Restoration and the reopening of the theatres.
[58] John Dryden, 'Of Heroic Plays; Prefixed to *The Conquest of Granada* (1672)' in *Dryden: Of Dramatic Poesy and Other Critical Essays*, ed. by George Watson (London: J. M. Dent and Sons, Ltd., 1962), i, pp. 157–8.

Just five years after this essay appeared, Dryden published *The State of Innocence: An Opera* (1677), the first libretto in England to be published as such.[59] However, this 'opera' was never set to music.

The use of the word 'opera' in essays and titles gives the modern student a fair idea of the seventeenth-century conception of this genre in England. A music setting was not crucial. An opera was defined by the content and style of the text. More than twenty years before Dryden's *Innocence*, Richard Flecknoe had published his *Ariadne . . .: A Dramatick Piece Apted for Recitative Musick* (1654). Again, there is, and most probably was, no musical setting, even though Flecknoe himself had meant to provide one. Nevertheless, the style of the text is directed toward a musical setting and is specifically discussed in the Preface.[60] *The Siege of Rhodes*, on the other hand, was not an opera but a 'just drama' performed with music out of necessity. Dryden described *The State of Innocence* as 'an opera which was never acted', not an opera which was never *sung*.[61]

The concept of an opera as a literary form rather than a musical genre is crucial to an understanding of seventeenth-century English opera. It was rarely sung throughout. Definite sections were set aside for musical composition. In his preface to *King Arthur* (1691), a drama set to music by Henry Purcell, Dryden dubbed this English type 'dramatick opera'.

The subjects of these dramatic operas were, to the near exclusion of all else, heroic. Haun recognizes this as one of Davenant's ideals[62] and already part of Dryden's concept of opera when he wrote *The State of Innocence* (1677).[63] Dent discusses 'the evolution of the peculiarly English heroic opera'.[64] Even Purcell's 'operas are at their core plays built around the heroic ideal.'[65] This consensus on the heroic nature of seventeenth-century English opera is undoubtedly correct. What is surprising, however, is the equally general consensus that this kind of opera developed out of the English masque.

'The germ of English opera is to be found not in the drama proper but in the masques of the early seventeenth century.'[66] 'The libretti of the dramatic opera derives from the libretti of the dramatic masque . . .'[67]

---

[59] Haun, *Libretti*, p. 120.
[60] Ibid., Chapt. ii, pp. 24–49.
[61] Ibid., p. 124. See also, Dryden, *Critical Essays*, i, 195.
[62] Haun, *Libretti*, p. 94.
[63] Ibid., pp. 124–5.
[64] Dent, *Foundations*, p. 104.
[65] Robert Etheridge Moore, *Henry Purcell and the Restoration Theatre* (London: Heinemann, 1961), p. 14.
[66] Dent, *Foundations*, p. 3.
[67] Haun, *Libretti*, p. 22.

Although the birth of opera in Italy coincided with an epoch where theatre and music flourished at London, the germ of English opera should not be looked for in the spoken drama. . . . It is indeed elsewhere that we should look for the germ of English opera. We ought to direct ourselves towards the masques.[68]

The reason for this strongly held but incorrect belief is most probably the equally strong French influence on both the late Caroline court masque and the operatic developments of the Restoration.

When Charles I married Henrietta Maria of France it had the effect of encouraging all things French in both arts and letters, just as the marriage of Henrietta Maria's father, Henry IV, to Maria de'Medici had in France encouraged the Italian. It was during Charles I's reign that Ben Jonson was dismissed, in itself a move away from the English literary masque to the French *ballet de Cour*. Davenant and others of Jonson's successors never cherished any hope of making the masque a literary type. Their intention was to please. 'D'Avenant's treatment of the masque is from some points of view retrograde; but there can be no doubt that he gave his audiences what they wanted. Besides, he gave them what was in fashion at the French court, and that was naturally above criticism.'[69] The institution of the Commonwealth, the execution of Charles I, and the exile of the queen and her eldest son (Charles II) in France interrupted the growing taste for things French, but it returned with an added impact at the Restoration.

Only three years after Charles II ascended the English throne, he sent one of his most promising choir boys, Pelham Humfrey, to France that he might absorb the French style by studying with Lully. After his return, Humfrey's French predilections exerted much influence on later court composers John Blow and Henry Purcell. In addition, Charles II blatantly imitated the French court by acquiring a band of 'twenty-four violins' modelled on the *vingt-quatre violons* of Louis XIV.

Thus it should come as no surprise that in 1674 the French opera *Ariane*, with a text by Perrin and music by Grabut, was performed at court to celebrate the marriage of the Duke of York to Princess Mary of Modena. Nor that Shadwell and Locke would choose to adapt a French *comédie-ballet* less than a year later. The original *Psyche* was performed in France in 1671, a play by Molière in which the sections to be set to music by Lully were added by Quinault. It seems extremely

---

[68] Francoise Matthieu-Arth, 'Du Masque à l'opera anglais,' *IMS*, x (1967), pp. 149–50.

[69] Dent, *Foundations*, p. 43. See also Gombosi, 'Musical Aspects,' pp. 10–11, where he makes the same point.

foolish, in light of the historical evidence, to protest that the French
model exerted little influence on the English adaptation.

> . . . It would seem that Professor Schelling regards *Psyche* as a new type of
> operatic play on the English stage directly imitative of French opera. It can be
> shewn, however, that the essential characteristics of this piece developed
> naturally from earlier native types of drama. An early prototype may be seen
> in *The Araygnement of Paris* (1584) of George Peele, which . . . exhibits the
> English form with its variety of pastoral and masque-like entertainments.[70]

Peele's play, as noted above, had all the elements necessary for the
development of an English opera. However, the planted seed never
germinated. Moreover, neither the pastoral nor the music drama were
native to England but derived from Italy. To connect this isolated work
with one taken from France almost a century later seems far-fetched at
best. It also inhibits an understanding of why Dryden sought the
French composer Grabut to compose *Albion and Albanius* (1685), the
first of Dryden's 'operas' to be set.

In the preface to this opera, Dryden attempts to define the genre.

> An opera is a poetical tale or fiction, represented by vocal and instrumental
> music, adorned with scenes, machines, and dancing. The supposed persons of
> this musical drama are generally supernatural, as gods, and goddesses, and
> heroes, which at least are descended from them, and are in due time to be
> adopted into their number. The subject therefore being extended beyond the
> limits of human nature, admits of that sort of marvellous and surprising
> conduct which is rejected in other plays.[71]

Dryden here allies the English form much more closely with the contemporary French operatic style than with the Italian.

> This definition to some extent fitted Lully's French operas. . . . However, it
> was quite out of date with reference to the more recent Venetian operas with
> historical subjects and suggests that Dryden either was unaware of trends in
> Venetian opera or else chose to ignore them.[72]

With the court masque during the era of Queen Henrietta Maria
leaning so heavily on the form and style of the French *ballet de Cour* and
the French influence being so strong in the musical sections of the
Restoration heroic drama, the relationship between these two forms is
at once obvious; but it is superficial. The English background for the
'dramatic opera' of the second half of the seventeenth century resided
quite clearly in the spoken drama of the Jacobean and Caroline eras.

First, the vast majority of these 'dramatic operas' were adapted from

---

[70] Walmsley, 'Influence of Foreign Opera,' pp. 39–40.
[71] Dryden, 'Preface to *Albion and Albanius* (1685)' in *Critical Essays*, ii, 35.
[72] Robinson, *Opera Before Mozart*, p. 84.

plays either by Shakespeare: *Macbeth* (1672), *The Tempest* (1674; Purcell's version, 1695), and *A Midsummer Night's Dream* (*The Fairy Queen*, 1692); or Fletcher: *The Prophetess* (*Dioclesian*, 1695), *Bonduca* (1695), *The Island Princess* (1699), and *The Mad Lover* (1701). More importantly, however, the strict conventions regulating the addition of musical sections were identical. 'The singers in *The Tempest* [1674] have no major part in the dramatic action, with the exceptions of Ariel and Milcha. This seems to mark one of the first appearances in English musical drama of the convention which dictated that singers should not be the actors, or vice versa.'[73] Exactly the same aesthetic has been seen above to govern the musical additions to all plays before the Commonwealth. Furthermore, the growth of 'production numbers' and masque-like insertions also follows the pattern begun in the spoken plays at that time. The conventions regarding the insertion of music, the type of music added, and the subjects available for such treatment derived quite explicitly from English spoken drama. The influence of the late court masque can be seen in the music of both the early plays and the Restoration 'dramatic opera' but the entire aesthetic of these later productions evolved from that of the drama.

This pattern remains clear throughout most of Purcell's dramatic music. In none of his dramatic adaptations do the principal characters sing.[74] Historians of music regularly apologize for this convention and protest that although dramatic operas did not adhere to the continental standards they were indeed a type of opera. Perhaps they 'protest too much'. No one feels a similar need to explain that *Die Zauberflöte* or *Fidelio* are 'real operas'! Spoken dialogue itself is no impediment toward attaining the status of opera. It is only when the principal actors are deprived entirely of musical expression that one's sense of what is an opera begins to waver. The 'dramatic opera' of England cannot be called opera in any modern sense of the term.

Dramatic opera derived from a literary form and remained a literary form. The musical insertions were meant as entertainments. They were generally not integral to the plot nor dramatically integrated in themselves. Their style derived, as did that of their pre-Commonwealth ancestors, from the typically undramatic and episodic French-style masque. The generic form of the English 'opera', however, grew out of the spoken drama.

A true operatic form depends on an integrated dramatic event wherein the emotional level is heightened, not relieved, by the music. The masques of Ben Jonson provide such an example. Although the development

---

[73] Haun, *Libretti*, p. 107.
[74] For example, see Moore, *Purcell*, pp. 76 and 152. Moore continually describes this convention with amazement. He does not appear to recognize its derivation.

sought by Jonson was largely inhibited by the tastes of the court, the impetus toward an integrated musical-dramatic event remained alive. Produced neither in the court nor on the public stage, these later masque-like, dramatic entertainments appeared principally at small, private functions, often performed by amateurs.[75] It is striking that the most important of this genre maintain a definite pastoral atmosphere. In these operatic masques the accepted verisimilitude of having those in pastoral pursuits express themselves in song continued to exert its powerful influence.

TABLE 4

Seventeenth-century English Operatic Masques

1633	*Arcades*	Milton-Lawes
1634	*Comus*	Milton-Lawes
1653	*Cupid and Death*	Shirley-Locke
1684	*Venus and Adonis*	? – Blow
1689	*Dido and Aeneas*	Tate-Purcell

Strangely, most modern commentators seem eager to prove that the pastoral played no part in the development of an English operatic style. It is one of the few points, for example, on which Dent and Haun agree.

The Puritan dominion was advantageous to English opera at least in one respect: no time was wasted over pastoral opera, for the Puritans would undoubtedly have condemned the amours of Arcadia as contrary to good morals. The classical divinities beloved of the Romans would have fared no better, and the result of these prejudices was the evolution of the peculiarly English heroic opera.[76]

. . . The British were not accustomed to plays in which gods and goddesses played principal parts. . . . Furthermore, there is the very practical consideration that the appearance onstage of pagan gods and goddesses would have brought down upon Davenant's head the leveling wrath of Parliament. To be heroic was perhaps acceptable; to be pagan, certainly not.[77]

In fact, the mythological pastoral is the most obvious operatic subject for those who yearn for realism. At the very least, it allows the principal characters to sing. Furthermore, this kind of topic remained very much in evidence throughout the Commonwealth.

For instance, the following Pastoral Plays all appeared during the Interregnum – 1649, Peaps, *Love in its Ecstasy*; 1651, Denny, *Sheepheard's Holiday*, and

[75] Welsford, *Masque, pp.* 215–16.
[76] Dent, *Foundations*, p. 104.
[77] Haun, *Libretti*, p. 68.

Willan, *Astrea*; 1654, Flecknoe, *Love's Dominion*; same year, *The Extravagant Shepherd*; 1655, a translation of Bonarelli, *Phillis of Scyros*; 1656, Cox, *Actaeon and Diana*; 1658, *La Fida Pastora* (translation of Fletcher's *Faithful Shepherdess*); 1658, Lower, *The Enchanted Lovers*. . . .[78]

This is not to say, on the other hand, that the pastoral, previously a notable failure on the public stage, suddenly achieved widespread success during the Commonwealth. Of the nine works listed above, two were printed translations, and none were ever acted. The pastoral continued to be an unpopular subject on the stage, but the subject remained very much alive. When the need arose for a small theatrical work to be set to music and performed privately, the pastoral recommended itself as an apt topic. In a footnote Haun concedes, 'One was allowed perhaps to be pagan in one's own house or at a private party.'[79]

The contribution made to the history of English opera by the collaboration of John Milton and Henry Lawes has gone too long unnoticed. Even their larger work, *Comus*, finds no place in the texts of the general histories. Dent dismisses the work in a footnote as having 'no bearing on the development of English opera'.[80] In fact, it probably had no effect on the development of the 'dramatic opera', derived as it was from a different tradition, but *Comus* nevertheless plays a very special role in the history of English dramatic music.

Comus presented one of the earliest examples of 'the substantive theatre masque'. 'Much more full-bodied than the intercalary lopped masque of the drama, it was likewise distinguished from the highly ornate court masque which had inspired it, not only by the simplicity of its mounting but by its closer approach to dramatic form.'[81] This type of masque, growing out of Jonson's earlier efforts, illustrates a compromise between the dramatic unity of the spoken drama and the musical ornamentation of the court masque. The balance of these elements and the frequent pastoral subjects encouraged the development of an operatic form. *Comus* exemplifies this.

The collaboration of Milton and Lawes was bound to be special; both men were sensitive to the other's art. Milton's father had been a musician of no mean standing, and one can picture the son surrounded by music and musicians from his childhood.[82] Lawes was regularly

---

[78] Percy A. Scholes, 'Jordan's Interregnum Masques,' *TLS* (14 June, 1934), p. 424.
[79] Haun, *Libretti*, p. 197, n. 34.
[80] Dent, *Foundations*, p. 38, n. 1.
[81] William J. Lawrence, 'The Origins of the Substantive Theatre Masque' in *Pre-Restoration Stage Studies* (Cambridge: Harvard University Press, 1927), p. 325.
[82] See Spaeth, Chapt. II, 'The Life of Milton as a Musician' in *Milton's Knowledge*, pp. 12–27.

praised by contemporary poets for setting their verses so sympathetic-
ally. Eight such commendations written by six different authors
appeared before any of Lawes' music was published.[83]

Arcades (1633) was the first product of this union. It is a slight work
containing but three songs integrated with a single dance and a long
recitation by the Genius of the Wood, played by Lawes himself.
Arcades was 'no doubt, as the superscription explicitly informs us, but
"part of an entertainment presented to the Countess Dowager of
Darby".'[84]

Nevertheless, the integrity of the drama and the general dependence
on the masque format clearly indicate that 'Jonson is the presiding
influence in *Arcades*'.[85] The music, however, is lost, and it is impossible
to reconstruct exactly how much of this small production was sung.[86]
At any rate, the production was a great success. *Comus*, written in the
following year for the same family by the same artists, relied on the
same masque-derived style and pastoral subject matter.

Comus is a major work residing outside any major tradition. Clearly,
like *Arcades*, it is indebted to Jonson's vision of the masque as a literary
form. Its immediate models, however, are amorphous. On the one hand,
it reaches back to the early seventeenth-century masque.[87] On the other
it reflects a more contemporary format. 'The framework of Comus is so
nearly identical with that of *Coelum Britannicum* [by Thomas Carew
(1632), music by Lawes] one might suspect that Lawes urged the
younger collaborator to follow the pattern devised by the older . . . .'[88]
But it has also been contended that *Comus* 'is far from being a full
masque',[89] and that its 'divagations from proper-masque form' are
'well-known'.[90] As much as anything else, the pastoral aspects of
Comus separate it from the English masque tradition.[91] Because *Comus*

---

[83] See Eric Ford Hart, 'Introduction to Henry Lawes,' *ML*, xxxii (1951), p. 217 and
Richard McGrady, 'Henry Lawes and the Concept of "Just Note and Accent," ' *ML*, l (1969),
p. 87. McGrady's article covers no new ground.

[84] Greg, *Pastoral*, p. 389.

[85] Frank Templeton Prince, *The Italian Element in Milton's Verses* (Oxford: Clarendon
Press, 1954), p. 66.

[86] Willa McClurg Evans, *Henry Lawes, Musician and Friend of Poets* (New York:
Modern Language Association of America, 1941), p. 66. One assumes the three lyrical
sections were set as solo songs, although *Comus*, see below, proves this cannot be held as an
infallible guide. There is no way of knowing whether the recitation by the Genius of the
Wood was performed in *stilo recitativo* or spoken. The one positive indication of its being
sung resides in the portrayal of the role by the composer.

[87] See Prince, *Italian Element*, p. 69.

[88] Evans, *Henry Lawes*, p. 96.

[89] Gombosi, 'Musical Aspects,' p. 10.

[90] Eugene Haun, 'An Inquiry into the Genre of *Comus*', *Vanderbuilt Studies in the Humanities*, ii (1955), p. 222.

[91] See Greg, *Pastoral*, p. 396.

does not 'depend upon dance and setting as essential features of the entertainment', and because it is 'more genuinely pastoral' than the English masque,[92] a few critics have turned toward Italy in their search for a source.

The most interesting of these studies is a provocative but little acknowledged essay by Gretchen Ludke Finney.[93] Her thesis is that *Comus* is in fact an opera, a *dramma per musica*, modelled specifically on the Roman opera *La Catena d'Adone* (1626) by Ottario Tronsarelli and Domenico Mazzochi, which itself is based upon two episodes from Giambattista Marino's *L'Adone* (published 1623).

The combination of the English masque with the Italian *dramma per musica*, and the use of a mythological pastoral theme, 'localized . . . , making it, as far as possible, British',[94] would appear the perfect compromise directed toward a truly national operatic form in England. Its possible influence on the three major 'operatic experiments' which followed – *Cupid and Death, Venus and Adonis*, and *Dido and Aeneas* – cannot be overlooked.[95]

Five songs by Lawes are extant from this production. Most commentators, without fully committing themselves, assume these songs represent only a portion of Lawes' contribution. In the text itself clear divisions exist between song and narrative indicated superficially by the use of italic print and internally by the use of rhyme. In the extant songs these divisions are not strictly adhered to. On the one hand, the first half of the epilogue, not a lyrical section, was set to music and used in lieu of Milton's own prologue. The second section was also set and served as the truncated finale. On the other hand, one of Milton's five designated songs, 'By the rushy-fringed bank' ('Sabrina rises, attended by water-nymphs, and sings'), is lacking; and the fourth and fifth songs, 'Back Shepherds, Back' and 'Noble Lord and Lady Bright', are combined in one setting. Lawes apparently did not feel governed by the textual divisions presented to him. Only a few writers, therefore, feel assured that the extant music is complete.[96] The general consensus is that there was much more.[97] Finney even raises the possibility of the whole having been set to music.[98] And certainly,

---

[92] Gretchen Ludke Finney, '*Comus*, Dramma per Musica', *Studies in Philology*, xxxvii (1940), p. 482.

[93] Ibid., pp. 482–500; republished in *Musical Backgrounds for English Literature* (New Brunswick: Rutgers University Press, 1962).

[94] Ibid., p. 491.

[95] See, for example, Gombosi, 'Musical Aspects', p. 10.

[96] One such statement is made by Evans, *Henry Lawes*, p. 97.

[97] See Haun, 'An Inquiry', p. 236.

[98] Finney, '*Comus*', p. 486.

if one notes all the musical cues in the text, this possibility is not far-fetched.

    1. After 1. 92: 'Comus enters . . .; with him a rout of monsters . . .; they come in making a riotous and unruly noise, with torches in their hands.'[99]

    2. 11. 102–104: 'Mean while welcome Joy and Feast,/ Midnight Shout and Revelry,/Tipsy Dance and Jollity.'

    3. 11. 143–144: 'Come, knit hands, and beat the ground/In a light fantastic round.'

    4. After 1. 144: 'The Measure.'[100]

    5. 11. 145–146: 'Break off, break off, I feel the different pace/of some chaste footing near about this ground.

    6. After 1. 658: 'Soft music.'

    7. After 1. 957: 'Then come in country dancers.'[101]

    8. 11. 958–959: 'Back shepherds, back anough (sic) your play/till the next sunshine holiday.'[102]

    9. 1. 966: 'Noble Lord and Lady bright.'[103]

    10. 11. 974–975: a 'victorious dance/O'er sensual Folly and Intemperance.'[104]

Furthermore, indications of musical form appear in the verse patterns and repetitions. These have been best explained by Haun. For example,

This song ['Sabrina faire'] is followed by a set of verses in which each of the two brothers and the Demon have a part, building up to a second invocation by the Demon to Sabrina, which concludes with the same line that the song does, 'Listen and save.'[105]

After Sabrina's arrival there exists a 'little three-speech scene' between Sabrina and the Demon.

---

[99] This direction obviously implies an anti-masque, a dramatic technique very popular at this time.

[100] The title signifies one of the main dances in the court masque. See Gombosi, 'Musical Aspects', on its use and importance.

[101] This would conclude the main dancing.

[102] This song, set by Lawes, is extant.

[103] This song, also extant in a setting by Lawes, replaced the Revels. Here the three Egerton children who had played major roles were formally presented to their parents – after safely escaping from Comus. They do not reappear in the drama. As in the Revels, their action served to overcome the barriers between performers and the audience.

[104] This corresponds to the Last or Departing Dance.

[105] Haun, *Libretti*, p. 233.

... It will be obvious that Milton composed the whole piece as a unit. The last line of Sabrina's song ['By the rushy-fringed bank'] rhymes with the first line of the Demon's plea. In addition, the -est rhyme which is introduced in her song ('gentle swayne at thy request') is not tagged until the Demon speaks 'of true virgin heere distrest'; it is then taken up again by Sabrina the second time she speaks and is repeated. ('Shepherd tis my office best . . . thus I sprinkle on this brest') To carry over the rhyme without carrying over the music would have been an error in taste which Milton with his sensitivity and Lawes with his knowledge of masque-technique would not have been likely to have committed. It is significant that such rhyme-patterns are not to be found in any other part of the masque. [106]

Finally, the words of the attendant Spirit, Thyrsis, a role which, it has been assumed, was played by Lawes himself, refer continually to the sung word. In fact the whole role could have been in *stilo recitativo* and remained within the conventions of seventeenth-century English drama. Three examples of textual references to music will suffice to illustrate this possibility.

1. *From the prologue*, 11. 82–8:

> ... But first I must put off
> These my sky robes spun out of Iris wooff,
> And take the weeds and likeness of a swain
> That to the service of this house belongs,
> Who with his soft pipe, and smooth-dittied song
> Well knows to still the wild winds when they roar,
> And hust the waving woods. ...

2. *Thyrsis greeted by the elder brother*, 11. 494–7:

> Thyrsis? Whose artful strains have oft delay'd
> The huddling brook to hear his madrigals,
> And sweetened every muskrose of the dale!
> How cam'st thou here good swain?

3. *Thyrsis describing his own singing, the dance of Comus and the monsters, and the song 'Sweet Echo' sung by the Lady*, 11. 543–67:

> I sat me down to watch upon a bank
> With ivy canopied, and interwove
> With flaunting honey-suckle, and began,
> Wrapt in a pleasing fit of melancholy,
> To meditate my rural minstrelsy,
> Till fancy had her fill; but ere a close
> The wanted roar was up amidst the woods
> And fill'd the air with barbarous dissonance:
> At which I ceased, and listen'd them a while
> Till an unusual stop of sudden silence

[106] Ibid., p. 235.

Gave respite to the drowsy-frighted steeds
That draw the litter of close-curtain'd sleep.
At last a soft and solemn-breathing sound
Rose like a stream of rich distill'd perfumes
And stole upon the air, that even Silence
Was took ere she was ware and wish'd she might
Deny her nature and be never more,
Still to be so displaced. I was all ear,
And took in strains that might create a soul
Under the ribs of Death. But, O! ere long
Too well I did perceive it was the voice
Of my most honour'd Lady, your dear sister:
Amazed I stood, harrow'd with grief and fear,
And 'O poor hapless nightingale,' Thought I,
'How sweet thou sing'st, how near the deadly snare!'

The implications in *Comus* for a complete musical setting are manifold. Without the music, however, the most important aspect of *Comus* for posterity remains its libretto, a perfect vehicle for an operatic production. The combination of the supernatural and the pastoral, placed, of course, into an English location, and the persistent allusions to dance and song as natural occurrences, would have made a musical setting particularly apt and acceptable. But in the politically unstable period just before the establishment of the Commonwealth, there existed little chance for such a development. In a different era, this text served as the basis of two operas, one adapted in 1737 by Paolo Rolli, a librettist also for Handel, for Nicola Porpora, and one by John Dalton in 1738 for Thomas Arne.[107]

The first production after *Comus* to follow the same musical–dramatic form was *Cupid and Death* (1653) by James Shirley and Matthew Locke. Locke's contributions to this score fall early in a career which later would be involved with the most important musical-dramatic productions of the century. He would write the music for the fourth act of Davenant's *Siege of Rhodes* (Henry Lawes contributed the settings of Acts I and V), and sing the part of the Admiral. He would write instrumental music for the first two Shakespearean adaptations, *The Tempest* and *Macbeth*, and compose the entire score of Shadwell's *Psyche*, based on a French model. Thus, Locke ultimately was associated with all the operatic trends of the century, from theatre masque, to heroic play, Elizabethan adaptation, and French imitation.

The question of whether the score for *Cupid and Death* is Locke's first effort can be reduced to whether Locke wrote his music for the 1653 private performance of the masque, in honour of the visiting Portuguese

---

[107] See Ernest Brennecke, Review of *Musica Britannica*, Vols. II and III, *MQ*, xxxviii (1952), pp. 621–5. These works are discussed in Chapter VI, below.

ambassador, or for the 1659 performance at 'the military ground in Leicester fields'. The later production followed *The Siege of Rhodes* (1656).

The extant manuscript dates from the second performance and attributes the music to both Matthew Locke and Christopher Gibbons. Most critics feel that Gibbons' compositions originate with the first production and that Locke's were added to the second. This belief derives in part from the respective ages of the composers (Gibbons was about fifteen years older) and from the assumption that the success of *The Siege of Rhodes* led to the revival of *Cupid and Death* with a more elaborate setting.[108]

Paul Morgan, in a master's thesis for the University of Chicago, takes exception to this view. He points out that the two largest contributions by Gibbons are 'superfluous to the continuity of the score or text'.[109] On this basis he concludes that Locke's music was written in 1653, Gibbons' added in 1659. To cloud the issue further, R. G. Howarth, noting that 'finis, 1659' is written at the end of the extant manuscript, assumes 'the work of [both] Locke and Gibbons was done for a performance in 1659 . . .'[110]

An investigation of these arguments shows that none is entirely conclusive. First, it is just as likely, if not more so, that the success of *Cupid and Death* led Davenant to allow Locke a single act to compose. None of the other composers of this work were unknown in the field of dramatic music.[111] The superfluous nature of Gibbons' contributions, however, is more in keeping with the conventions of the period than Locke's through-composed score, and their apparent interruption of Locke's tonal continuity could well be on account of a temporal priority. Finally, the 'finis, 1659' could simply refer to this specific manuscript copy. Thus, evidence is lacking for a definitive answer.[112]

---

[108] Dent, *Foundations*, p. 85. Matthieu-Arth ('Masque', p. 153), among others, completely concurs.

[109] Paul Morgan, *A Study of 'Cupid and Death': A Masque by James Shirley* (Master's thesis, University of Chicago, 1951), p. 19.

[110] R. G. Howarth, 'Shirley's Cupid and Death', *TLS* (15 November 1934), p. 795.

[111] Both Henry Lawes and Captain Cooke were allowed two acts. Both were personally known to Davenant through their compositions for *The First Day's Entertainment*. Lawes had been composing for the court masques in the reign of Charles I while Davenant was court poet, and was well known in literary circles, see above, not only for his setting of *Comus*. For more information on Cooke, see Richard J. McGrady, 'Captain Cooke: A Tercentenary Tribute', *MT*, cxiii (1972), pp. 659–60.

[112] The entire reason for worrying so over the date of Locke's contributions seems to be the desire to label either *Cupid and Death* or *The Siege of Rhodes* the first through-composed English opera. However, neither holds this honour. At least two of Ben Jonson's masques, *Lovers Made Men* (1617) and *The Vision of Delight* (1617) had been so set by Nicholas Lanier by the time of their publication in 1640. Lanier, in fact, was responsible for many

Cupid and Death owes no small debt to the French *ballet de Cour*. Divided into five entries, each with at least one comic *entrée* or antimasque, it ends with the typically French *grand ballet finale*. The score consists of 'the instrumental entries and dances, the "songs" and the recitatives'.[113] These are similarly grouped in each entry.

Entry I
1. instrumental entry (dialogue)
2. antimasque: Cupid, Folly, Madness, Host
3. solo song with chorus

Entry II
1. instrumental entry
2. Death's dance
(dialogue)
(instrumental ayres)
3. solo song with chorus

Entry III
1. instrumental entry (dialogue)
2. solo song with chorus

Entry IV
1. instrumental entry
(recitative)
2. antimasque: old men and women
3. solo song with chorus
4. antimasque: six gentlemen
(instrumental ayres)
5. solo song with chorus

Entry V
1. instrumental entry
(recitative and dialogue)
2. antimasque: satyr and apes
(instrumental music covering Mercury's entrance)
(recitative)
(instrumental music covering the discovery of Elysium Fields)
(recitative)
3. solo song with chorus
(recitative)
4. 'Grand Dance' (recitative)
'Grand Chorus'

The coherent structural plan is obvious. The first two entries are parallel and introductory. The third is musically abbreviated but

innovations in the English dramatic-musical style which were influential in the development of both Henry Lawes' and Matthew Locke's styles. See Emslie, 'Lanier's Innovations'.

The labelling of England's first opera is an impossible task. Many, from Lanier's compositions to Purcell's *Dido and Aeneas* (1689), have been so called. The fact remains that no strong operatic tradition developed in seventeenth-century England. Both *The Siege* and *Dido*, moreover, fall outside the conventions of 'dramatic opera', which was the strongest of the various trends. The six-year span between the two productions of *Cupid and Death* simply has no bearing on the subsequent history of English opera.

[113] Dent, *Foundations*, p. 85.

contains the crux of the masque: the switching of Cupid's and Death's
arrows. The fourth presents the horrors resultant from this mix-up
and includes two antimasques, thus balancing by extension the abbreviation of the third entry. The last includes the punishment of the chamberlain, perpetrator of the switch, and the resolution (*deus ex machina*) of
the problem. As a monumental coda to the dramatic action there is a
Grand Dance and Grand Chorus.

The repetitive and episodic nature of the libretto is perfectly mirrored
in Locke's portion of the score. Each entry, conceived as a separate,
static block, is set in one key repeated for every musical section.
Gibbons' music, except in the fifth centry, interrupts this plan, illustrated as follows.[114]

TABLE 5

Harmonic Structure of *Cupid and Death*

Entry	I	IIa	b	III	IVa	b	Va	b	c
Key	G	A	G/e	F	d	g	D	e	A
Composer	ML	ML	CG	ML	ML	CG	ML	ML	CG/ML

The harmonic plan contains no continuity from entry to entry but a
harmonic stability within each entry. Only the fifth divides from within;
and this, again, effects not a continuity but a vivid sectionalization. The
chamberlain's dilemma is presented in D major; the *deus ex machina*
provided by Mercury in E minor, and the Elysium Fields section in
A major.

By ignoring its episodic and repetitive nature, Dent misunderstands
the implications of the score and attempts to place this substantive
masque within the tradition of the English court masque. He labels as
antimasques: 1. Cupid's dance, 2. the dance of the Old Men and
Women, and 3. the dance of the Satyr and the Apes. The entry dance
of the grand masquers would be the Gentlemen's Dance; rediscovered
in Elysium they dance the grand dance.[115] This interpretation does not
explain all of the music (Death's Dance, for example) and makes a mess
of the obvious symmetry.

The structure of Cupid and Death is dependent on the French *ballet
de Cour*. Unlike many contemporary authors, however, Shirley kept a
tight control over the drama. The plot, of course, is not strictly pastoral
but is in that vein. The settings are first 'A forest, on the side of a hill,
a house . . . ,' then 'a pleasant garden, a fountain in the midst of it;

---

[114] Capital letters represent major keys; lower case letters, minor keys.
[115] Dent, *Foundations*, pp. 83–4.

5*

walks and arbours delightfully expressed.' The chorus refers to the
stories of *Apollo and Daphne* and *Venus and Mars*; they relay such sentiments as 'O let the weeping virgins strow, Instead of rose and myrtle
boughs, Sad yew and fun'ral cypress now.' The Elysium Fields are
vividly described as an Arcadian paradise:

> Open, blest Elysium grove,
> Where an eternal spring of love
> Keeps each beauty fair; these shades
> No chill or frost invades,
> Look, look how the flowers and every tree
> Pregnant with ambrosia be,
> Near banks of violets springs appear,
> Weeping out nectar ev'ry tear,
> While the once harmonious spheres,
> Turn'd all to ears,
> Now listen to the birds whose quire
> Sing ev'ry charming accent higher,
> If this place be not heaven, one thought can make it,
> And Gods by their own wonder led mistake it.

The combination of the pastoral vein with the coherent dramatic
plan and the extensive musical setting has persuaded many modern
commentators to call this work an opera. It is indeed operatic, but that
in itself was hardly innovative in 1653. This masque remains true to the
musical-dramatic plan of *Comus*, presented twenty years earlier, and
other 'substantive theatre masques', even though at this date the French
influence is predominant. Like *Comus*, this masque was presented
privately, probably by amateurs.[116] The two masques, however, cannot
be connected. They represent similar but independent responses to
contemporary influences on the masque. Blow's *Venus and Adonis*
(*c.* 1685), another unconnected example of this form, illustrates that
the developing dramatic and musical form of this masque type was
frozen by the time of the Commonwealth. From that time and throughout the Restoration, the 'dramatic opera', based on a different source,
took over the mainstream of musical-dramatic efforts.

Venus and Adonis, then, is backward-looking. It was performed at
court as 'masque for the entertainment of the King'. Although the date
of this performance is unknown, the king referred to is undoubtedly
King Charles II. The part of Venus was played by his mistress, and that
of Cupid by their illegitimate daughter. Even this 'court masque',
therefore, was performed by amateurs and included a child in a leading
role. The plan of *Venus and Adonis* can be compared with that of *Cupid
and Death*. It is coherent, repetitive, and French in accent. An important

[116] Ibid., p. 82.

difference, however, is the lack of a concluding dance in the score. This single omission shifts the basic emphasis away from dance toward a more vocal context; the masque-derivation of the form, however, is still obvious.

Prologue: 1. overture
2. vocal solo (Cupid)
3a. solo songs with choral response
(shepherds and shepherdesses)
3b. dance by shepherd and shepherdess
(during chorus)
4. dance (Cupid)

Act 1: 1. act tune
2. vocal scena (Venus and Adonis)
3. solo songs with choral response
(hunters)
4. dance (hunters)

Act II: 1. act tune
2. vocal scena (Cupid and Venus)
3. solo songs with choral response
(little cupids)
4. dance (little cupids)
5. vocal duet (Cupid and Venus)
6. choral response (graces)
7. dance (graces)

Act III: 1. act tune
2. vocal scena (Venus and Adonis)
3. choral response (little cupids)

The plan, even in the prologue, is evident. An instrumental introduction is followed by the solo singing which carries the slender plot. The entrance of the chorus precedes the concluding dance. The double presentation of the programme in the penultimate act recalls the similar extension in the penultimate entry of *Cupid and Death*.

Most modern commentators relabel this masque an opera. In seventeenth-century English terminology it simply was not. The prominence of those taking the route of 'dramatic opera' prevented a general recognition of the operatic possibilities inherent in the masque form. The greatest of the English seventeenth-century composers, however, seem to have realized the limitations of a 'dramatic opera' where the playwright controlled the characterization and the plot. Whenever the opportunity appeared to write for a private, amateur production, these limitations were ignored.

The pastoral played a large role in the development of the operatic tendencies growing out of the ballet-dominated masque. Pastoral-type characters and their mythological relatives could freely express themselves in song. In *Comus* and *Cupid and Death* the composers began to be comfortable with this freedom. In *Venus and Adonis*, Blow takes an important step toward a vocally dominated score by eliminating the concluding dance. The episodic nature of *Cupid and Death* is also lessened. Rather than five entries, *Venus and Adonis* contains a prologue and three acts. The dramatic continuity is thus increased as is the harmonic balance. Whereas Locke appears content in having put each entry in one key with no connection between them, Blow attempts harmonic bridges.

The Prologue of the masque begins firmly in C major modulating, after repeated cadences on the dominant of C major, to G major. Cupid closes this Prologue with a sixteen-measure arioso. After the long association with the major tonalities of C and G, the sudden modulation in this final section to A minor is shocking.[117] It would appear a strange harmonic ending to the Prologue. Act I, however, begins firmly in A minor and, with a few cadences to the dominant and relative major, remains in that key throughout.

After the principals exit in Act I there is a dance for the hunters based on the previously heard hunters' music. Both are in C major. The second act, nevertheless, begins where the singing in Act I left off – in A minor. The vocal entry immediately changes the tonic to F major. After an extended section in C minor, F major returns only to have the act end suddenly in D minor. Act III begins in D minor, remaining in that key through the death of Adonis. The third act and entire opera close in G minor.

Thus, just as in *Cupid and Death*, each major section is harmonically identified. The Prologue emphasizes C and G major. Act I is in A minor, Act II in F major. Act III emphasizes D and G minor. In every case, however, Blow tried to provide a connection between these large sections. The last eight measures of the Prologue modulate to A minor, which tonality is maintained through the act tune of the second act. The second act, mainly in F major, concludes with the chorus and Dance of the Graces in D minor.

TABLE 6

Harmonic Structure of *Venus and Adonis*

Prologue	I		II	III
C *major*/G *major* (A minor	⟶	⟵	A minor) F *major* (D minor	⟶) G *minor*
	A-minor			

[117] Even though the intermediate cadence in the eighth measure is in the dominant of G major, the lowered leading-tone, F natural, appears as a bass note by the third measure. The D major cadence, of course, leads to the dominant of A in the progression IV–V–I.

Such harmonic methods seem in retrospect quite naïve. This hindsight cannot, however, diminish the magnitude of Blow's vision. With the libretto clearly based on the episodic-ballet tradition, Blow chose to emphasize harmonically not the structural sectionalism but the dramatic continuity. Combined with his apparent elimination of the final ballet, this little masque moved a giant step away from a ballet-dominated, episodic structure to a vocally dominated, continuous drama. In the work of Henry Purcell, Blow's prize student, this move is strikingly continued.

A study of the libretto for *Dido and Aeneas* (1689) reveals that Purcell was presented with the same structural elements as his predecessors. In this opera-masque, however, the balance of these elements moves even further in the direction taken by Blow. That this can be attributed entirely to Purcell, and not to his librettist Nahum Tate, is immediately evident from a comparison of the libretto with the extant score.

Tate's libretto is divided into three acts with an opening prologue. Phoebus, Venus, Spring, and assorted Nereids, Tritons, Nymphs, and Shepherds, Shepherdesses, and Country Maids populate this short prologue. Like the prologue of *Venus and Adonis* and the first two entries of *Cupid and Death*, it sets up the nature and actions of the gods who will determine the crisis of the plot. Thus, after one of the Nereids spies Venus rising from the sea, Phoebus speaks to the Nereid about her:

> Whose lustre does out-shine
> Your fainter beams, and half eclipses mine,
> Give *Phoebus* leave to prophecy.
> Phoebus all events can see.
> Ten thousand harmes,
> From such prevailing charmes,
> To Gods and men must instantly ensue (11. 14–20)

The prologue also bows in the direction of Josiah Priest, a dancing-master, for whose boarding-school girls this piece was adapted. Into a mere eighty-one lines are incorporated directions for six dances and one instrumental interlude.

> 1) after 1. 11: *Venus* descends in her chariot, the *Tritons* out of the sea, *The Tritons Dance.*
> 2) after 1. 37: *The Nereids Dance.*
> 3) after 1. 41: *Exit, Phoe. Ven. Soft Musick.*
> 4) after 1. 47: *The Spring and Nymphs Dance.*
> 5) after 1. 53: *The Shepherds and Shepherdesses Dance.*
> 6) after 1. 59: *The Nymphs Dance.*
> 7) after 1. 81: *The Country Maids Dance*

The three acts of the main body of the work are also dance-oriented. Each act ends with a large dance. In Act II, which the libretto divides into two scenes, each scene ends with a dance. Indications for further, specific dances are given throughout: in Act I, 'the Baske' and 'A dance gittars chacony'; in Act II, 1, 'Enter Two Drunken Saylors, a Dance'; in Act II, ii, 'Gittar Ground a Dance', and 'A dance to Entertain Aeneas'; and in Act III, 'The Saylors Dance', and 'Jack of the Lanthorn Leads the Spaniards Out of Their Way Among the Inchanteresses. A Dance.' As opposed to the previous substantive masques, the remaining musical parts of *Dido*, the choruses and solos, are given no strict dramatic shape beyond having choruses precede the four concluding dances. Their words comment on the action and prepare for the ballet.

The primary manuscript score preserved in the Library of St. Michael's College, Tenbury Wells, contains a number of important discrepancies from the extant libretto.[118] The entire Prologue is lacking. Of eleven dances specifically called for in the three main acts, four are set. Some of the omissions are striking. As in Blow's earlier masque, there is no final dance. Moreover, all the dances in Tate's first act are lacking but the concluding Triumphing Dance. Also the dance of the drunken sailors, which interrupts the scene of the witches (II, i) in the manner of an antimasque, is deleted, leaving in this scene only the witches' concluding Echo Dance. Missing as well are three dances in Act II, ii. The second act ends with the arioso of Aeneas, omitting also, therefore, the final chorus.

It has become common practice in discussions and editions of *Dido and Aeneas*, indeed it has almost become a competitive sport, to see who can come up with the most 'complete' score by replacing the 'missing' material with compositions either newly composed or parodied from Purcell's other œuvre. 'With such a brief piece such as *Dido*, the common question of "What can we cut?" becomes for once "What shall we add?"'[119] This situation has arisen because of the unquestioned assumption that the extant music in the Tenbury manuscript is not complete. Indeed, the Tenbury manuscript can be dated no earlier than the second half of the eighteenth century; it is thought to represent a truncated and cut-up version of the opera which was inserted into various stage dramas of 1700 in piecemeal fashion. Thus Tate's libretto has been taken to stand as an authoritative guide to the true score of 1689. However, there are reasons to question these commonly-held beliefs.

---

[118] The Oki Ms., preserved at the Nanki Music Library, is apparently a later source and includes only minor variants. See Imogen Holst, 'A Note on the Nanki Collection of Purcell's Works', in *Henry Purcell (1659–1695): Essays on his Music*, ed. by Imogen Holst (London: Oxford University Press, 1959), pp. 127–30.
[119] Roger Savage, 'Producing *Dido and Aeneas*,' *Early Music*, iv (1976), p. 395.

First of all, the presumed date of the Tenbury manuscript, the earliest
manuscript source, is so much later than even the theatrical representations of *Dido and Aeneas* that there is no reason to believe it associated
with them rather than with Purcell's original score. Second, the additional lines set to music (perhaps by Daniel Purcell)[120] in the theatrical
versions are at least as conspicuously lacking in the surviving manuscript score as those assumed to be missing according to Tate's libretto.
Third, although the distribution of scenes in the manuscript does not
correspond to Tate's libretto, it relates even less to that of the later
representations where the second and third scenes were not simply
labelled differently but actually reversed.[121] Finally, there are many
differences between Tate's libretto and the surviving musical sources
besides the obvious omissions. These seem designed, and all have been
taken unquestioningly, or at least without comment, to represent Purcell's improvement of the libretto. It is not immediately clear why
other changes and omissions could not derive from Purcell as well as
these.

For example, it is clearly Purcell who makes Belinda into a chorus
leader.[122] Where Tate writes (in Act I) a separate and completely
rounded-off lyric for Belinda followed by a choral couplet:

> *Bel.* Shake the cloud from off your brow,
> Fate your wishes do allow.
> > Empire growing,
> > Pleasures flowing,
> Fortune smiles and so should you,
> Shake the cloud from off your brow,
>
> *Cho.* Banish sorrow, banish care,
> Grief should ne'er approach the fair

Purcell fuses the two together into one number, the chorus's music
growing logically out of Belinda's music and completing it.

Often Belinda's part grows on account of Purcell's conception of it.
In Act I, Tate writes:

> *Bel.*   Grief encreasing, by concealing
> *Dido.*   Mine admits of no revealing

<hr>

[120] Eric Walter White, 'New Light on *Dido and Aeneas*,' in *Purcell*, pp. 50–2.

[121] In Tate's libretto the second and third scenes are labelled Act II, i and ii. In the manuscript score they are labelled Act I, ii, and Act II. See below, p. 133. In the theatrical representations they have no corresponding labels but appear in reverse order.

[122] This appellation derives from Dent, *Foundations*, p. 188: 'But although for the most
part the chorus in *Dido and Aeneas* does no more than repeat exactly the airs sung by the
ubiquitous Belinda, its presence is constantly felt as a factor in the drama, and in some places
the mere suppression of Belinda's solos would give to the choruses an unexpected and striking
individuality. We must regard Belinda in fact not as a definite person, but merely as a chorus
leader. . . .' The opposite, however, is equally true. The suppression of the chorus would
give Belinda 'an unexpected and striking individuality.'

> *Bel.*   Then let me speak the Trojan guest,
>   Into your tender thoughts has prest.
>
> 2 *women.* The greatest blessing fate can give.
>   Our *Carthage* to secure, and *Troy* revive.

Purcell sets this as dialogue in recitative between the hesitant Queen and her encouraging, forthright handmaiden. Belinda acquires the lines of the '2 women', increasing the personal and dramatic intensity of the situation.

There exist in the score several similar examples.

1. In the recitative: 'Whence could so much virtue', Belinda alone responds to her mistress where Tate gives some of the lines to '2 women'.

2. In the solo-chorus, 'Fear No Danger', Tate writes one line for Belinda, one for the '2 women' and four for the chorus. Purcell sets all six lines as a duet between Belinda and one other woman (later called the attendant), then repeats the entire piece for chorus.

3. In the solo-chorus: 'Thanks to these Lovesome Vailes', Tate gives Belinda one line, the chorus three. Purcell has Belinda sing all the four followed by a repetition for the chorus.

4. In Tate's libretto (Act II, ii), Dido sings,

> The skies are clouded, heark how thunder
> Rends the mountain oaks asunder,
> Hast, hast, to town this open field,
> No shelter from the storm can yield.

Purcell gives Dido the first two lines, concluding them with a short recitative by Aeneas. Then Belinda sings the next two, as usual leading in the full chorus. This creates a particularly pleasing dramatic effect with the entire hunting party urging one another off the stage.

Belinda becomes in Purcell's hands the spokeswoman for the townspeople who, initially dumb, respond enthusiastically to all she says. A similar effect is made in the separate scenes for the witches and for the sailors. Purcell creates, respectively, a first and second witch and a first sailor. These accepted textual alterations of *Dido and Aeneas* suggest a closer look at other differences between the libretto and score is necessary.

Of the so-called missing dances, at least two may only be hidden. 'The Baske' in Act I may well have been performed to the chorus, 'Fear no danger'. The use of a danced chorus would hardly be an innovation. In addition, the long instrumental postlude to the attendant's aria in Act II, ii, may have been used for the dance 'to entertain Aeneas'. However, it is the missing chorus at the conclusion of Tate's Act II that represents the thorniest problem for Purcell's would-be revisers; there are now at least three 'solutions' available to modern performers.[123] The felt necessity for these appears to neglect important internal evidence. For example, there is a musical parallel between the concluding arioso of Aeneas and Dido's Lament at the conclusion of the following act. At the moments of their greatest stress, in each case resultant from their imminent separation, both characters break into non-literate vocalizations. The settings are identical, emphasizing the structural importance of the two laments.

Ex.1

Although it seems never to have been thought possible that the scenic divisions in the manuscript score might represent an authentic version, it is necessary to look again at the implications of these.

Where Tate writes three well-balanced acts, the second in two scenes, the manuscript score contains three acts of widely varying lengths created by the placement of two scenes in Act I.

Tate	*Tenbury Ms.*
Act I	Act I, i
Act II, i	Act I, ii
Act II, ii	Act II
Act III	Act III

Thus the manuscript's first act is approximately half again the size of Tate's. The second act is less than half as long since the final chorus and ballet are omitted as well. The third acts are about the same in length.[124] A graphic presentation of these differences is:

---

[123] The Boosey and Hawkes edition by Britten and Holst and the Purcell Society (Novello) edition by Dart and Laurie both make use of other music by Purcell to which they fit Tate's text as a contrafactus. In Savage, 'Producing *Dido and Aeneas*,' pp. 405–6, Michael Tilmouth offers a newly-composed finale.

[124] They are not *identical* for line attributions are altered and the concluding ballet is omitted, as noted above.

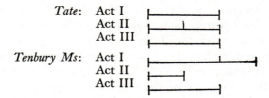

Dent mentions the alteration of the first two acts and concludes that 'the difference is of no importance'.[125] But the symmetry of the opera is apparently ruined. A closer examination reveals that the layout of the manuscript may not be as unimportant as has generally been thought.

The larger musical structure of the score implies not three major sections, as in the libretto, but two of equal length. With minor differences these exhibit a very similar plan.[126]

TABLE 7

Dramatic Structure of Dido and Aeneas

Part I:	I Ç S r Ç r	Ç r C r S C D	[pr] C[rCrC] S C D
Part II:	I Ç [Sp] r Ç r	[pÇ] D r S C D	r C r S C

I:	separate instrumental piece
Ç:	chorus with solo introductions
C:	chorus
D:	dance
S:	solo
r:	recitative
p:	instrumental postlude or prelude attached to another piece
[ ]:	a unit made up of multiple parts.

This visual layout brings into relief certain other facets of the surviving musical sources. There are only two independent instrumental symphonies – one at the beginning of each major section. At more minor divisions (the beginnings of Tate's Act II and III), an instrumental prelude is substituted. In the layout of the two parallel sections conflicting musical types coincide only once – a chorus with a dance in the second sections. One does not interpret this lack of symmetry as a major breach, however, and it may well explain why there survives only one setting of an intermediate dance movement.

[125] Dent, *Foundations*, p. 180.
[126] There are three divisions in each section. With the sections indicated by Roman numeral and the divisions by letter, the divisions in the libretto (L) and score (S) are as follows:

Part:	IA	IB	IC	IIA	IIB	IIC
L:	I		II, i	II, ii	III	
S:	I, i		I, ii	II	III	

The musical group [rCrC] in the last division of the first part parallels the recitative in the second part since the choral sections consist simply of interruptive laughter. They are not independent; the music is continuous. In another recitative (after the dance in the second division of the second part) laughing is similarly incorporated in smaller patches. Finally, the omission, at the end of Tate's second act, of the chorus and dance can be attributed as much to a desire for symmetry as to a dramatic urge to end with Aeneas' despair; and the musical relationship between this recitative and Dido's Lament ties together the dramatic thrust of Part II after which follows the Grand Choral Finale to the entire opera.

Each large section is divided into three parts. In two cases these divisions are marked by act or scene changes to a new locale. Moreover, each section has its own tonal centre. The introduction of Dido, which depicts her hesitation to submit to her feelings is written in C minor (section 1). The key changes to C major for the optimism of Belinda *et al.*, the entrance of Aeneas, and the triumph of emotion over both reason and destiny (section 2). The resolution of the witches to destroy this new-found happiness evolves in the tonal centre of F major (section 3). The hunt (section 4) emphasizes D minor/D major. When the sailors prepare to depart, and the witches see their success (section 5), the centre moves to B♭ major. Finally, Dido's anguish and death (section 6) conclude the opera in G minor.

Assuming that the score (but not the libretto) was planned in two large and parallel sections, each one includes three dramatic and tonal divisions. Dramatically the six sections form a perfect arch.

1. Dido's anguish
2. Aeneas's renunciation of his destiny; Dido and Aeneas unite
3. The witches plot against the pair
4. The witches carry out their plan
5. Aeneas's acceptance of his destiny; Dido and Aeneas separate
6. Dido's anguish

Harmonically the first three sections move from the key of the minor dominant to the major dominant to the major tonic in the key of F. The second three sections follow the same progression, with the interpolation of a major-mediant section, in the key of G minor. Thus instead of having each section in one key as does Locke, or making rather primitive efforts at connecting separate tonal sections, as does Blow, Purcell writes two sections in independent tonic areas with parallel and logical harmonic progressions. Benjamin Britten's argument that the

'second act' is proven incomplete because the tonality demands a return
to the key of the beginning of the act (F major) or its relative minor
(D minor) not only depends on an implicit trust in Tate's act divisions
but on a tonal scheme in advance of Purcell's music.[127]

The care with which Purcell put this work together is astonishing.
Equally astonishing is Dent's comment: '[*Dido and Aeneas*] conforms
to no tradition; it has no sense of style; but it is saved from falling
into the merely picturesque by its robust direction.'[128] The opera is
clearly based on the masque tradition and grows quite naturally out of
works by Lawes, Locke, and Blow. Blow had already brought about
an important re-orientation in the form; Purcell, Blow's student, continued in that direction. Both deprive the dance of its primary position.
As opposed to the often unconnected entrées of the *ballet de Cour* and
the popularity of a parallel antimasque tradition in England, one wit-
nesses a new trend toward dramatic unity. The movement from the
five entrées in *Cupid and Death* to the three acts and a prologue in *Venus
and Adonis* to the two large musical sections in *Dido and Aeneas*, is one
obvious result of this trend. The growing harmonic sophistication in
the scores of Locke, Blow, and Purcell further reflects it. Locke emphasizes each of his sections with distinct and unrelated tonal centres. Blow
attempts to relate the sections with hasty modulations at their beginnings or ends. Still, however, there exists no overall harmonic direction.
Purcell, like Locke, emphasizes his sectionalization with distinct tonal
centres. Each section, however, is not static but includes direct harmonic motion toward its own tonic. Purcell's division of the score into
halves also serves to emphasize the arch form of the drama, a complete
renunciation of the episodic plot.

Finally, it must be emphasized that *Dido and Aeneas* follows not only
the form of the early theatre masques but the choice of subject as well.
It is pastoral. Many recent commentators, however, have tried to place
it within the mould of the heroic play. One might attach that label to
Tate's *Brutus of Alba* from which the libretto derives, but the masque-
opera is pastoral in tone, topic, and length. The statement that 'in *Dido
and Aeneas* . . . the heroic figure is the heroine, yet the theme like that
of all the others [built on the heroic ideal] is the conflict between love
and honour'[129] just does not ring true. The opera revolves around Dido
and her emotions. At no point is she torn between love and honour. She
is torn by love alone.[130] Only Aeneas must worry about the dual call to

---

[127] Britten and Holst, eds., *Dido and Aeneas*, p. v.
[128] Dent, *Foundations*, p. 188.   [129] Moore, *Purcell*, p. 14.
[130] Cody (*Landscape*, p. 130) notes that in *Midsummer Night's Dream* Lysander's pledge of
fidelity to Hermia includes a reference to 'the false Trojan'. He aptly remarks, 'In the pastoral,
Aeneas is the false Trojan, and dying in the flames of love the more reasonable way to live.'
This reflects exactly the pastoralization of the story which occurs in *Dido and Aeneas*.

love and honour. The crisis of the masque, however, derives not from this conflict, as in the original story, but is artificially brought on by witches. Such supernatural plot motivation was hardly typical in the heroic play which generally depended solely on the strength and action of its heroic protagonist.

In *Dido and Aeneas*, the gods of Roman mythology are constantly on call. Phoebus and Venus appear in the Prologue as do a group of pastoral figures who bring it to its conclusion. Aeneas is described as having 'Anchises' valour mixt with Venus' charms'. During the hunt there is reference to Diana, Actaeon, and Venus. And a couplet from a chorus in the first act:

> *Cupid* strew your path with flowers,
> Gathered from *Elizian* bowers.

can be compared with a couplet in the choral finale:

> With drooping wings you *Cupids* come,
> To scatter roses on her tomb.

The story of *Dido and Aeneas* exists in the realm of the pastoral. It derives from the 'substantive masque' tradition in tone, subject matter, and musical setting. *Dido and Aeneas* illustrates how far composers of these masques had moved from the creation of an entertaining divertissement toward a true music drama. For this development the librettists cannot be given the credit. On the public stage the dramatist, with public taste on his side, could control the musical aspects to a great extent. For private performances he could not. The texts of Milton were as altered by Henry Lawes as Tate's text was by Purcell.

The distance travelled by these few compositions is evident from the modern belief that *Dido and Aeneas* derived from no tradition. Only a careful study of the operatic tendencies in stage dramas, court masques, and the cultural effects of the Commonwealth, together with analysis of librettos and scores, can reveal the conventions with which Tate and Purcell were working and the manner in which these were transformed.

As modern scholars have missed the traditions out of which *Dido and Aeneas* clearly sprang, so Purcell's contemporaries appeared able to overlook its innovation. In its first public performances this operatic masque was broken up and inserted piecemeal into a spoken drama just as if it formed the musical, masque portion of a typical dramatic opera.

In 1700 the work was 'inserted – a point to note – as a *masque* in Gildon's adaptation of *Measure for Measure*. . . .'[131] In January 1704 the

---

[131] Haun, *Libretti*, p. 131.

following notice appeared in the *Daily Courant* for the performance of *The Anatomist*, or *The Sham-Doctor*:

At the desire of several persons of quality. . . . With the masque of Mars and Venus. And an additional masque of *Aeneas* and *Dido*, compos'd by the late Mr. Henry Purcell.[132]

A similar notice appeared for *The Man of Mode*, or *Sir Topling Flutter*:

At the desire of several persons of quality. . . . With the masque of Aeneas and Dido, in several musical entertainments compos'd by the late Mr. Henry Purcell. . . .[133]

In both of these 1704 productions the opera was presented continuously as an afterpiece.

The accepted position that the Tenbury manuscript preserves *Dido and Aeneas* in an incomplete form is based on the presumption that it was copied from the score used in the 1704 representations of the opera. The argument is as follows. In the theatrical productions of 1700, when sections of the opera were inserted into a play, the two scenes of Tate's Act II were reversed, perhaps in order to conclude with a magical incantation scene.[134] Furthermore, the scene now first (Tate's II, ii) was augmented after Aeneas' recitative to include a discussion about the opposing forces of Love and Honour between Aeneas and two of his friends. This was followed as in Tate's libretto by the entrance of the witches and a concluding chorus and dance. The prologue was inserted last and altered so that it ends not with pastoral material but with a newly written duet between Mars and Peace. 'This provides a much stronger ending, in the classical as opposed to the pastoral vein.'[135] In fact, all of the alterations in *Dido* for its appearance as a dramatic opera in 1700 seem designed to give it the heroic qualities lacking in the original and thought more appropriate to the English operatic genre.

In its use as an afterpiece in 1704, these changes were dropped, and the opera reverted to a form 'approximating' the original. The scenes of Tate's second act were repositioned correctly, but presumably mis-labelled in such a way that Act II, i, still ended an act, although now Act I, and Act II, ii, still began an act. The added material in Act II, ii,

---

[132] Quoted in Emmett A. Avery and A. H. Scouten, 'A Tentative Calendar of Daily Theatrical Performances in London, 1700–1701 to 1704–1705,' *PMLA*, lxiii (1948), p. 139. See also William Van Lennep, et al., eds., *The London Stage 1660–1800: A Calendar of Plays, Entertainments and Afterpieces Together with Casts, Bar-Receipts and Contemporary Comment*, 5 vols. (Carbondale, Ill.: Southern Illinois University Press, 1965–8).
[133] Avery, 'A Tentative Calendar', p. 147.
[134] White, 'New Light', pp. 23–4.
[135] Ibid., p. 28.

was omitted, as was the entire prologue in any form.[136] The assumption seems to be that in dropping the added material, the original ending of the scene, purportedly still included in 1700, was also dropped. This, as stated above, is the most troublesome problem for modern editors of *Dido and Aeneas*, all of whom assume that the production of 1689 did include the numbers at the end of Act II. No one, however, has stated clearly whether these numbers were included in 1704. The reasoning seems to be that since the Tenbury manuscript is based on that performance and does not include those numbers, then they were not performed in 1704. However, the 'omission' of the numbers from the end of Act II seems to be the reason for assuming that the Tenbury manuscript represents the 1704 productions, making the arguments tautological. Indeed, there seems no reason whatsoever to assume that the productions of *Dido and Aeneas* in 1704 differed in any appreciable way from the original. It seems doubly odd to argue that the 1704 productions represent Purcell's intentions except for the end of this one scene when there are so many other textual variants from Tate's libretto as well.

Contrary to common opinion, then, there is sufficient reason to assume that the score of *Dido and Aeneas* as it has been preserved, except perhaps for the missing Prologue, reflects Purcell's original intentions. Even the manuscript evidence can be seen to point in that direction. Eric Walter White says of the Tenbury score, 'not only it is clean and clear, but internal evidence shows it was based on a very early score – possibly Purcell's own original manuscript as adapted for use in the theatre. The style of notation and the restricted use of figuration imply that the original must date from the end of the seventeenth or beginning of the eighteenth century.'[137] White thus seems to leave open the possibility that the source for the Tenbury manuscript copy could predate the theatrical revivals of 1700 and 1704. When he discusses the absence of the 1700 additions, however, he holds on to the view that they were *deleted*, either by the Tenbury scribe or at some prior time. Apparently because of the missing numbers at the end of Tate's Act II, White rejects the possibility that the source from which the scribe copied represented a version previous to the additions of 1700.

The extra music that was used in *The Loves of Dido and Aeneas* in 1700 does not appear to have survived. It is even doubtful whether it was carried over into the 1704 revivals, for there is no trace of any consciousness on the part of the Tenbury MS. scribe that there were omissions in the score from which

---

[136] John Buttrey has explained that this omission is an obvious consequence of the intervening accession of Queen Anne. The Prologue was written specifically with William and Mary in mind.

[137] White, 'New Light', p. 15.

he was copying. It is always possible that this extra music may turn up; but the likelihood now seems rather remote.[138]

And White's conclusions adhere to the traditional view, connecting by default the added music of 1700 with the numbers at the end of Tate's Act II.

Meanwhile, any modern edition of the opera (such as Britten's) that attempts to fill the gaps in the score as it has come down to us with appropriate music by Purcell is to be welcomed as a step towards the fuller realization of the true nature of the operatic masterpiece that Tate and Purcell planned and created together.[139]

The analysis given here, dividing *Dido and Aeneas* into two equal parts, highlights some of the problems inherent in the traditional view of Purcell's opera as incomplete. It also emphasizes the fact that the difficulty in dating the surviving sources hinges not on these manuscripts themselves but on the lost sources from which they were copied. Until clearer evidence is found, however, it seems most unlikely that the symmetry apparent in this two-part division could be the accidental result of mutilations made more than a decade after Purcell composed his original score for *Dido and Aeneas*.

In 1711, when Handel arrived in England, there did indeed exist an English pastoral genre in music, and *Dido and Aeneas* represented its highest achievement. Like the Italian form, it was diminutive; but it was a diminution, not of the contemporary dramatic opera as the Italian form was a reduction of the *opera seria*, but of the late Caroline court masque. Thus the English musical pastoral was closer in format to the earlier Italian operas, themselves musically derivative from the *intermedii*, and, therefore, close to the German pastoral. These three national musical-pastoral forms may be schematized.

TABLE 8

Musical Pastoral Forms

Format	Length	
	Extensive	*Diminutive*
Celebratory, festive – including chorus, ballet, and ensemble	German	English
Simple, refined – including a few soloists, without ensembles		Italian

[138] Ibid., p. 34.
[139] Ibid.

The German and Italian forms, both known and used by Handel, were dramatically opposed. The English musical pastoral was one possible compromise between them. Handel was to learn this third style of pastoral setting, and he was to compose according to its traditions. But he would never be restricted by it, nor would he favour it in its native land. In England Handel ultimately became his own judge.

CHAPTER V

Handel's Pastorals in the German, Italian, and English Styles

HANDEL'S GERMAN PASTORALS

When Handel arrived in Hamburg in 1703 at the age of eighteen German baroque opera was at its peak. Here Handel acquired first-hand knowledge of dramatic vocal music and began to compose in the operatic genre.[1] During the next three years, he wrote five large vocal works, four of them operas: *The St. John Passion* (1704),[2] *Almira* (1705), *Nero* (1705), and *Florindo* and *Daphne* (composed *c.* 1706, performed 1708).[3] The librettists of these works were Christian Heinrich Postel (*St. John Passion*), Christian Friedrich Feustking (*Almira* and *Nero*), and Hinrich Hinsch (*Florindo* and *Daphne*). *Florindo* and *Daphne* are clearly pastoral in their subject matter, but, except for a few extant fragments, the music for these, as well as for *Nero*, is lost.[4]

In Hamburg Handel came in contact with a large number of respected

[1] The only extant work now thought to predate the Hamburg period is the set of sonatas for two oboes (*Handel's Werke*, xxvii), but Paul Henry Lang (*George Frideric Handel*, New York: W. W. Norton & Company, Inc., 1966, p. 23), for one, places it later on stylistic grounds. One vocal work also seems belong to this period, 'Laudate pueri Dominum' (*Handel's Werke*, xxxviii). (See James S. Hall, 'The Problem of Handel's Latin Church Music,' *The Musical Times*, c (1959) and 'Handel among the Carmelites,' *Dublin Review*, ccxxxiii (1959).) In his *Chronological Thematic Catalogue* (Darley, England: Grian-Aig Press, 1972), A. Craig Bell lists both early works as well as a set of German Lieder as pre-Hamburg. For none does he give any justification.

[2] The authenticity of this passion has been questioned.

[3] *Florindo* and *Daphne* were composed as one opera, set to one libretto. On account of the length of the finished composition, the work was divided into two parts. (See Deutsch, *Handel*, p. 20, for the librettist's explanation.) This was not an unique happenstance in the history of elaborate, German pastoral opera: Keiser's *Orpheus* was performed as one opera in Brunswick (1698) and as two operas in Brunswick (1699) and in Hamburg (1702).

[4] Four fragments identified with *Florindo* appear in the Flower Collection at Manchester. See Arthur D. Walker, *George Frideric Handel: The Newman Flower Collection in the Henry Watson Music Library* (The Manchester Public Libraries, 1972). David R. B. Kimbell, in 'A Critical Study of Handel's Early Operas: 1704–1717' (Ph.D. dissertation, Oxford University, 1968), attempts a reconstruction of three of these fragments. At a meeting of the Royal Musical Association (16 March 1977) Winton Dean announced the possible discovery of additional fragments.

artists in addition to his librettists. He certainly would have known many of the people connected with the opera, such as Reinhard Keiser, the director of the Hamburg opera (1695–1718); Christian Friedrich Hunold ('Menantes') who was the librettist for two of Keiser's operas in 1703 and 1704; Barthold Feind, who was the librettist for five of Keiser's operas in 1705 and 1706; and Johann Mattheson, composer of one opera (1704) during this time and, along with Handel, one of the opera's cembalists. All of these men were directly related to the operatic pastoral tradition in Germany. Three have left treatises which give explicit definitions of the musical pastoral, and the fourth, Keiser, was perhaps the most active composer in this genre.

There can be little question that Keiser felt keenly competitive with his younger colleague due to the immediate success of Handel's first opera, *Almira*. Keiser composed the sequel to Handel's libretto, *Der Genius von Europa*, and then 'in 1706, probably out of jealousy, composed the same libretto [Feustking's *Almira*], altered by Barthold Feind.'[5] A similar set of circumstances also surrounded Handel's next production. Feustking's *Nero* and Feind's *Octavia* were written in competition, and these librettos were composed in competition by Handel and Keiser. This time Handel's efforts were less successful.

Perhaps due to the failure of *Nero* and also to a competitive spirit which would begin to affect his creative output more and more, Handel seems to have tried his hand at the one German operatic style opposite from the heroic drama. Accordingly, his last opera for the Hamburg stage was a pastoral, and nothing allies it more obviously to the German traditions than the necessity of dividing the finishing score into two evenings' entertainments. Although he was presumably responding to a challenge and attempting to outdo his competitor on various fronts, Handel did not remain in Hamburg for the performance of his opera *Florindo und Daphne*. His departure before the performance hints at some intrigue, and the opera was temporarily shelved. There can be little doubt, however, that this eminently German pastoral libretto was composed in Hamburg. Its performance in 1708 may simply reflect a growing awareness of Handel's successes in Italian operatic circles.

Florindo is long. Nothing in it appears to be on a diminutive scale. There are large choral scenes, dances, and ensembles which seem well-integrated into the line of the story. There are also several sections of simple recitative-aria alternation. The duets in general call for the two singers to have different words and, often, to portray opposing emotions.

---

[5] Deutsch, *Documentary Biography*, p. 14.

These probably were set in the consecutively-voiced duet style rather than as ensembles. The duets are usually, the larger ensembles always, in German, but the solos are, with only two exceptions in Act I, in Italian. This distinction may imply more than the obvious conclusion that the soloists were imported whereas the choruses were local. There was no precedent in contemporary Italian opera for large choral scenes, and librettos which otherwise might be Italian in origin would need these scenes newly written and interpolated into an otherwise Italian libretto. The choral scenes are particularly German and especially pastoral. The first act of *Florindo*, for example, opens with such a scene for which the entire text is German even though many of the soloists, who later switch to Italian in their arias, are introduced for the first time.

The libretto gives the following description of the first scene.

The scene takes place in a beautiful countryside in Thessaly where the nymphs and shepherds have erected a triumphal arch of fresh flowers for Phoebus; and to thank him because he killed the horrible and destructive serpent Python, they have arranged to hold a thanksgiving to Pythia [the priestess of Apollo at Delphi].[6]

The action begins with a chorus singing the praises of Phoebus ('Ihr muthigen Hörner, verdoppelt den Schall'). This encomium is then continued in what is clearly a unified set of movements. First Daphne, Florindo, and Alfirena sing a trio followed by a dance. Then Damon and Lycoris sing a duet followed by a dance. Not only is it likely that the dances would be musically related, but the two ensemble sections are themselves connected clearly as well. Both have the same trochaic metre, with four feet per line, and the same rhyme scheme (*ababcc*). The texts also closely parallel one another; note the similarities of the first lines:

> *trio* 'Ihr Nympffen, die ihr umb die Wipffel'
> *duet* '   Nympffen, die ihr in den Gründen'[7]

After these movements the scene continues with recitative and closes with a single choral line ('Das alles kommt von deinen Bogen her'). This line, in iambic ($\cup -$) pentameter is not clearly related

---

[6] Hinrich Hinsch, *Der beglückte Florindo* (Hamburg: n.p., 1708), I: i. 'Der Schauplatz stellet eine schöne Gegend in Thessalien vor, allwo die Nympffen und Schäffer dem Phoebus eine Ehren-Pforte von lauter Bluhmen auffgerichtet, und ihm zum Gedächtnitz, wegen des erlegten grausamen und schädlichen Drachens des Pythons: das dazu geordnete Danckfest Pythia halten.'

[7] Some of the verses in the trio begin with an upbeat which is optional in the trochaic pattern and easily accommodated in the strophic form.

either to the earlier set of numbers nor to the opening chorus with its repeated amphibrach ($\cup - \cup$) rhythm having from one to four feet per line—which is not to say, however, that Handel did not make a musical relationship. It is not far-fetched to assume that the entire scene of rejoicing was musically integrated. The central kernel of four movements certainly was.

Another chorus appears in Act I, iii, serving to close the festivities upon which the beginning of this opera revolves. It also serves as a massive exit number, the chorus leaving the stage for the first time, after which Phoebus only remains. That this develops into a small scene of its own is clear from the directions for a dance following the chorus. In this case the musical relationship between the chorus and the dance is made clear from the identification of the former as a chorus 'wird getantzet'.[8]

Act II opens by introducing new characters, the fathers of Florindo and Daphne. Both are river-gods, and each has one 'attendant'. There is no action in this scene, merely a lyric presentation which opens and closes with full quartets, both of which are in trochaic tetrameter and have identical rhyme schemes, *ababcc*. They were probably set to the same music. In between these each father sings a duet with his own attendant. The poetic differences in these duets imply settings different from each other and from the quartets. Both are trochaic tetrameter, but the rhyme scheme of the first is *abba*, whereas the second is *aabbcc*.

At the end of the second scene, Act II, during which Florindo asks for and receives the hand of Daphne in marriage, the river-gods and their attendants sing once again. The first and last lines are for all four and have identical texts. Surely these were set to the same music. The intervening eight lines are evenly divided as solos. The overall rhyme scheme is *ababacacaa*, and one can safely assume that the musical setting reflected this repetitive form in some way. There follows a general rejoicing in the form of a grand ballet by all the naiads and tritons risen out of the water.[9] The two opening scenes of Act II, therefore, function similarly to the first three of Act I. They set the tone for the remainder of the act, and they seem to prepare the listener for the solo arias to follow. Their form and style are unfamiliar to heroic opera; their presence aligns Hinsch's text closely with German pastoral traditions.

---

[8] Kimbell has hypothesized that this set of movements corresponds to one of the Manchester fragments and has reconstructed one possible musical interpretation from the existing bass line.

[9] The word 'Ballet' is actually in the libretto in contrast to the more familiar 'Tantz'. The difference seems to lie in the elaborateness of this dance which probably was not choreographed to the music of the preceding chorus but had a score of its own. According to the directions in the libretto, this ballet incorporated a change of scene.

The text of *Daphne* seems a good deal shorter than *Florindo*, but of course one cannot account for its musical elaboration. It is well always to keep in mind that the two operas were written and composed by Hinsch and Handel as one opera and divided later. Like *Florindo*, *Daphne* opens with an important choral scene. In *Florindo*, the occasion was a celebration in honour of Phoebus for slaying the Python. In *Daphne*, the occasion is the wedding of Florindo and Daphne. First comes a hymn to Hymen sung by the Thessalians during which, according to the stage directions, the priests perform the appropriate ceremonies. There then follows a choral song directed to the young couple. This is followed by a dance (to the same music) during which Cupid enters and (unperceived by all) wounds Daphne with one of Vulcan's arrows of chastity. She is immediately repulsed by all love. The chorus begins a second strophe (as can be inferred both from the poetic metre and the similarity of the formal outline of this scene with that of the opening of *Florindo*), but it is interrupted by Daphne who calls off the whole proceeding on account of her newly aroused feelings.[10] This abrupt change in the drama ends the choral scene in its pre-sumptive middle. It is never completed. In Act II, iii, there appears a storm scene with a dance, always a good operatic and especially pastoral device.[11] The opera, of course, ends with chorus.

From the librettos of *Florindo* and *Daphne*, one can confidently surmise that both operas fit into the generic pastoral tradition which existed in Germany. One should ask, however, if these librettos differ from the non-pastoral operas which Handel also composed in Hamburg.

Almira, for which both libretto and score survive, was Handel's first opera. It does include dances, but these generally occur in contrived

---

[10] The text of this scene up to the interruption reads:

Chorus:	Thalasia
	Hymen, lass die glimmen Hertzen
	Brennen mehr als diese Kertzen,
	Bis die Flamm den Sternen nah,
	Thalasia.
(Strophe 1.)	Streue, O Bräutigam, grünenden Nüsse,
	Sammle dafür die vergnügende Küsse,
	Welche die Liebste dir freudig gewährt;
	Theilet zusammen so Glücke als Brodt;
	Bleibet verbunden in Freude und Noth;
	Bis euch Elyseus Gefilde ernährt!
(Strophe 2.)	Knüpffe den Gürtel du schönste der Schönen. . . .
Daphne:	Halt ein, verwegne Faust'
	Ich wil hinfort der Liebe nicht mehr fröhnen. . . .

[11] One immediately can think of famous examples from both vocal and instrumental pastoral compositions, such as occur in Purcell's *Dido and Aeneas*, Haydn's *The Seasons*, and Beethoven's *Pastoral Symphony*. There is also a thunderstorm in Keiser's non-pastoral *Octavia* (1705).

'shows' within the operatic plot and are not particularly integral to the continuing action. Mostly there is social dancing; there are no large choral scenes. For example, the Spanish ladies and gentlemen of the court dance a Chaconne and a Saraband in celebration of Almira's virtues. At the end of Act I there is a ball during which there is playing, dancing, and singing on stage. The Courante, Bourrée and Rigaudon are sung; the Menuet and Rondeau are danced. At the beginning of Act III there is a Ballet of the Continents staged for the members of the court, during which the various entries are each represented by one song and dance: (1) Europe – Entrée Da Capo, (2) Africa – Rigaudon, (3) Asia – Saraband and (4) the clowns – Gigue. Aside from these, there is the usual 'Schluss-Chor'.

Nero (1705) is extant only in its libretto. Its title page lists five dances: 'von Cambattanten oder Fechtern', 'von Priestern', 'von Arlequens und Policionellens', 'von Mordbrennern', and 'von Cavalliers und Dames'. Unlike those in *Almira*, these are not entertainments planned for the opera's characters. And unlike those in the pastorals, they are not integrated into the action.[12] They are extraneous ballets which add spectacle and diversion to an opera made up mostly of arias and recitative. If it were necessary, as in the case of Keiser's *Croesus*, they could be omitted without detriment to the story.

Without the scores it is impossible to judge whether or not Handel altered his musical settings for a pastoral text, but one can say with assurance that he reserved the use of choral scenes, with the chorus as an active participant, especially for the pastoral. To a large extent, of course, it was the librettist who determined an opera's basic structure. It was the composer, however, who was capable of unifying a scene into an integrated whole or leaving it a string of detachable entertainments. With Handel's first pastoral it is necessary to guess what the music might have added. Judging from the pastoral text itself and from Handel's later operatic scores, it seems most likely that even the young Handel did not let the opportunity to exert some control over his libretto pass unheeded.

HANDEL AND THE ITALIAN PASTORAL TRADITION

While in Germany Handel adhered to the German pastoral tradition. Upon arriving in Italy, however, he was faced with the necessity of adopting an entirely different pastoral style. That he was capable of doing this within a very short time illustrates Handel's sensitivity to

---

[12] It is notable that the dances in *Florindo* and *Daphne*, as frequent and more important that those in *Nero*, are not listed on the title page. Thoy are not extravagant 'extras'.

national, musical dialects; it also bears witness to the Italian foundations of the generalized baroque musical language. Handel did not need to alter drastically his compositional practice. Rather, he needed to polish and refine it, especially in the settings of pastoral texts. Handel's secular cantatas, which were mainly written during his first two years in Italy and are almost entirely pastoral in nature, stand as a testimony to the stylistic changes which did take place.

Happily for the modern student, a chronology of Handel's years in Italy is no longer pure guesswork.[13] Without attempting to revise or supplement the known documentary evidence, it is nevertheless possible and worthwhile to summarize here the results of recent research, perhaps for the first time. Although gaps still exist, a much clearer picture emerges of Handel's movements during the years 1706–1710.

[13] See the references to Ewerhart, Fabbri, Hall, Kirkendale, Montalto, Strohm, and Zanetti in the following bibliography.

TABLE 9

Handel in Italy

Year	Date and/or Month	Place	Occupation	Associates	Reference
1706	Autumn	Florence	Travels to Italy from Hamburg with an invitation from Ferdinand de'Medici of Florence		Strohm, *RIM* (1974)
	?	Rome	Handel's autograph signature with the notation 'Rome, 1706', places him in that city before the end of the year[14]		Timms, *MT* (1973)
1707	14 January	Rome	'A German prince arrived in this city.' – Valesio diary		Flower, *Handel* (1947)
	4 April	Rome	*Dixit Dominus* finished (see 16 July 1707)	Cardinal Colonna	Hall, *MT* (1959)
	before 14 May	Rome	*Il Delirio amoroso* and *Il Trionfo del Tempo* (librettist: Panfili)	Cardinal Panfili	Montalto, *Un Mecenate* (1955)
	14 May	Rome	Description of weekly concerts at Card. Ottoboni's palace. Handel's presence at these meetings is assumed. – Blanville diary	Cardinal Ottoboni, Corelli, Caldara, A. Scarlatti	Streatfeild, *Handel* (1917)
	May–October	Rome	'regulated employment' by Ruspoli – Fondo Ruspoli; 20 works by Handel mentioned in copyists' bills dated 16 May, 30 June, 22 September, 10 October	Ruspoli, Margarita Durastante, Scarlatti (24 April – *Il Giardino di Rose*)	Kirkendale, *JAMS* (1967)
	16 May	Vignanello	8 cantatas copied for Ruspoli at his country estate		Kirkendale, *JAMS* (1967)
	12 June	Vignanello	*O qualis de coelo sonus*	Ruspoli	,,
	c. 12 June	Vignanello	*Salve Regina* (performed)	Ruspoli	,,
	12 June	Rome–Vignanello	'*Coelistis dum Spirat aura/* In festo S. Antonii de Padua . . . 1707' performed (Feast of Sant' Antonio)	Ruspoli	Ewerhart, *HJ* (1960); Kirkendale, *JAMS*, (1967)

[14] In a paper presented to the Royal Musical Association Anthony Hicks suggests that this notation by Handel may have been in error. He points out that the '1706' in the autograph signature of *Dixit Dominus* (4 April 1707) was later smudged out and replaced by '1707'. One is most likely to be confused about the year just after it changes, and Hicks thus proposes that Handel was using the Julian calendar in which the new year begins 25 March. Thus the date found by Timms may not be substantially earlier than the date for *Dixit Dominus*. See Anthony Hicks, 'Handel's Early Musical Development' *PRMA* (1976–7) pp. 80–9.

TABLE 9 – *continued*

Handel in Italy

Year	Date and/or Month	Place	Occupation	Associates	Reference
	30 June	Rome	2 cantatas copied	Ruspoli	Kirkendale, *JAMS*(1967)
	8 July	Rome	*Laudate pueri* finished (see 16 July 1707)	Cardinal Colonna	Hall, *MT* (1959)
	13 July	Rome	*Nisi Dominus* finished (see 16 July 1707)	Cardinal Colonna	Hall, *MT* (1959)
	16 July	Rome	Feast of the Madonna del Carmine, vesper service. Music by Handel:[15] 1 [*Salve Regina*] 2 *Haec est Regina virginum* 3 *Te decus virginum* 4 *Seviat tellus* 5 *Dixit Dominus* 6 *Laudate Pueri* 7 *Nisi Dominus*	Cardinal Colonna	Hall, *MT* (1959)
	22 September	Rome	6 cantatas copied	Ruspoli	Kirkendale, *JAMS*(1967)
	24 September	Rome	Handel acclaimed virtuoso at houses of Cardinals Colonna and Ottoboni – Merlini letter		Streatfeild, *Musical Antiquary* (1909/10)
	November (?)	Florence	Performance of *Rodrigo* (*Vincer stesso se è la maggior vittoria*)	Prince Ferdinand	Strohm, *RIM* (1974)
1708	November– February	Venice (?)		meets D. Scarlatti (?)	Strohm, *RIM* (1974)
	February – *c.* 30 April	Rome	'regulated employment' by Ruspoli (1) Cantata with b.c. (copied 26 February) (2) *Lungi dal mio ben* (finished 3 March) (3) *Resurrezione* (8 April)	Ruspoli, Grimani, Scarlatti (26 February *Il Giardino di rose*), Chiccheri (tenor), Pasqualino (alto); Scarlatti (25 March: 'Ora per la SS^ma annuziata'), Pippo (soprano), Cristofano (bass); Scarlatti (4 April: 'Passione' at Ottoboni's)	Flower, *Handel*; Kirkendale, *JAMS* (1967) Strohm, *RIM* (1974)

[15] Hicks places the cantata *Donna che in ciel* at this time on stylistic grounds. Strohm, connecting it with the Spanish War of Succession, places it in 1709. Ewerhart dates it 1708.

TABLE 9 – *continued*

Handel in Italy

Year	Date and/or Month	Place	Occupation	Associates	Reference
	after 30 April	Naples	Travels from Rome to Naples		
	16 June	Naples	*Aci* finished at house of Duke of Alvito (not present for wedding, 19 July)	Duke of Alvito	Barclay Squire, *Catalogue* (1927) Kirkendale, *JAMS*(1967)
	12 July	Naples	*Se tu non lasci amore* finished	?	
	14 July– c. 24 November	Rome	'regulated employment' by Ruspoli		Kirkendale, *JAMS*(1967)
	9 August	Rome	*Hendel non può* (librettist: Panfili) copied with 7 other cantatas (for Arcadian meetings)	Ruspoli	Kirkendale, *JAMS* (1967)
	28 August	Rome	5 cantatas copied (for Arcadian meetings)	Ruspoli	,,
	9 September	Rome	*Il Tebro* performed (for Arcadian meetings) 'Olinto' was Arcadian name for Ruspoli		,,
	November– December	Florence (?)	?	?	Strohm, *RIM* (1974)
1709	January–March	Rome (?)	?	?	,,
	⌈1 March	Rome	Caldara hired by Ruspoli⌉		Kirkendale, *JAMS*(1967)
	29 March	Siena	*Il Pianto di Maria* – Manucci diary[16]	for Prince Ferdinand de' Medici	Ewerhart, *HJ* 1960); Zanetti, *L'Approdo* (1960); Fabbri, *Chigiana* (1964)
	March– November	Florence (?)		?	Strohm, *RIM* (1974)
	November c. 9 November	from Florence	With letter of recommendation to Prince Karl von Neuberg in Innsbruck		Fabbri, *Chigiana* (1964)
	from 26 December	Venice	*Agrippina* performed 27 times		
1710	9 March	from Innsbruck	Letter to Ferdinando from Prince Karl		Fabbri, *Chigiana* (1964)
	16 June		Appointed Chapel Master at Hanover		Fabbri, *et al.*
	13 September	from Dusseldorf	Letter to Ferdinando from Elector Johann Wilhelm		Fabbri, *Chigiana* (1964)
	?	to Hanover	?	?	

[16] Hicks doubts the authenticity of this composition on stylistic grounds.

An examination of the foregoing table suggests that Handel travelled directly to Florence at the behest of the Medici family, although no documentary evidence for this long-held belief has yet been discovered. A recently published article by Reinhard Strohm, however, does lend greater credibility than ever before to this assumption.[17] After a stay in Rome, Handel returned to the court of the Medici in the autumn of 1707 for the production of *Rodrigo*, originally titled *Vincer stesso se è la maggior vittoria*. Strohm reasonably hypothesizes that Handel returned to Florence for a third autumn in 1708. In the spring of 1709 Handel was once again in the Tuscan area and associated with Prince Ferdinand. Only two compositions, however, *Rodrigo* and *Il Pianto di Maria* (29 March 1709) have been connected with these Tuscan visits, and the second is of doubtful authenticity.

Handel's stay in Naples was brief, only about ten weeks, and not 'a third of his time in Italy' as had been previously thought.[18] His trips to Venice were probably equally brief. Handel spent most of his time in Italy in Rome and in the specific employ of the Marquis Ruspoli.

A definite number of compositions was expected from him; by (probably) informal agreement he was obliged to remain and do his duties. This has to be said expressly to correct the romantic picture of the pampered youngster who wrote music or appeared 'in the academies' only when the spirit moved him. It confirms Mainwaring's remark, 'Handel was desired to furnish his quota,' a remark which does not have the flavor of an anecdote. In this position Handel was Caldara's immediate predecessor, no chapel master having been employed before March 1709.[19]

During these Roman tenures Handel also fulfilled specific commissions from Cardinals Colonna and Panfili; he definitely set librettos of the latter. Handel also appeared as a virtuoso performer at the house of Cardinal Ottoboni, and it is likely that some, if not many, of the texts for the 100 Italian cantatas composed by Handel were written by this man, an esteemed man of letters. Ruspoli, Panfili, and Ottoboni were also important members of the Arcadian Academy of Rome. These men gathered together not only for the regular meetings of the Academy but for the weekly *conversazione* at the houses of Colonna, Ottoboni, Panfili, and Ruspoli.[20] One must assume that all these meetings

---

[17] 'Handel in Italia: Nuovi contributi,' *Rivista Italiana di Musicologia*, IX (1974), 152–74. Strohm clarifies many of the problems surrounding Handel's Florentine visits. Especially noteworthy has been his discovery of the original libretto for Handel's first Italian opera, *Rodrigo*.

[18] Lang, *Handel*, p. 87. Of course, Lang's book appeared before the publication of the Ruspoli documents. Lang's placement of Handel into the cultural background of his time remains exemplary.

[19] Ursula Kirkendale, 'The Ruspoli Documents on Handel,' *JAMS*, xx (1967), p. 251.

[20] Ibid., p. 250, n. 101.

were infected by a similar atmosphere dictated by the more formal Academy.

During the summer of 1708 Handel can be definitely associated with the Arcadian Academy. Ruspoli, his employer, was then 'the host of the Arcadians', having succeeded Prince Giustiniani, the previous host, in September 1707.[21] The annual meetings were usually held in the warmer months (1 May to 1 October) so that these aristocratic shepherds might convene out-of-doors in true shepherdly fashion. Christmas, the birthday of the Arcadians' protector, was celebrated at the first general meeting each year.[22] Kirkendale convincingly argues that Handel's cantata *Arresta il passo* (14 July 1708) served this Christmas function in Ruspoli's first summer as host.[23] It can be assumed that the other cantatas copied during this summer period of 1708 were also written specifically for the Arcadian meetings.[24] Kirkendale has demonstrated that the instrumental cantata *O come chiare e belle* (10 September 1708) was written in honour of the Arcadian's host and Handel's employer under his assumed pastoral name, 'Olinto'.[25] No doubt it was at these meetings that Handel and Cardinal Panfili extemporized the cantata praising the young composer, *Hendel non può mia musa* (9 August 1708).[26]

---

[21] Ibid., p. 241.

[22] Ibid., p. 240.

[23] Ibid. A 'Cantata pastorale per la Nativita di nostro signore Gesu Cristo' by Alessandro Scarlatti with a text by Cardinal Ottoboni was presumably written for the same celebration in an earlier (?) year. A translation of the third and last recitative and aria reads:

Happy shepherds, whom the voices of angels did summon first of all men, Haste ye now to adore him, Our Redeemer and Saviour, who now is born on earth for our salvation! To celebrate his birth haste at once to the stable. Your pipes bring with you too, your music, your rustic airs shall soothe Him while He slumbers.

> The first ye were to hear the angel voices,
> Because tonight is born the Lamb of God on earth.
> Then haste ye on your way, and kneel before Him,
> With rustic pipe and song adore Him.

> Then leave your flocks and leave your mountain hut,
> Abandon now the favourites among your sheep,
> And follow Him who would deceive you not,
> Who will lead you to a place among the stars.

The translation of the recitative and first strophe of the aria appears in a modern edition of this work edited by Edward Dent (London: Oxford University Press, 1945). The second strophe of the aria has been translated by the author.

[24] Kirkendale, 'Ruspoli', pp. 245 and 250.

[25] Ibid., p. 242.

[26] Such improvisations have been described by the academy's founder, first president and historian, Giovanni Maria Crescimbeni. One such involving Giovan Battista Felice Zappi and Alessandro Scarlatti, both Arcadian members, has been translated and paraphrased from *Arcadia*, Lib. vii, Prosa v, by Dent, *Scarlatti*, pp. 89–90, and in R. A. Streitfeild, *Handel* (New York: Da Capo Press, 1964), pp. 35–36.

Thanks to the detailed research of Ursula Kirkendale, then, it is now known that Handel composed the majority of his cantatas in Rome for the Marquis Ruspoli during an interrupted period of employment which lasted approximately from the spring of 1707 to the autumn of 1708. During the last three months, when Ruspoli was its host, Handel's dated compositions can be directly associated with the Arcadian Academy. It is no surprise, therefore, that Handel's cantatas reflect his adoption of the Italian pastoral style most clearly. Using the Ruspoli documents as a guide, it is possible to trace chronologically Handel's stylistic development within the cantatas.

The years in which Handel's cantatas were copied for Ruspoli include 1707, 1708, 1709, and 1711. The copyist's dates for the first two years, during Handel's employment by Ruspoli, are presumably connected with the date of composition – 'for these months we can generally assume that the copyist's work was done only days or weeks after the composer's'.[27] Such is not the case for the later dates. Those from 1711 are certainly for second performances; the cantatas copied in 1709 were probably composed during the previous two years and copied for later performances or as gifts. The only dated works, then, which may be studied closely for evidence of Handel's stylistic development in Italy are those of 1707 and 1708, a period covering only about eighteen months. One can hardly expect revolutionary changes. Nevertheless, one can see certain trends, of which the most important is a movement toward greater simplicity, brevity, and economy of style, a distinct movement toward the Italian pastoral style.

The modern scholar knows less, perhaps, about these cantatas than about any of Handel's other works. What he does know, aside from the general notion that they served Handel as a musical reservoir in his later and larger works, is in general stylistically unrepresentative. It is hardly surprising, when a large collection of music is so little studied and discussed, that the unusual should stand out. Most writers, if they discuss Handel's cantatas at all, write about the large operatic scenas, such as *Agrippina condotta a morire* and *Armida abbandonata*, or the 'revolutionary scheme' of a cantata like *Udite il mio consiglio*, with its arioso refrains. According to the Ruspoli documents, however, two of these (and probably the third) were written before the end of June, 1707, when Handel had been in Rome for less than six months. Rather than being a product of his Italianization, as is so often claimed, they are more a product of Handel's training in Germany.

Handel did not learn about drama in Italy; he learned about lyricism and melodic refinement. The modern scholar must be always wary of

---

[27] Kirkendale, 'Ruspoli', p. 245.

choosing the 'most interesting' compositions as representative of a composer's output. In his cantatas Handel sought to learn a lyrical style, to conform with the Arcadians' tastes. Thus, the music from the end of his Italian tenure is more conventionalized, smoother, less dramatic.[28] That is to say, Handel approached the Italian lyric ideal through the writing of pastoral cantatas.

In the earlier works, dated from May to September of 1707, many of the stylistic elements may be described as complex and experimental. The rhythms are fussy, the harmony bold to the point of strangeness, and the melodies often jagged and replete with unusual leaps. Much lengthy figuration appears in the ritornellos, the bass line, and the vocal coloratura. Periodic structures are rare. Instead there is substantial use of baroque *Fortspinnung*, counterpoint, and sequence. The most daring formal structures derive from this period, as do the strongest and most dramatic contrasts. It is easy to see why many of these earlier pieces are those which have been singled out as the most interesting of Handel's Italian period.

Udite il mio consiglio 51:67 (16 May 1707), one of the first and most representative cantatas from the early period, illustrates clearly Handel's experimental style.[29] This continuo cantata begins with a recitative that at once reveals a bold, if somewhat awkward, harmonic plan: a series of fifth relations separated by the distance of a minor third effect a shortened trip around the circle of fifths from B minor to the dominant of B minor (the key of the succeeding arioso). That is, starting in B minor there is a shift to the super-tonic, C♯ major, which becomes the dominant of F♯ minor. By moving up a minor third Handel reaches A major as the dominant of D major. Then shifting down a minor third, B major becomes the dominant of E major. Once more moving down a minor third, C♯ major prepares the key of F♯ major which concludes the recitative and serves as the dominant to the B minor arioso which follows.

recit: b [c♯→f♯]   [A→D]   [B→E]   [C♯→F♯] aria: b
          m 3   m 3   m 3
          ↑   ↓   ↓

---

[28] Dent, *Scarlatti*, p. 63, remarks that Scarlatti's melodies also become more and more conventional.

[29] In Chrysander's four volumes containing the Italian cantatas, the ones with basso continuo accompaniment are presented alphabetically in volumes 50 and 51; the instrumental cantatas are presented in the same way in volumes 52A and 52B. The cantatas are sequentially numbered throughout each of the two sets. At the first reference to each cantata in this study, the volume and number of the cantata will be given, for example: *Dalla guerra amorosa* 50:8. The cantatas with continuo accompaniment will be referred to as continuo cantatas; those with instrumental accompaniment as instrumental cantatas.

The arioso 'Innocente rassembra' also includes an example of harmonic boldness by having the voice make its final cadence to the dominant; two measures later the continuo reaches the tonic.

Ex.1

This arioso of *Udite il mio consiglio* illustrates still another aspect of Handel's early Italian style — his predilection for aria forms other than the *da capo*. 'Innocente rassembra' is divided into three sections each with the same texts and similar musical material. Despite differences in their working out, all incorporate the opening auxiliary note figure followed by a sequential pattern in invertible counterpoint. As it first appears, the melody, and later the bass, includes the jagged melodic contours typical of the early period. The melody of the first section is illustrative of the style.

Ex.2

To give another example, both arias of *Ne' tuoi lumi, o bella Clori* 50:38 (22 September 1707) also exhibit the sequential repetition, chromaticism, and disjunct melodic line typical of the earlier period.

Ex. 3

Other continuo cantatas datable to Handel's early Italian period furnish additional examples of Handel's use of aria forms other than the *da capo*. *Aure soavi e liete* 50:3 (16 May 1707) has only two arias. Neither is a regular *da capo*. The first aria, 'Care luci', is simply through-composed in two sections.[30] The second aria, 'Un aura flebile',

---

[30] Anthony Lewis writes, 'In the first aria, "Care luci," there is no conventional *da capo*, but the effect of recapitulation is obtained by ending with part of the music of the first section adapted to the second couplet of the words – a skilful and telling device' ('The songs and Chamber Cantatas' in *Handel: A Symposium*, ed. by Gerald Abraham (London: Oxford University Press, 1954), p. 181). This is simply not apparent in the music.

6*

is designated *da capo*, but it is entitled an *Arietta* indicating its diminutive size. Actually the aria is a vocal adaptation of the French dance in the manner of Kusser and Keiser (see above, Chapter III). It is in 3/8, and has a bipartite A section with each part repeated. Thus its overall form may be schematized: a : ‖ : b ‖ : ‖ c: a : ‖ : b : ‖. Of all the commentators on Handel's cantatas, only Leichtentritt has recognized that such dance-like pieces, especially when used as a conclusion, such as in Kusser's *Erindo*, are in Handel's music Germanic in origin.

> *Aure soave* includes in addition to the above-mentioned beautiful aria 'Care luci' one of those charming ariettes ('Un aura flebile') in 3/8, with the dance-like, minuet character, that one finds not seldom in the cantatas. . . . Reinhard Keiser is a master of this lovely genre, and with a view to Keiser's ariettes, minuets, and so forth, Handel had a mind to be especially devoted to this manner of writing for a while.[31]

Because the score of *Florindo und Daphne* is not extant, it was impossible to determine whether Handel used traditional German aria forms as well as large choral scenes in his German pastoral opera. However, his frequent use of the dance aria in his earliest Italian pastorals, in a manner much like Kusser, indicates that he probably did the same in his German opera. In his later Italian pastorals the dance aria drops out in favour of the Italianate monothematic *da capo*.

At the beginning of his Italian tenure Handel uses the dance aria, like Kusser, as a conclusion, a punctuation mark. Without exception the concluding bipartite form is a sign of an earlier (1707) cantata. For example, Handel uses this form to end *Menzognere speranze* 51:3 (22 September 1707). Other cantatas can be assigned to this period on account of its use. *Dalla guerra amorosa* 50:8 (31 August 1709) undoubtedly dates from 1707; among other early stylistic features its last aria is simple bipartite dance form, a: ‖:b, unmodified to the *da capo*. In *Clori, degli occhi miei* 50:7, such an adaptation does occur, but the aria still fits clearly into the concluding minuet type. *Se per fatal destino* 51:60 (16 May 1707) shows some awareness of Italian taste by the substitution of a simple siciliano for the closing bipartite dance. Its unusually diminutive size makes this association clear. However, the positioning at the end is not Italian, and Handel came later to use the siciliano more traditionally by rarely placing it in pastoral compositions.[32]

---

[31] Hugo Leichtentritt, *Händel* (Berlin: Deutsche Verlags-Anstalt, 1924), p. 566.

[32] The siciliano was never an integral part of the Italian genre. It served with a number of other aria types to lend some diversity to the string of *da capos* in contemporary heroic opera. (For a full description of these types, see 'Aria' in *Grove*, I, pp. 197–8.) The use of sicilianos no more 'made' a pastoral than bravura arias 'made' an opera seria. In time Handel learned this. There are no sicilianos in *Il pastor fido* (London, 1712), an operatic adaptation of the most important literary contribution ever made to pastoral drama.

All of the examples of cadential dance movements above, except the already exceptional siciliano, exhibit another feature of Handel's early cantata style. They have no opening ritornellos. In Handel's early continuo cantatas the ritornello tends to be either totally lacking, as in these pieces, or very long and extended. As in almost all of the early stylistic features moderation is rare.

Another feature of the continuo line in the early cantatas is the use of a repetitious or sequential bass pattern. Repeated rhythmic patterns are especially prevalent. The dotted rhythms in the bass of the first aria in *Ne' tuoi lumi*, mentioned above, are typical.

Ex.4

The opening ritornello of the second aria, 'Superbetti occhi amorosi', from the same cantata shows not only the sequential patterning but also the typically extended length of the continuo introduction.

Often the busy figuration of the bass line can be found as well in the enthusiastic figuration of the vocal line. This is particularly true of those arias from the early period which do follow the regular *da capo* pattern. For example, the second aria, 'Non le scherzate', from *Udite il mio consiglio*, also mentioned above, is filled with figuration based on conjunct or triadic motives. In the A section thirty-two of the sixty-nine texted measures are vocalizations. This aria also illustrates another important aspect of the early cantatas – the strong contrast made between the A and B sections of the *da capo*. In 'Non le scherzate' the A section is in 3/8 and utilizes the generally smooth figuration described above. The B section changes into common time, includes no figuration, and possesses a jagged melodic line which at one point plummets down a ninth by thirds and then jumps up again in a single leap.

Similar contrasts are found in the first aria, 'Ride il fiore in seno al prato', of *Nella stagion che, di viole e rose* 50:37 (16 May 1707). The A section is effectively in 12/8; the B section is in common time. The A section is diatonic; the B section is chromatic. Other early features include the metric complexity of the A section caused by the implied vacillation between 4/4 and 12/8,[33] and the leaps of a ninth which occur in both sections.

Ex.5

(a)

[33] Although it seems obvious that in performance one should adjust simultaneous metrical clashes – ♪♪♪ occurring concurrently with ♪·♪ in another voice would make the latter ♩♪ – this does not answer the question of apparent changes of metre in succession. One has to assume in 'Ride il fiore', example 5, that Handel wanted 12/8 in measures 3–6, 4/4 in measures 7–8, and a pattern which changes by beat in measures 1–2. Otherwise there is no way to explain why Handel did not notate the entire aria in 12/8 as he obviously could have and, when he wanted to, did. Moreover, in 'Bel piacere' from *Agrippina* (Venice, 1709) Handel actually notates the metrical changes between 3/8 and 2/4, giving the modern scholar and performer ample reason to assume that, at least in his early years, Handel enjoyed such metrical vagaries. Finally, other metrical complexities, such as hemiola, are also favoured during this time. See 'Si crudel, ti lasciero' (Example 10 below) from *Tu fedel? tu costante?* (16 May 1707) reused with different texts in *Rodrigo* (Florence, 1707), and *Teseo* (London, 1713). When it ultimately found its way into *Susanna* (London, 1749) the metre was evened out into a constant 3/4.

Sometimes the contrast is built into the aria. The first aria, 'Lascia di più', of *Menzognere speranze,* mentioned above, is illustrative of Handel's textural experimentation during this early period. Not only are the voice and continuo set antiphonally, but an additional contrast is provided by a striking change of texture in the second of three settings of the text. This in effect makes the A section of the *da capo* into a musical (not textual) *da capo* of its own.

Ex. 6

The early continuo cantatas which do not end with a dance aria often end with a recitative. This is another stylistic feature exclusive to 1707. *Udite il mio consiglio*, the prototype of all early cantatas, ends with a recitative which both textually and musically recalls the opening recitative and arioso. Thus it ties together the whole composition.[34]

Ex.7

[34] The aria, 'Allor chè sorge', which Chrysander appends to this cantata does not belong with it; it does not appear in the autograph (British Library RM 20.d.12) as Chrysander states in his preface. Only in what appears to have been a primary source for Chrysander, Royal College of Music Ms 257, does this aria directly follow *Udite il mio consiglio*, but even here it is carefully allocated a new number.

Sarei troppo felice 51:53 (22 September 1707) also ends with recitative although this, together with the preceding recitative and aria are lacking in Chrysander's edition.[35] As in *Udite il mio consiglio* the final recitative quotes from the opening recitative and rounds off the form.

Ex.8

Final Recitative

Ah! che un cie-co ho per gui-da e un Dio ti-ran-no   ha del mio cor l'im-pe-ro

Sa - rei   trop - po fe - li - ce   s'io po - tes - si dar

first four measures of opening recitative, last four measures of opening recitative, and last four measures of intermediate recitative.

Sa - rei   trop - po fe - li - ce   s'io po - tes - si dar

leg - ge   al mio pen - sie - ro.

leg - ge   al mio pen - sie - ro.

Dalla guerra amorosa, associated above with the early period for other reasons, also ends with a recitative and arioso which recall an earlier recitative.

Many of the characteristics that appear in the early continuo cantatas may be found in the instrumental cantatas as well. The earliest of those that can be dated, *Delirio amoroso* 52A:12 (14 May 1707),[36] is often

---

[35] See R. A. Streatfeild, 'The Granville Collection of Handel Manuscripts', *Musical Antiquary*, ii (1911), p. 221, and Rudolf Ewerhart, 'Die Handel-Handschriften der Santini-Bibliothek, in Münster', *Handel Jahrbuch*, vi (1960), pp. 144–5. Only the first missing recitative and aria appear in British Library Add. 29, 484 and Add. 14, 182. All additions are in BL Eg. 2942.

[36] The copyist's bill for this work was published by Lina Montalto, *Un Mecenate in Roma barocca: Il Cardinale Benedetto Pamphili: 1653–1730* (Florence: Sansoni, 1955), pp. 325 (facsimile) and 335. The cantata was written for Cardinal Panfili; perhaps the text is by him.

singled out for emphasis because it includes two independent instrumental movements apart from its *Introduzione*. It is the only cantata to
do so. One wonders about the occasion for which it might have been
written, but the fact that it is from early in Handel's Italian residence
is obvious even without the copyist's date. The two instrumental
movements entitled with the French *Entrée* and *Menuet* are typical of
the dance-pantomime movements inserted in serious operas in Hamburg. *Almira* itself is an example. Such insertions were not in favour in
Italy, and Handel completely abandoned them in his later Italian works,
including both operas.

The arias of this cantata reflect Handel's early lack of moderation.
The ritornello of the first, 'Un pensiero', illustrates an adaptation of the
concerto grosso to the aria.[37] The opening ritornello includes extensive
figuration for the solo violin. The expansiveness of the movement is
obvious; the A section alone has seventy-two measures. A very similar
style obtains in the third aria where the repetitive and non-directional
figuration carries the A section for seventy-five measures.

The exuberant length of the early cantatas is also witnessed in *Tu
fedel? Tu costante?* 52B:22 (16 May 1707) where the ritornellos of the
first and third arias are long and sequential. The first aria has imitation

Ex. 9

[37] Lang writes on the influence of Corelli's concertos: 'Handel, like everyone else, was
deeply indebted to Corelli and his own concertos were a direct continuation of the Italian's
work. But the significance of the concerto as form and principle was not restricted to the
genre itself. . . . The type we might call 'concerto grosso aria' is already present in some of
the Italian cantatas Handel composed in Rome.' (*Handel*, p. 54.) The example from *Delirio
amoroso* is the earliest known of Handel's use of this form. It well illustrates the exaggerated
enthusiasm of an initial experiment. A more moderated example in Caldara's *Dafne* has been
mentioned above (see Chapter II).

between the voice and instrumental accompaniment, a contrapuntal technique which, like the invertible counterpoint in *Udite il mio consiglio*, Handel later avoids in his pastoral compositions (Example 9).

The last aria of this cantata is a two-part dance form, again without ritornello, which alternates between 3/8 and 3/4 (Example 10). The simplicity of the form and the alternation of the metric divisions make an interesting combination of early traits.

Ex.10

The last vocal piece of *Delirio amoroso* is also a concluding dance movement. It is a texted version of the instrumental menuet which both precedes and follows it. Thus this closing section is simply an extended type of the bipartite dance form ending which, like many other features of this cantata, is similar to those already noted in other cantatas from 1707.

Un'alma innamorata 52B:23 (30 June 1707) gives another example of a concluding dance form, this time moulded to the *da capo*: a :‖: b :‖̂ c‖ a :‖: b :‖. *Aure soave e liete* (16 May 1707) included an earlier example of this formal adaptation in a continuo cantata.

Unlike all of the preceding cantatas, *Armida abbandonata* 52A:3 (30 June 1707) does not have a pastoral text but one that is in the heroic vein, dramatic and tragic. Its musical style, however, is basically the same. This is because in his first year in Italy Handel had yet to develop an Italian pastoral style different from his regular dramatic vocal style. The German pastoral style, manifested mainly in large, choral scenes, was inappropriate to the diminutive Italian canatata. Its presence can only be felt in the frequent use of binary dance movements. In Handel's second year in Italy, during which the composer can be specifically associated with the Arcadians, Handel avoided such dramatic texts (or simply was not given them) and perfected the Italian pastoral idiom. Presumably his conception for *Armida* would not have changed.

Armida is often singled out as typical of Handel's entire cantata corpus. However, it does not illustrate what Handel learned from his Italian tenure, and neither is it unique. The dramatic scheme of *Udite il mio consiglio* (16 May 1707) is at least as unusual as *Armida*'s formal plan, and *Se per fatal destino* (16 May 1707) provides an earlier example of a siciliano. Thus, *Armida* is not particularly Italianate in its text, style, or dramatic form.

The Spanish cantata, *No se emendera jamas* 52B:18 (22 September 1707) and the French song *Sans y penser* (22 September 1707) also do not strictly belong in a study of Handel's pastoral style. But the new information that these are both early works and of Roman origin provides proof of Handel's interest during his first Italian year in the unusual, experimental, or bizarre. The Spanish cantata, written for voice, continuo, and 'chitarre', and notated in white notes with a few interspersed black neumes, even looks like an academic experiment – perhaps for one of Ruspoli's intellectual, but non-Arcadian club meetings. At any rate it is difficult to believe it is the kind of thing Handel would write for a Spanish princess.[38]

Clori, Tirsi, e Fileno or *Cor fedel* 52B:25 (14 October 1707) is the latest known work from Handel's first Italian year.[39] It is also the first cantata for more than one voice. There are twelve solo pieces published in the complete edition, including three duets (one in each possible combination) and one trio. Like the other cantatas from 1707 it is infused with stylistic traits and formal characteristics of Handel's early Italian period.

One of the arias, 'Amo Tirsi', is a bi-partite dance moulded into a *da*

---

[38] Lewis, 'Cantatas', p. 190.

[39] The beginning of the first aria, lacking in Chrysander's Handel edition, is printed in full in G. E. D. Arkwright, 'Handel's Cantata, *Conosco che mi piaci*', *Musical Antiquary*, i (1909–10), pp. 154–5. Additional movements, also lacking in the complete edition may be found in the Santini collection at Münster. See Ewerhart, 'Handel', pp. 128–31.

capo. Another, 'Un sospiretto', has, like those discussed by Leichtentritt
(see above), the character of a fragile dance movement. Finally, the aria
'Barbaro, tu non credi' stands out in Handel's use of novel styles and
strong contrasting moods during this period. Throughout the A section
there is a continual vacillation between a wild *presto, stile agitato*, and a
lyrical *adagio*. In fact, the entire cantata, with its great variety of aria
styles, is a study in contrasts, itself an early trait. Nevertheless, it is
in *Clori* that the first glimmers of Handel's new, 'Italian' style are
seen. This style may best be described by what it lacks of the earlier
style, and thus in many of the arias and duets the regular use of
repetitive figuration in the ritornellos and voice parts appears
somewhat moderated. The new style was to blossom in the following
year.

Arresta il passo 52A:3 (performed on 14 July 1708) is the earliest
datable Roman cantata from 1708.[40] It served to celebrate the
Arcadians' annual 'Christmas in July'.[41] An instrumental cantata, it
follows by nine months its predecessor of 1707, *Clori, Tirsi, e Fileno. La
resurrezione* (8 April 1708), Handel's largest Italian oratorio, had been
written and performed in the spring; and *Aci, Galatea e Polifemo*
(finished 16 June 1708; performed 19 July 1708), Handel's largest
Italian pastoral composition, had been written for festivities in Naples.
Arresta il passo and the remainder of Handel's known compositions for
Ruspoli datable through September of 1708 were probably written to
be performed at the summer meetings of the Arcadian Academy.
Handel's close association with the Academy at this time, in addition
to his continuing Italian experiences, most likely prompted the final
distillation of Handel's new pastoral style.

In these works from the summer of 1708, the melodies and instrumental accompaniments are smoother, the use of sequential repetitive
figuration less persistent. The total lack of rhythmic complexity, the
clear phrases, and, most importantly, the breathing spaces in the
musical flow point to the changes taking place in Handel's style. These
affect both the vocal and instrumental lines. The ritornellos tend to be
shorter (but rarely lacking altogether) and usually based on the opening
vocal material. Patterned figuration in the bass line is found less and
less often. The *da capo* becomes the standard form in which the B
sections are little valued for the chance they provide for contrast. The
middle sections seem rather to wither away; they are shortened,
deprived of ritornellos, and often melodically derived from the A
section. This, then, is perhaps the most striking change, and the one

[40] *Chi ben ama non paventa*, printed by Chrysander as a fragment, ought to be included in
this work immediately before the duet finale.
[41] Kirkendale, 'Ruspoli', pp. 240–1.

which is not simply a negation of earlier traits. It represents Handel's obvious assimilation of the monothematic *da capo* form appropriate to the Italian pastoral cantata.

Both of the arias in the continuo cantata *Quando sperasti, o cora* 51:51 (9 August 1708) illustrate the characteristics of this later style. With the same kinds of motives as in earlier works a completely new structure is created. In both arias the ritornellos are very short, and there is only a single instrumental measure between the two statements of the text in the A section. There are no cadenzas and there is an emphasis on a syllabic-type setting. In the siciliano 'Non brilla tanto il fior' the opening motive of the B section is derived from the one that opens the second part of the A section.

Ex. 11

In 'Voglio darti a mille dolci baci', the two motives developed in the B section are taken even more obviously from the corresponding two parts of the A section.

Ex. 12
(a)

(Ex. 12)

(b)

Similarly, in 'Si, piangete, o mie pupille' of *Lungi n'ando Fileno* 50:29 (22 August 1708), the ritornello is a perfunctory three and one-half measures long. The melody of the B section is clearly borrowed from the A section.

Ex. 13

In general these stylistic modifications apply to all of the 1708 cantatas, and it is unnecessary to multiply the examples. The ritornellos are shorter; generally three measures rather than ten. There are fewer vocal cadenzas and less 'spinning out' of motives. The melodic line becomes more conjunct or triadic and more syllabic; there are fewer dramatic contrasts between sections. In single cantatas, however, especially the longer ones, there appear arias which must be excluded from this description. 'Per trofei di mia costanza', from *Ah! crudel, nel pianto mio* 52A:1 (28 August 1708) is one example. Elaborate and long, it fits easily into the earlier stylistic period. Nevertheless, the general characteristics of most of these cantatas from 1708 remain quite different. That this is not always the case, however, deserves explanation.

One may point first to the brevity of the time span under discussion. The eighteen-month period is too short, and within Handel's life too integrated, to expect within it clear and distinct stylistic changes. One also has to point, however, to the difficulties of the dating system itself. The copyist's dates from 1707 can be considered close to the compositional dates without doubt. With those cantatas copied in 1708, however, there always exists the possibility that they were written earlier. This problem is compounded by the fact that many of the cantatas dated by the Ruspoli documents to 1708 exist in multiple versions. In such cases it is not always possible to know which version is meant. For example, if a 1708 copy refers to a second version, the cantata itself could have originated in 1707. Thus some of those cantatas copied in 1708 which seem to fall into the earlier period stylistically may actually derive from that period, for it is unlikely, from the biographical information known about him, that in 1708 Handel would have had the leisure both to write and rewrite the cantatas which exist in more than one version. It is more likely that, in order to fulfil all that was required of him, Handel returned to compositions already written, perhaps ones that had been intended as exercises and never performed, and reworked them as necessary.

Although the Ruspoli documents offer no example of a cantata now extant in multiple versions which reappears in 1708 after an entry for 1707, they do show three secular cantatas of 1707, *Aure soavi*, *Sarei troppo felice*, and *Tu fedel? tu costante?* recopied at the height of Handel's Arcadian summer (9 August 1708), indicating demand in excess of Handel's production. Certainly the eight months from March to October 1708 were Handel's busiest in Italy. One regards the number of compositions from this period, *La resurrezione*, the numerous Neapolitan works written in such a short time, and the cantatas composed immediately after for the Arcadian summer meetings, with a certain awe. It would be no surprise if Handel, while moving toward the development of a new lyric style, sometimes fell back on a few earlier compositions.

Those cantatas which first appear in the account books in 1708 cannot, therefore, be accepted without question as originating in that year. When cantatas first appear after 1708, the documents offer no basis whatsoever for determining their year of origin. In all such cases the problems are compounded when the cantata exists in multiple versions. To take but one example, *Ninfe e pastori* 51:40, 41, 42 (28 February 1709) exists in three versions. Its first aria, 'È una tiranna', is particularly indicative of Handel's early Italian period. The form itself is a feature of this early style; it is dance derived and has no opening ritornello: a : ‖ b : ‖A͡‖cA *da capo* (where the upper case letters represent ritornellos). Also indicative of the early period is the metric alternation between 3/8 and 3/4. Yet the opening bars of the middle section are so close to being a perfect inversion of the A motive that one could hardly call it a coincidence.[42] That the sections are related would normally imply a later period, but the contrapuntal device points to the earlier period.

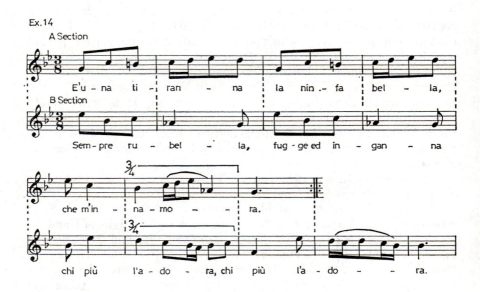

Ex.14

This aria appears only in cantatas 40 and 41.[43] Cantata 41, however, which does not exist in autograph, is simply a copy of the cantata (40) for soprano transposed into the alto range. Thus the difficulty of finding a chronology for these cantatas can be limited to two versions. Considering only the form and style of the opening aria in number 40, one would place this version most likely in 1707, perhaps toward the end

---

[42] It is interesting to note that many of Handel's first approaches to the monothematic Italian pastoral aria occur in dance-type pieces. This probably reflects Handel's concept of the similarity of their functions.

[43] Handel's autograph for number 40 (BL RM 20.d.11) contains the first aria with the repetition indicated by 'da capo'. Chrysander has apparently taken his version of number 40, where this aria is written out, from RCM 257. See above, n. 34.

of that year.[44] If, then, this aria was later deleted to form cantata 42, cantata 40 is the earlier. Indeed, the autograph of number 42 is in much neater and smaller script than cantata 40, an indication that Handel was no longer 'composing'.[45] However, even with the omission of the first aria, traces remain of the original compositional period. For example, the last aria in both versions is a little 3/8 canzonetta-like piece especially familiar from the 1707 compositions. Thus regardless of the time of its revision, all versions of *Ninfe e pastori* retain important features of its original early style.

It is important to emphasize that one cannot talk about qualitative differences between these style periods. What Handel accomplished in Italy was the assimilation of an additional style which was smoother, more lyrical, and associated particularly with the pastoral. The vast majority of texts for these cantatas were of course pastoral, and the most striking difference between the earlier and later works, therefore, is Handel's adoption of the Italian pastoral aria form. Except for the stylized dances, Handel's earlier style represents a more heroic approach to the text. The early cantatas, however, appear not to have found disfavour even in Italy. According to the Ruspoli documents many of these were recopied more than once. Nevertheless, it would be difficult not to see the trend away from this style in Handel's later cantatas. Throughout his life, however, Handel would draw freely from both types. Handel clearly did not feel one of these styles to be superior, but he saw that in separate instances, one or the other was more appropriate.

For example, when Handel was called upon during the Arcadian summer of 1708 to compose *Mentre il tutto è in furore* 50:31 (22 August

Ex.15

la bel - li - ca   trom — — — — — — — — —

— — — ba, la bel- li- ca   trom - ba,

[44] The Santini collection at Münster preserves many of the manuscripts originating in Ruspoli's household. The only copy of *Ninfe e pastori* extant there is the first version, number 40. Even if this relates to the copy made in 1709 it presents no chronological difficulty, for many of Handel's 1707 cantatas were recopied at that time.

[45] One may assume that the order in which Chrysander printed the variant readings reflects his thoughts on their chronology. In all but one case where the versions are identically titled, a stylistic consideration of their relative features always yields a chronology which follows Chrysander's ordering.

1708), a poem celebrating Ruspoli's military successes in the Spanish War of Succession,[46] he wrote a battle piece for soprano with the singer imitating horn calls in the first aria (Example 15), and accompanied in *stile agitato* in the second.

For a piece such as this Handel did not use his newly-acquired but inappropriate pastoral style. Handel's complete awareness of the specific nature of the pastoral style, however, is most clearly seen in the intra-cantata borrowings of 1708–1710. *Io languisco* 52A:4, a celebratory piece in honour of Charles III, sent from the Hapsburg Empire as the presumed King of Spain, and two pastoral compositions: *Apollo e Dafne* 52B:16, and *Arresta il passo* 52A:3 illustrate Handel's careful use of the pastoral and heroic styles. The last, according to the Ruspoli documents, dates from the summer of 1708 in Rome; *Apollo e Dafne* fits stylistically into the later period as well (probably 1709); and the paper evidence of *Io languisco* places it in England (*c.* 1710).[47] Thus all the compositions can be dated after the time when the pastoral and non-pastoral styles were clearly defined in Handel's works.

Two arias from *Apollo e Dafne* appear in *Io languisco* with different texts: 'Come rosa e su spina' becomes 'Se qu'il ciel' and 'Ardi ardor' becomes 'Anche il ciel'. In both cases the only difference lies in the extension of phrases to allow for more fioritura in the celebratory *Io languisco*. This varies from a minor elongation (Example 16) to the addition of an elaborate cadenza lacking in the pastoral (Example 17).

Ex.16

Apollo e Dafne

Tal con - fu - ga re - pen - ti - na pas-sa il fior del-la bel - tà,   tal con - fu - ga re - pen-

Io languisco

Se col d'or, fuor del suo a - bis- so   lie-to o - mai ri - sor- ge- rà,   se col d'or fuor del suo a-

[46] Strohm, 'Handel', p. 171.

[47] Strohm (Ibid., pp. 171–2), places it in early 1709. In any case it certainly follows *Apollo e Dafne*.

-ti – na, tal con-fu-ga re-pen – ti – na   pas-sa il fior del-la bel-tà

– bis-so, lie-to o-mai ri-sor-ge – rà,_____ ri-sor-ge – rà

Ex.17

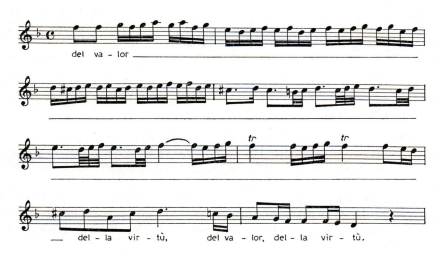

del va – lor _____

_____ del – la vir – tù,   del va – lor, del – la vir – tù.

The duets 'Per abbatter' from *Arresta il passo* and 'Non più barbaro' from *Io languisco* are essentially the same throughout the A sections. In the B sections there is no similarity. In the B section of *Io languisco*, a strong contrast is made both melodically and texturally. It is wholly without a ritornello, and the instrumental accompaniment is reduced to continuo. There is no relationship of musical material. In the pastoral, however, Handel carefully places the fermata after the A section at the vocal cadenza.[48] The ritornello in the tonic then becomes introductory, balancing the two sections in a manner so familiar from Caldara. This may possibly be Handel's only use of Caldara's practice, and it implies

[48] Handel so often omits notating the fermata altogether in his autographs that its special placement here must be accepted without question.

a new awareness of Caldara's style.[49] Handel further emphasizes the balance and strophic relations between the sections by starting the voices in the B section with the initial vocal theme of the A section in the tonic and only making the modulation to the relative minor clear at the fifth note. He also retains the instrumental forces of the A section. Thus the differences between these two *da capo* duets lies solely in the treatment of their B sections or in the manner in which their heroic or pastoral texts are emphasized. One may schematically compare the two formal plans:

'Per abbatter'   A B A' c b a b d ⌢‖ A' B' A''   c' c' | da capo

'Non più barbaro'   A B A' c b a b d   A B A' ⌢‖ e | da capo

Thus Handel left Italy with a new style at his disposal. That it was connected with the pastoral is clear. However, it was diametrically opposed to the style he had used for the pastoral in Germany, which generally called for an enlarged format. In Italy, the pastoral called for a simple, non-dramatic style and a reduced size. In England Handel was to make use of both forms.

HANDEL'S ITALIAN PASTORAL OPERA

While in Italy Handel did not apparently have the opportunity of composing a pastoral opera. His two operas written during these years, *Rodrigo* (Florence, 1707) and *Agrippina* (Venice, 1709) both adhere to an heroic model. One might argue that Handel was not prepared to write an Italian pastoral opera at this time, at least certainly not in 1707. The large number of pastoral cantatas composed during these years, however, had served as a proving ground for the Italian pastoral style. By 1710, when *Io languisco* was probably written, Handel had clearly sorted out the Italian pastoral and heroic traits in his compositions. After leaving Italy he did not wait long to put this knowledge to operatic use.

Within only two years of first stepping foot on British soil[50] Handel wrote and produced his first two operas for English audiences. Each represented one of the two styles which Handel had acquired in Italy. *Rinaldo* (24 February 1711), its story marginally derived from Tasso's epic *Jerusalemme liberata*, was long and heroic. Although ridiculed in print,[51] *Rinaldo* was greeted with popular acclaim. *Il pastor fido* (22 November 1712), based on Guarini's pastoral, differed radically from

---

[49] In less than a year Caldara would take over as Maestro di cappella for Ruspoli
[50] This is presumed to have been in October or November of 1710.
[51] Deutsch, *Handel*, pp. 35–7.

the dramatic and expansive style of *Rinaldo*. It was smaller, lyrical, and without surprises in form or format. It failed miserably.

During these two years Handel was formally employed as *Maestro di cappella* at the Hanoverian Court. His time in England was officially reckoned as leave, which most likely created pressure on the young composer to work quickly. According to his librettist, Giacomo Rossi, Handel completed the score to *Rinaldo* in two weeks.[52] By 27 June 1712 he temporarily resumed his duties in Hanover, returning to London in October of the same year. The score for *Il pastor fido* was 'finished Oct 24'.[53] Within a month the opera was produced.

In neither score does Handel cater to English taste. In his hurry to present London with his best efforts, he had no time to study the English musical style. When Aaron Hill sketched out the story of *Rinaldo*, however, from which Rossi constructed the Italian libretto, he kept in mind the possibility of deriving an indigenous English opera from elements of the heroic dramatic opera.[54] The magical and spectacular aspects of the libretto, which led Winton Dean to classify *Rinaldo* in a special category of an opera based on magic,[55] especially reflect Hill's conception. Handel's score does not.

Handel had learned to write in two basic operatic styles, the heroic and the pastoral. His concept of the latter changed drastically in Italy, but the number of general styles open to him did not. As he had in Hamburg, Handel attempted to show London his talents in both operatic fields. The score for *Rinaldo* (HW 58) represents Handel's heroic or dramatic style, a part of his compositional practice since his days in Hamburg and essentially unchanged since *Almira* (1705). *Il pastor fido* (HW 59), on the other hand, is a perfect example of the lyrical Italian pastoral. A comparison of the two scores makes their differences apparent, and illustrates Handel's well-defined conception of this difference. Whereas the first focuses on the achievement of diversity and a wide range of colour, the latter strives for the simplicity and consistency found in the pastoral operas of Pollaroli, A. Scarlatti, and Caldara. Handel's one hundred cantatas had prepared him for this moment.

Both *Rinaldo* and *Il pastor fido* contain six main characters represented by three sopranos, two altos, and a bass. In *Rinaldo* the arias are

---

[52] See the preface to the opera, described in *HW*, lviii, p. iii, and given in full in Deutsch, *Handel*, pp. 33–4.

[53] Lang, *Handel*, p. 128; Deutsch, *Handel*, p. 49.

[54] See the letter to Handel in which Hill offers his ideas on a national operatic form, in Deutsch, *Handel*, p. 299. Hill was the manager of the Haymarket Theatre where *Rinaldo* was performed.

[55] Dean, *Opera*, Chapt. 6, 'Magic Opera', pp. 77–97.

almost equally divided among these ranges. In *Il pastor fido*, the bass enters only to sing the final aria, performing the function of a *deus ex machina*. Moreover the ranges of the sopranos and altos are so nearly equal that before his entrance the entire vocal compass has been less than two octaves. Although in *Il pastor fido* Handel maintains this absolute consistency of tone colour, in *Rinaldo* he varies it throughout.

In a recent article, the limited vocal range of *Il pastor fido* has been attributed to an English dramatic convention. 'The distancing effect of Guarini's stately formalism was partly replaced on the London stage by the all-female or all-child convention. Handel seems to have accepted this device in his use of five high voices for the principal roles: a countertenor, a male alto, a contralto and two sopranos.'[56] This theory overlooks the Italian operatic practice which regularly utilized high voices in both male and female leading roles. It neglects the evidence of *Rinaldo* where the principal characters are assigned the same vocal registers. The vocal ranges in *Silla* (London, 1714) are even closer to those in *Il pastor fido* than *Rinaldo*, the bass being used only once. *Teseo* (London, 1713) and *Amadigi* (London, 1715) use similar ranges. Obviously one is dealing here not only with an Italian operatic convention but also with the ranges of specific singers in the operatic company. The difference in *Il pastor fido* appears in the consistency of the range. This consistency reflects the simplification inherent in the Italian pastoral mode. Handel emphasizes consistency, simplicity, and diminution throughout this pastoral opera.

Whereas *Rinaldo* contains thirty arias, a duet in each act, two sinfonias, two marches, and a 'Battaglia', *Il pastor fido* has twenty-three arias, one duet, and two sinfonias related to the sacrificial ceremony. As a result, *Rinaldo* includes twelve to sixteen numbers in an act, and *Il pastor fido* averages eight. The pastoral therefore is only about half the size of the heroic drama. On 26 November 1712, Francis Colman wrote in his 'Opera Register':

The stage and scenes at ye Opera Theatre in ye Haymarket, having been altered and emended during ye vacant Season. They open'd ye House Nov.R ye 26th 1712. with a New Pastorall Opera called The Faithful Shepherd. ye musick composed by Mr. Hendel. . . . The Scene represented only ye Country of Arcadia. ye Habits were old. – ye Opera Short.[57]

Handel limited *Il pastor fido* in size. He also restricted complexity in its composition. About thirty per cent (7/23) of the arias in this pastoral are accompanied only by continuo, compared with about

---

[56] Duncan Chisholm, 'The English Origins of Handel's *Pastor Fido*', *MT*, cxv (1974), p. 653.
[57] Quoted in Deutsch, *Handel*, p. 50.

seventeen per cent (5/30) in *Rinaldo*. Handel's operas show a pattern wherein the continuo aria gradually decreases in importance until by *Amadigi* (1715) it was practically non-existent. In *Almira* (1705), this type of accompaniment accounted for half the arias, in *Rodrigo* (1707) a third, in *Agrippina* (1709) a fourth, and in *Rinaldo* (1711) a sixth.[58] The sudden resurgence of the continuo aria in *Il pastor fido* specifically reflects the simplicity of the Italian pastoral idiom.

The reduced dimensions of *Il pastor fido* are even apparent in its orchestrally accompanied arias. Two out of sixteen, 'Augelletti, ruscelletti' and 'Ho un non sò che nel cor', are *arie all'unisono* – that is, accompanied at pitch by the violins with no continuo support. Another, 'Di goder', is without continuo throughout the vocal sections, the first violins often playing in unison while the seconds provide the harmony. In the cadenzas, however, the voice is virtually unaccompanied, the violins serving apparently to mark pitch and time.

Ex. 18

---

[58] Bruno Flögel, 'Studien zur Arientechnik in den Opern Händels', *HJ*, ii (1929), pp. 120–1.

In a fourth aria, 'D'allor trionfante', there are also long passages of *unisono*.

Handel never uses the *aria all'unisono* extensively. As with the continuo aria, he can be seen moving away from an earlier practice. Of *Rinaldo*'s twenty-five orchestral arias, only two, 'No, no, che quest'alma' and 'Bel piacer', utilize this technique. A third, 'Il Tricerbero humilato' uses a different but related accompaniment; the voice and orchestra move in octaves throughout, creating a ponderous, not lightening effect. This accompaniment continues to reappear in Handel's compositions; a later and more familiar example occurs in the *Messiah*, 'The people that walked in darkness'. In general, however, the *unisono* accompaniment lost its appeal. Its use in *Il pastor fido* reflects the pastoral idiom. Even Burney in his contemporary *History* comments on the unusual number of continuo and *unisono* accompaniments in this opera.

Handel has been accused of crouding some of his songs with too much harmony; but that is so far from being the case in this opera, that he not only often leaves the voice without any other accompaniment than a violoncello, but sometimes even silences that. In ['Se m'ami, o caro'], the singer is frequently left alone, or with only a violin in unison; and when the voice is good and the performer knows how to use it, this is always acceptable to the undepraved part of an audience.[59]

[59] Charles Burney, *A General History of Music* (London: printed for the author, 1789; new critical edition edited by Frank Mercer, New York: Harcourt, Brace and Co., 1935), II, p. 682. Burney's *History* was originally published in 1789. The aria 'Se m'ami, o caro' as it

Handel's final method of keeping the pastoral simple is his use of the monothematic *da capo* aria. In seven numbers, including the final chorus, the B section approaches a variation or development of earlier material. 'Augelletti, ruscelletti' and 'Ho un non sò che nel cor' make use simply of transposed melodic repetition. 'Allor che sorge', 'Tu nel piagarmi il seno', 'Secondaste al fine', and 'Quel ch'il Cielo' combine melodic variation with strict rhythmic repetition. The B section of 'Ritorna adesso Amor' develops an inversion of the aria's head motive.

Many commentators on Handel's style have observed the composer's predilection for a close relationship between sections of the *da capo* aria. 'Basically Handel regards the *da capo* aria as thematically homogeneous, with the second part continuing the same material as the first.'[60] 'The standard form of the *da capo* aria in Handel, insofar as there is such a thing, comprises a first part with ritornello at the beginning and end and subsidiary ritornellos between the vocal paragraphs, and a shorter second part founded on a related key, usually the relative minor or major, developing the material of the first and modulating more freely.'[61] It is important to observe, however, that this was a style he learned in Italy where it specifically related to the Italian pastoral genre. Only after Handel ceased to compose in the Italian pastoral vein, did he integrate this style into other compositional types. For example, whereas in fully thirty per cent of the arias in *Il pastor fido* the sections of the *da capo* are closely related, in *Rinaldo* this occurs clearly only once, in 'Il vostro maggio de' bei verdianni'. In 'Basta che sol tu chieda' and 'Lascia ch'io pianga', the technique also seems present to a lesser degree. None of these appears in a heroic situation; all three, in fact, take place in the distinctly pastoral settings of the second act – either on the shore of a peaceful sea or in Armida's pleasure garden. Moreover, it is interesting to note that all three of these arias were borrowed by Handel from earlier compositions.

Indeed, the question of borrowing in these two operas raises some important issues. Since no codification of Handel's operatic borrowings

---

appeared in *Il pastor fido* contained only continuo accompaniment. In its first use, in *Aci, Galatea e Polifemo* (1708), Handel explicitly called for two cellos and continuo, which rarely diverge from a single line. In *Il pastor fido*, as well, there is no indication of a violin *unisono*. However, when the aria was borrowed into *Acis and Galatea* of 1732 a *unisono* for *tutti violini* was indicated without being written out. Either Burney remembered the latest version or he has divulged an interesting titbit about performance practice. It is possible that in continuo arias with instrumental ritornellos the violins were expected to play along with the voice throughout the vocal section.

[60] Anthony Lewis, 'Handel and the Aria', *PRMA*, lxxv (1958–9), p. 105.
[61] Dean, *Opera*, p. 156.

7

has appeared in print,[62] unsubstantiated statements abound. A true
believer in the printed word might well develop the notion that between
1705 and 1712 Handel composed only one opera – his first. 'Rodrigo
was scarcely more than an experiment, since the body of the work,
especially the arias, was taken from the score [of *Almira*].'[63] 'Nearly
two-thirds of the vocal movements [in *Rinaldo*] are based in whole or
part on earlier music.'[64] 'The music [of *Il pastor fido*] is mostly a
pasticcio from previous works.'[65] This, of course, represents an exaggeration that even the authors cited did not intend. But the constant
emphasis on borrowing in Handel's scores does obfuscate the care taken
by the composer with each of his works. In *Rodrigo*, for example,
Handel only seems to borrow twice from *Almira*. Most of the borrowings derive from his cantatas of 1707, which are of course still not
adapted to the Italian pastoral style. In his next opera, *Agrippina*,
which is also heroic, and rarely mentioned as a score using previous
material, Handel depends much more heavily on his Germanic heritage,
borrowing seven numbers from Keiser's *Octavia*. He also borrows,
among others, three arias from *Rodrigo*, two from *Duella amorosa*, a
cantata of 1707,[66] and three from *La resurrezione*.[67] The emphasis on
non-pastoral sources is obvious. In fact in a complete list of sources for
this opera, the pastoral cantatas of 1708 play by far the smallest part.[68]
The suitability of his borrowed material would be a concern to Handel
throughout his career. Nevertheless, if *Il pastor fido* consists mostly of
borrowed material, then one could question whether its 'pastoral'
qualities (especially à propos continuo and *unisono* accompaniments) do
not simply derive from a concentration of pieces in an earlier style. The
answer lies in the fact that *Rinaldo*, with which the pastoral is in such
contrast, also relies heavily on borrowings with a totally different
result.

As in *Agrippina* the sources for *Rinaldo* are almost entirely from
heroic, or at least not Italian pastoral, compositions. The list includes
Almira, *Rodrigo*, and *Agrippina*, as well as cantatas from 1707, *La
resurrezione*, and *Il trionfo del tempo*. Handel borrows some from *Aci,
Galatea e Polifemo* (1708); however, the clearest instance, where both

---

[62] Kimbell, 'A Critical Study,' attempts a complete listing for Handel's first eight (extant)
operas. See also Bernd Baselt, "Zum Parodie verfahren in Händels frühen Opern," *HJ*,
xxi–xxii (1975–6), pp. 19–40, for a newly-published list of Handel's self-borrowings in his
early operas.
[63] Lang, *Handel*, p. 85.
[64] Dean, *Opera*, p. 29.
[65] Edward J. Dent, 'The Operas' in *Symposium*, p. 24.
[66] See Ewerhart, 'Handel,' pp. 125–6.
[67] These are the main datable sources.
[68] There are two clear borrowings from *Arresta il passo* (14 July 1708).

music and text are taken, derives from an aria for the monster Polifemo
which, of course, was never intended to be pastoral. Polifemo stands in
contrast to his pastoral surroundings.[69]

With *Il pastor fido* the situation is different. Only two arias, 'Fato
crudel' (used as 'Quillt ihr überhäuften' in *Almira* and as 'Sommi Dei'
in *Rodrigo*) and 'Nel mio core' (used as 'Es streiten' in Keiser's *Octavia*
and as 'Dell' Iberia' in *Rodrigo*), originate in previous operas. All other
sources derive from the Italian works between 1707 and 1709. Even
among these, however, Handel makes important changes to adapt the
style better to a pastoral. Especially interesting are those arias which
were used, also borrowed, in the celebratory cantata of 1710, *Io
languisco*.

The second aria of *Il pastor fido*, 'Augelletti, ruscelletti', was used
with just about the same text by Handel in *La resurrezione* (1708) and
then with different words, 'Un sol angolo', in *Io languisco*. Except for
changes in key, the A sections of all three *da capo* arias are almost
identical. The B sections are all different. In the oratorio, where the
aria originates, the *all'unisono* accompaniment of the A section is maintained unchanged in the B section. This section develops a rhythmic
and melodic motive rather persistently which, although it is not a
quotation from the A section, is definitely related to it. This is
emphasized, of course, by the unchanging texture.

In 'Un sol angolo' of *Io languisco* the B section changes from
all'unisono (senza continuo) to simple continuo accompaniment, as
complete a textural alteration as is possible. The jagged melodic and
rhythmic contour of the B section is also in complete contrast to the
preceding part. When Handel uses this aria in *Il pastor fido* he rewrites
the B section a third time, making it texturally and melodically a
quotation of the A section.

Ex.19

(a) A Section

Au - gel - let - ti, ru - scel - let - ti

B Section

Che tro - var sol può ri - sto - ro

---

[69] This distinction is made in some way in all of Handel's settings of this mythological
story. See below.

(Ex. 19)

In the neutral oratorio Handel uses his common procedure of linking the sections in an ambiguous, casual way. In the heroic celebratory cantata, he rewrites the B section to emphasize the contrast with the A section. In the pastoral opera, Handel makes the two sections almost identical.

Sometimes the changes are more subtle, but recognizable nevertheless. 'Secondaste al fine' from *Il pastor fido* is a binary dance piece adapted to the *da capo* form. The A section is dominated by a melodic turn which occurs in each measure. In the B section this is changed to a scale pattern, then to an auxiliary note figure. In the introductory ritornello, repeated identically before the B section, Handel alternates the turn with the scale pattern, thus setting up both sections of his aria.

When Handel used this aria previously in *Io languisco*, 'Col valor', he emphasized the distinction by introducing the A section with the turn only, the B section with only the scale.

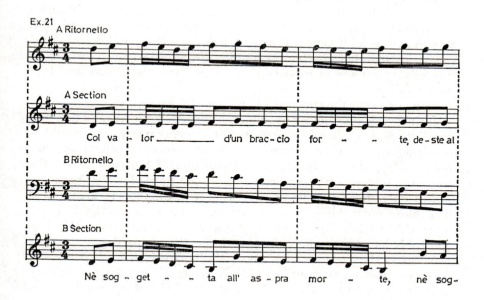

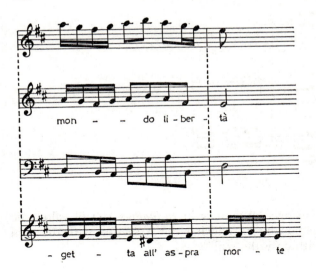

In its original form, 'Fra pensieri' from *Fra pensieri* 50:21 (31 August 1709), probably written late in 1707, there is no opening ritornello, but turn and scale patterns appear in the voice part in both sections. In this work Handel was just starting to link the sections of his pastoral *da capo* arias together. In *Io languisco* he distinguished the two sections carefully by his use of motives in the voice part and ritornellos. In *Il pastor fido* he arrives at the sophisticated device of linking the two sections by using the ritornello to prepare the motivic change.

Il pastor fido offers other examples of changes made in arias that have come through an heroic source, but it is unnecessary, and would be overbearing, to discuss them all. Most, however, illustrate some unique adaptation to the Italian pastoral ideal.[70] Suffice it to say that when the source is pastoral in both text and music Handel in general makes only those alterations necessary to accommodate a new text. The most outstanding example is the creation of the final chorus, 'Quel ch'il Cielo', from the closing aria of *Un' alma inamorata* 52B:23 (probably late 1707) where the text begins 'Ben impari'.

What is the most striking about the borrowings in *Il pastor fido*, however, is that just about half of them are taken intact with no change in their original text. That is, if two-thirds of *Il pastor fido* is borrowed

---

[70] 'Ho, un no sò che nel cor,' used identically in *La resurrezione*, *Agrippina*, and *Il pastor fido* with the same text and music is one exception. Another example of subtle alteration occurs in the changes made in moving 'Più non spero' in *O! come chiare* to 'Con linfe' in *Io languisco* to 'Se un ombre' in *Il pastor fido*.

musically, then about one-third of the libretto derives from Handel's previous librettos, and, one must assume, from Handel's choice. Statements such as the following, therefore, totally miss the implications of the score.

Rossi's libretto is silly, it fearfully mangles Guarini's original, and the librettist failed to provide any dramatic interest.[71]

Giacomo Rossi reduced Guarini's famous play so drastically that very little of its poetry is left, and Rossi's own arias contrast very awkwardly with the exquisite sixteenth-century language of Guarini.[72]

One cannot fault Rossi for a book he apparently had so little a hand in. The analysis, below, of Handel's 1732 revision of *Acis and Galatea* will better illustrate Handel's finesse in putting together a drama, but his control over *Il pastor fido* is, nevertheless, clear. When more than a fourth of the text, as well as more than half of the music is pre-existent in the composer's previous repertoire, it is quite obvious where the control lies.[73]

Knowing little of English tastes, and misjudging the international importance of the Italian pastoral form, Handel quite naturally would have wanted to present to the enthusiastic English audiences of *Rinaldo* the other side of his compositional coin. One can assume that Handel deliberately chose pieces from among his popular Italian compositions for display. Most likely Rossi was asked to write connective recitative along with a few new texts. Perhaps Handel even recommended the plot of *Il pastor fido* to him. Certainly, the pastoral conceits expressed in most of these arias fit interchangeably into any typical pastoral context. The pastoral dramas, after all, were hardly notable for their individuality: the entire literary mode consisted of stereotyped situations. With a little juggling of arias, some new texts, and new recitative, one could just as easily have *Aminta*, or any similar pastoral for that matter, as *Il pastor fido*.[74]

To understand Handel's compositional practice one must understand Handel's position in his collaborations. He did not write *Il pastor fido*

---

[71] Lang, *Handel*, p. 128.

[72] Dent, 'The Operas', p. 24.

[73] Although it is often impossible to say to what extent a composer has affected his libretto, there is some evidence in Handel's case that this was something he never left completely to the librettist. See the letters surrounding the composition of *Belshazzar* (1745) in Dean, *Oratorio*, pp. 434–5, the further assumptions of Dean concerning the operas (*Opera*, pp. 41–3), and negatively the evidence of librettists chafing under Handel's yoke (Deutsch, *Handel*, pp. 112–15 and 185–6 about Rolli, and pp. 851–3, about Morell).

[74] Handel's own juggling of these arias in the 1732 *Acis* and the 1734 revision of *Il pastor fido* makes this abundantly clear. See below.

as an Italian pastoral because he was given such a book. Handel chose his own direction. Nothing, however, could be further from the truth than to say about *Il pastor fido* that 'a study of the English predecessors of Handel's pastoral opera sheds some light on his choice of subject. . . .'[75] If Handel had been aware of English precedents he would not have written *Il pastor fido* in the style he did. If he had been aware of English taste, he probably would not have written it at all.

THE OPERATIC PASTORAL IN ENGLAND AT THE
BEGINNING OF THE EIGHTEENTH CENTURY

The pastoral in England had never been popular on the public stage: not in Jacobean or Caroline drama, not in Restoration opera, not even in the court masques. It only had succeeded as a kind of hybrid entertainment for private functions for families and schools. With very few exceptions, every attempt at publicly producing an operatic pastoral in England had been a failure.[76] The contemporary criticism of the pastoral was continuous, consistent and, often, contemptuous.

In 1702 Francois Raguenet (1660–1722) had published in France a dissertation extolling the virtues of Italian opera to the disadvantage of the French. The nationalists immediately took offence and set the machinery in motion for a lengthy series of rebuttals and defences. The resulting controversy was of interest wherever the operatic form had spread. England was treated to a translation of the original work in 1709. Moreover, the anonymous translator, thought by Hawkins to be J. E. Galliard, annotated his translation heavily and added 'A Critical Discourse upon Opera's in England, and a means Proposed for their Improvement'. In this commentary he leaves no room for doubt about the English taste for pastorals.

The Theatre in the *Hay-Market* opened with a Pastoral Compos'd by *Gia [com]o Gr[ebe]r*, A *German*, who had Study'd Composition in *Italy*. This was the first Pastoral that had ever been Presented on the *English* stage, and prov'd fatal to that Theatre, and so indeed have all the rest, for none of 'em ever Took; so that the Undertakers of the Opera ought to tremble at the very Name of Pastoral. . . .[77]

---

[75] Chisholm, 'English Origins', p. 651.
[76] Even Chisholm in arguing for the English origins of *Il pastor fido* is forced to admit this. He describes the failure of almost every eighteenth-century attempt: *Aminta* (adapted by Oldmixon, 1698), p. 651; *The Fickle Shepherdess* (1703), p. 652; *The Loves of Ergasto* (1705), p. 652; *The Temple of Love* (1706), p. 652; and *Alarbus* (1709), p. 652.
[77] *A Critical Discourse Upon Opera's in England and a Means Proposed for Their Improvement* in François Raguenet, *A Comparison Between the French and Italian Musick and Opera's*, *Translated from the French, with Some Remarks*. (London: n.p., 1709), facsimile edition. introduction by Charles Cudworth (Farnborough: Gregg International Publishers, 1968), p. 66.

The Loves of Ergasto (April 1705), was quickly followed by another pastoral, *The Temple of Love* (March 1706) with a score by the Italian, Giuseppe Fedeli Saggione. The author of *The Discourse* claims 'that probably it might have pass'd Muster in the *Indies*, or some other barbarous countries where musick was hardly ever heard of, but 'twas impossible it shou'd take in *London*. . . ?[78] 'The third pastoral opera to appear in as many years, *Love's Triumph* (February 1708), draws more specific commentary. P. A. Motteux adapted *Love's Triumph* from *La pastorella*, a pastoral drama by Cardinal Ottoboni. The author of *The Discourse* describes its Italian presentation as a concert in adjunct to a puppet show. He then describes the operatic arrangement of this piece by Valentino for the English stage:

This Musick being some time after brought into *England*, it came into Signior *Val[entin]o*'s Head to put it on the Stage; without considering it was Originally Design'd to be Sung in a Room, with the parts in the Singers Hands, and not to be Perform'd off hand on a Theatre; and since the Styles proper for the Chamber and the Stage are perfectly different, it was impossible it cou'd have any good Effect; besides this, he left out almost all the Recitative, and added a great number of Noisie Airs, that seemed to vie with each other which shou'd be loudest; to these he join'd chorus's and dances in abundance, after the *French* Fashion; insomuch that this pastoral was perfectly changed from its former Being and that soft Milk which nourishes the happy Shepherds on the fertile *Arcadian* Plains, grew hard and sower, and so curdled in the Stomachs of those that Tasted it, that they were Surfeited with the first Meal, and dar'd not venture a second time on such disagreeable unwholsome Food.[79]

The criticisms presented by this author form a fascinating commentary on the national forms taken by the pastoral at the beginning of the eighteenth century.

The Italian pastoral by Ottoboni would surely have reflected Arcadian principles whether or not it originated in that Academy. It is even possible that Handel heard or knew of this composition. The original score was diminutive, 'Design'd to be sung in a room' in the style 'proper for the chamber.'[80] It was not acted; probably none of Handel's Italian pastorals were either.

---

[78] Ibid.

[79] Ibid., p. 74.

[80] Each of this opera's three acts was set by a different composer: Act i by Carlo Cesarini, Act ii by Giannino (Giovanni detta del Violone), and Act iii by Giovanni Battista Bononcini, with additions by Alessandro Scarlatti. Although such collaboration implies a large scope, the extant arias (BL add. 22101) from this opera illustrate the Italian pastoral style. There are in all only twenty-eight arias (divided 12–8–8). About a third of these relate to the monothematic style of the Italian pastoral.

7*

In adapting this fragile pastoral to the stage, Valentino disregarded its essential nature, rooted in the Italian pastoral convention. He added 'noisie airs' and 'chorus's and dances in abundance'. Thus 'this pastoral was perfectly chang'd from its former being.' The mismatch of styles caused the opera's failure. 'This is an instance of the nice taste of the English, who cou'd not endure an *Italian* piece *Frenchefied* as this was. . . .'[81]

Like the Italian pastoral, the style and size of the English pastoral was diminutive. It included the use of chorus and dance, rarely as a spectacular addition, but as an integrated element, essential and natural to the portrayal of the shepherdly life. The active ensemble participated as well in the larger German pastoral form. Although Hunold emphasized the more formal and celebratory aspects of the pastoral, he implied the importance of integration and relevance in the use of ensembles. On the other hand, *Love's Triumph* 'being stuff'd out with dance and chorus, after the *French* fashion, was so disrelish'd by the audience, that the second night of its representation, the whole town in a manner forsook it.'[82]

The large and contemporary group of prominent English essayists did not let this almost annual failure of a pastoral opera go unnoticed. Their wit and writing in such periodicals as the *Tatler*, *Guardian*, *Spectator*, and *Rambler* had become the 'indicators of good taste in literature and the arts.'[83] When the season approached in early March of 1710, Richard Steele placed a wonderfully sarcastic notice in the *Tatler*.

Advertisements.
To all Gentlemen, Ladies, and Others, that
delight in soft lines.

These are to give notice, that the proper time of the year for writing pastorals now drawing near, there is a stage-coach settled from the One Bell in the Strand to Dorchester, which sets out twice a week, and passes through Basingstoke, Sutton, Stockbridge, Salisbury, Blandford, and so to Dorchester, over the finest downs in England. At all of which places, there are accommodations of spreading beeches, beds of flowers, turf seats, and purling streams, for happy swains; and thunderstruck oaks, and left-handed ravens, to foretell misfortunes to those that please to be wretched; with all other necessaries for pensive passion.

---

[81] Raguenet, *Comparison*, p. 8, n. 6.
[82] Ibid., p. 8, n. 7.
[83] Bonamy Dobrée, *English Literature in the Early Eighteenth Century: 1700–1740*, Vol. vii of *The Oxford History of English Literature*, edited by F. P. Wilson and Bonamy Dobrée, 12 vols (Oxford: Clarendon Press, 1959), p. 76.

And for the convenience of such whose affairs will not permit them to leave this town, at the same place they may be furnished, during the season, with opening buds, flowering thyme, warbling birds, sporting lambkins, and fountain water, right and good, and bottled on the spot, by one sent down on purpose.[84]

The essayists' most important contribution to pastoral criticism depended not so much on opera *per se* as on an important contemporary controversy concerning the true literary form of this genre. This nevertheless had its effect on operatic taste and production.

The close publication of two sets of pastoral poetry – one in a realistic, rustic style by Ambrose Philips (1708), the other in the classical, Arcadian style by Alexander Pope (1709) – had instigated the arguments. 'The Pope – Philips quarrel over the proper criteria for pastoral was one of the most famous and fierce literary disputes of the eighteenth century: it focuses for us the whole question of what traditions a poet should properly employ in writing about the country, and in what way it is proper for him to employ them?'[85] The essayists, Richard Steele, Joseph Addison, and Thomas Tickell, lined up behind Philips. The men who would later form the Scriblerus Club,[86] John Arbuthnot, Jonathan Swift, and John Gay (among others), supported their colleague, Pope. Notably, both factions in this controversy condemned Guarini's *Il pastor fido*.

The rationalists turned their backs on both masters of the Italian Renaissance pastoral. Thomas Tickell set forth the main tenets of this critique in four *Guardian* papers.[87]

The Italians were the first amongst the moderns that fell into pastoral writing. It is observed, that the people of this nation are very profound and abstruse in their poetry. . . . There are two pastoral plays in this language, which they boast of as the most elegant performances in poetry that the latter ages have produced, the *Aminta* of Tasso, and Guarini's *Il Pastor Fido*. In these the names of the persons are indeed pastoral, and the sylvan gods, the dryads, and the satyrs, appointed with the equipage of antiquity; but neither the language, sentiments, passions or designs, [are] like those of the pretty

[84] *The Tatler*, ed. by George A. Aitken (London: Duckworth and Co., 1899), iii, No. 143 (9 March, 1709–10), pp. 157–8.
[85] Patricia Meyer Spacks, *John Gay* (New York: Twayne Publishers, Inc., 1965), p. 30.
[86] This association was 'formed in 1714 . . . to combat pedantry and the abuses of learning' (William Rose Benét, *The Reader's Encyclopedia*, (New York: Thomas Y. Crowell Co., 1965, p. 909).
[87] *The Guardian* (London: Jones and Co., 1829), no. 22 (6 April 1713); No. 23 (7 April 1713); No. 28 (13 April 1713); and No. 30 (15 April 1713).

triflers in Virgil and Theocritus. . . . Whoever can bear these, may be assured he hath no taste for pastoral.[88]

Tickell concludes by recommending England 'as a proper scene for pastoral'. Thus, habits, customs, and climate should be Anglicized. 'By the same rule, the difference of the soil, of fruits, and flowers, is to be observed.' Classical mythology should bow to 'our own rustical superstition of hob-thrushes, fairies, goblins and witches'. 'It is easy to be observed that these rules are drawn from what our countrymen Spenser and Philips have performed in this way.'[89]

Although the strict neo-classicists based their theory on the pastorals of the Italian Renaissance, they usually separated the achievements of Tasso and Guarini, accepting only the work of the former.[90] Thinking about writing a pastoral drama, Pope stated, 'I should certainly displease all those who are charm'd with *Guarini* and *Bonarelli*, and imitate *Tasso* not only in the simplicity of his thoughts, but in that of the *Fable* too.'[91] Pope found fault with Guarini's baroque sensibilities; he condemned his use of 'wit', 'conceit', and 'intrigue'. Only in Tasso did he find 'a certain majesty in simplicity which is far above all the quaintness of wit.'

When Handel came to compose *Il pastor fido* for England in 1712, the antecedents were devastating. Thus, it is unnecessary to say that there was 'more than a touch of cabal in the opera's failure.'[92] Guarini's pastoral was condemned on all sides. Previous operatic pastorals in 1705, 1706, and 1708 had failed miserably. The mismatching of Italian and French styles was condemned; nevertheless, Handel's strict Italian pastoral fared no better. In the Italian style, the English expected grand opera. Whereas *Love's Triumph* had been 'stuff'd out' too much, *Il pastor fido* was too little. 'Ye opera was short.' Burney's critique shows a better understanding of international style than Colman's one-liner: 'In the first place, it was a *pastoral* drama, in

---

[88] Ibid., No. 28, p. 42.

[89] Ibid., No. 30, pp. 44–45.

[90] In the 'Neo-classicism' of the Italian Arcadian academy, the line was drawn *after* Guarini but before Marino. (See Chapt. II.) The English neo-classicists follow the French lead of Rapin and Fontenelle in condemning Guarini's pastoral. An excellent exposition of these viewpoints appears in Congleton, *Theories*.

[91] Nicolas J. Perella, 'Pope's Judgment of the *Pastor Fido* and a Case of Plagiarism,' *Philological Quarterly*, xl (1961), p. 446.

[92] Chisholm, 'English Origins', p. 653.

which simplicity was propriety.'[93] Yet even he is undone by the opera's tedium. Throughout his discussion Burney uses the words 'short', 'trivial', 'plain', and 'common'. He writes, for example, 'act second contains nine songs, three of which are short and inconsiderable.'[94] Finally, Burney, for all his attempts to give a good review, concludes, '[Handel's *Il pastor fido*], upon the whole, is inferior in solidarity and invention to almost all his other dramatic productions.'[95]

The pastoral form to which English audiences were accustomed was highly varied and quite dramatic. Although it might be termed 'simple' in relation to the elaborate court masque from which it derived, a better word would be 'direct'. Certainly it was short. In the beginning of the eighteenth century the pastoral 'masque' appeared most regularly as an afterpiece to a non-musical dramatic presentation. Sometimes, such as the use of *Dido and Aeneas* in a production of Shakespeare's *Measure for Measure* in 1700, these pastorals were broken up and placed piecemeal throughout a spoken drama. In this way the separate trends of the dramatic opera and the theatre masque briefly converged. However, these little pastoral masques, directly descendent from *Dido and Aeneas*, never lost their dramatic continuity. They never degenerated into beautiful but unrelated episodes, like the masques from Purcell's *Fairy Queen*. When used as interludes, they functioned not as spectacle but as a unified subplot, often with comic intent. On rare occasions, the pastoral masque was still performed alone as a single entity. But regardless of its manner of performance, as interlude, end-piece, or entity – and *Dido and Aeneas* was variously performed each way – the masque remained the only pastoral type in the years before *Il pastor fido* which was successful on the English stage.

THE PASTORAL MASQUE IN ENGLAND AT THE BEGINNING OF THE EIGHTEENTH CENTURY

In the first decade of the eighteenth century London watched as four different types of operatic productions vied with one another. Each type had its faction. First there was the Italian import. Initially sung in translation, the earliest to appear was *Arsinoe* (1705) by Stanzani, translated by Motteux. The next step was taken in 1706 with *Camilla*, composed by A. M. Bononcini, which was sung half in English, half in Italian. That is, the various parts were divided among English- and Italian-

---

[93] Burney, *History*, II, p. 684.
[94] Ibid., p. 682.
[95] Ibid., p. 684.

speaking performers. By 1710, and perhaps earlier, these operas were entirely given over to Italian composers, librettists, and artists. G. Bononcini's *Almahide* (1710) is usually credited (or denounced) as the first on the evidence of a statement by Burney: 'This was the first opera performed in England, *wholly in Italian and by Italian singers.*'[96] Although the music critics (such as Burney) and essayists joined in railing against this rude import, they were to lose the battle. The public liked Italian heroic opera. Handel produced *Rinaldo* (1711) on the crest of a wave.

The second type of operatic composition was thrown up in direct competition. This was an English opera in the Italian practice. The most famous example is *Rosamund* (1707) by Joseph Addison and Thomas Clayton. The failure of this movement can be attributed to a lack of expertise on the part of English artists compared with the skilled Italian artisans who overran and conquered the British Isle. Burney is definitive on this matter.

But, to judges of music, nothing more need be said of Mr. Addison's abilities to decide concerning the comparative degrees of national excellence in the art, and the merit of particular masters, than his predilection for the productions of Clayton, and insensibility to the force and originality of Handel's compositions in *Rinaldo*, with which every real judge and lover of music seems to have been captivated.

This opera, in spite of all its poetical merit, and the partiality of a considerable part of the nation for English music and English singing, as well as fervent wish to establish this elegant species of music in our country without the assistance of foreigners, after supporting with great difficulty only three representations, was laid aside and never again performed to the same music.[97]

The third type was represented by a small but vocal group who demanded not a 'nationalized' Italian opera, but a continuation of the 'true' English operatic genre – the dramatic opera. There were revivals of the Purcellian models, and in 1699, Motteux added his own adaptation of Fletcher's *The Island Princess*, set by Jeremiah Clarke, Richard Leveridge, and Daniel Purcell. One supporter of this solution, John Dennis, published a pamphlet entitled, *An Essay on the Opera's After the Italian Manner, Which are About to be Established on the English Stage With Some Reflections on the Damage Which They May Bring to the Publick* (1706).

Dennis feared that the 'soft and effeminate' Italian music would soften the natural English heroic temperament. He called for England to claim victory in the cultural war on the homefront as resolutely as

[96] Ibid., p. 664.
[97] Ibid., p. 658.

she did in political wars on foreign soil. Although he suspected all music, Dennis admitted the likelihood of its continued existence and thus decried what he considered the worst. 'This small treatise is only levell'd against those opera's which are entirely Musical; for those which are Drammatical may be partly defended by the Examples of the ancients.'[98] Throughout the treatise, however, the tone taken is that of procuring a cure rather than a preventative. Of the four operatic types, this was the only one not through-composed. It did not survive the decade.

The fourth type, the English pastoral masque, was most heavily represented. Motteux's *Mars and Venus* (1696), composed by Godfrey Finger and John Eccles, was mounted three times as an afterpiece (with two different plays) in 1704. The same author's *Acis and Galatea* (1701), composed by Eccles, was heard fourteen times between 1702 and 1709 as an endpiece to twelve different plays.

Pastoral masques continued to be the only indigenous English operatic work thoroughly set to music. That they now served as interludes or end-pieces to spoken drama indicates at once their heritage in smaller dramatic masques of the Caroline era and their continued low profile in English musical history. The only self-standing productions had been for private functions, but the use of Purcell's *Dido and Aeneas* in this era as an interlude and afterpiece emphasizes the similar contemporary conception of all the examples. The libretto of *Mars and Venus* (with prologue and three acts) lends additional credence to the theory of a continued tradition. The format of the prologue is typical of the libretto in general.

> Overture: 'Symphony of trumpets, kettledrums, violins, and hautbois'
> Instrumental Entry Music
> *Erato*: solo with choral repetition
> 1st attendant: solo
> 'Ritornel of Flutes'
> 2nd attendant: solo
> 'Ritornel of violins'
> duet of two other attendants
> 'Ritornel of violins'
> *Erato*: solo I
>   solo II
> 'Ritornel of violins'
> *Thalia*: solo
> 'Ritornel'

---

[98] Dennis, 'Preface' in *Essay*, p. [1]. The 'Ancients' seem unlimited in their ability to legitimatize modern artistic practices.

Terpsichore: solo
'To treble the pleasures,
With regular measures,
   My train shall advance:
Some joyn in a chorus;
While gayly before us,
Some joyn in a dance'
'Ritornel'
GRAND CHORUS
   'While the Grand Chorus is performing, there is an
entry of Dancing-masters. . . .'

Like the examples from the seventeenth century, this masque section
opens with instrumental music followed by a dramatic chorus with
solo. The centre of the prologue is filled with vocal solos and duets with
various instrumental ensembles. The entire section closes with a
Grand Choral Finale which accompanies a ballet. The dance element,
at one point integral to the form, had remained after Purcell completely subservient to the vocal. Although *Mars and Venus* was never
performed as a self-standing entity, its relationship to the earlier
masques is strong. This is equally true in the only masque of the
decade intended to stand alone, *The Judgment of Paris*. As might be
expected, the particulars of its composition were somewhat unusual.

On 21 March 1700 the *London Gazette* printed the notice of a
contest: 'Several persons of quality having for the encouragement of
musick advanced 200 guineas to be distributed in four prizes . . . to
each master as shall be judged to compose the best.'[99] The composers
entering were given William Congreve's *The Judgment of Paris*. It was
surely no coincidence that a contest in 1700 purporting to encourage
the English composition of dramatic music used a pastoral libretto.
The pastoral masque was the only healthy English musical dramatic
form.

The winning scores were by John Weldon, John Eccles, Daniel
Purcell, and Godfrey Finger. 'Walsh published two of them – those of
Eccles and Purcell – in full score, a sign of public interest very rare in
that period.'[100] Performances were quickly mounted.[101]

March 1701:	Eccles
March 1701:	Finger
May 1701:	Weldon
December 1702:	Purcell

[99] Stoddard Lincoln, 'A Congreve Masque', *MT*, cxiii (1972), p. 1078.
[100] Dean, *Oratorio*, p. 154.
[101] For detailed information on performances in this period see Van Lennep, *et al.*, *The London Stage*, ii, No. 1.

After those initial performances, however, the compositions were never again produced independently:

                January 1704:   Weldon at a concert
                February 1704: Weldon at a concert
                March 1705:   ?   in *King of Portugal*
                March 1706:   Eccles in *The Provok'd Wife*
                April 1706:   Eccles in *The Fatal Marriage*

Perhaps due to the popularity of these pastoral masques, theatre managers attempted to mount pastoral opera. However, the productions resulted in total failure. The one person closely connected with both ventures was Pierre Motteux, author of *Mars and Venus*, author of *The Temple of Love* (1706), and translator of *Love's Triumph* (1708). Motteux also represented the dramatic opera with his adaptation (1699) of *The Island Princess* by Fletcher.

Born in France in 1663, Motteux did not emigrate to England until he was twenty-two. Although his French background may have been influential in his frequent choice of pastoral texts, Motteux was explicitly searching for an acceptable path to an indigenous English opera. In the epilogue to *The Temple of Love* (1708), he complains that contemporary productions

> Get cloaths, tho' the Actors with half-pay dispense,
> Get scenes, get Whims, get anything – but Sense.
> Our Author, who stood by, thought this unkind,
> And tho' 'tis hard, wou'd strive a way to find,
> To treat your Ear, yet not disgust your Mind,
> Too much the *English* Fair in wit abound,
> To bear with Dulness for the sake of sound.

For the most part, Motteux's efforts failed. But his attempts may have had a lasting effect on English operatic efforts. In the first decade of the eighteenth century dramatic opera reached a dead end. Attempts at translating or imitating the Italian operatic librettos were unsuccessful. Tne English pastoral masques, however, were popular, and their very existence may have suggested a path opposite the imported Italian heroic opera. Their subjects differed, as did their styles. English composers could compete on their own turf, so to speak, without setting themselves up for direct comparisons. By the second decade of the eighteenth century this dichotomy became clear. Italian opera in the *opera seria* convention was heroic; English opera, based on the masque tradition, was pastoral.

Congreve, author of *The Judgment of Paris*, continued to be active in the musical-dramatic milieu of the early eighteenth century. In 1702 he and Eccles, one of the contest's winners, collaborated on an Ode for

St. Cecilia's Day, *The Hymn to Harmony*. By 1703, he and John Vanbrugh were thinking of opening a theatre in the Haymarket. The premiere actually occurred in 1705 with *The Loves of Ergasto*. There is reason to believe, however, that Congreve had hoped to open the theatre with a work of his own.[102] This must have been *Semele*. Probably the music, again by Eccles, was not completed in time. By the end of 1707 when it announced that the finished opera was 'ready to be practic'd', Congreve was no longer attached to the Haymarket and the operatic situation had changed.[103] *Semele*, the 'first' English opera, was never produced.

In the same year as *Il pastor fido*, John Hughes and J. E. Galliard produced what may have been the last attempt at English opera for more than a decade and a half. Like the others, *Calypso and Telemachus* was a pastoral. Also like the others, it failed.

Best known to modern Handelians as the author of the little cantata *Venus and Adonis* (1711?), generally considered the first English text set by the composer,[104] Hughes was a prominent member of the literary group called the Scriblerus Club. Formed about 1713 when the arguments concerning pastoral theory were in their heyday, and including in its membership Hughes, Pope, Congreve, Jonathan Swift, John Arbuthnot, and John Gay, the club concentrated much of its energy on the fray. Firm believers in the classical pastoral, as written and discussed by Pope and written by Hughes and Congreve, the Scriblerians took two paths. First, they buttressed their own stance by continuing to write classical-mythological pastorals. Second, they ridiculed the pastorals of their opponents.

Throughout this war, from the inception of the Scriblerus Club to the production of Handel's *Acis and Galatea* (1718) at the Cannons residence of the Duke of Chandos, the composer and the Scriblerians were in close association. From 1712 to 1714 their activity centred on the London house of Richard Boyle, Lord of Burlington; afterwards, at Cannons. During this time, when these were apparently his only two places of residence, Handel assimilated the English musical style. *Acis and Galatea* stands as the culmination both of this study and of Handel's association with the leading literary figures of England.

Because of the continued importance of the classical-mythological pastoral in English music drama, the direction of the battle about

---

[102] Stoddard Lincoln, 'The First Setting of Congreve's *Semele*', *ML*, xciv (1963), p. 105. Handel was to set an adaptation of this libretto in 1744.

[103] Ibid., pp. 105–6.

[104] See the correspondence in Deutsch, *Handel*, pp. 44–5. In both arias, 'Dear Adonis' and 'Transporting Joy', of this little pastoral cantata written even before *Il pastor fido*, Handel not surprisingly uses the strict monothematic aria form of the Italian pastoral.

pastoral theory had often depended on operatic developments. For example, when *Calypso and Telemachus* failed, the proponents of the classical pastoral retreated to the smaller and more popular masque.

In 1715 Colley Cibber and John Pepusch collaborated on a production of the story of *Venus and Adonis*. It was produced twenty-two times (always appended to a play) within a year. Cibber and Pepusch also collaborated on *Myrtillo* (1715). Hughes and Pepusch produced *Apollo and Daphne* in 1716. As Dean writes, 'Colley Cibber's preface to *Venus and Adonis* . . . leaves no doubt that the movement of 1715–18 was a conscious act in the operatic war.'[105]

The following entertainment is an attempt to give the town a little good music in a language they understand: For no theatrical performance can be absolutely good, that is not proper; and how can we judge of its propriety, when we know not one word of the voice's meaning? . . . And thus, by slavishly giving up our language to the despotic power of sound only, we are so far from establishing theatrical music in *England*, that the very exhibition or silence of it seems entirely to depend upon the arrival or absence of some eminent foreign performer. . . . And (though the insolent charms of the *Opera* seem to be above it) why should we suppose that a little plain sense should do music any more harm, than virtue does a beautiful woman? . . . It is therefore hoped, that this undertaking if encourag'd, may in time reconcile music to the *English* tongue. . . . And at worst, it will be an easier matter to instruct two or three performers in tolerable *English* than to teach a whole nation *Italian*.[106]

The beginnings of this 'movement' may be traced back to Motteux, then to Purcell and Tate, and finally to John Milton in his *Arcadia* and *Comus*.

THE ENGLISH APPRENTICESHIP

The text of Handel's *Acis and Galatea* (1718) comes naturally out of this tradition. Written, composed, and performed privately at Cannons, where Pepusch was master of music, the libretto for the masque was a joint effort of the Scriblerians. Attributed mainly to Gay, both Hughes and Pope had a hand in it as well. The chorus 'Wretched lovers' and the trio 'The flocks shall leave the mountain' are adaptations from Pope's published works, the latter from his pastorals.[107] Hughes contributed 'Would you gain the tender creature?' and it is apparent

---

[105] *Oratorio*, pp. 155–6.
[106] 'The Preface' to *Venus and Adonis* in Colley Cibber, *The Dramatic Works* (London: J. Rivington and Sons, 1777), v, 213–14.
[107] Dean, *Oratorio*, p. 161.

that many of the other texts derive specifically from his *Apollo and Daphne*.[108]

The main contributor was John Gay. Although glossed over by most modern literary historians, *Acis and Galatea* represents an important step in Gay's development of the pastoral genre. Before its composition, Gay had thrown all of his efforts toward the pastoral vein into ridiculing the pastoral realists; his most famous burlesque had followed quickly upon the heels of the pastoral arguments presented in the *Guardian* in 1713. *The Shepherd's Week* (1714) was intended to illustrate the hilarious result of following the English realists' own rules.

The title and the character's names, Cuddy, Hobbinol, Diggon, etc., point to the first author of an English pastoral, Edmund Spenser. And although Gay does not hesitate to make fun of one long dead,

Yet further of many of Maister *Spencer*'s Eclogues it may be observed; though Months they be called, of the said Months therein, nothing is specified; wherein I have also esteemed him worthy mine Imitation,[109]

he means more to burlesque his contemporaries, Thomas Tickell and Ambrose Philips.

Other poet travailing in this plain High-way of Pastoral know I none. Yet, Certes, such it behoveth a Pastoral to be, as Nature in the Country affordeth; and the Manners also meetly copied from the rustical Folk therein. In this also my Love to my native Country *Britain* much pricketh me forward to describe aright the Manners of our own honest and laborious Ploughmen, in no wise sure more unworthy a *British* Poet's imitation, than those of *Sicily* or *Arcadie*. . . . Thou wilt not find my Shepherdesses idly piping on oaten Reeds, but milking the Kine, tying up the Sheaves, or if the Hogs are astray driving them to their Styes.[110]

Gay achieves a feeling in *The Shepherd's Week* very close in spirit to the pastoral burlesque in *As You Like It* written a century before. But Gay was not to stop here. Taking the next logical step in his *Trivia* (January 1716), he chose to sing not of native shepherdesses 'milking the kine' but of the natives of London itself. After all, if it is realism that is desired, if Arcadia and Sicily are to be abandoned, then why choose the country as the object of one's panegyric? In writing of the 'beauties' of city life, Gay makes his realism strike home. As in most pastorals, Gay writes of the weather:

---

[108] Ibid., pp. 157–8.
[109] John Gay, 'The Proeme' in *The Shepherd's Week* (London: Ferd. Burleigh, 1714), p. [iv].
[110] Ibid., pp. [i–iii].

When sleep is first disturbed by morning cries;
From sure prognosticks learn to know the skies,
Lest you of rheums and coughs at night complain;
Surpriz'd in dreary fogs, or driving rain.
When suffocating mists obscure the morn,
Let thy worst wig, long us'd to storms, be worn;
This knows the powder'd footman, and with care,
Beneath his flapping hat secures his hair,
Be thou, for every season, justly drest,
Nor brave the piercing frost with open breast;
And when the bursting clouds a deluge pour,
Let thy *Surtout* defend the drenching show'r.[111]

and of the seasons:

Winter my theme confines, whose nitry wind
Shall crust the slooby mire, and kennels bind;
She bids the snow descend in flaky sheets,
And in her hoary mantle cloath the streets,
Let not the virgin tread these slippery roads,
The gathering fleece the hollow patten loads,
But if thy footstep slide with clotted frost,
Strike off the breaking balls against the post.[112]

Pastoral ridicule proved a fertile vein for Gay. After *The Shepherd's Week* and *Trivia*, the *Town Eclogues* appeared in 1720. More importantly, however, the *Trivia* were predecessors of *The Beggar's Opera* (1728). Swift brought up the idea, after the success of *Trivia*, in a letter (August 1716) to Pope: 'I believe further that the pastoral ridicule is not exhausted, and that a porter, foot-man, or chair-man's pastoral might do well. Or what do you think of a Newgate pastoral, among the whores and thieves there?'[113]

In an attempt to illustrate the superiority of the Graeco-Roman pastoral, however, ridicule of the realistic pastoral represented only half of the picture. The other, of course, was the penning of proper, classical pastorals. Collaborating on the pastoral masque, *Acis and Galatea*, allowed the Scriblerians to work with the one form in which the Classical pastoral had succeeded. It is possible, however, that this exercise was intended as a warm-up for the production of a true dramatic pastoral. In 1720 Gay finished such a work. 'Since the summer of 1718. . . . Gay had been fascinated by his reading in foreign pastorals,

---

[111] John Gay, *Trivia* i: 121–32, in *The Poetical, Dramatic, and Miscellaneous Works of John Gay* (London: Edward Jeffery, 1745), ii, p. 139.
[112] Gay, *Trivia* ii, pp. 319–26, in Ibid., p. 162.
[113] Quoted in Dobrée, *English Literature*, p. 132.

in the novels of Cervantes, and in the plays of Tasso and Guarini, and his enthusiasm for these stories was now to bear fruit in a new pastoral tragedy, *Dione*.'[114] It is clear from the prologue that Gay feared for his pastoral.

> When Paris on the three his judgment pass'd;
> I hope, you'll own the shepherd show'd his taste:
>
> . . . . . .
>
> Yet still methinks our author's fate I dread,
> Were it not safer beaten paths to tread
> Of tragedy, than o'er wide heaths to stray,
> And seeking strange adventures lose his way?
> No trumpet's clangour makes his heroine start,
> And tears the soldier from her bleeding heart;
> He, foolish bard! nor pomp nor show regards.
> Without the witness of a hundred guards
> His lovers sigh their vows. – If sleep should take ye,
> He has no battle, no loud drum to wake ye.
> What, no such shifts? there's danger in't, 'tis true;
> Yet spare him, as he gives you something new.[115]

Indeed the play was never performed, although it was printed twice in the *Collected Poems*, in 1720 and 1731, and twice published separately in 1733 and 1763.[116] Both *Dione* and *Acis and Galatea* followed the fates of their predecessors. The pastoral drama was unpopular, the pastoral masque a success.

Like the earlier theatre masques of Blow and Purcell, *Acis and Galatea* (HW 3) depends on the chorus as a structural force. In the interim productions set by Eccles and Pepusch, the chorus had not been so used; but these works were generally not intended to stand alone. While keeping alive the pastoral masque tradition, they did nothing to further it. This function was left for Handel. In circumstances very similar to those in the seventeenth century which called for a private self-standing production, Handel succeeded.

Originally performed in one act, *Acis and Galatea* is naturally

---

[114] William Henry Irving, *John Gay: Favorite of the Wits* (Durham, N. C.: Duke University Press, 1940), p. 175.

[115] John Gay, *The Poetical Works of John Gay*, ed., with a life and notes, by John Underhill (London: Lawrence and Bullen, 1893), ii, p. 41.

[116] Irving, *Gay*, p. 177. Interestingly, Irving notes that the play was translated into German by J. O. P. Müchler and published around the middle of the century. The Germans had continued to cultivate the classical pastoral, both foreign and native. The 1733 printing in England was surely occasioned by the musical setting of *Dione* by John Lampe in that year. (See Chapter VI.)

divided by its choruses into three parts.[117] The first chorus sets the idyllic pastoral scene.

> Oh, the pleasure of the plains
> Happy nymphs and happy swains,
> Harmless, merry, free and gay,
> Dance and sport the hours away.

Following this is an exposition of those 'happy nymphs and swains' in five *da capo* arias: (1) Galatea looking for Acis, (2) Acis looking for Galatea, (3) Damon counselling Acis, (4) Acis finding Galatea, and (5) Galatea finding Acis. The culmination of this exposition (one can hardly call it action) is expressed in the duet of Acis and Galatea, 'Happy We'.

In the second part, the chorus again signals the mood, which now changes abruptly.

> Wretched lovers! fate has past
> This sad decree: no joy shall last.

The entrance of the villain-monster Polyphemus creates this sudden disruption. There again follow five *da capo* arias: (1) Polyphemus praising Galatea's beauty, (2) Polyphemus denouncing Galatea's coldness, (3) Damon counselling Polyphemus, (4) Acis denouncing the suit of Polyphemus and (5) Damon counselling Acis. The culmination of this second exposition of feelings is expressed in the trio 'The flocks shall leave the mountains'. The only 'action' in the entire pastoral occurs at the end of the trio when Polyphemus puts an end to his rival with the 'massy ruin'.

After the death of Acis there follows the third part which may be compared to the Grand Choral Finales in the masques of Blow and Purcell. 'Mourn all ye muses' for full chorus is followed by 'Must I my Acis still bemoan' which begins as a strict air for Galatea. After what appears to be the first statement of the text, the chorus interrupts with consolation, and finally advice. In 'Heart, the seat of soft delight' Galatea transforms the dead Acis into a 'bubbling fountain'. Handel toys with the listener's expectation of the *da capo* form, but does not

---

[117] Handel's autograph from the Cannons period is through-composed without the chorus 'Happy We'. In revivals the work, often with additions, was often presented in three acts. The chorus following the duet ('Happy We') is presumed to have been added in 1739, the year when Gay's authorship was first publicly recognized. From this date, the English *Acis* was generally performed in two acts with the chorus ('Happy We') making a firm ending to Part I. See William C. Smith, '*Acis and Galatea*' in *Concerning Handel: His Life and Works* (London: Cassell and Co., Ltd., 1948), pp. 197–268 and Dean, 'History and Text of *Acis and Galatea*' in *Oratorio*, pp. 171–9. In editions of Gay's works, which include *Acis* only after 1739, the pastoral always appears in two acts with the choral 'appendage' to the first. Without a libretto or literary edition from the Cannons period, it is impossible to assess the original *literary* form of the masque and Handel's hand, if any, in altering it.

exactly fulfil it, a theme used both in the ritornello and voice part (but
not the head motive) returns only to be extended and developed, and
thus gives meaning to the action and words of Galatea, 'through the
plains he joys to rove, murm'ring still his gentle love'. Acis (like the
A section) will not return, but the fountain will continually express his
love (its motives). In fact, the 'murm'ring' in an accompanimental
figure continues throughout the following and final chorus, 'Galatea,
dry thy tears'.[118] The last two lines of text in this chorus repeat the
last two lines of the air, quoted above. At this textual repetition Handel
brings the chorus to a recapitulation of its first theme originally sung to
'Galatea, dry thy tears,/Acis now a god appears!' and alters the
'murm'ring' in the accompaniment to an exact reproduction of that in
the air. The air and the chorus, therefore, function as a unit, the finale
of the chorus giving the 'da capo' to the solo. The simultaneity of these
recapitulations creates a strong conclusion to the masque.

Throughout the masque Handel manipulates his compositional
practice to underscore dramatic points. In the first exposition, which
fixes the nature of the relationship between Acis and Galatea, Handel
uses only the *da capo* form. This is a throw-back to the Italian pastoral
which emphasized regularity and consistency as musical and Arcadian
virtues. In the first air, 'Hush ye pretty warbling choir', Handel
further relies on that mode by writing a melodic repetition of the main
theme from the A section at the opening of the B section.[119]

Ex. 22

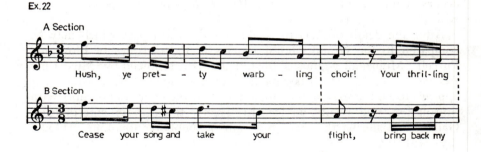

---

[118] Chrysander's edition has omitted nineteen bars of this last chorus which are given in:
Rudolf Steglich, 'Der Schlusschor von Händels *Acis und Galatea*, Ergänzung und Analyse',
HJ, iii (1930), pp. 154–56.

[119] In a moment of misguided enthusiasm, Lang (*Handel*, p. 274) writes, 'But "Hush ye
pretty warbling choir" is English pastoral *in excelsis*.' Not only is the style in itself wholly
Italian, but this aria represents one of the few cases in *Acis* in which borrowing plays a part.
'Hush ye pretty warbling choir' arrives in the English masque after appearances in *Delirio
amoroso* (1707) and *Aci, Galatea e Polifemo* (1708), but originates in Keiser's (!) *Octavia*
(1705). See Dean, *Oratorio*, p. 641.

strains a-wake my pains

A - cis to my sight

The second exposition introduces the one disruptive element. Notably its introductory chorus, 'Wretched lovers', is the first movement of the masque not in *da capo* form. Furthermore, the only piece besides the first to connect melodically the two sections of the *da capo* is the final aria of this section, 'Consider fond shepherd', the last piece of pastoralism before the tragic dénouement.

Ex. 23

A Section

Con - si - der, fond shep - herd, how fleet - ing's ___ the plea-sure

B Section

The joys ___ that at - tend ___ it, by mo - ments ___ we mea-sure

The concluding trio, of course, concludes with the violent action of Polyphemus. It is not a *da capo*. Arcadia has been shattered. No movement from here to the end of the masque has a true *da capo*. Although Handel ties its use to a dramatic purpose, the prevalent use of this form in the expository sections of *Acis and Galatea* has presented a constant problem to commentators eager to emphasize the beauties and English nature of the score. 'Nevertheless the single discoverable blemish on this lovely work is its formal regularity, especially in Act I. Even where page after page is of outstanding beauty the domination of the *da capo* begins to be irksome.'[120]

However, Handel does not use the *da capo* in *Acis* in a way that

---

[120] Dean, *Oratorio*, p. 166. See also Lang, *Handel*, pp. 274–5.

reflects the *opera seria* tradition. The form represents the Arcadian mood. Although he borrows from the Italian practice, Handel moulds the musical structures to a dramatic purpose.

In a similar manner, the tonal plan of the masque serves both its structure and the drama; the opening choruses of the two parallel sections are in B♭ major as is the final chorus. B♭ major is thus the major tonality for the masque. In the first exposition Handel uses the major keys on the fifth, fourth, and second scale degrees. In the second exposition he emphasizes the minor keys on the third, sixth, and second degrees. Major tonalities are also used on the second and sixth degrees. The movements of the choral finale present a plagal cadence in the tonic key. The whole of *Acis and Galatea* may thus be diagrammed:

Arcadia Statement A:

chorus	air	air	air	air	air	duet
da capo	da capo	da capo	da capo	da capo	da capo	da capo
B♭	F	c	B♭	E♭	F	C

Disruptive Elements B:

chorus	air	air	air	air	air	trio
through	da capo	da capo	da capo	da capo	da capo	through
B♭	g	d	G	C	G	c

Choral Finale C:

Chorus	solo with chorus	air	chorus
f	F	E♭	B♭

The harmonic structure, like Handel's use of overall and individual forms, represents a dramatic concept. In *Acis*, Handel realizes his plan by picturing Arcadia not only in major but in the major scales of the tonic, subdominant, and dominant degrees. In the second part, where the atmosphere changes, he emphasizes the mediant degrees instead. Every movement in which Polyphemus takes part is in minor. When Galatea and the chorus come to an acceptable conclusion, the major tonalities on the dominant degrees return.

Although many of the elements used by Handel in *Acis and Galatea* are derived from the Italian pastoral, the impact is strictly English and issues directly from the masque tradition. Handel's composition illustrates an awareness of the same kinds of structures, dependent on a build-up toward an ensemble, culminating in a Grand Choral Finale. It telescopes the form from Purcell's two main sections to one and increases the harmonic continuity. The English nature of *Acis* is further revealed in its melodic turns and certain harmonic quirks. On such grounds E. D. Rendall develops the relationship of Handel's score with Purcellian antecedents at some length.[121] Dean suggests

[121] E. D. Rendall, 'The Influence of Henry Purcell on Handel, traced in *Acis and Galatea*', *MT* xxxvi (1895), pp. 293–6.

that Handel studied the works of Pepusch.[122] Yet there is little direct borrowing in *Acis* from any source, none from Purcell or Pepusch, and only a single case outside Handel's own works (an accompanimental figure in 'Hush ye pretty warbling choir').[123]

One can be sure, nevertheless, that during his years with the Scriblerians Handel was studying English music. He asked Hughes (see above) for English words to set (1711) and during his 'English apprenticeship' produced not only *Acis*, but *Queen Anne's Birthday Ode* (1713), *Utrecht Te deum* and *Jubilate* (1713), and the twelve *Chandos Anthems* (1717–20). The similar period with the Arcadians in Rome produced even more concrete evidence of Handel's study of national musical forms. That he succeeded in acquiring the general aura as well as specific stylistic traits of the English style, however, is probably most clear from the regularly inspired (but regularly fruitless) searches for the specific English models used in these pieces. It is also obvious from a comparison of *Acis* with the Italian pastoral *Il pastor fido* or the Neapolitan *Aci, Galatea e Polifemo* (HW 53) (1708).

In neither Italian work is there a chorus. The *da capo* form is given no dramatic meaning; its constant use is due to convention. In both Italian works the emphasis is on the high vocal ranges. In *Aci*, the young shepherd is a soprano castrato who sings above Galatea. In *Acis*, the soloists include one soprano, two tenors, and a bass. In the Italian works continuo arias appear with regularity. There are none in *Acis*. Furthermore, the humorous characterization of Polyphemus in 'I rage, I melt, I burn' is totally new, and is in complete accord with the thinking of the Scriblerians. In *Aci*, Polifemo sings typical Italian rage arias. Two short examples will suffice to show the extent of this change on the melodic characteristics of the arias. Where Polifemo is grotesque, Polyphemus is a buffoon. Polifemo is represented by melodic fragments plummeting down more than an octave and a half. The range and the awkwardness, coupled with the sheer force, of these motives present a horrific picture of the monster.

[122] Dean, *Oratorio*, pp. 158–9.
[123] Ibid., p. 641.

Ex. 24

Fra l'om - bree gl'or - ro - ri, fra l'om - bree gl'or - ro - ri far-
- fal - la con - fu - sa già spen - ta_ la_ fa - ce non
sà mai_ go-der, non_ sà mai _ go-der

On the other hand, Polyphemus becomes a pleasant bungler who
repeats himself constantly and runs in tight circles without getting
anywhere.

Ex. 25

O rud-dier than the cher-ry, o sweet-er than the
ber - ry, o rud-dier than the cher- ry, o sweet-er than the
ber - ry, o nymph more bright than moonshine night, like kindlings bright and mer-ry.

In *Acis* Handel adopts the English pastoral genre in structure (both
harmonic and formal), style, and even in characterization.

By 1718 Handel was well-versed in three different pastoral traditions. Although England was to become his permanent home, the
English pastoral mode was not to predominate in his musical corpus.
One reason for this was that Handel had never intended to commit
himself to an English style. He had planned solely to write Italian operas
for the English stage.

The one attempt Handel made to produce an Italian pastoral in England failed miserably. The experiment was never repeated. *Amadigi* (1715) which contains a distinctly pastoral atmosphere already shows modifications, discussed in detail below. By 1715, moreover, Handel had been living among the Burlington circle for two years.

Perhaps Handel might have continued to write Italian *opere serie* and English pastorals, but circumstances demanded a different solution. The German pastoral form represented an appropriate compromise. Constructed on an operatic scale, it depended on a basically Italianate (but not necessarily pastoral) style. In format, however, it equalled an enlarged English pastoral, and the structural foundation thus assured that it would not be simply an Italian pastoral 'stuff'd out'.

Already Handel had transferred specific stylistic elements from the Italian pastoral into the English masque. The similarity of the finished product to a miniature German pastoral must have been apparent to him. As the German and English forms depended mostly on structural elements and the Italian on stylistic elements, a combination of modes could easily be achieved. In many respects Mattheson's definition in *Der vollkommene Kapellmeister* (1739) reflects such a synthesis. Even so, Handel might not have come to this decision if his hand had not been forced. Between 1718 and 1732, he ignored the pastoral form altogether.

CHAPTER VI

Handel's Stylistic Maturity:

The Place of the Pastoral in Handel's Later Operatic Compositions

BACK TO GERMAN TRADITIONS: A SYNTHESIS

Toward the end of Handel's service for the Duke of Chandos plans were already being made to create an academy where Italian opera might be regularly performed.[1] By May, 1719, Handel had been ordered to the continent to secure the proper voices for this undertaking, and a list of the subscribers had been published. To be a subscriber, one needed to pledge £200, the amount of one share. The largest sum pledged, £1,000, or five shares, was made by the first governor of the academy, Thomas Holles, Duke of Newcastle, and also by 'James Duke of Chandois', and 'Richard Earl of Burlington'. Even John Arbuthnot, Esq., pledged one share. This Italian venture, then, created no obvious break in Handel's relations with his English patrons and colleagues. Perhaps the failure of English opera had led them to the second step of at least assuring themselves that the Italian opera would be the best available. Handel's association with the academy gave them that assurance.

Radamisto (27 April 1720) was the first in a series of fourteen operas Handel wrote for the Royal Academy of Music in the eight years of its existence. This was a period of great creativity for Handel. With a singleness of purpose rarely surpassed he wrote one beautiful work after another, often two in a year. Handel borrowed infrequently in this period; the quality of his musical invention remained consistently high. None of these operas is a 'pasticcio' of earlier works, such as *Il pastor fido*, and during this time Handel arranged only one pasticcio out of another composer's work.[2]

---

[1] See Deutsch, *Handel*, pp. 83–6.

[2] *Elpidia* (1725) was Handel's first arrangement of another composer's entire opera. The libretto was by Zeno, the music principally by Vinci. Handel added new recitatives. See Reinhard Strohm, 'Handels Pasticci', *Analecta Musicologica*, XIV (1974), 208–67, and Deutsch, *Handel*, p. 181.

During this period Handel was in his preferred element. The management of the academy was at times a ticklish business, but Handel was given the opportunity to write operas, to vanquish his colleagues Bononcini and Ariosti, and to enjoy a large personal success. The reception of the first two operas Handel wrote for England may well have directed this present course. The operas for the academy are all of the heroic type; there occurs as well 'a disappearance of the magical element'.[3]

After the failure of this company in 1728 – due to a combination of financial difficulties and problems with personnel – Handel quickly went about organizing another. He must have felt that his own part in the academy represented an overwhelming success. Handel was eager to find new singers and continue with his proven formula. The early operas from this Second Academy illustrate the musical continuity which existed for Handel between these two ventures.

Lotario (1729), the first opera, was 'a throwback to the academy manner'.[4] In 1731 and 1732, Handel continued his Metastasio 'series', begun with *Siroe* (1728), with *Poro* and *Ezio. Sosarme* (1732) also revolves around the dynastic-heroic plots familiar from the earlier academy. Only *Partenope* (1730) varies this pattern. A comedy which satirizes some of the conventions of heroic opera, it nevertheless depends on that tradition for its existence. *Flavio* (1723) from the first academy is a predecessor to this kind of parody, but in this earlier instance is so lightly handled that its point has often been misunderstood.[5]

Handel's real break with the traditions of the first academy came in 1732 with the production of *Acis and Galatea* – not the Cannons version, but a new production derived from a combination of sources. This not only represented 'the first stirrings of pastoral and oratorio since the Cannons days',[6] it was the first pastoral publicly produced by Handel since 1712.

Handel's revival-revision of *Acis and Galatea* (10 June 1732) marks the beginning of a particularly active period of pastoral composition. Of the six newly composed operatic works between 1732 and 1736 all are pastoral in design. The major revision of *Il pastor fido* falls into these years as well. The reasons for Handel's sudden change of direction are many and complex. However, the immediate incentives for the first production, *Acis and Galatea*, are clear.

---

[3] Dean, *Opera*, p. 30.
[4] Ibid., p. 31.
[5] Ibid., p. 30. The chapter 'Antiheroic Operas' in *Opera*, pp. 100–22, covers a facet of Handel's operas that has been little investigated. Dean's categories, however, are not clearly drawn – especially in this discussion and that on magic operas. See below.
[6] Lang, *Handel*, p. 240.

The Cannons *Acis* had been written for a private presentation, perhaps for a special occasion. Handel seemed unaware of its public potential, and, concentrating on his operatic endeavours, allowed the score to lie fallow. Twice between its first performance and 1732, the masque had been presented as a benefit: first, in Bristol on 22 November 1727 for Nathaniel Priest, an organist; then in London at Lincoln's Inn Theatre on 26 March 1731 for Philip Rochetti, a tenor. The first performance contained only parts of the score in a concert performance; the second is presumed to have been complete and fully staged.[7] It is not clear whether or not these performances had Handel's sanction before-the-fact. Neither seems to have disturbed the composer in any way. Handel regarded the fate of fellow musicians an important concern. He was 'both an original member and generous benefactor' of the Fund for the Support of Decayed Musicians (founded 1738).[8] Furthermore, at least parts of the score, the songs (without an ascription to Handel), had been in the public domain since their publication in 1722.

In 1732, however, the situation changed. Thomas Arne, impresario and father to the composer of the same name, perhaps impressed by the Rochetti benefit in 1731, mounted an elaborate and profitable stage production of *Acis and Galatea* at the New Theatre in the Haymarket. This was in direct competition with Handel's academy at the King's (Haymarket) Theatre. The performance was generally true to the Cannons version, but divided into three acts. The first intermission came after the duet 'Happy We', the second disturbed the composer's design by breaking after the fourth aria, 'Love sounds the alarm', of the second set. However, this is not utterly destructive of the score. No other position for a break, granting the necessity of one, between the second section and the 'choral finale' could have been better. At least this choice enabled the second part to close in C, following Handel's harmonic intentions; the second and third parts to end and begin, respectively, with a concerted piece rather than recitative (which would have been the case with any other choice), and the entire finale from 'Mourn, all ye Muses' to remain both thematically and harmonically intact. To break after 'Mourn, all ye Muses', for example, would have mutilated Handel's musical concept even more than was done. Moreover, it hardly lacks drama for an 'act' which begins with the entrance of Polyphemus to end with Acis' jealous call for revenge. With the full realization that the best choice, musically and dramatically, would have been to take no break after 'Happy We', the decision made by Arne is certainly

---

[7] Comprehensive information on the chequered career of the score to *Acis* appears in Smith, '*Acis and Galatea*' in *Concerning Handel*, pp. 197–268; and Dean, '*Acis and Galatea*: History and Text' in *Oratorio*, pp. 171–90.

[8] Dean, *Oratorio*, p. 83.

not as inharmonious as it first appears.[9] At any rate the two performances, on 17 and 19 May, appear to have been publicly well-received.

Handel, generous though he might have been, did not allow his charitable nature to take precedence over his business sense. It is a preposterous situation, and one that was to occur to Handel with increasing regularity, to be put in competition with oneself.[10] Within sixteen days of the second of Arne's performances, the King's Theatre began to advertise its own production of *Acis and Galatea* fully revised by the composer. This revival, notably successful in its day, has been universally criticized since as the 'antithesis of the Cannons *Acis*', acclaimed by most as a masterpiece.[11] Consider for a moment Handel's position.

There is some thought that Handel's opera season of 1732 was financially in distress, that, in fact, it was short of a promised production.[12] Then a competitor succeeds with a pirated version of one of Handel's own compositions. Handel could not well retaliate by presenting the same piece, nor would he want to present his 'other *Acis*', the Neapolitan serenata, as it stood, remembering the failure of the Italian pastoral style in England. To write a new work would take too long, and the venture would be too risky. Handel did, then, what must have seemed the natural thing. He took his two previous compositions based on this story and blended them, using the framework of the traditional German pastoral.

Handel's synthesis of the various pastoral genres had already begun in the Cannons *Acis* with a combination of English and Italian elements. The Italian style was similarly appropriate to the German genre, as witnessed in Keiser's *L'Inganno fedele* (1714), and the German pastoral, except in dimension, resembled the English form. Furthermore, with the German pastoral in mind, Handel would not have thought the polyglot libretto for the version to be 'grotesque in its linguistic discontinuity'.[13] *Florindo* and *Daphne* had such librettos; they were common in Hamburg.

Handel derived the score for the 1732 production from two principal sources: *Aci, Galatea e Polifemo* (Naples, 1708) and *Acis and Galatea*

---

[9] See Dean, *Oratorio*, p. 183, where he, like others, emphasizes the ineptitude of this division.

[10] Handel was similarly motivated to produce *Esther* earlier in 1732 on account of a competitive and pirated production.

[11] Dean, *Oratorio*, p. 173. See also Lang, *Handel*, pp. 281–82.

[12] However, a certain amount of doubt surrounds these assertions. See Smith, *Concerning Handel*, p. 216, and Dean, *Oratorio*, p. 172.

[13] Lang, *Handel*, p. 282.

8

(Cannons, 1718). In order to make a German pastoral out of his Italian and English compositions, however, Handel enlarged the cast. *Aci* (1708) had only three characters; *Acis* (1718) has four; *Acis* (1732) has eight. This in itself provides a broader framework. Thus Handel fills out the Arcadian landscape with a new group of shepherds and shepherdesses. Their names – Clori, Filli, Sylvio, Dorindo, and Eurilla – are familiar to the student of pastoral literature. The last three had appeared in Handel's *Il pastor fido*; the first two were clearly taken from the cantata *Cor fedele* (1707), also called *Clori, Tirsi, e Fileno*. The pieces written for these characters often derive from the compositions in which their names first appear. The added soloists lend more of a pastoral background, or tableau, against which the actions of the three protagonists move. They also take over the role of Damon from the Cannons *Acis*. They give perspective.

Both of the previous scores had been set in one act. The 1732 revision had three, which were clearly delineated. Each was bounded by a set of choruses, more appropriately termed choral scenes. In the end it is the choruses which define the German pastoral form, and it is for these that Handel borrows almost exclusively from outside his preexistent Acis fund. In addition and more importantly, the choral movements present the only situations for which Handel writes wholly new material. Every act begins and ends with a chorus. Only the first and the last are taken from *Acis* (1718).

At the end of the first act, Handel borrows a duet with chorus from the *Birthday Ode* (1713). The original words,

> The day that gave great Anna birth
> Who fix'd a lasting peace on earth,

appear seven times throughout the Ode as a choral refrain, but Handel chose the only setting which includes a duet as part of the chorus. This was crucial to Handel's aim, for the German pastoral particularly emphasized scenes of interaction between the soloists and the chorus. Thus this scene replaces the private rapture of 'Happy we' in *Acis* (1718). The new words

> Love promises content only
> to him who remains faithful in his heart[14]

are sung by Acis and Galatea, then by the company at large. Handel adds to this borrowing a newly composed homophonic choral conclusion, 'Lieto esulti'.

---

[14] 'Contento sol promette Amor
A chi fedel conserva il cor.'

The second act begins with a movement for soprano and chorus from the *Brockes Passion* (1716). Here the new words depict Galatea coyly describing her total contentment.

> Galatea: Would you like to see
> 　　　　　where there is calmness,
> 　　　　　Would you like to find
> 　　　　　the seat of love?
> 　　　　　Come —
> Chorus:　Where?
> Galatea: In this breast . . .[15]

Again, however, Handel is not content with an exact borrowing, He adds a seven-measure choral finale with the text 'Jove gives a long and happy life to the faithful lover'. Polifemo's entrance, which immediately follows this optimistic declaration, dispels the reverie.

The second act ends with a newly composed chorus whose text indicates just how far the Arcadians have fallen from their innocent rejoicing in Jove's blessing. They plead with Venus for intercession. The musical form of the scene derives from the German pastoral. The outer, duplicate choral movements represent the A section of a *da capo*. The B section consists of a solo for Clori, which in itself is a *da capo* whose form derives from the dance: $\| : a : \| : b : \| \, \overset{\frown}{\|} \, c \, \|$ da capo. The composition in its entirety is reminiscent of finales in German pastorals and specifically of those in Kusser's *Erindo*.

The third act begins with another new composition, partly derived, however, from two sources: the final trio of *Clori, Tirsi, e Fileno*, 'Viver' e non amar', and the opening theme of 'Wretched lovers' in *Acis* (1718). The A section of this *da capo*, written for the eight soloists with a chorus of tenors and basses who sing in unison with Silvio and Polifemo, presents the theme from the cantata. The B section, for five-part chorus, develops the original theme against that from 'Wretched lovers'.

Handel's choice of pre-existent material for the *Acis* revision was far from haphazard. Nevertheless, the finished product has caused Handel scholars no little pain. To its continued disadvantage, the 1732 *Acis* is measured by the yardstick of the 1718 *Acis*. Two quotations will illustrate the general nature of the complaints.

---

[15] Galatea: Vuoi veder dov'è la calma
　　　　　　Vuoi trovar d'Amor la palma
　　　　　　Vien —
　Coro:　　Dov'è
　Galatea: In questo sen . . .

Quite apart from its two languages, Handel's 1732 Serenata was a pre-posterous affair. It is immensely long, cumbersome, and unbalanced, the antithesis of the Cannons *Acis*. He threw together a considerable part of the Naples and Cannons settings and added excerpts from several other works, sacred and secular, without bothering to fit them into the context or, in some cases, to alter the words. A good deal of transposition was necessary.[16]

[Acis and Galatea (1732)] was an immediate success and was repeated seven times, causing the Little Theatre production to fold up after two performances. The price of the victory was heavy, though it did not seem so to Handel. As was usual in such cases, the hurried reworking did not result in improvement; as a matter of fact, Handel made an unholy mess of this graceful score. In order to bring to bear his heaviest weapons, the celebrated Italian singers of his troupe, he had the unfortunate idea of combining the English *Acis and Galatea* with *Aci, Galatea, e Polifemo*, the earlier serenata, thus taking an unpardonable step to bilingual performances. The result of the uncritical mixing of the two versions, the haphazard transpositions and adaptations, created a fearful jumble in which all the grace of the English pastoral disappeared.[17]

Perhaps the edition of Chrysander is the real target for most of this abuse, for, as Dean and Lang are quick to point out, he has made it next to impossible to reconstruct Handel's score. However, no commentator has yet understood even what Handel intended to create. It is clear from the libretto that the basic source was not the Cannons *Acis* at all, but the Neapolitan Serenata. In an obvious reference to its origin, Handel also called the revision a Serenata. The thread of the drama, the recitatives, are mostly adapted from this earlier text; other arias and choruses are fitted into this framework (see Table 10).[18]

---

[16] Dean, *Oratorio*, p. 173.
[17] Lang, *Handel*, pp. 281–2.
[18] In Table 15 none of the secco recitative from *Acis* (1718) is shown. In the original it is of minimal proportions. None is borrowed in the revision.

TABLE 10

Acis and Galatea (1732) and its Sources

Aci (1708)	Acis (1718)	Other	Acis (1732)
	Chor.: 'O the pleasures'		I. Chor.: 'O the pleasures'
	Aria: 'Hush ye pretty'		Aria: 'Hush, ye pretty'
Duet: 'Sorge il di'			Duet: 'Sorge il di'
Recit: 'Vanti, o cara'			Recit: 'Vanti, o cara'
	Aria: 'Where shall I seek?'		Aria: 'Lontan da te'
Recit: 'Se di perte'			Recit: 'Se di perte'
	Aria: 'As when the dove'	New?	Aria: 'Si lagna augel'
			Recit: 'Pastor, guarda'
	Aria: 'Say what art thou pursuing?'		Aria: 'O pastor'
	Aria: 'Love in her eyes'		Aria: 'Stanno in quegli'
		New?	Recit: 'Bella, non ben'
		Clori, Tirsi (1707): 'Come la rondinella'	Aria: 'Come la rondinella'
		New?	Recit: 'Quanto del'
		Clori, Tirsi (1707): 'Un sospiretto'	Aria: 'Un sospiretto'
		Arresta il passo (1708): 'È un foco'	Aria: 'È un foco'
		Birthday Ode (1713): 'The day that gave'	Solos/chorus: 'Contento'
		New	Chorus: 'Lieto esulti'
Aria: 'Sforzano'	Duet: 'Happy we'		II. Chorus: 'Vuoi veder'
Recit: 'È qual nuovo'			
Aria: 'Che non può'			
Accomp. recit: 'Ma qual horrido'	Accomp. recit: 'I rage'	*Brockes Passion* (1716): Eilt, ihr'	Accomp. recit: 'Ma qual horrido'
Aria: 'Sibilar l'angui'			
	Aria: 'O ruddier than the cherry'		Aria: 'Ferito son d'amore'
Recit: 'Deh! lascia'			Recit: 'Deh! lascia'
	Aria: 'Cease to beauty'		
	Aria: 'Would you gain?'		Aria: 'Would you gain?'
Aria: 'Benche tuoni'			
Recit: 'Cadrai'			Recit: 'No, cadrai'
Aria: 'Non sempre, no'			Aria: 'Non sempre, no'
Recit: 'Folle, quanto'			Recit: 'Folle, quanto'
Aria: 'Dell'aquila'			Aria: 'Dell'aquila'
Recit: 'Meglio spiega'			Recit: 'Meglio spiega'

TABLE 10 – *continued*

Acis and Galatea (1732) and its Sources

Aci (1708)	*Acis* (1718)	*Other*	*Acis* (1732)
Aria: 'Precipitoso'			
Recit: 'Si t'intendo'			
Aria: 'S'agita in mezzo'			
Recit: 'So che' – 'Senti'			Recit: 'Senti quando'
Trio: 'Proverà'			Trio: 'Proverà'
Recit: 'Ingrata'			Recit: 'Ingrata'
		New	Chor: 'Smiling Venus'
Aria: 'Fra l'ombre'	Aria: 'Love sounds'		
	Chor: 'Wretched lovers'		
			III. Solos/chorus: 'Viver'e non'
		Clori, Tirsi (1707) 'Vivere e non'	
Recit: 'Ma che?' – 'Ah, Stella'			Recit: 'Ah! cruda Stella'
Aria: 'Qui l'augel'			Aria: 'Qui l'augel'
			Recit: 'Nell'impero'
		New?	Aria: 'Di goder'
		Il pastor (1712) 'Di goder'	
Recit: 'Giunsi al fin'			Recit: 'Giunsi al fin'
Aria: 'Se m'ami'			Aria: 'Se m'ami'
Recit: 'Qui sull'alto'			Recit: 'Qui sull'alto'
	Aria: 'Consider fond shepherd'		Aria: 'Consider fond shepherd'
Recit: 'Lascia bocca'			Recit: 'Caro sino' – 'Lascia bocca'
Trio: 'Dolce amico'	Trio: 'The flocks shall leave'		Trio: 'Delfin vivrà sul'
Recit: 'Or poichè' – 'O dio'			Recit: 'O, Dei'
Aria: 'Verso già l'alma'			Aria: 'Verso già l'alma'
	Accomp: 'Help, Galatea'		
	Chor: 'Mourn all ye'		
	Solo/chorus: 'Must I'		
	Aria: 'Heart, the seat'		
Recit: 'Misera'			Recit: 'Misera'
Aria: 'Impara, ingrata'		New	
Recit: 'Ah tiranno'			
Aria: 'Del mar'			Aria: 'Del mar'
			Recit: 'Ma il mio'
Recit: 'Ferma'			
Trio: 'Chi ben ama'	Chor: 'Galatea, dry thy tears'		Chor: 'Galatea, dry thy tears'

This choice necessitated a great deal of rewriting because of the different vocal ranges used in the three versions. For example, in 1708 Acis was a soprano, in 1718 a tenor, and in 1732 an alto. Handel takes the opportunity, however, to tighten and condense the drama.

Almost all of the recitatives are shortened. The reduction of the passage following the trio 'Proverà lo sdegno' is typical.

1708	1732
Pol. Ingrata se mi nieghi	*Pol.* Ingrata, se mi nieghi
ciò che sperar potrei	ciò che sperar potrei
come tuo dono,	come tuo dono,
io che schernito sono	
ottener lo saprò come rapina.	ottener lo saprò come rapina.
Gal. Poichè il ciel già destina,	*Gal.* Poichè il cielo destina,
che ti lasci, oh mio bene,	che ti lasci, o mio bene,
corro in braccio a Nereo	corro in braccio a Nereo

Pol. Dolci catene
  ti faran queste braccia.
Aci. Empio, t'arresta
Gal. Tormentosa, e funesta
  pria m'accolga la parea.
Pol. Ecco al mio seno ti stringo.
Gal. Ah – genitore!
  col tuo duro tridente corri
  e svena il tiranno il traditore.
Aci. Non ti smarrir mio vita.
Gal. In libertà gradita
  ecco al fin che già sono,
Pol. Ah! crudo fato,
  tu pur fuggi, o crudel!
Aci. Respiro.
Gal. Addio;
  precipito nell'onde,   precipito nell'onde,
  idolo mio.   idolo mio!

Before Aci's aria 'Dell'aquila l'arti' the dialogue is cut from twenty-one measures to eleven, before Aci's 'Qui l'augel da pianta', from twenty-three to six, etc. The continual editing belies the notion that Handel uncritically threw together a mass of pre-existent material. Into this revised framework Handel carefully added arias and choruses from his previous pastorals.

Neither of the Acis scores is mutilated. With only one exception, both appear intact in their original order. Duplicate situations are avoided, and for such moments as Polifemo's entrance, the climactic trio, and Acis' death Handel makes a choice between sources. With a constant awareness of dramatic necessities, Handel has arranged his new score with a great deal of finesse.

Thus the opera (for such it is) opens with the Cannons chorus, 'O the pleasures of the plains'. Clori, with no intervening recitative, at once dispels the notion that all Arcadian nymphs 'dance and sport the hours away' by singing 'Hush, ye pretty warbling choir!' The altered words of the B section lead the audience to the entrance of Acis and Galatea.

1718	1732
Cease your song,	Cease your song,
and take your flight,	and seek the grove,
Bring back my Acis	Where some happy
to my sight.	lovers rove.

Again without connective recitative, Acis and Galatea enter with the opening duet from the Naples *Aci*, 'Sorge il dì'.[19]

These three numbers form an introduction to the drama wherein, with no intermediate narrative or dialogue, Handel shows the audience that the inhabitants of this generally idyllic atmosphere can be inflicted with pain but that none has reached the happy couple. Neither of the previous works had so effectively and quickly set the background for the development of the plot.

Handel next gives each of the young lovers a solo aria, thus maintaining the format of the 1708 *Aci*. However, the music from the serenata is discarded in favour of two airs from the English masque. In this first instance here a choice between dramatically parallel situations is necessary, Handel uses the recitative from *Aci* which directly follows the duet. He interrupts it, however, after Aci's lines with 'Lontan da tè'. In this aria, borrowed from *Acis* (1718), 'Where shall I seek the charming fair?' the words are altered to adjust to the stage presence, rather than absence, of 'the charming fair'. Galatea then sings her part of recitative from *Aci*, followed by 'Si lagna augel' from *Acis* ('As when the dove'). Representing the only case of a piece from either source used out of order, this aria provides a convenient way of giving Galatea a solo at the right moment without going outside the previous Acis compositions. The act continues and ends with interaction among others of the Arcadian residents – Silvio, Filli, and Dorindo. With only one exception the 'outside' borrowing is limited to this extension of Act I.

Polifemo enters in Act II. At this point in both of the previous scores Handel had made an exceptional use of accompanied recitative. In *Acis* (1732) he chooses to use neither source intact but to combine them. Instead of the triadic trumpet calls of *Aci* (1708) or the *stile agitato* of *Acis* (1718), Handel derives the accompagnato from Polyphemus' first

---

[19] In the Naples version, Aci was a soprano, Galatea an alto. This was reversed in 1732. Their parts in the duets and trios have been switched.

vocal line in *Acis* (1718) (Ex. 1a), using it as a musical symbol for the entrance of the blustering English-style monster (Ex. 1b and c).

Ex. 1

(a)

I rage, _____

(b)

(c)

Av - vam — — — — — — — po

He is first noticed, however, as in the 1708 *Aci*, by the young couple, not by the chorus. To the text of the 1708 production Handel then appends a new text for Polifemo, partly modelled on the 1718 version. This recitative leads to the comic 'O ruddier than the cherry' ("Ferito son d'amore') which replaces the bravura aria from *Aci* (1708), 'Sibilar l'angui d'Aletto'. The serious villain of the Italian pastoral would have been no more appropriate to the German form than it had been to the English masque.[20] The continuation of the second act, nevertheless, depends heavily on the *Aci* score.

The first act of the revision derives mostly from *Acis* (1718), the second from *Aci* (1708). The third act skilfully combines the dénouements of both. Although the chorus from *Acis*, 'Wretched lovers', is

---

[20] Although a secondary reason for its replacement may have been the previous use of this aria in *Rinaldo*, characterization appears the more important cause. 'Precipitoso nel mare,' another of Polifemo's arias in *Aci* (1708), is also omitted, and not because Handel had previously used it or because it had ceased to please him a quarter of a century after its composition. In fact, its omission was apparently so conscious to him that 'Precipitoso' was resuscitated less than a year later as 'Swift inundation' in *Deborah* (February, 1733).

omitted, its primary theme finds its way into the first chorus. 'The flocks shall leave the mountain' ('Delfin vivra sul monte') from *Acis* (1718) substitutes for the trio from the serenata, 'Dolce amico'. Although this is followed by the Italian aria, 'Verso già l'alma' rather than the accompanied recitative from the masque, the opera closes with the final chorus from that work.

The opera is structurally organized around B♭ major. The first act concludes in the key of the mediant (D), the second in the dominant (F), the third in the tonic (B♭).[21] The first movement emphasizes the tonic with its mediant minor harmonies (g and d) and the dominant. This pattern is clear throughout the first act. The opening chorus is in B♭ (g); the first aria, F(a); the duet, B♭(d). None of these works, deriving from both of the previous *Acis* scores, is transposed. The next aria interrupts a section of dialogue from *Aci* which section originally cadenced in C. Handel rewrites the entire recitative, maintains the C cadence, and transposes 'Lontan da tè' ('Where shall I seek?') up a fourth to f(c). 'Come la rondinella' from *Clori* remains untransposed in F(a), the aria from *Arresta il passo*, 'È un foco', untransposed in g(B♭). The chorus from the *Birthday Ode* remains in d; Handel writes the new choral finale in D. Thus, the first act, in spite of its many sources and necessary transpositions displays a clear tonal structure.

The second act moves away from the tonic by emphasizing the dominant with the minor keys built on its third and fifth degrees (F–a–c) and the sub-mediant with the minor keys built on its third and fifth (G–b–d). Moreover, the dominant group seems to represent Arcadia, whereas the sub-mediant group depicts Polifemo. Thus, the opening chorus from the *Brockes Passion* is transposed from g to a. As this change makes little difference to the comfort of the singers, the transposition can only have been necessitated by the association of the sub-mediant with Polifemo. Indeed, Polifemo's two succeeding arias are in G minor; Eurilla's intermediary 'advice' aria is in G major, transposed up a ninth from the Cannons aria, 'Would you gain the tender creature?' After this section of Polifemo dominated arias in the sub-mediant, the second act ends squarely in the Arcadian dominant. Thus, Handel transposes the aria of Aci from 1708, 'Dell'aquila', down a third from A(c♯) to F(a), and writes the newly-composed chorus in F(c).

In the last act Handel begins on the major tonality built on the leading note, the scale degree the furthest away from the tonic by the circle of fifths. Through a progression of secondary dominants, Handel moves

---

[21] Throughout this section, capital letters refer to major tonalities, lower case letters to minor. The key of the B section of *da capo* forms will be given in parentheses following the primary tonality. For example, 'Hush, ye pretty warbling choir' is in F(a).

relentlessly towards a firm conclusion in the tonic. The various transpositions work into the plan. 'Qui l'augel' (the second movement) is
transposed down a seventh from C(a) to D(f♯). 'Se m'ami' (No. 4) is
transposed up a minor third from e(G) to g(B♭). The fifth movement
appears in its original key G(♭), as does the sixth movement – in c. In
the last three movements the tonic and dominant are reiterated. 'Verso
già l'alma' (No. 7) is transposed down a fifth from F(C) to B♭(F); 'Del
mar fra l'onde' (No. 8) moves up a diminished fifth from E(B) to
B♭(F). The final chorus remains in its original key (B♭).

Throughout the opera, the transpositions are regularly adjusted to
the tonal structure. The arias for Acis, for example, which have been
taken from the earlier serenata are not transposed by any set interval.
They are moved down a third, seventh, fourth, and fifth, respectively.
Transpositions by sevenths and ninths make one question why they
are not the easier octave, and as an interval of transposition the diminished fifth is probably quite rare. Vocal requirements provide insuffi-
cient reason to explain these differences, especially when in each case
the aria fits into an overall tonal structure.

Handel's 1732 revision may well be 'the antithesis of the Cannons
Acis', but it was meant to be. It certainly was not a 'fearful jumble'.
The dramatic framework (the recitatives) derived from a single work,
the Neapolitan serenata. Into this framework Handel inserted some of
the music from the Cannons masque and other compositions. He
enlarged the structure and added large choral movements. Handel
intended to and succeeded in creating a German pastoral.

It is silly to assume that Handel was not totally conscious of what he
was doing and pleased with the result. The finished product need not
be 'defended' by saying that 'the Anglo-Italian version of *Acis and
Galatea* was certainly not an idea of Handel's choosing. It had been
forced on him by the challenge of Arne's pirated production of the
Cannons masque.'[22] In fact, Handel was responding to far more than
the single production of *Acis*. He was answering to a renewed assault
of English pastoral opera upon the Italian heroic ideal.

Before 1728, Handel had had the English operatic stage practically
to himself. The Royal Academy had faced no direct competition in
Italian opera, and English opera, since the rebuff of *Calypso and Telemachus* (1712), had been practically non-existent. The production of
The Beggar's Opera inadvertently changed that. On the heels of its
success, the Royal Academy closed, Handel was forced to start again,
and English opera revived.

Indeed, Arne's production of Handel's *Acis* was only one part of his

---

[22] Julian Herbage, 'The Secular Oratorios and Cantatas', in *Symposium*, pp. 136–7.

larger effort to re-establish English opera upon the London stage. 'The years 1732–33 saw the most energetic of all attempts to float English opera as a going concern in London. In March 1732 Thomas Arne (senior), Henry Carey, and J. F. Lampe opened a season at the New Theatre in the Haymarket, and the campaign was continued at other theatres.'[23]

Their first production (March, 1732) was *Amelia: A New English Opera* by Henry Carey and J. F. Lampe. Their second was the pirated version of *Acis*. Third was a second collaboration by Carey and Lampe, *Teraminta* (November, 1732). Both *Amelia* and *Teraminta*, romantic tragicomedies, are in the realm of the pastoral. In *Teraminta* this is especially pronounced.[24] The first production in 1733 (February), again by Lampe, was a setting of Gay's pastoral tragedy, *Dione*.

Handel's response to this competition was immediate and twofold. First he retaliated with his own production of a Germanic-style *Acis*. Second, he strove to emphasize the pastoral atmosphere in his theatre. From his revision of *Acis* to 1736, Handel never returned to the strictly heroic texts used exclusively in the first Royal Academy. A study of each of his new productions and revivals during this period reveals Handel's competitive strategy and his increasing utilization of the German pastoral conventions.

THE PASTORAL REAWAKENING

Many commentators have been at a loss to explain the production of a pastoral by Bononcini in Handel's realm, the Haymarket Theatre, in June 1732, but Lang is correct in assessing that 'there was nothing to be feared from Bononcini; he had shot his bolt and could no longer challenge Handel.'[25] What is interesting, of course, was that at this particular moment the Bononcini opera happened to be a pastoral.[26] In between his revision of *Acis* and the production of a new opera, Handel used Bononcini's pastoral to help turn the competition in his favour by adding variety to the programming. From their April production of *Acis* to the November production of *Teraminta*, the men at the New Theatre had had nothing new to offer.

By January of the new year Handel's opera was ready. *Orlando* was a

[23] Dean, *Oratorio*, p. 265.
[24] See Allardyce Nicoll, *A History of English Drama: 1660–1900*, ii (Cambridge: Cambridge University Press, 1968), 235–6.
[25] Lang, *Handel*, p. 243.
[26] The pastoral serenata by Bonocini preserved at the British Library (Rm 20.b.11) perhaps represents this production. Its four characters divide just seven arias and join in a final ensemble. It is as Italian in style as in size.

fantastic success. To say this composition shows that 'Handel neither recognized the significance of the warm reception of the English works nor was he inclined to give up opera for anything else'[27] overlooks the decisive action which was taken. *Orlando* is Handel's first opera after nineteen consecutive *opere serie* to return to the realm of the pastoral.

Dean labels *Orlando* as one of five Handelian operas based on magic; they are *Rinaldo* (1711), *Teseo* (1713), *Amadigi* (1715), *Orlando* (1733), and *Alcina* (1735). Certainly magic plays a part in all of these operas. As a basic category, however, it lacks consistency. *Orlando*, for example, is the first of a trilogy of operas based on *Orlando Furioso* by Ariosto. Dean calls two magical. The third, *Ariodante* (1735), does not fit into any of his categories.

A more important opera is *Ariodante*, whose plot, like those of *Orlando* and *Alcina*, comes from Ariosto. It contains a good deal of pageantry, including a tournament in the lists and some big scenes for ballet and chorus, with a wind-band on the stage in the last act. But unlike the other operas based on Renaissance epics it has no supernatural or magic content; and the temper is neither heroic, despite the characters, nor anti-heroic.[28]

All of the Ariosto operas belong in the pastoral vein. Traditionally this is how they had been conceived and how Handel would have viewed them.

Pastoral dramas, as they developed in the court of Ferrara, had a special relationship to the pastoral sections of the narrative epic. Operatic plots borrowed from epics almost always involved these pastoral sections. In fact, pastoral sections from narrative epics became the first major source for opera librettos after the early spate of mythologically-based pastorals. In Florence in 1619, Salvadori and Gagliano collaborated on *Il Medoro*, based on the same section of *Orlando Furioso* as Handel's *Orlando*. In 1625, Florence saw a second production, *La Liberazione* by Saracinelli and Caccini, taken from *Orlando Furioso*. In 1626 Rome witnessed *La Catene d'Adone* by Tronsarelli and Mazzochi based on Marino's *Adone*. This was followed in Rome by *Erminia* (1733), a pastoral opera by Rospigliosi and Rossi, based on a combination of Tasso's *Gerusalemme Liberata* and *Aminta*. As late as 1642, Rospigliosi and Rossi collaborated on another pastoral, *Il palazzo incantato*, this time taken from *Orlando Furioso*.[29] In 1658, *Il Medoro*, a completely new opera by Auretti and Luccio based on the same material as the 1619 version appeared in Venice.

---

[27] Lang, *Handel*, pp. 240–1.
[28] Dean, *Opera*, p. 102.
[29] Murata, 'Operas for the Papal Court,' pp. 37–8, 67, 80, 97.

Handel's *Rinaldo* (1711), based on sections from Tasso's *Gerusalemme Liberata*, is one of what must be very few exceptions to this tradition. Notably, however, its dependence on Tasso is minimal. Furthermore, in sketching out the plot, Aaron Hill strove to please English tastes. Thus by focusing on martial and magical elements, the libretto of *Rinaldo* reflects the earlier tradition of the heroic dramatic operas, seen especially in *King Arthur* by Dryden and Purcell. Handel's response to this dramatic libretto firmly lay, as seen above, in the tradition of the *opera seria* as he loosely interpreted that form. Similar to *Almira* (1705), *Rodrigo* (1707), and *Agrippina* (1709), it contrasts strongly with *Florindo* (1708), *Daphne* (1708), and *Il pastor fido* (1712). The magical element in *Rinaldo* was simply not Handel's focus.

With *Amadigi* (1715), however, Handel returned, at least in part, to a pastoral mode. Based on the Spanish epic *Amadis de Gaula* of uncertain authorship, as it appeared in a French libretto by Antoine de la Motte (1699),[30] the martial and heroic aspects of *Rinaldo* are totally absent. In true pastoral fashion Amadigi and Orianna are in love, but their path to eternal bliss is temporarily blocked by Melissa, who loves Amadigi, and Dardano, who loves Orianna. The sole distinction of this story is that Melissa happens to be a sorceress, and thus Dean chooses the magical element as this opera's primary focus. Handel, however, set it as a pastoral.

Amadigi followed quickly on the heels of *Il pastor fido*'s failure. Thus it is no surprise that it moves slightly toward the German conception of the pastoral in its construction. Although still substantially smaller than *Rinaldo*, *Amadigi* is somewhat more expansive than *Il pastor fido*. Notably, however, it is Handel's first opera, with the possible exceptions of *Florindo* and *Daphne*, to make use of a combined chorus and solo finale. This scene, 'Godete, oh cori amanti', is in *da capo* form. The A section is sung both times by the chorus, the B section as a duet by Amadigi and Orianna. Even more striking, the ballet which follows is based entirely on the music of the chorus. This finale, therefore, also provides the first extant example in Handel's music of a thematically unified scena of solo, chorus, and ballet. The reason is the opera's pastoral atmosphere and, perhaps, its French libretto.[31] The French influence, however, had strongly permeated German musical traditions, and Handel would naturally have responded to this libretto with the experience of his own German musical background, not out of a desire to sound French.

<hr>

[30] David Kimbell, 'The *Amadis* Operas of Destouches and Handel,' *ML*, xlix (1968), p. 329.
[31] See Kimbell, op. cit., for a discussion of this libretto's French relations.

In the years following *Amadigi*, as Handel moved away from writing pastorals, he began slowly to incorporate more of the stylistic features of these pastorals into his heroic dramas. The Italian monothematic pastoral aria has already been mentioned in this context. In three of his later Academy operas, Handel also experimented with enlarged finales.[32] Only in the next decade, however, did this become a significant feature of Handel's operatic style, and its most expansive development occurs specifically in relation to the pastoral compositions of 1732 through 1737.

Although some important modifications toward the German pastoral conventions first appear in *Amadigi*, they remained in this early opera subservient to the Italian pastoral. 'Act I in particular,' Dean writes, 'suffers from monotony of rhythm, texture, and tonality; eight of its eleven arias are in B flat or G minor, and in most of them in triple time. Four times in the opera (twice in succession in the second act) we find two consecutive arias in the same key, a situation avoided in mature operas.'[33] These traits are not so much immature as they reflect a specific style. By placing *Rinaldo*, *Amadigi*, and *Orlando* into one group on the one hand and detaching *Ariodante* from the Ariosto trilogy on the other, one can easily overlook the differing conventions by which these operas were constructed.

Orlando, Handel's first new opera to be produced after the success of the *Acis* revision, stands out as a striking departure from its predecessors of almost two decades. It is the first opera since *Amadigi* (1715) to be based on a legendary epic. Surely, this was no mere accident of fate. Competing as he was with the revival of the pastoral English opera, Handel moved his compositions in that direction. Although still tied somewhat to the Italian *opera seria* tradition, *Orlando* illustrates a distinct loosening of its constraints. This is due, specifically, to its pastoral design and to the movement taking place in Handel's conception of the genre back to the German form.

The finales of all three acts are representative of this conception. Act I concludes with a trio sung by Angelica, Dorindo, and Medoro. Each of the singers has different words according to his or her situation. Handel's setting reflects this in the music. Reminiscent of the fine trios in *Aci* (1708) and *Acis* (1718), 'it is the first example in Handel, or

---

[32] See Dean, *Opera*, pp. 148–9. The three operas are *Radamisto* (1720), *Giulio Cesare* (1724), and *Alessandro* (1726). Such finales would not be foreign to the modified form of the German *opera seria*. In contrast to the Italian conventions of *Il pastor fido*, for example, the score of *Rinaldo*, following the traditions of German heroic opera, was bigger and more full of choral and symphonic numbers. In the period of transition between Handel's use of the Italian pastoral forms and his return to the German style, some of these distinctions are blurred.

[33] Dean, *Opera*, pp. 88–9.

indeed in any opera of the period, so far as I am aware, of a trio as a
finale to an act.'[34]

Act II concludes with a solo scene for Orlando in which he halluci-
nates about the underworld. The final aria is not *da capo* but rondo.
The primary musical section is heard three times; there are two episodes. The text of the final repetition of the rondo theme, however,
does not repeat the original words but borrows from the second episode. This drawing together of text and music creates a firm conclusion
totally unlike that created by a normal *da capo*.

$$\text{Text} \quad \text{A} \quad \text{B} \quad \text{A} \quad \text{C} \rightarrow \text{C}^1$$
$$\text{Music} \quad \text{A} \quad \text{B} \quad \text{A} \quad \text{C} \quad \text{A}$$

The listener simultaneously perceives a dramatic continuity and a
musically closed form.[35]

In the finale to the opera, the integration of the soloists and chorus
reminds one of similar compositions placed into the *Acis* revision (1732).
Primarily in a varied strophic form, this finale also borrows certain
formal aspects from the rondo finale of Act II. The opening ritornello
of twelve measures presents the main theme. Orlando sings the first
strophe. The setting (sixteen measures) essentially follows the instrumental introduction. The second strophe, sung as a duet by Angelica
and Medoro, begins with the same text and head motive. The musical
and textual continuations, however, develop differently from the first
verse. Again, the strophe is sixteen measures.

The third strophe, beginning again with the same head motive, is
totally different textually and, aside from the head motive, appears
similar to a rondo episode or B section of a *da capo*. Dorinda sings this
strophe which is twenty-five measures long.

The last strophe in five parts is labelled *Coro*, but was certainly sung
by the soloists. The title, however, implies Handel's conception of the
movement. The strophe is repeated, the second presentation extended to
twenty measures from the sixteen of the first. In many respects these
choral verses approach a recapitulation of the opening verses. In the
first presentation the continuo line from Orlando's strophe is repeated;
in the second both the melodic line and continuo parts are approxi-
mated from the duet.

[34] Dent, 'The Operas', p. 48. Of course, the trio in *Acis* clearly ends the second section.
[35] Indeed, the only similar construction by Handel may be found in the last two pieces of
Acis. See pp. 203–4, above.

Ex. 2
(a)

(b)

The harmony is continuous throughout. Based in B♭ major, the six
sections cadence in B♭ major, F major, G major, D major, F major,
and B♭ major, or I–V–VI–III–V–I. The text has the structural form:
A A′ B C C. The musical form is harder to assess; basically it may be
visualized: A₁ A₁ ′ A₂ B A₁ ″ A₂ ′. That is, the ritornello precedes the
first verse which is based on it. The second verse derives from the first.
The third, except for the head motive, is basically new material. The
first presentation of the fourth verse returns in varied form to the first,
the second presentation to the second.

The combination of strong harmonic direction with textual development and repetition and melodic variation is not totally different from
the techniques used by Handel in creating the rondo finale of Act II.
These structural methods were part of Handel's compositional techniques upon leaving Hamburg,[36] they were generally associated by him
with pastoral compositions. After Handel had learned the Italian pastoral style, he abandoned the German techniques for many years. Only

[36] An early example of similar formal structure appears in 'Innocente rassembra' in the
cantata *Udite il mio consiglio* (1707). See Chapter V.

from the time of the *Acis* revision (1732) do they reappear and begin to play a larger and larger role in Handel's entire œuvre.

Handel's direction in pastoral compositions away from the Italian tradition can be seen in an increased use of nature scenes and sicilianos, totally lacking in many Italianate pastorals, including Handel's own *Il pastor fido*. Moreover, many stylistic features of *Orlando* reflect specifically the freedom of the German pastoral tradition. The aria forms are not totally dependent on the *da capo*; there is an abundance of arioso and accompanied recitative. Little instrumental sinfonias or codas occur throughout to be accompanied by pantomimed action. Essential to the drama, they represent the missing element of chorus and ballet. They occur when Zoroaster shows Orlando the palace of Cupid (I, ii), at the Sinfonia to Act III, and where Zoroaster and the four genies restore Orlando to his sanity (III, ix). Dent believes further that the final movement (gigue) of the overture was intended as a ballet.[37]

In fact, the pastoral nature of this operatic libretto can be seen clearly in these opening scenes, beginning with the ballet and moving through Zoroaster's presentation of the Throne of Love and his exhortation of Orlando to arms. Orlando chooses love; he specifically chooses to give up his glory because 'the sound of the war bugle will frighten Pan and the nymphs away from the woods.'[38] *Orlando* is a setting of the famous pastoral oasis from *Orlando furioso* as an entity in itself, and thus as a pastoral.

Orlando's innovative aspects and its success did not forestall the collapse of Handel's second venture. The competition Handel now faced was stupendous. A rival Italian academy was being forced among political lines. King George II continued to support Handel while his son, Prince of Wales, with whom the king was in conflict, conceived of the notion of attacking his father through his favoured musician. Thus the Opera of the Nobility, armed with Handel's best singers, librettist Paolo Rolli, and composer Nicola Porpora, set out to conquer the *opera seria* audience of London.

Meanwhile the assault from the revived English pastoral opera continued with strengthened ranks. No longer a simple company across the street, English pastorals began appearing in all the theatres. This growth was due, at least in part, not to their inherent success but to the royal nuptials in 1734 of Princess Anne, and in 1736 of the Prince of Wales. Both were celebrated by a wave of celebratory English pastorals, including in 1733, *The Happy Nuptials* by Carey and Lampe; in 1734, *Bacchus and Ariadne*, *Nuptial Masque* set by Galliard, *Aurora's Nuptials*

---

[37] Dent, 'The Operas', p. 47.
[38] Poggioli, *The Oaten Flute*, p. 34.

by Lampe, and *The New Festival*; and in 1736, *A Grand Epithalamium* by Arne. At the height of this renewed interest in the pastoral, Fan-shawe's translation of *Il pastor fido* was reissued, for the only time in the eighteenth century, in 1736.

Faced with the competition in *opera seria* from the Opera of the Nobility on the one hand, and English pastoral opera on the other, Handel nevertheless reorganized his forces for a third operatic venture. He continued to move in the direction of the German pastoral. While the grand size of these operas put them on a par with the *operia sera*, their subject and structure vied against the English offerings.

Handel's first new offering for his reorganized company was *Arianna in Creta* (produced 26 January 1734). The story depicts one incident in the elaborate legends concerning Theseus. Handel had earlier set an-other episode of Theseus' life in *Teseo* (1714) where the young man first arrives in Athens. Medea, who is both a witch and counsellor to King Aegeus (some legends make her his wife), unsuccessfully tries to poison the hero. Jealousies of affection and political intrigue are over-come on the discovery that Theseus is Aegeus' only son.

In *Arianna*, these difficulties surmounted, Theseus sets off for Crete in hopes of slaying the Cretan minotaur, a monster to whom a yearly Athenian tribute of seven maidens is sacrificed. Seven Athenian youths are likewise sacrificed at the Androgean games named in honour of the murdered Prince of Crete. Theseus succeeds not only in abolishing the odious tribute but in winning the heart of Ariadne, princess of Crete.

The Opera of the Nobility, catching wind of Handel's production of *Arianna*, rushed out an opera based on a third aspect of the Theseus legend, *Arianna in Nassos*, in which Theseus deserts Ariadne on the Island of Naxos. This part of the legend was familiar to opera from the time of Monteverdi's setting of Rinuccini's libretto on the same subject (*Arianna*, 1608). Although considered the first *tragedia in musica*, the story of Ariadne was and continued to be in an ambiguous position between the heroic and pastoral drama. This certainly had been the case in the German settings by Conradi and Kusser in 1690 and 1691.[39] England was also familiar with the tragic story as retold in Flecknoe's *Ariadne Deserted* and in Lawes' famous setting of 'Ariadne's Lament'.

Of the three sections of the Theseus legend, only those concerning Ariadne approach the pastoral vein. Dean categorizes *Teseo* as magical, thus linking it with *Orlando*, and considers *Arianna* heroic – presumably by default, as it is neither anti-heroic nor magical. These classifications, however, simply do not fit the operas. Certainly magic is used in *Teseo*,

---

[39] See the discussion above about the Monteverdi setting, pp. 26–7, and about the Conradi and Kusser settings, p. 74.

but it is an extra trick held by Medea and used to further her personal and political goals. The opera does not take place in the realm of the supernatural, as does *Amadigi*, nor rely heavily on a pastoral atmosphere, as does *Orlando*. Even Dean seems to become uncomfortable with his categories, for he ultimately describes *Teseo* as 'a hybrid between the classical-heroic and magic types'.[40]

Arianna, on the other hand, has many points in common with traditional pastoral drama. It is probably no coincidence that the story, which often emphasizes these specific moments, had recently been re-written by an Englishman. Francis Colman's use (for Pisa, 1733) of the legend reflects the importance of pastoral operatic traditions in England.[40a]

In Handel's *Arianna*, the love of Ariadne and Theseus is mirrored by that of Carilda and Alceste; both Theseus and Carilda are members of the Athenian sacrificial party. The intrigue is enhanced by making Ariadne and Carilda close friends and by having Carilda beloved by a villainous Cretan general, Tauride. King Minos represents the unbending law. Ariadne, thought to be the daughter of Archeus, Prince of Thebes, turns out to be King Minos' own daughter, kidnapped shortly after birth. At first glance this may not seem pastoral, but the story includes more than a few plot elements distinctly connected with baroque pastoral drama.

In the initial chapter of this book an attempt has been made to define pastoral drama without limiting its possibilities. For example, mythological and legendary stories not indigenous to the pastoral landscape could often be re-rooted in Arcadian soil and take on luxuriant growth. Thus the adventurousness, or heroism, of *Arianna* cannot be regarded as distinctly unpastoral. After all, hunters had always been an important part of the pastoral population. In describing the plot of the third most important and famous of the Ferrarese pastoral plays, *Filli di Sciro* by Guidubaldo Bonarelli della Rovere (Ferrara, 1607), Greg touches on this relationship.

The plot of the play is highly intricate, and shows a tendency towards the introduction of an adventurious element; it turns upon the tribute of youths and maidens extracted from the island of Scyros by the King of Thrace. The figure of the satyr is replaced by a centaur who carries off one of the nymphs. Her cries attract two youths who succeed in driving off the monster, but are severely wounded in the encounter. The nymph, Celia, thereupon falls in love with both her rescuers at once and it is only when one of them proves to be her long-lost brother that she is able to make up her mind between them. This brother had been carried off as a child by the Thracians together with his betrothed Filli, and having escaped was lately returned to his native land. . . .[41]

---

[40] Dean, *Opera*, p. 83.
[40a] See Reinhard Strohm, 'Händel und seine italienischen Operntexte', *HJ* (1975–6), p. 137.
[41] Greg, *Pastoral*, p. 213.

The resemblances between the story of Ariadne and Bonarelli's pastoral are striking. Both revolve around an annual tribute of youths and maidens from one country to another. In both cases this tribute is abolished by the end of the story. The Cretan minotaur, of course, replaces the Centaur. And there is the typical play of mistaken parenthood. Finally, both take place on islands that therefore seem isolated from true civilization; Scyros is contrasted with Thrace as Crete is with Greece. The island had always played a large and important role in lending the proper atmosphere to the pastoral, beginning with Sicily. Scyros and Crete are closely related.

The story of *Filli di Sciro* was known in England; it had been translated into English in 1630 and 1657. Handel's librettist, then, not only had the tradition begun with Rinuccini of using the pastoral convention in operatic adaptations of the Ariadne legend, but he had the almost parallel story of *Filli di Sciro*.

Indeed, both *Filli* and *Arianna* have plot elements in common with *Il pastor fido* as well. All hinge on strict sacrificial laws. In *Il pastor fido* 'these comprise an edict of Diana to the effect that any nymph found guilty of a breach of faith shall suffer death at the altar unless someone offers to die in her place; likewise a custom whereby a nymph between fifteen and twenty years of age is annually sacrificed to the goddess.'[42] In all three dramas one or more of the four young lovers is led to the sacrifice; in all the intended victim is spared, and the sacrificial laws ended. Other similarities between *Il pastor fido* and *Arianna* are that the heroine's father must, because of his position, condemn (knowingly or unknowingly) his own daughter and that a long-standing confusion about parental heritage is resolved. Such plot elements, as general as they may seem, were important to the pastoral; their existence determined which stories from renaissance epics or medieval romances might be eligible for remaking in the pastoral vein. Handel's heroic operas include similarities in the general outline of their plots as well; these are, of course, different from those in the pastorals.

Most heroic librettos play against the background of an active war. In pastorals wars may be mentioned as having happened, or as happening elsewhere, but the pastoral landscape itself is free from such terrors. Instead, the inhabitants of Arcadia are likely to face monsters of various types, ranging from the fearsome dragon who takes an annual human meal to the rather humorous lusty satyr who runs off with nymphs and shepherdesses. Such characters do not appear in heroic drama.

Although both pastoral and heroic dramas may well turn on a love

---

[42] Ibid, p. 96.

story, only in the pastoral is this an end in itself. In heroic dramas, the girl usually comes with a kingdom. Indeed, the kingdom and not the girl is generally the focus of the story. Many of Handel's heroic operas represent a deposed or captive queen; usually she is being forced to marry against her will. In *Floridante* and *Siroe*, the queens (Elmiras both) are sole survivors of family massacres, but they finally ascend to their rightful positions with their preferred mates. In *Tamerlano*, *Lotario*, *Scipione*, and *Riccardo*, the queens (or princess) have been taken prisoner by tyrants who demand them in marriage. In *Rodelinda* a similar situation occurs through the belief that the rightful king (and husband) has been murdered. Whole societies hang on the outcome of these love affairs. The only pastoral equivalent of such situations is the burden of a ritual sacrifice with which the heroine is usually threatened; when she is released, the kingdom is freed from its need to pay tribute. But these situations, both affecting whole societies, are different: one represents the overthrow of a human, tyrannical rule; the other illustrates the continuing will of the gods, first in punishment, then in forgiveness.[43]

The political affairs of man play a large role in heroic dramas. Whereas in pastoral operas the rule of Arcadia is never threatened, in heroic dramas this is constantly the case. In *Siroe*, *Tolomeo*, and *Sosarme* a rivalry between brothers for the throne is induced by the favouritism of the reigning parent. Two monarchs are in conflict in *Tamerlano*, *Giulio Cesare*, *Rinaldo*, *Riccardo*, *Lotario*, and *Floridante*. In *Agrippina* and *Teseo* there is the question of a son's succession. These political aspects are notably lacking in the pastoral.

A librettist considering a story for an opera during the late seventeenth and early eighteenth centuries would likely try to place it in either the heroic or the pastoral moulds. The composer would do the same, and the choice would determine many of the opera's structural and stylistic features. In *Arianna* the king's rule is not in question. Minos represents the unbending, unyielding law, but he is not a tyrant. He is treated by all with honour and respect; his reign is never threatened. The closest character to a tyrant is the General Tauride and he is actually more like the resident satyr of Arcadia. The regular, ritual sacrifice is also present, performed by a monster and condoned by the gods through an oracle. Their will is symbolically represented by the stones of marble on which the sacrificial laws are inscribed. Dramatically, *Arianna* is a pastoral, the island of Crete substituting for Sicily

---

[43] Poggioli (*The Oaten Flute*, pp. 230–1) writes, 'Even when they are not alone in their paradise, the pastoral lovers forget society and the world. . . . From this viewpoint the most antibucolic pair of lovers in history and poetry are Anthony and Cleopatra – not only for their tragic end but also because they stage their passion in the great theatre of the world.'

or the mythological Arcadia. That Handel understood this is clear from the musical score.

The curtain rises on the final movement of the overture during which the fourteen proposed victims from Athens disembark at Crete. After the opening recitative, during which the sacrificial laws are read, the marble tablets fall to the ground and break. An eight-bar Sinfonia accompanies 'four little cupids with garlands and olive branches in their hands flying through the air'. This opening structure, heavily dependent on pantomime, is similar to the beginning of *Orlando*.

Act II opens with a marvellous dream sequence for Theseus, unified by a recurring instrumental ritornello, in which Sleep enters to show Theseus that he will slay the Minotaur. Theseus awakens filled with new resolve. Made up of two scenes this sequence is actually one *da capo*, first extended, then interrupted. After an accompanied recitative which opens the act, the A section, a *larghetto* in 3/8, begins with an eleven-measure ritornello cadencing in F major. Theseus sings through a typical double presentation of the text.

> God of ever grateful rest/Drive my anxious cares away.
> O'er me your downy wings display/And ease my troubled breast.

During the repetition of the ritornello at the close of the A section, however, he falls asleep. The accompanied recitative of Sonno in D minor represents the B section, after which, in true *da capo* fashion, the ritornello reappears for the third time. Theseus cannot, of course, repeat the text of the A section. He awakens, and breaking the ritornello off in its middle, sings of his resolve in a *furioso accompagnato*, dropping into secco at the entrance of Alceste. Like a dream itself, the *da capo* form fades away.

Large and unified solo scenes like Theseus's dream and Orlando's vision seem to grow naturally out of the thematically unified choral scenes of the pastoral. Placed at the opening or end of an act they are used to replace the ensembles, such as those used in the *Acis* revision. Similar structures in Scarlatti's pastorals also seemed to replace the choral scenes lacking in the contemporary Italian form. Thus the unified solo scenes seem to be yet another example of Handel's synthesis of national pastoral traditions. He presumably did not have a chorus at his disposal for most of his pastoral operas. Thus Handel relied on the use of these solo scenas and their pantomimed ballet to replace the pastoral's concerted numbers.

At the ends of the operas, however, Handel could rally his soloists and create an ensemble finale as he did in *Orlando*. In the penultimate scene of *Arianna*, Theseus and Ariadne sing an extended duet, 'Mira adesso'. Theseus follows this with 'Belle sorge', which appears to be a straight *da capo* aria until after the complete vocal repetition of the A section. Then the final ritornello is replaced by a three-part chorus based on the music and text of the aria. Whenever possible in these operas, Handel used the solo-choral scena, the main constituent of the German pastoral form. Both *Orlando* and *Arianna*, structurally so similar, move distinctly toward this form. Shortly after the performance of the latter, Handel was able to reimmerse himself in it, as he had in *Acis* (1732).

Parnasso in festa (13 March 1734) was Handel's offering to Princess Anne upon her wedding. Like *Acis* it was performed without action and utilized a large chorus. Much of the score was borrowed from the biblical oratorio *Athalia* (1733) written for Oxford and not yet heard in London. Handel, however, added important new items and made some some striking alterations in the borrowed material.

Parnasso can be called a choral opera, for the chorus plays an integral role throughout. It is not relegated to festive beginnings and finales. Table 11 shows the contents of *Parnasso* in relation to *Athalia*.

TABLE 11

A Comparison of *Parnasso in festa*
with its primary source, *Athalia*

Parnasso in festa (1734)		Athalia (1733)
I.		
aria	Virginette dotti e belle	Blooming virgins
chorus	Corriamo pronti	The traitor if you there descry
aria/	Deh! cantate	Tyrants would in impious throng
chorus	Esco, ne da stimolo	Tyrants ye in vain conspire
aria	Spira il sen	Softest sounds
aria/	Gran Tonate	
chorus	Già vien da lui	The cloudy scene
aria	Con un vesso	Soothing tyrant
duet	Non portò/Sin le grazie	Joys in gentle trains
aria	Quanto breve	Faithful cares
chorus	Cantiamo a Bacco	Cheer her o Baal
aria	Del Nume Lieo	
aria/	Sciolga dunque	
chorus/	S'accenda pur di festa	
chorus	Replicati al ballo	
II.		
solo/		
chorus	Nel petto	The rising world
aria	Torni pure	
aria	Nel spiegar	Through the land
chorus/	Oh! quanto bella	
aria/	Tra sentier	
chorus	Oh! quanto bella	
aria	Già le furie	Hark! Hark his thunders
recit/	Dopo d'aver	
aria/	Hò perso	O Lord whom we adore
chorus	S' unisce al tuo	Hear from thy mercy seat
duet	Cangia in gioja	Cease thy anguish
chorus	Coralli e perle	The gods who chosen
III. Sinfonia		
chorus/		
aria	Si parli	When storms
aria	Da sorgente	Joys in gentle strains
aria	Sempre aspira	Gloomy tyrants
aria/	Non tardate	
chorus	Accorriam	
aria	Circondin	My vengeance wakes me
aria	Han mente	
aria/	Lunga serie	
chorus	Giove il vuole	

The first aria, 'Virginette dotti e belle', adopts only the A section of the *da capo* aria 'Blooming Virgins'. It leads into the entrance of the chorus. This scena with Apollo derives entirely from *Athalia*. The next choral scene, again with Apollo, uses material from *Athalia*, but the solo lead-in 'Gran Tonate' replaces the instrumental introduction to the English 'The cloudy scene' ('Già vien da lui'). 'Quanto breve' borrowed from 'Faithful cares' gives the opera its first *da capo*. The new aria 'Del Nume Lieo' is also in that form.

The finale to Act I is entirely new. Apollo sings the *da capo* aria 'Sciolga dunque' in E(A). The chorus enters with 'S'accenda pur di festa' containing separate solo sections for bass, two sopranos, and alto, and including a choral refrain. The final chorus in A major 'Replicate al ballo' repeats the A section of Apollo's aria 'Sciolga dunque' fitted into the familiar closing dance pattern: ‖ : A : ‖ : B A : ‖ . Thus, the entire set of three movements forms a giant repetitive structure (see Table 12).

TABLE 12

Parnasso in festa: Form of Act I Finale

	Aria	Ensemble with Choral Refrain	Chorus
individual form	*da capo*	*rondo*	rounded binary
function in larger form	A	B	A'
key	E	A	A

In Act II, Handel adds another wholly new choral scene. The hunting chorus, 'Oh! quanto bella', a written-out *da capo* ($A_1A_2BA_2'$) in G(D) precedes the *da capo* aria 'Trà sentier di amene', also in G(D). Then Handel recapitulates only the *da capo* of 'Oh! quanto bella'. This technique reminds one of the 'Smiling Venus' from *Acis* (1732), also newly composed, which form has been seen to derive from the German pastoral.

The second large choral scene of Act II, 'Hò perso', is borrowed intact from *Athalia*. The *da capo* aria with which it begins follows a normal course through the B section. Instead of returning to opening material, however, the chorus enters with a repetition of the B section in the primary key.

The third act begins with the choral scena 'Si parli'. In adapting the material borrowed from *Athalia*, Handel adds a choral introduction and two choral interruptions to the solo aria. Thus he creates an active solo-choral interchange from a solo aria that had a choral conclusion.

In Apollo's siciliano, 'Non tardate, Fauni ancora', from Act III, Handel brings in the chorus near the end, Apollo, however, continues to sing as well. The finale, 'Lunga serie'/'Giove il vuole', includes a solo for Apollo almost in the manner of an *obbligato*.

Parnasso is clearly based on the German pastoral practice. The English audiences enjoyed it immensely. Even the Prince of Wales was in attendance.[44] As in his Italian pastoral period, when Handel

[44] Ven Lennep, *et al.*, *The London Stage*, Part 3, i, p. 376.

altered his arias to comply with the Italian practice, here he carefully alters the arias from *Athalia* to comply with the German pastoral practice. Handel was following a course of action which was proving successful. He finished out his season with revivals, including *Acis* (1732) and *Il pastor fido,* the latter thoroughly revised. By now it should be clear that the revival of this Italian pastoral did not reflect 'a curious choice',[45] especially as Handel's alterations made this pastoral over according to the German conventions. The two versions are compared in Table 13.

The first, and most obvious change involves the addition of choruses, without exception borrowed from *Parnasso in festa.* Only one of these, however, '(S'unisce al tuo', Act III) originated in *Athalia* (see Table 11, above). Most of the choral additions are used to conclude the acts. Thus Act I ends with Silvio and the hunters, on their way to the hunt, singing the larger 'Oh! quanto bella'. Mirtillo leads the shepherds in 'Accorete o voi Pastori' (in *Parnasso,* 'Non tardate, Fauni ancora') to end Act II. In the last act the choral additions are not limited to the finale.

At the beginning of Act III Silvio enters with his band of hunters. He talks of the splendours of hunting. In the 1712 version a stage direction indicates 'suonano li corni di caccia'. In 1734, the shortened 'Oh! quanto bella' from Act I replaces that direction. Similarly the choral response 'S'unisce al tuo' substitutes for an instrumental sinfonia at the point of Mirtillo's offer of self-sacrifice to save Amarilli. The opera ends amid general rejoicing with the thematically related aria and chorus, 'Sciolga dunque al ballo' and 'Replicati al ballo'.

Another and similar change involves the addition of an introductory Sinfonia to Acts II and III. These and the choruses serve to enlarge the structure of the opera. Moreover, all of the structural changes help to change the Italian opera into a German pastoral. There are other, more specific changes as well.

---

[45] *Lang, Handel,* p. 250.

TABLE 13
The First Two Versions of *Il Pastor Fido*

Il pastor fido (1712)	Il pastor fido (1734A)	Comments
I	I	
overture	overture	in 1734: greatly shortened
'Fato crudel, Amor'	'Fato crudel, Amor'	different settings –
		in 1734, orchestral (through-composed)
		in 1712, continuo (da capo)
recit: 'Ah! nò'	recit: 'Ah! nò'	
'Augelletti, ruscelletti'	'Fra gelsomini'	1712: unisono, borrowed unaltered from *La Resurrezione* (1708)
		1734: new, orchestral
recit: 'Ah! infelice'	recit: 'Ah! infelice'	1712: secco
		1734: accompanied
recit: 'Son di Mirtillo!'	recit: 'Son di Mirtillo!'	
'Son come navicella'	'D'amor a fier'	1712: continuo, borrowed unaltered from *Lungi dal mio* (1707)
		1734: new, orchestral
recit: 'Come viver'	recit: 'Come viver'	
recit: 'Ferma, Mirtillo'	recit: 'Ferma, Mirtillo'	in 1734: last two measures redirected to B (rather than G). Mirtillo's lines intact; Eurilla's rewritten lower.
'Lontan del mio'	'Lontan del mio'	in 1734: transposed down a minor third.
recit: 'Ah! che sperar'	recit: 'Ah! che sperar'	in 1734: transposed down a major third.
'Di goder'		1734: used later, out of order.
'Casta dea'	'Frode, sol a te'	same setting, different texts (original in *Rodrigo*).
recit: 'Tu sola'	recit: 'Tu sola'	after equivalent openings (in continuo and text, not melodic line),
	'Finchè un zeffiro'	in 1734: new text and music inserted. borrowed intact (words and music) from *Ezio* (1732).
recit: 'Respira'	recit: 'Respira'	in 1734: picks up where 1712 source broke off above (recit: 'Tu solo'), again interrupted before end with new conclusion. Dorinda's part at pitch; Silvio's transposed up.

TABLE 13 – continued

The First Two Versions of *Il Pastor Fido*

Il pastor fido (1712)	Il pastor fido (1734A)	Comments
'Mi lasci'	'Quanto mai'	1712 aria had been used intact in 1734 production of 1732 Acis. A continuo aria. 1734 borrowed intact from *Ezio*. An orchestral accompaniment.
recit: 'Cintia, mia'	recit: 'Nell'impero' 'Di goder'	new recit. in 1712: used earlier.
	recit: 'Cintia, mia' 'Quel Gelsomino'	in 1734: redirected to cadence in B (instead of A). 1734: new, orchestral.
'No vo'legarmi'		1712: music borrowed from *Clori*, *Tirsi* (1707), orchestral. This original used intact in *Acis* (1732).
	chorus: 'Oh! quanto bella'	borrowed intact (words and music) from *Parnasso in festa* (1734).
II	**II**	
	sinfonia	
recit: 'E ancor' 'Caro Amor'	recit: 'E ancor' 'Caro Amor'	1712: orchestral (through-composed) 1734: new, orchestral (same text, different (*da capo*) settings of A section.
'Occhi belli'		through-composed
recit: 'Già fortuna'	recit: 'Già fortuna'	same bass line; in 1734, rewritten lower (Eurilla)
	'Ho un non sò'	in 1712 comes later; in 1734, borrowed out of order, transposed down whole step (Eurilla).
recit: 'E chi tenta' 'Allor che sorge'	recit: 'E chi tenta' 'Torni pure'	in 1712: continuo, borrowed from *Rodrigo* (1707) used in 1732 Acis, kept for 1734 production. in 1734: borrowed intact from *Parnasso* (1734).
recit: 'Mi fian cari' 'Finte labbra'	recit: 'Mi fian cari' 'Finti labbra'	in 1734: greatly cut, bass line otherwise intact, as Dorinda's lines; Silvio transposed up.
recit: 'Vanne lunge'	recit: 'Vanne lunge'	

TABLE 13 – *continued*
The First Two Versions of *Il Pastor Fido*

Il pastor fido (1712)	Il pastor fido (1734A)	Comments
'Sol nel mezzo'	'Sol nel mezzo'	in 1734: transposed up fifth.
recit: 'Dorinda' –	recit:	
'Non mi fuggir'	'Non mi fuggir'	bass line intact; in 1734, opening lines omitted, first chord carefully altered from root position (E major) to first inversion (C major) to deal with the harmonic problem created by deletion. Otherwise identical.
'Se in ombre'	'Se in ombre'	
recit: 'Ed è pur'	recit: 'Ed è pur'	in 1734: identical but for last two quarter notes in continuo – to D (in 1712, to F).
'Nel mio core'	'Sì, revedrò'	in 1712: music borrowed from *Rodrigo* (1707), used in 1734 production of 1732 *Acis*, orchestral
recit: 'E tu stessa'	recit: 'E tu stessa'	in 1734: new, orchestral.
'No! non basta'	'Scherza in mar'	in 1734: bass line intact, Eurilla's part rewritten lower, Amarilli's intact. completely different. in 1734: aria borrowed intact from *Lotario* (1729) perhaps this aria substituted for 'Son come navicella' from 1712 version – cut in 1734. (See act I.) Both are for Amarilli.
recit: 'Ah! tepido'	recit: 'Ah! tepido'	text: begins same, diverges; different setting.
'Ritorna adesso'	'Accorrete, o voi'	1734: music borrowed from *Parnasso* (1734) to lead into this chorus (words and music from *Parnasso*).
	Chorus: 'Accorriam'	
III	III	
	sinfonia	
recit: 'Sventurato mio amore!'	recit: 'Sventurato mio amore!'	in 1734: used in Act II.
'Ho un non sò'		
recit: 'Miei fidi'	recit: 'Miei fidi'	in 1734: combines first line of recit from 1712 with previous recit. Silvio's part transposed up, harmonies rewritten.
['Suonano li corni di caccia!']	chorus: 'Oh! quanto bella'	borrowed intact from *Parnasso* (1734).

TABLE 13 – continued
The First Two Versions of *Il Pastor Fido*

Il pastor fido (1712)	Il pastor fido (1734A)	Comments
recit: 'Mà veggio'	recit: 'Mà veggio'	in 1734: picks up where chorus interrupted; text same; continuo same; vocal line rewritten higher.
	'Sento nel sen'	in 1734; new, orchestral.
recit: 'Ergiti, Silvio', 'Se m'ami, o caro'		in 1712: borrowed from *Aci* (1708), used in *Acis* (1732).
recit: 'Amor, se gloria', 'Tu nel piagarmi', 'D'allor trionfante'	recit: 'Già Amarilli' 'Secondaste al fine'	in 1712: new, orchestral.
recit: 'Già Amarilli' 'Secondaste al fine'	Sinfonia –	in 1712: new, orchestral.
Sinfonia –	arioso: 'Oh! Mirtillo!'	in 1734: first measure altered harmonically.
arioso: 'Oh! Mirtillo!'	'Ah! non son io'	in 1734: harmonic direction altered at end.
	recit: 'Sciogliete'	in 1734: borrowed intact from *Ezio* (1732).
recit: 'Sciogliete' duet: 'Per te, mio dolce'	duet: 'Per te, mio dolce'	in 1734: ending altered – to lead without break into chorus.
Sinfonia 'Risonar mi sento'	chorus: 'S'unisce al tuo' 'Dell'empia frode'	in 1734: borrowed unaltered from *Parnasso*. in 1712: new, orchestral; in 1734: borrowed: intact from *Riccardo* (1727), has higher tessitura.
recit: 'Cessate'	recit: 'Cessate'	in 1734: transposed up a whole step, some rewriting.
'Risonar mi sento' recit: 'E ti stringo'	'Dell'empia frode', recit: 'E ti stringo', duet: 'Caro/Cara', recit: 'Chiedo', aria: 'Sciolga dunque'	in 1734: tonal direction altered at end. borrowed intact from *Teseo* (1713) new recit. borrowed intact from *Parnasso*.
chorus: 'Quel ch'il Cielo'	chorus: 'Replicati al ballo'	in 1734: borrowed intact from *Parnasso*, thematically dependent on preceding aria. in 1712: music borrowed from aria in *Un Alma inamorata*.

Handel begins both operas with the same aria text. The settings, however, are entirely different. In 1712 it appears as a *da capo* continuo aria. In 1734, only the A section of the text is used, and the accompaniment is instrumental. In general Handel tries to get away from the abundance of continuo arias in the original opera which was rare even at the time. This change may be seen to represent a desire to avoid the specific elements of the Italian pastoral. The same desire explains some of the many aria substitutions.

In four cases, for example, Handel replaces a unisono or continuo aria with a new orchestral aria: 'Augelletti, ruscelletti' with 'Fra gelsomini', 'Son come navicella' with 'D'amor a fier', 'Mi lasci' with 'Quanto mai', and 'Allor che sorge' with 'Torni pure'. In some cases Handel replaces arias that had already been used in the *Acis* revision of 1732, or added to the second production of that revision on 7 May 1734; the revision of *Il pastor fido* opened less than two weeks later (18 May 1734). This involved replacements for 'Mi lasci' (used in 1734), 'No vo' legarmi' (this setting had been borrowed from an aria, 'Come la rondinella', in *Clori* (1707) which was used intact in the 1732 and 1734 *Acis* productions), 'Allor che sorge' (used in 1732 and 1734), 'Nel mio cor' (used in 1734) and 'Se m'ami, o caro' (used in 1732 and 1734).

Handel also adds arias to the original framework. This appears to serve two purposes. First, it adds to the general enlargement of the opera; second, it shortens long passages of recitative by interruption. He had done this also in the *Acis* revision, which uses many similar techniques. Thus 'Finchè un zeffiro' comes in the middle of a recitative passage from Act I. 'Ho un non sò', from the 1712 version, but used out of place in 1734, interrupts a recitative in Act II, as do 'Oh! quanto bella', 'Sento nel sen', and 'Ah' non son io' in Act III. All in all, counting arias, duets, choruses, and sinfonias, the 1734 version is more than 20 per cent larger than the original.[46] In neither work is there a clear tonal plan.[47]

In the two major revisions from this period, then, both pastoral, Handel uses very similar methods. In both he begins with the dramatic framework, or recitative, of an Italian pastoral. To both he adds substantial choral scenas. To enlarge the structure further, he adds arias from outside sources. Finally, in both revisions, Handel clearly works

---

[46] The 1712 version contains twenty-seven numbers; the 1734 version thirty-three.

[47] Dean (*Opera*, p. 103) notes that in 1712 Handel identified Amarilli with G major/minor. It has been shown above that Handel used a similar kind of tonal characterization for Polyphemus in 1718 and 1732, first identifying the monster with minor and then specifically with G major/minor. In the revision of *Il pastor fido*, no such tonal characterizations exist.

with the German pastoral in mind. With this form he hoped to win the operatic war.[48]

For the time being, however, the two Italian houses ended the season with a stalemate. London, the royalty aside, had found it difficult to support one opera house, let alone two or more. Moreover, Heidegger appeared to have dealt Handel's enterprise its death blow by rather underhandedly letting the King's theatre for the new season to the competition. Nevertheless, Handel seems always to have kept the lead, leaving the Opera of the Nobility trying to catch up. This situation began with the two *Ariannas* of 1733/34 and now continued with new force.

Handel's 1732 operatic revision of *Acis* had been prompted by the successful revival of the English *Acis* of 1718. The revision, too, proved a success. Moreover, it provided the impetus to Handel's continued use of German pastoral traditions throughout this decade and during this period was revived twice in London, on 7 May 1734 and 24 March 1736. It comes as no surprise, then, that Porpora and Rolli, probably after Handel's 1734 performance, decided to try their hand at the same legend. On 1 February 1735 the Opera of the Nobility offered its first performance of *Polifemo*. Within a three-year span, therefore, London was treated to three operatic productions of the Acis legend. The audiences, moreover, would have recognized more similarities between these works than their plots. In Arne's production and Handel's 1734 performance, the part of Polyphemus was played by Gustavus Waltz. In Handel's 1732 performances and Porpora's production, the part was played by Antonio Montagnana. Other casting similarities between Handel's first performances and Porpora's production included Senesino as Acis in the former and Ulisse in the latter, and Francesca Bertolli as Dorinda in the former and Calypso in the latter.

Handel's return to the German pastoral traditions is especially highlighted by the co-existence of these three operatic versions of the Acis legend each in a different national style. Whereas the *Acis* of 1718 does nicely with four soloists and only one couple, Handel's revision in the German tradition requires eight soloists even though keeping to the one couple. Both use chorus. Rolli's libretto for *Polifemo* calls for six soloists, and the story is expanded to include the story of Ulysses and the Cyclops (alias Polyphemus). It includes an additional nymph and fisherman whose existence adds to the intrigue within the story. Following the Ovidian legend, Polyphemus loves Galatea, Galatea loves Acis, Acis loves Galatea. Following the episode in Homer's

---

[48] The presence of the Prince of Wales at *Parnasso*, see above, may be explained by the royal function it celebrated. However, he was also in attendance at the revision of *Il pastor fido* (Ven Lennep, *et al.*, *The London Stage*, Part 3, i, p. 399).

Odyssey, Ulysses blinds the Cyclops, but here the act serves additionally as revenge for Acis' murder. Ulysses returns to his voyage having released his comrades from the Cyclops' cave and the Arcadians from the constant threat of Polyphemus's wrath. Acis and Galatea are reunited as gods.

Interestingly enough Rolli presents Porpora with a first scene framed by parallel texts for chorus, seven five-syllable lines with a rhyme scheme of *abbaccd*. Porpora omits the second chorus, however, destroying the opportunity for a rounded-off choral scene, and thereby adapts his text to the Italian pastoral conventions. The opening chorus, a typical feature of many *opere serie* whether heroic or pastoral, then stands as the last concerted ensemble until the obligatory short finale. There are about eleven arias in each act. Galatea's first aria, 'Se al campo', is an immediate and striking example of the Italian pastoral monothematic aria. Compare the opening lines of the two sections.

Ex. 3

Other examples occur throughout the opera and are sung by all of the characters except Polyphemus – illustrating that it is always the monster, never the hero (such as Orlando, Ruggiero, or Ulysses), who is a misfit on the Arcadian landscape. Three additional examples of the pastoral aria from Act I will serve to illustrate not only the use of this technique but the overall similarity of the melodic material. Contrast is avoided on all sides.

Ex. 4
(a)

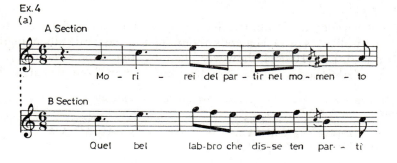

In what seems a natural outgrowth of the avoidance of contrasts, three arias in a row from Act I are in cavatina form. Generally equivalent to the A section of the *da capo*, these arias include a dual presentation of the text separated by a ritornello. The second part is musically similar to a varied strophe, and, in fact, two of the three arias have double texts in the score, indicating a strict strophic form. The overall structure of these arias would be *A A' A A'*.[49] Both the use of strophes and the early date of the opera tend to place these forms outside the later movement toward the more general use of the cavatina. These three consecutive arias from Act I are the only examples of such a form in all of *Polifemo*.

The Opera of the Nobility, having moved into Handel's theatre, begin to utilize as well Handel's theme of the pastoral, albeit in the Italian tradition. Handel, however, had by this time a better conception of the tastes of the London public. Far from defeated, he

[49] The difference between the 'strophic cavatina' and the monothematic *da capo* may be illustrated:

	cavatina				da capo				
music	A	A'	A	A'	A	A'	A"	A	A'
text	a	a	b	b	a	a	b	a	a

received permission to produce operas in the new theatre at Covent Garden. Moreover, he had gained the use of a ballet company headed by the French prima ballerina, Marie Sallé, and a small chorus. These helped to expedite his continued use of the German pastoral conventions.

Much has been made of Handel's use of these resources during the 1734–35 season. However, his two new operas for this season, *Ariodante* and *Alcina,* certainly do not represent 'a stylistic departure' dependent on Neapolitan and French influences.[50] Both operas fit clearly into the German pastoral mode used by Handel throughout this period. Although neither one uses the conventions as extensively as do the pastoral revisions or *Parnasso* they both follow the pattern seen in *Orlando* and *Arianna* of loosening the *opera seria* conventions through an approach to the German pastoral ideal.

Both operas, like *Orlando,* are based on Ariosto's epic. *Orlando, Ariodante,* and *Alcina* form a continuum. Each derives from Ariosto. Each moves closer to the form of the German pastoral. Thus at Covent Garden, Handel continued with his 'battle plan'. The ballet troupe and chorus fitted in nicely, but did not alter the composer's direction. The extent to which these operas from 1734–35 may be called French depends entirely on the earlier French influence on the German pastoral form.

Handel opened the new season in November with two revivals: *Il pastor fido* (November 8) and *Arianna* (November 21). It is notable that in choosing works from his entire corpus for performances to include ballet, Handel picked two pastorals. *Il pastor fido* had been his most recent production. For this second revival, Handel added a Prologue to be danced and sung. The plot was loosely woven around the story of Terpsichore, the muse of dance. The characters include Terpsichore, Apollo, the god of music, and Erato, the muse of love poetry. The form of this Prologue, called *Terpsichore,* is reminiscent of the German singend-Ballett. Such prologues were familiar in Germany. Moreover, a prologue based on the same subject had been used in Motteux's *Mars and Venus* (see above) and was given its last London performance in February 1724. With such English and German precedents, it becomes an unnecessary exercise to search for influences from across the Channel. The French musical forms had influenced German and English music at a much earlier date.

It is unclear what kind of literary help Handel received in forming this prologue. Of the eight vocal pieces, three are borrowed, text and music, from *Parnasso.* Such evidence tends to point toward Handel

---

[50] Lang, *Handel,* p. 251.

having the controlling hand in most of the revisions and contrafacta during this period – *Acis* (1732), *Parnasso* (1734), *Il pastor fido* (1734), and *Terpsichore* (1734) – as he must have earlier, for example, in *Il pastor fido* (1712). It is fascinating to speculate whether Handel may have written some of these texts himself.

Besides the new prologue for this revival of *Il pastor fido*, Handel makes a few additional changes in the body of the score. The entire first scene with Mirtillo is excised in favour of a recitative scene for Amarilli (beginning at scene ii, recit: 'Ah! infelice'), extended in the libretto by the use of quotations from Guarini's pastoral. Tireno's speech from the last act also includes new lines which paraphrase Guarini. Earlier, both Bressand and Zeno had used quotation in their German pastorals. This third version of Handel's *Il pastor fido*, however, is the only one of his to quote directly from the play.

Later in Act I, Handel takes the opportunity to replace or excise the last two of the arias which had appeared in the *Acis* revisions. 'Lontan del mio' (used in *Acis* 1732 and 1734) is replaced by the new 'Sento brillar'. 'Di goder' (used in 1732) is excised. The final aria of Act I, 'Quel gelsomino' is replaced by the new 'Non vo'mai seguitar' which is textually and thematically more akin to the chorus, 'Oh! quanto bella', which concludes the act. However, there exists no specific melodic relationship even though the atmosphere and effect of these pieces are quite similar. Between these movements Handel inserts a dance suite.

The second act concludes with a ballet suite; and a third ballet is placed between the thematically related aria and chorus which conclude the opera. Moreover, in this last case, Handel borrows the music for the final dance movement from the vocal numbers surrounding the suite, thus creating a massive, thematically unified finale.

Arianna was revived using a similar plan. Ballets were inserted at the finales.[51] It is worthwhile to remember that this opera already included much opportunity for dance pantomime, including the opening disembarkation and Theseus's dream, which could well have presented the ballet corps with additional opportunity.[52]

In January 1735 Handel was ready with *Ariodante*. He had written the first two acts without knowing of the move to Covent Garden.[53] Thus it is clear that the opportunity for dances and choruses had not

---

[51] Dean, *Opera*, p. 142.

[52] Mlle Sallé had performed in the ballet *Bacchus and Ariadne* at Covent Garden on 17 April and 7 May 1734. As this obviously depicted a portion of the Theseus legend not set in *Arianna in Creta*, it is unclear what effect, if any, it might have had on the choice of this opera for a new production.

[53] Dean, *Opera*, p. 142, discusses the sources for this opera in some detail.

affected Handel's choice of subject nor the major part of this opera's composition. Like *Il pastor fido* and *Arianna, Ariodante* was adjusted to the new situation by the addition of ballets to the act finales. The choruses already appear in Handel's original version written before he had learned of the impending move or his new resources.

Ariodante is based on one of the love episodes from *Orlando furioso*. It is dependent on a pastoral atmosphere. 'More than half of the action takes place in the open air.'[54] Act I, for example, ends in a 'Valle deliziosa' where Ariodante and Genevra cavort with the shepherds and shepherdesses.

> Ariodante: O happy denizens of this place, joyful nymphs
> and amorous shepherdesses, come and celebrate our
> joy with dance and song.[55]

There follows a pastoral sinfonia in the siciliano manner. Then the lovers sing a duet into which the shepherds join, ultimately alternating lines with the young lovers. This technique is totally familiar from Handel's previous pastorals. Although this opera may be the first since *Amadigi* to utilize a real chorus, not simply an ensemble of soloists, there is no change of method.[56]

When Handel inserted a ballet suite into this finale he integrated it by the use of thematic relationships, as he had in *Il pastor fido*. The first movement of the dance suite is, therefore, based on the theme of the preceding duet and chorus. A shortened version of the vocal piece which omits the initial duet follows the ballet.

Handel had used this technique in writing the chorus 'Oh! quanto bella' for *Parnasso*. When he borrowed it for *Il pastor fido*, however, he saved the shortened 'recapitulation' for a later moment in the opera, stretching thematic resemblances over three acts. Such long-term use of thematic repetition is very rare in operas of this period. In *Ariodante*, however, Handel goes even further by using the last movement of the overture as the first of the opera's final ballet suite. Both the characters and the music of the opera return by the end to the happy state which prevailed at the beginning. The opera's final dance movement which follows is repeated in a texted version by the chorus.

[54] Dean, *Opera*, p. 103.
[55] Act I, scene ii, translated by Dale McAdoo (RCA LSC–6200).
[56] Sirvart Poladian, 'Handel as Opera Composer,' (unpublished Ph.D. dissertation, Cornell University, 1946), assumes that choruses were used only in those operas where a tenor part occurs in the ensembles without a tenor soloist. This reasonable thesis leads to the conclusion that there was a break of twenty years in Handel's use of an operatic chorus (from *Amadigi* in 1715 to *Ariodante* in 1735). But this conclusion overlooks such interim compositions as the operatic revision of *Acis* (1732), *Parnasso* (1734), and the revision of *Il pastor fido* (1734). Furthermore, the choral technique was the same in *Orlando* (1733) and *Arianna* (1734) even if the ensembles were originally sung by the soloists. Handel's conception of the pastoral chorus did not falter.

As well as having pastoral characters, *Ariodante* includes pastoral elements in its story. Certainly the setting in Scotland would have appealed to British pastoral tastes. It had always been important to the English that Arcadia be located on the British Isles.[57] Moreover, not only is the general story similar to *Il pastor fido*, but certain additions to it are clearly borrowed from Guarini. These are the basic elements of the two plots.

Il pastor fido	*Ariodante*
Mirtillo and Amarilli are in love	Ariodante and Ginevra are in love
Corisca, a nymph without honour, loves Mirtillo	Polinesso, a courtier without honour, loves Ginevra
Corisca arranges to have Amarilli appear unfaithful	Polinesso arranges to have Ginevra appear unfaithful
The Arcadian laws condemn Amarilli to be sacrificed at the altar	The Scottish laws condemn Ginevra to burn at the stake

But while the dénouements are arranged somewhat differently, the evil is undone in both cases and innocent love triumphs.

Both stories derive a good deal of poignancy by having the girls' fathers forced by their position to uphold the law by condemning their own daughters. In *Ariodante* this poignancy is increased by tearing a page out of Guarini's pastoral:

Amarilli	*Ginevra*
Perchance some help may come. Father, dear father, dost thou leave me too? An onely daughters father, wilt thou do. Nothing to save me? Yet before I die. A parting kiss to me do not deny . . . Thy belov'd Daughter's *wedding* callst thou this? To-day a bride; to-day a sacrifice. (IV, v, −1. 3690–3701; trans. Fanshawe)	Father, ah, how sweet the name! I come to kneel at your feet, not to ask forgiveness, for I have not erred, . . . I ask not to die despised by you, for I die innocent. Grant that I may kiss the dear hand which signed my death warrant, then I shall be happy. (II, ii; trans. McAdoo)

---

[57] The use of Scotland as a land of mystery, romance, and pastoral atmosphere was not limited to the baroque era, examples ranging from *Lucia di Lammermoor* to *Brigadoon*.

The kissing incident does not appear in Ariosto.[58]

It is unnecessary to emphasize the pastoral nature of *Ariodante*. The story itself had always been especially popular in England and its pastoral connotations had always been recognized. By the time a complete translation of Ariosto's *Orlando furioso* was published in 1591, 'the story of Ariodante and Ginevra had already been translated twice and had supplied the subject for a play.'[59] The first of these, in rhyming couplets by Peter Beverley, emphasizes all of the pastoral possibilities. He even describes the Scottish setting in explicitly pastoral terms as an island, and, by implication, far more remote from Beverley's England than it could ever possibly be. Its apparently tamed landscape is almost magically fertile. Any indication of changing seasons or harsh winters is simply omitted.

> Amongst the vanquisht Regions, that
>   worthy brute did winne:
> There is a soyle in these our days,
>   with Ocean Seas cloasde in.
> That fertile is, and peopled well, and
>   stord with pleasant fields:
> And hath for tillage lucky land, that
>   yeerly profit yields.[60]

The pastoralism in the libretto of Handel's opera is evident enough without historical corroboration. All the King's subjects seem to be shepherds and shepherdesses, the action is concentrated out-of-doors, and a text taken from *Il pastor fido* is added to the original story. The relationship to Guarini's pastoral in general must have been obvious to Handel and his contemporaries.

Alcina (15 April 1735) is a continuation of the pastoral mode. It returns to the magic dominions of a sorceress as in *Amadigi*. Such magical situations were especially favoured in pastorals, and the enchantress, replacing the monster in other examples, always played a special role.[61]

---

[58] The libretto from which Handel's was adapted is by Antonio Salvi, first set to music by Perti (Pratolino, 1708), and the addition of the kissing incident is attributable to this source. The choruses, however, were new in Handel's version.

[59] Praz, 'The Flaming Heart', pp. 290–1.

[60] The complete translation is given in Charles T. Prouty, *The Sources of 'Much Ado about Nothing': A Critical Study, together with the Text of Peter Beverley's 'Ariodante and Jenevra'* (New Haven, Yale University Press, 1950).

[61] In *Rinaldo* and *Teseo* the magical realms of the enchantresses are oases or strictly illusionary. This expels them from the pastoral category. *Amadigi*, which is also somewhat of this cast, may be allowed because of its lack of martial and political motives and its generally more pastoral atmosphere. Melissa does create illusionary landscapes, but the entire opera is set in her territory. There is no vacillation.

In ancient literature, the primary danger to the consciousness inherent in the wilderness is manifested and symbolized in its animal inhabitants. . . . While the monster embodies the terror engendered by the hostility of featureless terrain to the rational process, the enchantress – the second major peril of the wilderness – incarnates its feminine seductiveness, the temptation for man to yield to antirational self-indulgences of the body and spirit, unbridled sexuality or slothful day-dreaming, away from the restraints of his community and its institutions.[62]

In fact, Ruggiero's abdication of his duties (both martial and marital) to live the life of sensual pleasure on Alcina's magic island is but a prelude to the main story in which he regains his sense of responsibility through the efforts of his true beloved, Bradamente, and repudiates the life of leisure. *Alcina* is a pastoral morality, like *Seelewig* where the characters actually take on allegorical names, but even more like *Comus*, 'a spiritualised Aminta' in which Tasso's pastoral becomes 'a morality in antique garb'.[63]

In both dramas enchantment is used to detain persons who stumble into the realm of the sorcerer. In both the sorcerer is able to turn unwanted persons into animals, and, in both this power is associated with Circe. Comus is Circe's son; Alcina performs her similar enchantments in the presence of a statue of Circe. Finally in both dramas the enslaved person is rescued by the return of a loved one.

The literary connection between *Comus* and *Alcina* is not a novel idea: it was certainly clear in Handel's time. It has been shown how the rivalries between Handel, English opera, and the Opera of the Nobility had encouraged direct competition. Handel had been spurred to turn to pastoral composition by the increased strength of the English operatic movement. When they failed with their production of Handel's *Acis*, the English group immediately turned to Gay's second classical pastoral and produced *Dione* (1733) with music by Lampe. In 1734 an English 'dramatic pastoral', *Florimel* by Maurice Greene, was privately produced.[64] The Opera of the Nobility had beaten Handel with a production of *Arianna* in 1733. In 1735 it followed Handel with *Polifemo*. As operatic rivalry engendered three pastoral productions of the Acis legend in differing national styles, so within less than three years *Alcina* provoked both rival companies to produce operatic versions of *Comus*.

As with Rolli's *Polifemo*, Rolli's *Sabrina* (26 April 1737) turned the

---

[62] Piehler, *The Visionary Landscape*, pp. 73–4.
[63] Praz, *The Flaming Heart*, pp. 330–1.
[64] See H. Diack Johnstone, 'Greene's first opera: "Florimel" or "Love's Revenge" (1734)', *MT*, cxiv (1973), pp. 1112–13.

story into an Italian pastoral. Instead of a sister with two brothers and no love interest, Rolli uses two brother and sister pairs. Each sister is betrothed to the other's brother, and the trip through the woods is *en route* to the location of their double wedding. Unfortunately the score of this opera is no longer extant, and it is even uncertain who might have composed it. Probably it was a pasticcio. The libretto calls for seven characters, the four lovers, Sabrina, Comus, and Thyrais, a shepherd. There is no chorus. There are about ten arias in each act.

As opposed to *Sabrina*, *Comus* (4 March 1738) follows the English traditions. The drama was adapted by John Dalton; Thomas Arne, son of the impresario, was the composer. The operatic adaptation of Milton's one-act masque closely follows the similar adaptation six years earlier by Arne Senior of Gay's one-act pastoral masque.

Dalton divides Milton's poetry of 1,023 lines almost exactly in thirds, breaking it at ll. 330 and 659. Act I, then, portrays the Lady and her confrontation with Comus. Act II presents the brothers and their rejection of Comus' crew. Act III blends and resolves the actions of the previous acts. In Act I, typical of all three acts, Dalton discards only twelve of 330 lines, while breaking up Milton's longer speeches into faster-paced dialogue. To facilitate the conversion Dalton adds an extra Spirit; he also adds seventy-seven new lines, many of which are simply descriptive, explanatory, or exclamatory. Dalton, however, also saw the need for additional musical opportunities, and this is where most of his interpolations fit. In Act I, he adds eight new lines for the duet, 'From tyrant laws and customs free', another eight for the solo, 'By the gayly circling glass', eight more for the solo, 'Fly swiftly, ye minutes', and four for the concluding chorus, 'Away, away'.

In the second act, Dalton's large interpolation of 136 lines occurs toward the very end to incorporate the entrance of Comus's throng in a scene akin to an antimasque. It includes two new songs, a trio, and a repetition of the choral ending to Act I. The third act includes the longest interpolation, beginning with twenty-six lines from Milton's own *L'Allegro*. Dalton then proceeds to add four songs and an opportunity for a dance. A little later, before returning definitely to Milton's text, he adds two more songs, one of which is danced. Finally, he closes the act with a chorus.

This English operatic adaptation of *Comus* thus returns to a somewhat earlier style. It incorporates spoken dialogue, and extra opportunities are made for the dance. Dalton was careful, however, to increase the purely musical moments of the libretto and to conclude his acts with choral finales. When this production was repeated in Exton in the spring of 1745, Handel was asked to provide some additional music, and his three songs connected with a choral refrain were used as a new epilogue.[65] At this time or perhaps later, some of Handel's music from *L'Allegro* (1740) was also introduced at the beginning of Act III where Dalton had first inserted lines from that poem.[66]

In the 1730s, however, Handel was still fighting for survival among three operatic traditions. In fact, the productions of the Italian *Sabrina* and the English *Comus* were most likely occasioned by competition with Handel's *Alcina* in the German pastoral tradition. *Alcina* begins by showing the audience the true state of affairs, the oasis-like nature of Alcina's pleasure garden. Ruggiero's rescuers, Bradamante and Melisso, arrive at a barren landscape closed in by steep mountains. To find Ruggiero they must enter the magical kingdom which for its inhabitants represents the entire world. In scene ii, amidst thunder and lightning, this world is opened up to them, represented by choruses who sing, 'This is the heaven of the contented, this is the centre of joy, this is the Elysium of the living, where heroes have their pleasure.' The job of Bradamante and Melisso will be to convince Ruggiero that this world is an illusion. The device of showing its illusionary nature, however, only emphasizes how real this world can appear for even the audience itself quickly accepts the delusion. This, of course, is just what happens to an initiate such as Ruggiero, 'who now considers the Garden of Deduit itself as the world. What was a moment ago but a part now becomes the whole.'[67]

Handel includes in this pastoral opera not only the 'spectacular revelation of Alcina's court in the second scene, with its life of endless pleasure celebrated in a seductive sequence of chorus and ballet movements',[68] but an extraordinary choral finale covering four scenes. Beginning with a chorus, 'Sin per le vie del sole', it includes the pantomime of the boy Oberto with his father-turned-lion and the boy's repudiation of Alcina. It continues in a climactic trio for Alcina, Ruggiero, and Bradamante, and the pantomime where Ruggiero breaks Alcina's urn, destroying her illusory kingdom. There follows a chorus for the released

[65] See Anthony Hicks, 'Handel's Music for *Comus*', *MT* cxvii (1976), pp. 28–9, for a complete description of this music newly discovered by Hicks. See also Betty Matthews, 'Unpublished Letters Concerning Handel', *ML*, xl (1959), pp. 261–8. Handel may have had a strong sense of fight, but he obviously held no grudges. After vanquishing Bononcini in the first academy, Handel performed an opera of his at the end of the 1731–1732 season. After surviving the blow of the *Beggar's Opera*, produced by John Rich, the father, he turned to John Rich, the son, for performance rights at Covent Garden in 1734. After squashing the pirated version of *Acis* and the English operatic revival directed by the elder Arne, he wrote music for a production of the younger. And after the Opera of the Nobility collapsed, Handel took Rolli back as a librettist for his last operas.

[66] See the Correspondence of Winton Dean, *ML*, xl (1959), p. 406.

[67] John V. Fleming, *The Roman de la Rose: a Study in Allegory and Iconography* (Princeton, N.J.: Princeton University Press, 1969), p. 65, describing the enchanted garden of that poem.

[68] Dean, *Opera*, p. 51.

prisoners who describe their former states – a wild animal, a stone, a tree, and a wave. A sequence of dances continues the action, the last of which is repeated in the concluding chorus.

Handel's last opera in this period of consecutive pastorals was written for the wedding of the Prince of Wales. *Atalanta* first appeared 12 May 1736. The story represents still another mythological legend pastoralized into an offshoot of Guarini's pastoral.[69] Atalanta (like Silvio in *Il pastor fido*) prefers hunting to love-making. A princess by birth, she flees into the Arcadian forest disguised as Amarillis, a shepherdess. Meleager, King of Aetolia and Atalanta's would-be lover, follows her there disguised as the shepherd Thirsis. By the end of the opera, Atalanta falls in love with Meleager, and their correct identities are revealed. Thus the happy royal nuptials ensue amid a spectacular fireworks display accompanied by the now-anticipated Grand Choral Finale.[70]

	Entrance of Mercury
	Sinfonia
	arioso: 'Del supremo Tonante'
	aria: 'Sol prova contenti'
	Chorus: 'Dalla stirpe degli Eroe'
A	Chorus: 'Gridiam, gridiam'
A'	Dance
B	Chorus: 'Viva la face'
B	Dance
B	Chorus: 'Viva la face'
B	Dance
A	Chorus: 'Con voce giuliva'

To return to ideas posed in the Introduction, it should be evident by now that Handel (and his librettist) did not add this huge choral finale, and a chorus at the beginning of Act II, only because *Atalanta* was

[69] A number of operas in the seventeenth and early eighteenth centuries had been based on this legend. It is possible to group them into 'families'. The largest, which was kindly pointed out to me by Duncan Chisholm, went under various titles including *La costanza in amor vince l'inganno*, *Felicita d'Imenei*, and *Attalanta* (sic) and occurs at least six times between 1694 and 1736. This libretto, however, is different from Handel's in a number of ways. There is, for example, an officially organized contest for the slaying of the wild boar. After Atalanta throws a dart but misses, Meleager saves her from the boar's attack. These librettos also contain the familiar pastoral devices of giving Meleager a confidant and having the lovers leave love notes on the trees. In Handel's libretto there are no love notes, no confidant, no contest, and Atalanta must save Meleager after *he* misses. The set of librettos from which Handel's derives is much smaller and newer than the family above. It may be traced back to *La caccia in Etolia* (Ferrara, 1715) by Valeriani, set by Chelleri. This opera was performed again in Heidelberg, 1722, and a new setting appeared by Buini in Venice, 1720. Only Handel's, of course, includes choruses. Another set which is German-oriented and culminates in Bressand's *Atalanta* (Brunswick, 1698), is also unrelated to Handel's libretto, although in the German tradition.

[70] The thematic repetitions used during these final movements are noted by the letters A and B.

written for a royal occasion. Otherwise there would be no way to explain similar choruses and finales in, for example, the Ariosto operas *Orlando*, *Ariodante*, and *Alcina*. Handel uses these large choral scenes in pastoral operas. When large choruses are appropriate to a festive occasion, the pastoral becomes the appropriate topic. The choruses were not added because of the festive occasion.

Some authors hold that the finale points to the influence of Rameau. Dean writes that Handel 'ended the opera with a string of choruses and instrumental movements in the manner of Rameau.'[71] The French influence may be there but it is filtered through a German sieve. Any influence of Rameau is most improbable. Rameau did not produce *Hippolyte*, his first opera, until 1733. His first opera-ballet was performed in 1735, in the midst of Handel's set of so-called ballet operas. There is no evidence that any dramatic work by Rameau was performed in London at all during the eighteenth century,[72] and it is hard to see what effect it might have had in any case. Handel's turn to the German pastoral traditions clearly begins in 1732.

Atalanta carries on the German pastoral tradition. The reason that this opera, along with *Orlando*, *Arianna*, *Ariodante*, and *Alcina*, appears to illustrate Handel's loosening of the *opera seria* conventions is that it, like the others, is not an *opera seria*. The heroic works of this type which Handel wrote for the first and second Academies do contain many unconventional details which reflect the generally looser traditions of Hamburg and are to many modern ears their most redeeming traits. Yet in discussing Handel's freedom from strict convention, modern scholars almost always turn to the period 1732–6 for examples. Although the specific choice varies from author to author, the comments are quite similar.

Heroic operas by Handel and other composers working in Germany and England sometimes show conservative influences. . . . Handel never forgot his younger days in Hamburg where *da capo* form had been far from obligatory and where *ariosos*, songs and instrumental sections had been used to create much freer overall structures than were possible in the Metastasian type of opera. The relatively free forms of much of his *Orlando furioso*, 1733, with its many *ariosos*, reflect the music of the Hamburg operas with which Handel was earlier acquainted.[73]

However, Handel would not have considered *Orlando*, or any of the others, heroic. The general freedom, the use of chorus and dance, ariosos and sinfonias, relates directly to these operas' pastoral character.

---

[71] Winton Dean, 'Handel's Wedding Opera', *MT*, cxi (1970), p. 705. See Lang, *Handel*, pp. 252–3, about the influence of French opera on *Alcina*.
[72] See Van Lennep, *et al.*, *The London Stage*.
[73] Robinson, *Opera before Mozart*, p. 122.

Much has been said to disparage German baroque opera. Einstein writes that at the time of Gluck, 'German opera did not yet exist', that what was performed at Hamburg and elsewhere in that country was 'a hybrid, an offshoot, a bastard form of French and Italian opera'.[74] In *Baroque Music* by Claude V. Palisca, the subject of German opera does not even appear.[75] Thus it comes as no surprise that any influence it might have had on Handel is regularly belittled. Nevertheless, Handel's music clearly reflects German conventions. What he wrote in Hamburg reflected the Hamburg tradition and, especially, Keiser. In Italy, he learned how to write Italianate compositions modelled on Scarlatti. After presenting himself to London Handel studied the English musical style descended from Purcell. However it remains true that Handel was born in Germany and received his musical training there.

In other countries Handel worked to learn the national conventions. Once this was accomplished he fitted what he had learned into his own personal compositional style which had the German tradition as its basis. It becomes, therefore, a treacherous business to try to identify specific national traits in Handel's style. Thus, the one piece chosen by Lang to epitomize the English style in *Acis* (1718) 'Hush ye pretty warbling choir' was borrowed from the Italian *Aci*; the accompaniment, moreover, originated in Keiser's *Octavia*.[76] Dent strongly implies that the arias in *Rodrigo* are Germanic, whereas '*Agrippina* was written mainly under the influence of Alessandro Scarlatti'.[77] In fact, *Agrippina* contains more borrowed German material than *Rodrigo*, and the one aria from *Agrippina* that Dent points out as strikingly advanced, 'Pensieri, voi mi tormente', was borrowed from *Rodrigo*.[78]

Keiser's music and the opera at Hamburg influenced Handel's music throughout his career. The pastoral form represents a specific example. Handel also learned and wrote in the Italian pastoral form. He composed an English pastoral masque. Yet after producing one of each type in London, he returned to the German convention; both *Acis* and *Il pastor fido* became German pastorals in their revisions. As Hamburg opera synthesized many outside influences, so did Handel. Into the German format he fitted the Grand Choral Finale of the English masque. He bent the Italian convention of the *da capo* aria with its thematically related sections to a dramatic end. In creating this

[74] Alfred Einstein, *Gluck*, trans, by Eric Blom (London: J. M. Dent and Sons, Ltd., 1954), p. 1.
[75] Englewood Cliffs, New Jersey: Prentice-Hall, Inc., 1968.
[76] See Lang, *Handel*, p. 274, and Dean, *Oratorio*, p. 641.
[77] Dent, 'Opera', pp. 20-1.
[78] Ibid., p. 22.

international synthesis, however, the basic framework remained German.

The stretch of time during which Handel returned to the German pastoral form is bounded by the major successes of two oratorios: *Athalia* (1733) and *Saul* (1738). Generally this period is reckoned as 'obscure and difficult'.[79] Before it, Handel may be considered solely in the light of *opera seria*; after it he becomes the composer of oratorios. No one seems to understand why Handel delayed this 'conversion' for five years.

A trend which is observable in retrospect is not always as easily observable at the time. Italian opera may have been doomed, but the years 1733 to 1738 formed the period of its most intense activity. It may have been clear that London would not support two Italian houses; but Handel could easily have expected to win this battle and continue alone with his supremacy proven. Dean writes:

> During the five years that separated *Athalia* from *Saul*, Handel produced nine new operas and expanded or altered several others. His activities were governed by the cut and thrust of the struggle with the Opera of the Nobility. . . . We must not expect to find evidence of a consistent artistic policy on either side.[80]

This, however, is exactly what one does find.

The confluence of incentives, including the renewed rivalry of English opera, a pirated performance, the competition from the Opera of Nobility, the availability of a ballet corps and chorus, and the two royal weddings, turned Handel's composition away from *opera seria* to the pastoral. He clearly saw this dramatic genre as a double-edged tool that could lure audiences away from the rival productions of Italian *opera seria* and English pastorals as well. The German pastoral functioned on a middle ground with elements of each form.

Handel's plan succeeded. This is clear even from a list of the operas performed by the Opera of the Nobility. Basically founded on a programme of heroic *opera seria*, in 1735 the academy began to borrow Handel's methods. The two new operas that year by Rolli and Porpora were *Polifemo* and *Ifigenia in Aulide*, a striking change of direction. In 1736, Porpora and Rolli came up with *Fest'Imeno* for the wedding of the Prince of Wales. After *Atalanta*, however, the prince deserted the company he had founded and reverted to Handel's camp. One of the last efforts of this company was Rolli's adaptation of Milton's *Comus*.

---

[79] Dean, *Oratorio*, p. 265.
[80] Ibid., p. 267.

Handel's life from 1733 to 1738 may be 'obscure and difficult' to modern commentators, but during this time Handel had a clear plan. This plan of pastoral compositions succeeded in defeating all operatic rivals; at the same time, it also led the way to Handel's oratorio style.

CHAPTER VII

Conclusions

HANDEL'S OPERAS FROM 1737 TO 1741

By the end of the seventeenth century the pastoral conventions of Italy, Germany, and England were distinct and clearly distinguishable from one another. In each of these countries the musical traits of the pastoral were closely related to the developing literary traditions, and it was the differences in these which gave each operatic type the specific style of its own. To a large extent, with the flexibility one must allow to any artistic genre, these three distinct literary and musical styles of pastoral composition remained extremely stable throughout the first half of the eighteenth century. In fact, during the 1730s all three types were set up in direct competition with one another on the London stage. Twice there appeared a complete set of three pastorals of differing nationalities based on the same story or on closely parallel stories.

During this decade Handel's dramatic compositions for London represented the German pastoral traditions. He returned to a reuse of these conventions through a direct rivalry with the English pastoral tradition, and the Italian opera company, the Opera of the Nobility, was led to produce pastorals of its own through competition with Handel. Only when the collapse of this company seemed imminent in 1737 did Handel interrupt his unbroken string of pastoral productions.

From 1732 to 1736 every new production (and the complete transformations of *Acis* and *Il pastor fido* belong in this category rather than with the revivals) had been clearly related to the German pastoral traditions. It is this alone which explains the increasing use of choral movements during these years and the extraordinary succession of built-up choral finales. External happenstance, such as the availability of Mlle. Sallé's dance company, simply did not affect Handel's programme, as the original version of *Ariodante* clearly illustrates. The chorus had already been given an integral role.

Perhaps during this time Handel still harboured the idea of returning, once the opposition was vanquished, to the uncontested production of heroic operas. At any rate he broke his run of pastorals suddenly in 1737 with three heroic operas, *Arminio*, *Giustino*, and *Berenice*. These represent Handel's greatest operatic failures. Nevertheless

Giustino is especially fascinating in its apparent rapprochement between pastoral style and heroic text. The opera opens with a large chorus, the first act includes a choral scene with Goddess Fortuna, the second act includes a chorus in praise of the love of the protagonists (similar to a situation later in *Solomon*), and the opera closes with a built-up finale incorporating chorus and soloists. Each situation in itself could easily be pastoral, but the opera as a whole simply is not. The specific incentive seems to come from the mention of the Golden Age, a definitely pastoral era, in the first chorus and the belief stated in the last chorus that it has been attained once more. Although Handel relates the last aria and final chorus of *Serse* (1738) through their accompaniments, and he derives the final chorus of *Faramondo* (1738) melodically from the previous aria, he would not again try the experiment of *Giustino*.

Meanwhile the pastoral was not forgotten. Rolli's *Sabrina* had been produced in 1737. Arne's *Comus* first appeared in 1738. In 1739 'a pastoral opera' by Giovanni Baptista Pescetti was produced in London (10 March 1739). Perhaps importantly, it told the same story as Handel's *Orlando* (1733) and used the libretto (with some substitutions for the original arias) of Porpora's *Angelica e Medoro* (1720) which title it retained. After the collapse of the Opera of the Nobility, Pescetti had apparently been hired to replace Porpora at Covent Garden.

Porpora's opera follows the Italian pastoral conventions in every way. Of the first eight arias in Act II, for example, only those three sung by the demented Orlando are not in the monothematic pastoral aria form. The others show not only striking melodic similarities between sections but usually include identical accompanimental forces in both sections as well. Two examples follow, both of which are instrumented for strings.

Ex 1

Pescetti's 1739 version is not as interesting for its use of the Italian conventions as for its bow to the English pastoral. In light, perhaps, of the success of Handel's pastorals and the English pastorals, and the collapse of the Opera of the Nobility (Rolli's *Sabrina* had been a dismal failure even after an intermezzo was added), Pescetti's libretto includes interesting variants from the original by Metastasio. It opens with a chorus. Four arias are omitted from Act I, and this first act closes with a new duet. Act II also opens with a chorus; there are five aria substitutions, one aria is omitted, and this act also closes with a chorus. The choral additions along with a general reduction of its dimensions point to an attempt to capture the English pastoral spirit. In size, at least, the Italian and English pastorals have a common ground from which they can proceed. The German pastoral, on the other hand, is diametrically opposed to the Italian tradition; it continued to be Handel's resource.

In 1739 Handel produced another German-style pastoral, *Jupiter in Argos* (1 May 1739).[1] Although Handel used a libretto new to him (*Giove in Argo* by Antonio Maria Lucchini), he maintained a compositional practice parallel to that in the revisions of *Acis* (1732) and *Il pastor fido*. In general using previously written compositions of his own, Handel takes the basic recitative structure of an Italian pastoral and transforms it according to German convention.[2] Most of the arias are borrowed. In his autograph Handel simply indicates the operas from which the arias should be taken and the necessary transpositions. The borrowings come from every period in Handel's career, from works including the Italian cantatas (1707–08), *Teseo* (1713), *Scipione* (1726), *Tolomeo* (1728), *Alcina* (1735), *Arminio* (1737), and *Giustinio* (1737). Often, as in earlier pasticcios, these appear with their original texts.

---

[1] The performance itself cannot be firmly verified. It was advertised in the *London Daily Post* from 26 April 1739 to 30 April 1739. See Jacob M. Coopersmith, 'The Libretto of Handel's *Jupiter in Argos*,' *ML*, xvii (1930), pp. 289–95.

[2] The most complete source, an autograph, which begins with Act II and contains only a fragment of Act III, may be found at the Fitzwilliam Museum, Cambridge (Fitz. 30 H 8).

A few points may be made about the choruses. These, of course, do not appear in the original libretto. The second act begins with chorus; another is called for in scene ii. The third act, of which only the last scenes exist, ends with a succession of choral movements, 'S'unisce al tuo martiro' and 'D'amor di Giove'. The first is borrowed from *Parnasso in festa*; the second is newly composed. The choruses in Act II, however, are both borrowed. The first, identified by Handel as 'Care selve', had been thought possibly to indicate a choral version of the opening arioso of *Alcina*, 'Care selve'.[3] Certainly this is not the case. It must refer to the chorus 'Smiling Venus, queen of love' from *Acis* (1732). Handel later added new Italian words in pencil to this conducting score; they begin 'Care selve, date al cor'. As these Italian words cannot be clearly attributed to any of the succeeding revivals of *Acis*, and because the aria which formed the middle section of this repeated chorus is not translated, one may assume the translation was made for *Jupiter in Argos*. And it leads one to postulate that the Italian text written over the autograph of 'Heart the seat of soft delight' (*Acis*, 1718) may also originate with this performance. Neither Italian text is a translation of the English; different dramatic situations are implied.

The second chorus in Act II, 'Oh! quanto bella gloria', is borrowed from *Parnasso in festa* from where it initially moved into *Il pastor fido* (1734). The mention of *Parnasso* (rather than *Il pastor fido*) may be revealing since, as in *Jupiter*, this chorus begins a scene devoted to hunting enthusiasts. (In *Il pastor fido* it closes the second act.) Indeed, in *Jupiter* it is followed by solo material for Diana, goddess of the hunt. At the end of this scene Handel writes, 'poi replica una parte . . .,' the rest of which has been lost in the trimming of the manuscript. But the sense is surely to repeat the shortened version of 'Oh! quanto bella' exactly as the scene had been rounded off in *Parnasso*. Like its pastoral predecessors, from which most of the choral material is borrowed, *Jupiter in Argos* belongs to the German tradition.

In 1740, Handel wrote only one opera, *Imeneo*, a pastoral. Perhaps incited by Pescetti's pastoral of 1739 (Handel's first and discarded manuscript for this opera dates from 1738), *Imeneo* adheres to English dimensions. It includes choruses − all the acts end with one − and an especially fine trio. In its size and reduced accompanimental forces, however, *Imeneo* moves away from German conventions. Just as when Handel returned to heroic opera in 1737 he failed, so too did his return to reduced pastoral dimensions fail to lure the London audiences.

[3] See Coopersmith, 'Libretto,' p. 291.

Handel's last opera, *Deidamia* (10 January 1741), in the heroic vein, also failed to please.[4]

Lang tries to describe Handel's thoughts at the end of this, his last operatic season. 'And now quiet settled down both on the theatre and on the house in Brook Street; Handel seemed at last to have acknowledged defeat and given up opera. What was his state of mind? He must have been baffled; neither oratorio nor opera was successful, only the pastorals found favor with the public.'[5] The pastoral form should not, however, be denigrated. The pastorals of the 1730s, in fact, served as the proving ground for Handel's later dramatic oratorios.

In Handel's production of oratorios there are two big gaps. The first and longer exists between *Athalia* (1733) and *Saul* (1738). The second occurs between *Saul* and *Samson* (1742). In 1732 for competitve reasons Handel had returned to the German pastoral for the first time since leaving Hamburg. During his first oratorio break, Handel continued to build on this tradition with an unbroken chain of pastorals in the German tradition culminating in 1736 with *Atalanta*. This represented a complete change of direction from his heroic operas of the 1720s.

After 1736 Handel experimented with the basic structure of the German pastoral. He applied it to a heroic opera in *Giustino*, he reduced it to English dimensions in *Imeneo*, but he was not successful in either case.[6] Although many have wondered, often in dismay, at Handel's persistence in the composition of operas during the 1730s, it is clear that this was no unconscious choice. Handel's pastoral decade separates the heroic decade of the 1720s from the oratorio decade of the 1740s. It also provides their link. Consider the wide gaps between Italian heroic opera and English oratorio bridged by Handel's German pastorals.

---

[4] Similar to *Giustino*, but far less revolutionary in its approach, *Deidamia* includes choruses at the end of Acts II and III, as well as a hunting chorus in Act II. The choral material in *Giustino* is more elaborate and generally integrated into the action.

[5] Lang, *Handel*, p. 326.

[6] At the end of the first and during this second 'break' Handel also composed his three most exquisite English odes, *Alexander's Feast* (1736) and *Ode to St. Cecilia* (1739) by Dryden, and *L'Allegro ed il Penseroso* (1740) by Milton. (He also made his first anglicization of Panfili's *Il trionfo*.) Related by their size and use of choruses to the English pastoral masque, these compositions may have influenced Handel's seeming adaptation of a more English pastoral format in *Imeneo* (1742). Yet, in the end, these odes, as full of pastoral sentiments as they are, are neither dramas nor pastorals, and their use of the chorus is, therefore, less dramatic than in the operas. These works are closer in style to the *Chandos Anthems* than to Handel's dramatic compositions and do not play an active role in the development of Handel's oratorio style.

SACRED AND SECULAR TEXTS

Discovering the correct derivation of the musical form found in Handel's oratorios has been hindered by what appears to many an insurmountable barrier between sacred and secular compositions. In the baroque era, however, the pastoral had many points of contact with sacred drama. In the conventions of dramaturgy, for example, they were considered two types of the same genre. Thus, Giambattista Doni (1593–1647) says explicitly that the pastoral and the spiritual drama make up the two types of tragicomedy.[7] The reason for this may well be that like Guarini, the fountainhead of all things pastoral in the baroque era, Doni traces the pastoral back specifically to the Hebrews.

I would allow the pastoral to have musical settings of all its parts, especially since gods, nymphs, and shepherds of that oldest century [the Golden Age] in which music was natural and speech almost poetic are introduced into it. We know, in fact, that the most ancient Greek writers were poets much before their art was codified, and even before them, the Hebrew patriarchs and prophets wrote poetry naturally as can be seen from the sublime canticle of Moses.[8]

The Biblical Hebrews, then, the subjects of the vast majority of Handel's oratorios, could be considered the earliest, and perhaps only, human pastoral civilization, parallel to the mythological nymphs and swains of the Golden Age. This relationship is clear enough in the parity of Handel's two oratorios of 1742, *Samson* and *Semele*.

Many links exist between sacred and pastoral drama. The similarities in their literary handling, for instance, led to their practically simultaneous use as the earliest opera librettos. *Euridice* by Peri and Rinuccini was produced in Florence on 16 October 1600. Cavalieri produced *La rappresentazione di anima e di corpo* in Rome in 1600. The arguments which ensued over the priority of one or the other of these works as the first opera continue today. Yet they do not concern the priority of the dramatic forms which sprang from a single source and often reverted to their combined form, the morality.

The use of didactic allegory in pastorals has been seen as a familiar device. *Eumelio: dramma pastorale* (Rome, 1606) by Agostino Agazzari 'is of an allegoric youth who is torn between the enticements of pleasure and vice and the appeals of reason and virtue.'[9] The earliest

[7] Doni, 'Trattato', p. 15.
[8] Ibid.
[9] Pirrotta, 'Early Opera', p. 75.

extant German opera, *Seelewig* (1644) by Staden and Harsdorffer, was subtitled 'geistliche Waldgedicht' or spiritual pastoral.

The close association between the pastoral and Christianity was also seen in the make-up of the Roman Arcadian Academy. In music this association is nowhere so clear as in the *siciliano*, which vacillates between picturing languorous nature scenes and the shepherds at Christ's Nativity. Handel's compositions provide specific examples. In fact the precedent for 'He shall feed his flock like a shepherd' from the *Messiah* appears to be the Musette which begins the ballet suite for the shepherds in the first act finale of *Ariodante*.

This link between pastoral and sacred associations crops up through-out Handel's oeuvre. The Chandos Anthems, for example, are full of nature painting. 'But the pastoral is as much in Handel's poetic make-up as it is characteristic of the Psalmists.'[10] Moreover, similarity of these two styles reflects itself in the pattern of Handel's borrowing. The *Brockes Passion* appears in *Acis* (1718). It reappears in the *Acis* revision. *La resurrezione* turns up in *Il pastor fido*. But most important, *Athalia* practically becomes *Parnasso*, which 'should warn those who see the oratorios as "sacred music" to be careful.'[11]

Opera in Hamburg began with a religious drama, *Der erschaffene, gefallene und wieder aufgerichte Mensch* (1678) by Christian Richter and Johann Theile. With the emergence of other dramatic types, this kind of opera retained its popularity. In 1703, Keiser and Hunold produced an opera about Solomon; in 1704 one about Nebuchadnezzar.[12] The year 1709 saw a production by Feind and Graupner about Samson.[13] These were not 'oratorios', but dramatic presentations.

Dean notes the close association between the literary style of the late oratorios and the pastoral masques of the early eighteenth century.

The reader is continually struck by verbal parallels between [the librettos of the early eighteenth-century English pastoral masques] and texts subse-quently set by Handel. Admittedly the emotions and the language of pastoral,

---

[10] Lang, *Handel*, p. 217.
[11] Ibid., p. 249.
[12] See Brockpähler, *Handbuch*, p. 204.
[13] Ibid., p. 205.

and of minor eighteenth-century poetry in general, are narrowly circum-
scribed; but there is enough evidence to suggest that Morell may have drawn
on these old masques in seeking inspiration for his oratorios. . . .

The first lines 'Gentle Morpheus, still relieve me', 'Softest strains of
musick sounding' and 'Conduct her to the gloomy shade' (all from *The Death
of Dido*) are each echoed in the first lines of late oratorio airs which were
certainly or probably the work of Morell; and the six-line air 'Thus the
brave from war returning' (*Venus and Adonis*) anticipated more than one of
Morell's, notably 'Heroes when with glory burning' (*Joshua*), in sentiment,
rhyme, and diction.[14]

Certainly there are associations in subject matter. Jephtha is called
upon to sacrifice his only daughter. Susanna is condemned to death on
trumped-up charges of infidelity. Didymus and Theodora, like Mirtillo
and Amarilli, argue over who will accept the death penalty. It is
significant as well that when Rolli writes a drama based on the subject
of David and Saul, another of Handel's topics, he calls it 'l'Eroe
pastore, melodramma sacro'.[15] Once again, the inclusion of *Semele*,
based on the old Congreve libretto and other pastoral-mythological
texts, among the so-called sacred oratorios graphically illustrates the
similar conventions surrounding biblical and pastoral subjects. *Parnasso
in festa*, *Atalanta*, and *Semele*, for example, and *Jephtha*, *Susanna*, and
Solomon all derive from the same literary category, and Handel sets
them with that in mind.

LANGUAGE AND STAGING

Another major obstacle in reconciling Handel's heroic operas with
his oratorios has been the distinction made between concert and staged
performances. To a certain extent it is a totally unnecessary obstacle.
The concert versions were forced on Handel, and the stage directions
in some of his autographs indicate clearly that he thought of the
oratorios in a dramatic sense. Yet it is also the pastorals which bridge
this gap.

Acis (1732), clearly a drama, was given in costume with no action.
Parnasso in festa (1734) and *Jupiter in Argos* (1739) were both concert
performances. And the only dramatized opera ever to be given later in
a concert version was *Imeneo* (1740) performed in Dublin 1742, the
year Handel began his oratorio decade.

This performance of *Imeneo* also bridged the gap between Italian
and English performances. For the concert version it was given in

[14] Dean, *Oratorio*, pp. 156–7.
[15] George E. Dorris, *Paolo Rolli and the Italian Circle in London: 1715–1744* (*Paris*,
Mouton & Co., 1967), p. 163.

English translation. The pastoral played an important role in English operatic traditions; moreover, all English opera in the 1730s was pastoral. Handel's *Acis* (1732) had also included English sections. The pastoral, which fluctuates naturally between languages, easily served to overcome the language barrier between Italian opera and English oratorio.

CHORUSES

The main difficulty in determining the stylistic origin of Handel's oratorios has centred on an apparent lack of precedent for the handling of the chorus. Reaching back into Handel's previous compositions, some commentators have pointed to the German passions, others to the choruses in the Italian psalm settings. Still more turn to the English anthem. It is certainly true that Handel wrote 'Anthem' oratorios.[16] They include *Israel in Egypt*, *Messiah*, and the *Occasional Oratorio*. These have little bearing, however, on the use of an active chorus in the dramatic oratorio.

The key to both the German pastoral and the dramatic oratorios lies in the role assigned to the chorus. The recent attempts to derive this choral function from Racine and Greek drama tend only to complicate the problem.

It was Racine's treatment of the chorus, deliberately modelled on that of Attic dramatists with their conception of drama on two levels, one enacted by the characters, the other carried by a chorus operating at once within and above the action — and they derive their peculiar power from the fact that they are participants before they are commentators — that transformed the fragmentary eloquence of the Italian operas into the sublime unity of the oratorios.[17]

Whereas it is certainly true that two of Handel's earliest oratorios, *Esther* and *Athalia*, have librettos adapted from dramas by Racine, this in itself would have played a very minor role in Handel's conception of their form. Otherwise one would expect a similar French influence in the setting of the French-derived opera librettos, *Teseo* (1713) from Quinault, *Amadigi* (1715) from de la Motte, *Flavio* (1723) from Corneille, and *Rodelinda* (1725) from Corneille. On the contrary, however, 'the specifically French qualities have been largely eliminated.'[18] The choruses are noticeably lacking. That is, Handel regarded these opera librettos, except for *Amadigi*, as heroic *opere serie*. He treated

---

[16] Jens Peter Larsen (*Handel's Messiah*, 2nd edition New York: W. W. Norton and Co., 1972, p. (21 coins this term, and it is a good one.

[17] Dean, *Oratorio*, p. 40. See also Lang, *Handel*, p. 283.

[18] David Kimbell, 'Libretto of Handel's *Teseo*', *ML*, xliv (1963), p. 379.

them as such. The reason *Amadigi* was not treated the same way was not because of its French origin, but because it was conceived as a pastoral.

The 'transformation' of Handel's style from opera to oratorio derives from the German pastoral conventions, from Handel's circumstantially motivated return to these during the years 1732 to 1736, and from the strong literary connection between pastoral and biblical texts. That is, the stylistic changes made in his operas during this 'difficult and obscure period' of the 1730s lead directly into the style used in the oratorios. Handel's pastoral period bridges the gap between the *opera seria* and the oratorio.

HANDEL'S CAREER: A SUMMARY

That Handel continued to depend throughout his life on the German conventions he absorbed in his youth might come as a surprise to many. The general consensus has been that his operas are entirely Italian – 'Four years in Italy (1706–1710) converted Handel almost exclusively to the melodious Italian manner . . .'[19] – and that his oratorios reflect (Racine's influence aside), his English naturalization.[20] Of course, there is truth in all these assertions.

Handel epitomizes the baroque. Born in Germany, he was totally familiar with German operatic conventions. He travelled to, and learned the conventions of operatic productions in Italy and England. Certainly he was aware of operatic practices in France. Moreover, the pastoral genre in Handel's corpus provides specific examples of the composer's separate use of these national styles.

In Hamburg, Handel set a pastoral text using the German conventions. Unfortunately the music for this divided opera, *Florindo* and *Daphne*, is lost, but a study of the libretto reveals to what extent the libretto adheres to the conventions and suggests ways in which it might have been set.

In Italy, Handel adopted the Italian pastoral mode completely. The stylistic alteration can be observed in the cantatas he wrote for Ruspoli during a two-year span. The larger cantatas and serenatas, such as *Aci, Galatea e Polifemo*, *Apollo e Dafne*, and *Clori, Tirsi, e Fileno*, illustrate this change.

Once in England Handel's initial productions included two operas in opposing styles: the freer form of the *opera seria* as practised in Hamburg and the stricter form of the Italian pastoral. The latter was a

---

[19] Palisca, *Baroque Music*, p. 188.
[20] Lang devotes an entire chapter to a rebuttal of the 'peculiar' German notion that Handel remained influenced by his German heritage (*Handel*, Chapt. xxvii, pp. 679–705).

total failure. In the period of the Royal Academy of Music, therefore, Handel depended totally on heroic opera.

In the years between 1732 and 1738, Handel was faced with a series of tremendous challenges which caused him to abandon his earlier methods. During these years Handel increasingly turned away from heroic subjects toward the operatic conventions of the German pastoral. The important transformations of *Acis and Galatea* and *Il pastor fido* into German-type pastorals both fall within this period as do the three Ariosto operas, *Orlando, Ariodante,* and *Alcina.*

This period has been troublesome for musicologists to explain. After the huge success of the English oratorio, *Athalia,* in 1733, the pause of five years before another appeared (*Saul,* 1738) seems at first inexplicable except in terms of Handel's shortsightedness or stubbornness. During this time that Handel fought ferociously with his competition, the direction he was to take became clear.

Both the pastoral operas and the oratorios depend on the musical and literary conventions of the German pastoral. Their common derivation may be explained by the close connection of the two dramatic types as examples of one literary category and by the continual association in music between pastoral and religious settings.

There can be no doubt of Handel's continued and 'lively intellectual interest in literary affairs. . . . Literature and the literary permanently attracted Handel.'[21] At times one must assume that the composer had a strong hand in the final forms of his librettos. Indeed Handel always seems to have surrounded himself not with musicians, but with writers. In Italy he was actively involved with the Roman Academy. In England, he cultivated the same kind of association with the Scriblerus Club. Other composers seem to have represented to Handel only a source of competition, or sometimes simply a source.

Handel's abiding literary interests explain in part why the compositions adhere as strictly as they do to literary conventions. In fact, Handel's artistic commitment to a relationship between the arts was already evident when, at the age of twelve, the composer signed a poem he had written on the death of his father:[22]

> Georg Friedrick Händel,
> dedicated to the liberal arts.

---

[21] Percy M. Young, 'Handel the Man,' in *Symposium,* pp. 3–4.
[22] The entire poem in the original German and English translation may be found in Deutsch, *Handel,* pp. 6–8.

Bibliography

Abraham, Gerald, ed. *Handel: A Symposium.* London: Oxford University Press, 1954.

Andreen, Gustav. *Studies in the Idyl in German Literature.* Rock Island, Illinois: Lutheran Augustana Book Concern, Printers, 1902.

Arkwright, G. E. P. 'Handel's Cantata, *Conosco che me piaci.' The Musica Antiquary,* i (1909–10), pp. 254–5.

Armstrong, A. Joseph. *Operatic Performances in England before Handel.* Waco, Texas: Baylor University Press, 1918.

Avery, Emmett L. and Scouten, A. H. 'A Tentative Calendar of Daily Theatrical Performances in London, 1700–1 to 1704–5.' *PMLA,* lxiii (1948), pp. 114–80.

Baker, C. H. Collins and Muriel I. *The Life and Circumstances of James Brydges – First Duke of Chandos.* Oxford: Clarendon Press, 1949.

Bannard, Yorke. 'Music of the Commonwealth.' *Music and Letters,* iii (1922), pp. 394–401.

Baretti, Joseph. *An Account of the Manners and Customs of Italy with Observations on the Mistakes of some Travellers with regard to that Country.* London: T. Davies, 1768.

Batt, Max. *The Treatment of Nature in German Literature from Günther to the Appearance of Goethe's 'Werther'.* Chicago: University of Chicago Press, 1902.

Bell, A. Craig. *Handel: Chronological Thematic Catalogue.* Darley, England: Grian-Aig Press, 1972.

⸻ : 'Handel in Italy.' *The Music Review,* xxviii (1967), pp. 85–101.

Bianconi, Lorenzo and Walker, Thomas. 'Dalla *Finta pazza* alla *Veremonda*: Storie di Febiarmonici.' *Rivista Italiana di Musicologia,* x (1975), pp. 379–454.

Bond, R. Warwick. 'Note on the Italian Influence in Lyly's Plays.' *The Complete Works of John Lyly.* Edited by R. W. Bond. Vol. ii. Oxford: Clarendon Press, 1902. Facsimile edition. Oxford: Clarendon Press, 1967.

Brand, C. P. *Torquato Tasso: A Study of the Poet and his Contribution to English Literature.* Cambridge: Cambridge University Press, 1965.

Brennécke, Ernest. 'Review of *Musica Britannica*, Vols. ii and iii.' *The Musical Quarterly,* xxxviii (1952), pp. 621–5.

Brenner, Rosamond Drooker. 'The Operas of Reinhard Keiser in their Relationship to the "Affectenlehre".' Unpublished Ph.D. dissertation, Brandeis University, 1968.

Brockpähler, Renate. *Handbuch zur Geschichte der Barockoper in Deutschland.* Emsdetten/Westfalen: Lechte Verlag, 1964.

Bruford, Walter Horace. *Germany in the Eighteenth Century: The Social Background of the Literary Revival.* Cambridge: Cambridge University Press, 1935.

Bryan, J. Ingram. *The feeling for Nature in English Pastoral Poetry*. Tokyo: Kyo-Bun-Kwan, 1908.

Buelow, George J. 'An evaluation of Johann Mattheson's opera *Cleopatra* (Hamburg 1704).' *Studies in Eighteenth-Century Music*. New York: Oxford University Press, 1970.

——: '*Die schöne und getreue Ariadne*, a lost opera by J. G. Conradi Rediscovered.' *Acta Musicologica*, xliv (1972), 108–21.

Bullough, Geoffrey. 'Sir Richard Fanshawe and Guarini,' *Studies in English Language and Literature presented to Karl Brunner*. Edited by Siegfried Korninger. Vienna: Wilhelm Braumüller, 1957.

Burney, Charles. *A General History of Music from the Earliest Ages to the Present Period*. London: printed for the author, 1789. Critical edition. Edited by Frank Mercer. New York: Harcourt, Brace and Co., 1935.

Burt, Nathaniel. 'Opera in Arcadia.' *The Musical Quarterly*, xli (1955), pp. 145–70.

Buttrey, John. 'Dating Purcell's *Dido and Aeneas*.' *Proceedings of the Royal Musical Association*, xciv (1967–8), pp. 51–62.

Cannon, Beekman C. *Johann Mattheson: Spectator in Music*. New Haven: Yale University Press, 1947.

Chisholm, Duncan. 'The English Origins of Handel's *Il Pastor Fido*.' *The Musical Times*, cxv (1974), pp. 650–3.

Chrysander, Friedrich, *G. F. Händel*. 3 vols. Leipzig: Breitkopf & Härtel, 1919.

Cibber, Colley. *The Dramatic Works*. 5 vols. London: J. Rivington and Sons, 1777.

Clarke, Henry Leland. 'John Blow: A Tercentenary Survey.' *The Musical Quarterly*, xxxv (1949), pp. 412–20.

Clubb, Louise George. 'The Making of the Pastoral Play: Italian Experiments between 1573 and 1590.' *Petrarch to Pirandello: Studies in Italian Literature in honour of Beatrice Corrigan*. Edited by Julius A. Molinaro. Toronto: University of Toronto Press, 1973.

Cody, Richard. *The Landscape of the Mind: Pastoralism and Platonic Theory in Tasso's 'Aminta' and Shakespeare's Early Comedies*. Oxford: Clarendon Press, 1969.

Compagnino, Gaetano; Nicastro, Guido; and Savoca, Giuseppe, eds. *Il Settecento: L'Arcadia e l'età della riforme*. Vol. vi, i, of *La Letteratura italiana: Storia e Testi*. Edited by Carlo Muscetta. 8 vols. Laterza: Bari, 1973.

Congleton, James E. *Theories of Pastoral Poetry in England: 1684–1748*. Gainsville, Florida: University of Florida Press, 1952.

Coopersmith, Jacob Maurice. 'Handel Lacunae: A Project.' *The Musical Quarterly*, xxi (1935), pp. 224–9.

——: 'The Libretto of Handel's '*Jupiter in Argos*', *Music and Letters* (1930), pp. 289–95.

Crescimbeni, Giovanni Maria. *La Bellezza della volgar poesia*. Rome: G. F. Buagni, 1700.

——: *Commentarii intorno all' Istoria della Poesia Italiana*. Vol. ii. London: Presso T. Becket, 1803.

——: *Storia dell' Academia degli Arcadi*. London: T. Becket, 1803.

Cullen, Patrick. *Spenser, Marvell, and Renaissance Pastoral*. Cambridge, Mass.: Harvard University Press, 1970.

Cummings, William H. 'Dr. John Blow.' *Proceedings of the Royal Musical Association*, xxxv (1908–9), pp. 69–86.

: 'Matthew Locke, Composer for the Church and Theatre.' *Sammelbände der Internationalen Musikgesellschaft*, xiii (1911–12), pp. 120–6.

Cunningham, Dolora. 'The Jonsonian Masque as a Literary Form.' *Ben Jonson: A Collection of Critical Essays*. Edited by Jonas A. Barish. Englewood Cliffs, New Jersey: Prentice-Hall Inc., 1963.

Cutts, John P. 'British Museum Additional MS. 31432: William Lawes' Writing for the Theatre and the Court.' *The Library*, 5th series, vii (1952), pp. 225–34.

: *La Musique de Scène de la Troupe de Shakespeare: The King's Men sous le Règne de Jacques Ier*. Paris: Centre National de la Recherche Scientifique, 1959.

: 'Robert Johnson and the Court Masque.' *Music and Letters*, xli (1960), pp. 111–26.

Daniel, Samuel. *The Complete Works in Verse and Prose*. Edited by Alexander B. Grosart. London: Hazell, Watson and Viney, Ltd, 1885.

Dean, Winton. *Handel's Dramatic Oratorios and Masques*. London: Oxford Unversity Press, 1959.

: *Handel and the Opera Seria*. Berkeley: University of California Press, 1969.

: 'Handel's Wedding Opera.' *The Musical Times*, cxi (1970), pp. 705–7.

Demuth, Norman. *French Opera, its development to the Revolution*. Sussex: Artemis Press, 1963.

Dennis, John. *An Essay on the Operas After the Italian Manner*. London: n.p., 1706.

Dent, Edward J. 'Italian Chamber Cantatas.' *The Musical Antiquary*, ii (1911), pp. 142–53, 185–99.

: *The Foundations of English Opera*. Cambridge: Cambridge University Press, 1928.

: 'A Pastoral Opera by Alessandro Scarlatti.' *The Music Review*, xii (1951), pp. 7–14.

: 'The Operas.' *Handel: A Symposium*. Edited by Gerald Abraham. London: Oxford University Press, 1954.

: *Alessandro Scarlatti: His Life and Works*. London: Edward Arnold, 1960.

Deutsch, Otto Erich. *Handel: A Documentary Biography*. London: Adam and Charles Black, 1955.

Dobrée, Bonamy. *English Literature in the Early Eighteenth Century: 1700–1740*. Vol. vii of *The Oxford History of English Literature*. Edited by F. P. Wilson and Bonamy Dobrée. 12 vols. Oxford: Clarendon Press, 1959.

Donadoni, Eugenio. *A History of Italian Literature*. Vol. i. New York: New York University Press, 1969.

Doni, Giambattista. 'Trattato della Musica Scenica.' *Lyra Barberina*. Edited by A. M. Bandini. Vol. ii. Florence: Typis Caesareis, 1763.

Dorris, George E. *Paolo Rolli and the Italian Circle in London (1715–1744)*. Paris: Mouton & Co., 1967.

Draper, R. P. 'Shakespeare's Pastoral Comedy.' *Études Anglais*, xi (1958), pp. 1–17.

Drayton, Michael. *The Works of Michael Drayton*. Edited by J. William Hekel. Oxford: Shakespeare Head Press, 1932.

Dryden, John. *Of Dramatic Poesy and other Critical Essays*. 2 vols. Edited by George Watson. London: J. M. Dent and Sons, Ltd., 1962.

Einstein, Alfred. '*Orlando Furioso* and *La Gerusalemme Liberata* as Set to Music During the 16th and 17th Centuries.' *Music Library Association Notes*, 2d Ser., viii (1950–1), pp. 623–30.

——: *Gluck*. Translated by Eric Blom. London: J. M. Dent and Sons, Ltd., 1954.

Eisenschmidt, Joachim. *Die szenische Darstellung der Opern Georg Friedrich Händels auf der Londoner Bühne seiner Zeit*. 2 vols. Berlin: Georg Kallmeyer Verlag, 1941.

Eitner, Robert. '*Seelewig*, das älteste bekannte deutsche Singspiel von Harsdörffer und S. G. Staden, 1644. Neudruck.' *Monatshefte für Musik-Geschichte*, xiii (1881), pp. 53–147.

Empson, William. *Some Versions of the Pastoral*. London: Chatto and Windus, 1935.

Emslie, McDonald. 'Nicholas Lanier's Innovations in English Song.' *Music and Letters*, xli (1960), pp. 3–27.

Evans, Herbert, ed. *English Masques*. London: Blackie and Son, 1897.

Evans, Willa McClurg. *Ben Jonson and Elizabethan Music*. Lancaster, Pa.: Lancaster Press, 1929.

——: *Henry Lawes, Musician and Friend of Poets*. New York: Modern Language Association of America, 1941.

Ewerhart, R. 'Die Händel-Handschriften der Santini Bibliothek in Münster.' *Händel Jahrbuch*, vi (1960), pp. 124–35.

Fabbri, Mario. 'Nuove luce sull'attività fiorentina di Giacomo Antonio Perti, Bartolomeo Cristofori, e Giorgio F. Hendel.' *Chigiana*, xxi (1964), pp. 148–9.

Fehr, Max. *Apostolo Zeno und die Reform des Operntextes*. Inaugural Dissertation, University of Zurich. Zurich: A. Tschopp, 1912.

Feind, Barthold. *Gedanken von der 'Opera'*. Hamburg: Verlegts Hinrich Brummer, 1708.

Fellowes, E. H., ed. *Songs and Lyrics from the Plays of Beaumont and Fletcher*. London: n.p., 1928. Facsimile edition. New York: Benjamin Blom, Inc., 1972.

Finney, Gretchen Ludke. '*Comus* Dramma per Musica.' *Studies in Philology*, xxxvii (1940), pp. 482–500.

——: *Musical Backgrounds for English Literature*. New Brunswick, N.J.: Rutgers University Press, 1962.

Fleming, John V. *The 'Roman de la Rose': A Study in Allegory and Iconography*. Princeton: Princeton University Press, 1969.

Flemming, Willi. *Die Oper. Deutsche Literatur: Sammlung literarscher Kunst= und Kulturdenkmäler in Entwicklungschreiben*. Edited by Walter Brecht, Dietrich Kralik, and Heinz Kinderman. Barock Reihe: Barockdrama. Vol. v. Leipzig: Philipp Reclam, jun., 1933.

Fletcher, John. *The Works of Francis Beaumont and John Fletcher*. Edited by Arnold Glover and A. R. Waller. 10 vols. Cambridge: Cambridge University Press, 1906.

Floegel, Bruno. 'Studien zur Arientechnik in den Opern Händels.' *Händel Jahrbuch*, ii (1929), pp. 50–156.

Ford, Walter. 'Handel's Cantatas.' *Proceedings of the Royal Musical Association*, lviii (1931–2), pp. 33–42.

Freeman, Robert. 'Opera Without Drama: Currents of Change in Italian

Opera. 1675–1725.' Unpublished Ph.D. dissertation, Princeton University, 1967.

: 'Apostolo Zeno's Reform of the Libretto.' *Journal of the American Musicological Society*, xxi (1968), pp. 321–41.

Fuller, Maitland J. A. 'Foreign Influence on Henry Purcell.' *The Musical Times*, xxxvii (1896), pp. 10–11.

Fürstenau, Moritz. *Zur Geschichte der Musik und des Theaters am Hofe zu Dresden*. Dresden: Rudolf Kuntze, 1861–62. Facsimile edition. Leipzig: Edition Peters, 1971.

Gardner, Helen. 'As You Like It.' *More Talking of Shakespeare*. Edited by John Garrett. London: Longman, Green and Co., 1959.

Gay, John. *The Poetical, Dramatic, and Miscellaneous Works of John Gay*. 6 vols. London: Edward Jeffry, 1745.

: *The Poetical Works of John Gay*. Edited with a life and notes by John Underhill. 2 vols. London: Lawrence and Bullen, 1893.

Gilbert, Allan. *Literary Criticism*. New York: American Book Co., 1940.

Girdlestone, Cuthbert. *Jean-Philippe Rameau: His Life and Work*. London: Cassell and Co. Ltd., 1957; rev. ed. New York: Dover Publications, Inc., 1969.

Gombosi, Otto. 'Some Musical Aspects of the English Court Masque.' *Journal of the American Musicological Society*, i (1948), pp. 3–19.

Gravina, Gianvincenzo. *Prose di Gianvincenzo Gravina*. Edited by Paolo Emiliani Giudici. Florence: Barbera, Bianchi e Co., 1857.

Gray, Alan. 'Purcell's Dramatic Music.' *Proceedings of the Royal Musical Association*, xliii (1916–17), pp. 51–62.

Greg, Walter Wilson. *Pastoral Poetry and Pastoral Drama*. London: A. H. Bullen, 1906.

Grillo, Giacomo. *Poets at the Court of Ferrara: Ariosto, Tasso and Guarini*. Boston: The Excelsior Press, Inc., 1943.

Grout, Donald J. *A Short History of Opera*. New York: Columbia University Press, 1947.

The Guardian. London: James and Co., 1829.

Hall, James S. 'Handel among the Carmelites.' *The Dublin Review*, ccxxxiii (1959), pp. 121–31.

: 'The Problem of Handel's Latin Church Music.' *The Musical Times*, c (1959), pp. 197–200, 600.

Hanning, Barbara Russano. 'Apologia pro Ottavio Rinuccini.' *Journal of the American Musicological Society*, xxvi (1973), pp. 240–62.

Harsdörffer, Georg Philipp. *Frauenzimmer Gesprächspiele*. 8 vols. Nuremberg: Wolfgang Endtern, 1643–57.

Hart, Eric Ford. 'Introduction to Henry Lawes.' *Music and Letters*, xxxii (1951), pp. 217–25, 328–44.

Hartmann, A., Jr. 'Battista Guarini and *Il Pastor Fido*.' *The Musical Quarterly*, xxix (1953), pp. 415–25.

Haun, Eugene. 'An Inquiry into the Genre of *Comus*.' *Vanderbilt Studies in the Humanities*, ii (1955), pp. 221–39.

: *But Hark! More Harmony: The Libretti of Restoration Opera in English*. Ypsilanti, Mich.: Eastern Michigan University Press, 1971.

Herbage, Julian. 'Handel in Rome.' *The Listener* (19 January 1938), pp. 820–1.

: 'The Oratorios,' *Handel: A Symposium*. Edited by Gerald Abraham. London: Oxford University Press, 1954.

: 'The Secular Oratorios and Cantatas.' *Handel: A Symposium.* Edited by Gerald Abraham. London: Oxford University Press, 1954.

Hicks, Anthony. 'Handel's Music for *Comus.' The Musical Times,* cxvii (1976), pp. 28–9.

Holmes, William C. 'Giancinto Andrea Cicognini's and Antonio Cesti's *Orontea,' New Looks at Italian Opera: Essays in Honor of Donald J. Grout.* Edited by William W. Austin. Ithaca, N.Y.: Cornell University Press, 1968.

Holst, Imogen, ed. *Henry Purcell (1659–1695): Essays on his Music.* London: Oxford University Press, 1959.

: 'Purcell's Librettist, Nahum Tate.' *Henry Purcell (1659–1695): Essays on his Music.* Edited by Imogen Holst. London: Oxford University Press, 1959.

Howarth, R. G. 'Shirley's Cupid and Death.' *Times Literary Supplement* (15 November 1934), p. 795.

Hunold, Christian Friedrich [Menantes]. *Die allerneueste Art, zur reinen und galanten Poesie zu gelangen.* Hamburg: G. Liebernickel, 1707.

Ingram, R. W. 'Operatic Tendencies in Stuart Drama.' *The Musical Quarterly,* xliv (1958), pp. 489–502.

Irving, William Henry. *John Gay: Favorite of the Wits.* Durham, N.C.: Duke University Press, 1940.

Jefferey, V. M. 'Italian Influence in Fletcher's *Faithful Shepherdess.' The Modern Language Review,* xxi (1926), pp. 147–58.

Jenkins, Harold. 'As You Like It.' *Shakespeare Survey,* viii (1955), pp. 40–51.

Johnstone, H. Diack. 'Greene's First Opera: *Florimel* or *Love's Revenge.' The Musical Times,* cxiv (1973), pp. 1112–13.

Jonson, Ben. 'Ben Jonson's *Sad Shepherd* with Waldron's Continuation.' *Materialien zur Kunde des älteren Englischen Dramas.* Edited by W. W. Greg. Louvain: A. Uystpruyst, 1905.

Kerman, Joseph. *Opera as Drama.* New York: Vintage Books, 1952.

Kimbell, David. 'The *Amadis* Operas of Destouches and Handel.' *Music and Letters,* xlix (1968), pp. 329–46.

: 'A Critical Study of Handel's Early Operas: 1704–1717.' Unpublished Ph.D. dissertation, Oxford University, 1968.

: 'Libretto of Handel's *Teseo.' Music and Letters,* xliv (1963), pp. 371–9.

Kirkendale, Ursula. *Antonio Caldara: Sein Leben und seine venezianisch-romischen Oratorien.* Graz: Hermann Böhlaus Nachf., 1966.

: 'The Ruspoli Documents on Handel.' *Journal of the American Musicological Society,* xx (1967), pp. 222–73.

Kretschmar, Hermann. *Geschichte der Oper.* Leipzig: Breitkopf & Härtel, 1919.

Kunitz, Stanley J. and Colby, Vineta. *European Authors: 1000–1900.* New York: The H. W. Wilson Co., 1967.

Lang, Paul Henry. *George Frideric Handel.* New York: W. W. Norton and Co., 1960.

Larson, Jens Peter. *Handel's 'Messiah.'* 2nd edition. New York: W. W. Norton and Co., 1972.

Lascelles, Mary. 'Shakespeare's Pastoral Comedy.' *More Talking of Shakespeare.* Edited by John Garrett. London: Longman, Green and Co., 1959.

Lawes, Henry, and Milton, John. *The Mask of Comus.* Edited by E. H. Visiak and Hubert J. Foss. London: The Nonesuch Press, 1937.

Lawrence, William J. 'The Origin of the Substantive Theatre Masque.'

Pre-Restoration Stage Studies. Cambridge, Mass.: Harvard University Press, 1927.

Lee, Vernon [Violet Paget]. *Studies of the Eighteenth Century in Italy*. London: T. F. Unwin, 1907.

Leichtentritt, Hugo. *Reinhard Keiser in seinen Opern*. Berlin: Tessarotypie-Actien-Gesellschaft, 1901.

: *Händel*. Stuttgart: Deutsche Verlags-Anstatt, 1924.

: 'Handel's Harmonic Art.' *The Musical Quarterly*, xxi (1935), pp. 208–23.

Lewis, Anthony. 'The Songs and Chamber Cantatas.' *Handel: A Symposium*. Edited by Gerald Abraham. London: Oxford University Press, 1954.

: 'Handel and the Aria.' *Proceedings of the Royal Musical Association*, lxxxv (1958–9), pp. 95–107.

Lewis, C. S. *The Allegory of Love: A Study in Medieval Tradition*. New York: Oxford University Press, 1958.

Libretti. Katalogue der Herzog August Bibliothek Wolfenbüttel, xiv. Frankfurt am Main: Vittorio Klostermann, 1970.

Lievsay, John Leon. 'Italian *Favole Boscaresce* and Jacobean Stage Pastoralism.' *Essays on Shakespeare and Elizabethan Drama*. Edited by Richard Hosley. Columbia, Miss.: University of Missouri Press, 1962.

Lincoln, Stoddard. 'The First Setting of Congreve's *Semele*.' *Music and Letters*, xliv (1963), pp. 103–17.

: A Congreve Masque.' *The Musical Times*, cxiii (1972), pp. 1078–81.

Lindsey, Edwin S. 'The Music of the Songs in Fletcher's Plays.' *Studies in Philology*, xxi (1924), pp. 325–55.

: 'The Music in Ben Jonson's Plays.' *Modern Language Notes*, xliv (1929), pp. 86–92.

Long, John H. *Shakespeare's Use of Music: A Study of the Music and Its Performance in the Original Production of Seven Comedies*. Gainsville, Fla.: University of Florida Press, 1955.

Lorenz, Alfred. *Alessandro Scarlatti's Jugendoper: ein Beitrag zur Geschichte der italienscher Opera*. 2 vols. Augsburg: Dr. Benno Filser Verlag G.M.B.H., 1927.

Lyly, John. *The Complete Works of John Lyly*. Edited by R. Warwick Bond. Oxford: Clarendon Press, 1902. Facsimile edition. Oxford: Clarendon Press, 1967.

Mainwaring, John. *Memoirs of the Life of George Frederick Handel*. London: Printed for R. and J. Dodsley, 1760. Facsimile edition. Amsterdam: F. A. M. Knuf, 1964.

Manifold, John Streeter. 'Theatre Music in the Sixteenth and Seventeenth Centuries.' *Music and Letters*, xxix (1948), pp. 366–98.

: *The Music in English Drama from Shakespeare to Purcell*. London: Rockliff, 1956.

Marcuse, Sibyl. *Musical Instruments: A Comprehensive Dictionary*. Garden City, New York: Doubleday and Co., Inc., 1964.

Mark, Jeffrey. 'The Jonsonian Masque.' *Music and Letters*, iii (1922), pp. 358–371.

: 'Dryden and the Beginnings of Opera in England.' *Music and Letters*, v (1924), pp. 247–52.

Marks, Jeanette. *English Pastoral Drama: From the Restoration to the Date of the Publication of the 'Lyrical Ballads' (1660–1798)*. London: Methuen and Co., 1908.

Mattheson, Johann. *Der vollkommene Kapellmeister*. Hamburg: C. Herold, 1739. Facsimile edition. Edited by Margarete Reimann. Kassel: Barenreiter Verlag, 1954.

Matthews, Betty. 'Unpublished Letters Concerning Handel.' *Music and Letters*, xl (1959), pp. 261–8.

Matthieu-Arth, Françoise. 'Du Masque à l'Opéra Anglais.' *International Musicological Society*, x (1967), pp. 149–58.

McCullen, J. T. 'The Functions of Songs Aroused by Madness in Elizabethan Drama.' *A Tribute to George Coffin Taylor*. Edited by Arnold Williams. North Carolina: University of North Carolina Press, 1952.

McGrady, Richard. 'Henry Lawes and the Concept of "Just Note and Accent".' *Music and Letters*, l (1969), pp. 86–102.

    : 'Captain Cooke: A Tercententary Tribute.' *The Musical Times*, cxiii (1972), pp. 659–60.

Montalto, Lina. *Un Mecenate in Roma barocca: Il Cardinale Benedetto Pamphili (1653–1730)*. Florence: Sansoni, 1955.

Menantes, see Hunold.

Montgomery, Franz. 'Early Criticism of Italian Opera in England.' *The Musical Quarterly*, xv (1929), pp. 415–25.

Moore, John Robert. 'The Function of the Songs in Shakespeare's Plays.' *Shakespeare Studies: by Members of the Department of English of the University of Wisconsin to Commemorate the Three Hundredth Anniversary of the Death of William Shakespeare, April 23, 1616*. Madison, Wisc.: University of Wisconsin Press, 1916.

Moore, Robert Etheridge. *Henry Purcell and the Restoration Theatre*. London: Heinemann, 1961.

Morgan, Paul. 'A Study of "Cupid and Death", a Masque by James Shirley.' Unpublished Master's thesis, University of Chicago, 1951.

Moser, Hans Joachim. *Heinrich Schütz: His Life and Work*. Translated by Carl F. Pfatteicher. St. Louis: Concordia Publishing House, 1959.

Müller von Asow, Erich H. *The Letters and Writings of George Frideric Handel*. London: Cassell and Co., 1935.

Murata, Margaret. 'Operas for the Papal Court with Texts by Giulio Rospigliosi.' Unpublished Ph.D. dissertation, University of Chicago, 1975.

Muratori, Lodovico Antonio. *Della perfetta Poesia Italiana*. Vol. ii. Venice: Coleti, 1770.

Myers, Robert Manson. 'Mr. Handel of London: A Study of George Frideric Handel's Place in Eighteenth Century Literature.' Unpublished Master's thesis, Columbia University, New York, 1942.

    : *Handel, Dryden and Milton: Being a Series of Observations on the Poems of Dryden and Milton, as Altered and Adapted by Various Hands, and Set to Music by Mr. Handel*. London: Bowes and Bowes, Publishers, Ltd., 1956.

Nicoll, Allardyce. *A History of English Drama: 1660–1900*. Vols. i and ii. Cambridge: Cambridge University Press, 1967–8.

Olschki, Leonardo. *Guarini's 'Pastor Fido' in Deutschland*. Leipzig: H. Haessel Verlag, 1908.

Orgel, Stephen. *The Jonsonian Masque*. Cambridge, Mass.: Harvard University Press, 1965.

Paget, see Lee.

Palisca, Claude V. 'The Alternati of Florence, Pioneers in the Theory of

Dramatic Music.' *New Looks at Italian Opera: Essays in Honor of Donald J. Grout.* Edited by William W. Austin. Ithaca, N.Y.: Cornell University Press, 1968.

: *Baroque Music.* Englewood Cliffs: Prentice-Hall Inc., 1968.

: 'Musical Asides in the Correspondence of Emilio De' Cavalieri.' *The Musical Quarterly.* xlix (1963), pp. 339–55.

Patrick, Rogers. 'Dating Acis and Galatea.' *The Musical Times,* cxiv (1973), p. 792.

Perella, Nicolas. 'Pope's Judgment of the *Pastor Fido* and a Case of Plagiarism.' *Philological Quarterly,* xl (1961), pp. 444–8.

: *The Critical Fortune of Battista Guarini's 'Il Pastor Fido.'* Florence: Leo S. Olschki, 1973.

Piehler, Paul. *The Visionary Landscape.* London: Edward Arnold, 1971.

Pirrotta, Nino. 'Temperaments and Tendencies in the Florentine Camarata.' *The Musical Quarterly,* xl (1954), pp. 169–89.

: 'Commedia dell'arte.' *The Musical Quarterly,* xlvii (1955), pp. 305–24.

: 'Early Opera and Aria.' *New Looks at Italian Opera: Essays in Honor of Donald J. Grout.* Edited by William W. Austin. Ithaca, N.Y.: Cornell University Press, 1968.

Poggioli, Renata. *The Oaten Flute: Essays on Pastoral Poetry and the Pastoral Ideal.* Cambridge, Mass.: Harvard University Press, 1975.

Poladian, Sirvart. 'Handel as Opera Composer.' Unpublished Ph.D. dissertation, Cornell University, 1946.

Portal, Emmanuele. *L'Arcadia.* Palermo: R. Sandron, 1922.

Praz, Mario. *The Flaming Heart: Essays on Crashaw, Machiavelli, and other Studies of the Relations between Italian and English Literature from Chaucer to T. S. Eliot.* 2nd ed., New York: W. W. Norton & Co., Inc., 1973.

Prendergast, Arthur. 'The Masque of the Seventeenth Century.' *Proceedings of the Royal Musical Association,* xxiii (1897), pp. 113–31.

Price, Lawrence Marsden. 'English > German Literary Influences: Bibliography and Survey.' *Modern Philology,* ix (1919–20), pp. 1–616.

Prince, Frank Templeton. *The Italian Element in Milton's Verses.* Oxford: Clarendon Press, 1954.

Prouty, Charles T. *The Sources of 'Much Ado about Nothing': A Critical Study Together with the Text of Peter Beverley's 'Ariodanto and Ieneura.'* New Haven, Conn.: Yale University Press, 1950.

Prunières, Henri. *Cavalli et l'Opéra Venetien au XVIIIe Siècle.* Paris: Les Editions Rieder, 1931.

Puttenham, George. *The Arte of English Poesie* (1589). I: 'Of Poets and Poesie,' Chapter XVIII: 'Of Shepheards or Pastorall Poesie called Eglogue, and to what purpose it was first invented and used.' *Elizabethan Critical Essays.* Edited by G. Gregory Smith. Vol. II. London: Oxford University Press, 1904.

Raguenet, François. *A Comparison between the French and Italian musick and opera's.* Translated from the French; with some remarks. To which is added *A Critical Discourse upon Opera's in England, and a means proposed for their improvement.* Introduction by Charles Cudworth. London: n.p., 1709. Facsimile edition. Farnborough: Gregg International Publishers, 1968.

The Rambler. Introduction by S. C. Roberts. London: J. M. Dent and Sons, Ltd., 1953.

Rees, Joan. *Samuel Daniel: A Critical and Biographical Study*. Liverpool: Liverpool University Press, 1964.

Reese, Gustav. *Music in the Renaissance*, 1st edition, revised. New York: W. W. Norton and Co., Inc., 1959.

Rendell, E. D. 'The Influence of Henry Purcell on Handel, traced in *Acis and Galatea*.' *The Musical Times*, xxxvi (1895), pp. 293–6.

: 'Some Notes on Purcell's Dramatic Music with Especial Reference to the *Fairy Queen*.' *Music and Letters*, i (1920), pp. 135–44.

Rimbault, Edward F. 'An Historical Sketch of the History of Dramatic Music in England From the Earliest Time to the Death of Purcell, Anno Domini 1695.' *Publications of the Musical Antiquarian Society*. Vol. vii. London: Chappell, 1842.

Robertson, J. G. *Studies in the Genesis of Romantic Theory in the Eighteenth Century*. Cambridge: Cambridge University Press, 1923.

: *A History of German Literature*. 6th edition. Edited by Dorothy Reich. London: William Blackwood, 1970.

Robinson, Michael F. *Opera before Mozart*. London: Hutchinson University Library, 1966.

: *Naples and Neapolitan Opera*. Oxford: Clarendon Press, 1972.

Rolland, Romain. *Some Musicians of Former Days*. Translated by Mary Blaiklock. New York: Henry Holt and Co., 1915.

Rose, Gloria. 'The Cantatas of Giacomo Carissimi.' *The Musical Quarterly*, xlviii (1962), pp. 204–15.

Sasse, Konrad. *Händel Bibliographie*. Leipzig: Uebdeutscher Verlag für Musik, 1967.

Savage, Roger. 'Producing *Dido and Aeneas*: an investigation into sixteen problems with a newly-composed finale to the Grove Scene by Michael Tilmouth.' *Early Music*, iv (1976), pp. 393–406.

Schmidt, Gustav Friedrich. *Die frühdeutsche Oper und die musikdramatische Kunst Georg Caspar Schürmann's*. Regensburg: Gustav Bosse Verlag, 1933.

: 'Johann Wolfgang Francks Singspiel *Die drey Tochter Cecrops*.' *Archiv für Musikforschung*, iv (1939), pp. 257–316.

Schmitz, Eugen. *Geschichte der Kantate und des Geistlichen Konzerts: Geschichte der weltlichen Solokantate*. Leipzig: Breitkopf & Härtel, 1914. Facsimile edition. Hildesheim: G. Olms, 1966.

Schneider, Constantin. *Geschichte der Musik in Salzburg von der Ältesten Zeit bis zur Gegenwart*. Salzburg: Verlag R. Kiesel, 1935.

Scholes, Percy A. 'Jordan's Interregnum Masques.' *Times Literary Supplement* (14 June 1934), p. 424.

Scott, Mary A. 'Elizabethan Translations from the Italian. Part II: Translations of Poetry, Plays and Metrical Romances.' *PMLA*, xi (1896), pp. 377–484.

Scott-Thomas, H. F. 'Nahum Tate and the Seventeenth Century.' *ELH*, i (1934), pp. 250–75.

Serauky, Walter. Das Ballet in G. F. Händels Opern.' *Händel Jahrbuch*, viii (1956), pp. 91–112.

Shaw, Harold Watkins. 'John Blow as Theorist.' *The Musical Times*, lxxvii (1936), pp. 835–6.

: 'The Secular Music of John Blow.' *Proceedings of the Royal Musical Association*, lxiii (1936–7), pp. 1–19.

: 'John Blow, Doctor of Music: A Biography.' *The Musical Times*, lxxviii (1937), pp. 865–7, 946–9, 1025–8.

: 'Blow's Use of the Ground Bass.' *The Musical Quarterly*, xxiv (1938), pp. 31–8.

: 'John Blow's Anthems.' *Music and Letters*, xix (1938), pp. 429–42.

Sidney, Sir Philip. *An Apologie for Poetry* (c. 1583, printed 1595). *Elizabethan Critical Essays*. Edited by G. Gregory Smith. Vol. I. London: Oxford University Press, 1904.

Smith, Alexander Brent. 'Henry Purcell.' *Music and Letters*, xviii (1937), pp. 162–8.

Smith, Homer. 'Pastoral Influence in the English Drama.' *PMLA*, xii (1897), pp. 355–460.

Smith, Patrick J. *The Tenth Muse: A Historical Study of the Opera Libretto*. New York: A. A. Knopf, 1970.

Smith, William C. *Concerning Handel. His Life and Works*. London: Cassell and Co. Ltd, 1948.

Solerti, Angelo. 'I precedenti del Melodramma.' *Rivista Musicale Italiana*, x (1903), pp. 207–33, 466–84.

: *Gli Albori del Melodramma*. 3 vols. Milan, 1904–5; reprinted ed., Hildesheim: G. Olms, 1969.

Spacks, Patricia Meyer, *John Gay*. New York: Twayne Publishers, Inc., 1965.

Spaeth, Sigmund Gottfried. *Milton's Knowledge of Music*. Weimar: R. Wagner Sohn, 1913.

The Spectator. Edited with an introduction and notes by Donald F. Bond. 5 vols. Oxford: Clarendon Press, 1965.

Squire, Barclay. 'Purcell's Dramatic Music.' *Sammelbände der Internationalen Musik-gesellschaft*, v (1903–4), pp. 489–563.

: 'Purcell's *Dido and Aeneas*.' *The Musical Times*, lix (1918), pp. 252–4.

Staton, Walter F. and Simeone, William E., eds. *A Critical Edition of Sir Richard Fanshawe's 1647 Translation of Giovanni Battista Guarini's 'Il Pastor Fido'*. Oxford: Clarendon Press, 1964.

Steglich, Rudolf. 'Der Schlusschor von Händels *Acis und Galatea*, Ergänzung und Analyse.' *Händel Jahrbuch*, iii (1930), pp. 145–59.

Streatfeild, F. A. 'The Granville Collection of Handel Manuscripts.' *The Musical Antiquary*, ii (1911), pp. 208–24.

: 'Handel at Cannons.' *The Musical Times*, lviii (1916), pp. 286–7.

: 'Handel, Rolli and Italian Opera in London in the Eighteenth Century.'' *The Musical Quarterly*, iii (1917), 428–45.

: *Handel*. Rev. 2 nd. ed. New York: Da Capo Press, 1964.

Strohm, Reinhard. 'Händel in Italia: Nuovi Contributi.' *Rivista Italiana di Musicologia*, ix (1974), pp. 152–74.

: 'Händels Pasticci.' *Analecta Musicologica*, xiv (1974), pp. 208–67.

The Tatler. Edited with introduction and notes by George A. Aitken. 4 vols. London: Duckworth and Co., 1899.

Thaler, Alwin. 'Milton in the Theatre.' *Studies in Philology*, xvii (1920), pp. 269–308.

Thorndike, Ashley H. 'The Pastoral Element in the English Drama before 1605.' *Modern Language Notes*, xiv (1899), pp. 228–46.

Timms, Colin. 'Handel and Steffani: A New Handel Signature.' *The Musical Times*, cxiv (1973), pp. 374–7.

Tomlinson, Gary. 'Ottavio Rinuccini and the *Favola Affetuosa.*' *Comitatus*, vi (1975), pp. 1–27.

Towneley Worsthorne, Simon. *Venetian Opera in the Seventeenth Century*. Oxford: Clarendon Press, 1954.

Van Lennep, William; Avery, Emmet L.; and Scouten, Arthur. *The London Stage 1660–1800: A Calendar of Plays, Entertainments and Afterpieces Together with Casts, Box-Receipts and Contemporary Comment*. 5 vols. Carbondale, Ill.: Southern Illinois University Press, 1965–8.

Walker, Arthur D. *George Frideric Handel: The Newman Flower Collection in the Henry Watson Music Library*. The Manchester Public Libraries, 1972.

Walmsley, D. M. 'The Influence of Foreign Opera on English Operatic Plays of the Restoration Period.' *Anglia*, lii (1928), pp. 37–50.

Weaver, Robert L. 'Opera in Florence.' *Studies in Musicology: Essays in the History, Style, and Bibliography of Music in Memory of Glen Hayden*. Edited by James W. Pruett. Chapel Hill: University of North Carolina Press, 1969.

Webbe, William. *A Discourse of English Poetrie (1586)*. *Elizabethan Critical Essays*. Edited by G. Gregory Smith. Vol. I. London: Oxford University Press, 1904.

Welsford, Enid. *The Court Masque: A Study in the Relationship between Poetry and the Revels*. New York: Russell and Russell, Inc., 1962.

West, Dorothy Irene. *Italian Opera in England (1660–1740), and Some of its Relationships to English Literature*. An Abstract of a Thesis. Urbana: University of Illinois, 1938.

Westrup, J. A. 'Purcell and Handel.' *Music and Letters*, xl (1959), pp. 103–8.

White, Eric Walter. 'New Light on Dido and Aeneas.' *Henry Purcell (1659–1695): Essays on His Music*. Edited by Imogen Holst. London: Oxford University Press, 1959.

Wolff, Helmuth Christian. *Die Barockoper in Hamburg (1678–1738)*. 2 vols. Wolfenbüttel: Möseler Verlag, 1957.

⸻ : *Die venezianische Oper in der zweiten hälfte des 17. Jahrhunderts*. Berlin: O. Elsner, 1957.

Wotquenne, Alfred. *Table alphabetique des morceaux mesures contenus dans les oeuvres dramatiques de Zeno, Metastasio et Goldoni*. Leipzig: Breitkopf & Härtel, 1905.

Young, Percy M. 'Handel the Man.' *Handel: A Symposium*. Edited by Gerald Abraham. London: Oxford University Press, 1954.

Zanetti, Emilia. 'Handel in Italia.' *L'Approdo Musicale*, iii (1960), pp. 3–40.

⸻ : 'Le musiche Italiane di Handel.' *L'Approdo Musicale*, iii (1960), pp. 41–46.

Zelm, Klaus. *Die Opern Reinhard Keisers: Studien zur Chronologie, Uberlieferung und Stilentwicklung*. Munich: Musikverlag Katzbichler, 1975.

Index

References to musical examples are given in italics. In general the complete listing of page-references for a musical work is given under the composer; the entry for the librettist will only give those pages on which he or his work is discussed and will include a parenthetical reference to the composer. Cross-references (such as 'Arcadia, *see also* Golden Age') are made in cases where an alternate entry is deemed complementary or especially useful.